ORGANIZATION THEORY

ORGANIZATION THEORY
Integrating Structure and Behavior

GARY DESSLER

School of Business and Organizational Sciences
Florida International University

PRENTICE-HALL, INC., *Englewood Cliffs, New Jersey 07632*

Library of Congress Cataloging in Publication Data

DESSLER, GARY.
  Organization theory.

  Includes bibliographical references and index.
  1. Organization. I. Title.
HD31.D4227   658.4   79-11380
ISBN 0-13-641886-4

Editorial/production supervision and
  interior design by Ann Marie McCarthy
Cover design by Wanda Lubelska Design
Manufacturing buyer: Harry P. Baisley

Printed in the United States of America

10 9 8 7 6 5 4

PRENTICE-HALL INTERNATONAL, INC., *London*
PRENTICE-HALL OF AUSTRALIA PTY. LIMITED, *Sydney*
PRENTICE-HALL OF CANADA, LTD., *Toronto*
PRENTICE-HALL OF INDIA PRIVATE LIMITED, *New Delhi*
PRENTICE-HALL OF JAPAN, INC., *Tokyo*
PRENTICE-HALL OF SOUTHEAST ASIA PTE. LTD., *Singapore*
WHITEHALL BOOKS LIMITED, *Wellington, New Zealand*

To Robert J. House

Contents

Chapter 3

Contemporary Organization Theories   34

CHAPTER OVERVIEW.
HUMAN-RELATIONS MANAGEMENT: THE PERIOD OF COLLISION.
BRIDGING THE ERAS: FOLLETT, BARNARD, AND SIMON.
THE BEHAVIORAL-SYSTEMS SCHOOL.   TOWARD A SITUATIONAL THEORY.
SUMMARY.

PART II

THE CONTEXT OF ORGANIZATIONS   57

Chapter 4

The Context of Organizations: Environment, Technology, Size   59

CHAPTER OVERVIEW.   ORGANIZATIONAL ENVIRONMENTS.
ENVIRONMENT AND ORGANIZATION.   TECHNOLOGY AND ORGANIZATION.
ORGANIZATION SIZE AND STRUCTURE.   SUMMARY.

Chapter 5

Decision Making and Communication   83

CHAPTER OVERVIEW.   TYPES OF DECISION MAKERS.   COMMUNICATION.
HUMAN INFORMATION PROCESSING.
ORGANIZATIONAL METHODS FOR HANDLING INFORMATION.   SUMMARY.

case for part II: the food canning company   *104*

PART III

ORGANIZATION STRUCTURE AND DESIGN   107

Chapter 6

Departmentation and Coordination   109

CHAPTER OVERVIEW.   DEPARTMENTATION.   LINE-STAFF STRUCTURE.
COORDINATION.   SUMMARY.

Contents

Chapter 7

Organizational Hierarchy and Delegation **136**

CHAPTER OVERVIEW. DELEGATION AND DECENTRALIZATION. HIERARCHICAL LEVELS AND THE SPAN OF CONTROL. SUMMARY.

case for part III: prebuilt, inc. *156*

PART IV

MOTIVATION AND COMPLIANCE IN ORGANIZATIONS **165**

Chapter 8

Motivation and Organization Theory **167**

CHAPTER OVERVIEW. IMPOSED VS. SELF-CONTROL IN ORGANIZATION THEORY. A SURVEY OF MOTIVATION THEORIES. SUMMARY.

Chapter 9

Authority, Control, and Reward Systems **193**

CHAPTER OVERVIEW. POWER AND AUTHORITY IN ORGANIZATIONS. CONTROL SYSTEMS. REWARD SYSTEMS. SUMMARY.

Chapter 10

Self-Control and Intrinsic Rewards **216**

CHAPTER OVERVIEW. INTRINSIC MOTIVATION IN ORGANIZATION THEORY. JOB ENRICHMENT. BUILDING COMMITMENT. THE USE OF PARTICIPATION. STAFFING AND INTRINSIC MOTIVATION. SUMMARY.

case for part IV: the lincoln electric company *248*

PART VI

ORGANIZATIONAL EFFECTIVENESS   *389*

Chapter 15

Organizational Effectiveness   *391*

CHAPTER OVERVIEW.   WHAT IS ORGANIZATIONAL EFFECTIVENESS?
QUESTIONS IN ORGANIZATION THEORY.   SUMMARY.

Preface

Organization Theory is intended for use in courses with titles such as Organization Theory, Organization Theory and Behavior, Organization Behavior, and Management and Organization Theory. The book was written to provide its readers with a research-based, integrated treatment of organization structure and behavior, presented within a framework that illustrates the close relationship between an organization's structure, behavior, and environment.

There is an ongoing dialogue concerning the topics a book like this should cover, and *Organization Theory: Integrating Structure and Behavior* reflects my own biases concerning what that subject matter should be. On the one hand is the argument that it should focus mostly on "macro" topics, and more specifically on questions of organization structure and design. On the other are those that tend to combine organization theory with organization behavior, and who therefore focus more on "micro" topics including individual and group behavior in organizations. My own bias is to treat this subject with more of a macro emphasis, but to recognize that in theory and in practice it is useful to try to integrate the macro and micro material. It is rare, for example, that an organization can be structured and designed without regard to the people and behavioral processes—individual needs, group processes, intergroup conflicts, and so on—that are involved. Similarly, it is rare that one can study and understand behavior in organizations without understanding the required relationships and structure within which that behavior is taking place. Readers of *Organization Theory: Integrating Structure and Behavior* will develop, I hope, a better appreciation of how the structure and behavior in an organization interact with and complement each other.

Readers of my earlier *Organization and Management: A Contingency Approach* will find some overlap between that book and this. Most importantly, Chapters 4 (Context: Environment, Technology, and Size), 6 (Departmentation and Coordination), and 7 (Organizational Hierarchy and Delegation) in the present book are based largely on the corresponding chapters of the earlier book, although the material has been updated, extended, and thoroughly revised.

Although I am, of course, solely responsible for the final product, I want to take this opportunity to acknowledge several people who contributed to the development of this book. Robert J. House, Shell Professor of Organizational Behavior at the University of Toronto, stimulated my initial interest in organizational behavior and theory, and his standards have been a guidepost to his many students and colleagues. I would like to thank H. Randolph Bobbitt, Ohio State University; Edwin A. Gerloff, University of Texas at Arlington; Lawrence R. Jauch, Southern Illinois University; and Arlyn J. Melcher, Kent State University, who were kind enough to review some or all of the manuscript as it developed. I want to especially thank Karl Magnusen at Florida International University for his valuable recommendations. Marian Blessing assisted me with the administrative details and typing of the project.

Finally, I want to thank my wife Claudia and son Derek for letting me borrow the time from them for seeing the book through to completion.

ORGANIZATION THEORY

PART I

*FOUNDATIONS
OF ORGANIZATION
THEORY*

Chapter 1

Introduction

to Organization Theory

CHAPTER OVERVIEW

The purpose of this chapter is to define *organization theory* and the plan of this book.

SCIENCE, THEORY, AND ORGANIZATION THEORY

In the most general sense, a science is a body of knowledge that is systematically acquired and arranged. Physics, biology, and chemistry are thus sciences, as are psychology and other behavioral sciences. The systematic observation and analysis of organizations might be termed *organizational science*, and its major end product an *organization theory* (or theories) aimed at explaining a set of organizational facts and their relation to one another. In this book we will see that over the past 50 years, many theories of organization have developed. These theories help us to understand the structure and behavior of organizations, and to predict how a change—such as widening the span of control—may influence the structure, behavior, and effectiveness of the organization.

A *hypothesis* is a "tentative theory," a theory that is to be tested but that has not yet received enough empirical support to gain the position of a full-fledged theory. Hypotheses are tested through the *scientific method*, and the origin of the word scientific helps explain the method's nature. *Scientific* comes from two Latin words—*scientia*, knowledge, and *facere*, to make—and so "scientific" literally means the creation of knowledge. Basically, the scientific method involves a cycle of observation, generalization, and experimentation; some phenomenon is observed, a general hypothesis is developed to explain this phenomenon, and an experiment is carried out to test the hypothesis. In practice, this cycle is never-ending, and the frontier of the science is pushed ever forward as scientists (through observation, generalization, and experimentation) collect new bits of information that are weaved into the tapestry of their evolving theories.

But there is more to the scientific method than simply observation, generalization, and experimentation, just as there is more to painting a picture than just following some multistep format. Science, as Warren Weaver points out,

> . . . is not technology, it is not gadgetry, it is not some mysterious cult, it is not a great mechanical monster. Science is an adventure of the human spirit. It is essentially an artistic enterprise, stimulated largely by disciplined imagination, and based largely on faith and reasonableness, order, and beauty of the universe of which man is a part.[1]

Science is thus a systematic body of knowledge, and *theories* are its major expressions, since they provide the general relationships or frameworks that allow us to understand, explain, and predict phenomena within the science we are focusing on. Theories are developed through the scientific method, which involves more than just observation, generalization, and experimentation. The scientific method is as much an attitude, an attitude characterized by curiosity, rationality, openmindedness, objectivity, and honesty, among other things.[2] Furthermore, we should not confuse the trappings of the scientific method with the scientific method itself. Test tubes, meters, slide rules, and questionnaires are useful scientific tools but are neither "science" nor "the scientific method"—just aids.

Finally, remember that although the scientific method usually involves a rather routine series of experimental steps, this is not always the case. Scientists do try to carry out experiments as carefully as possible to ensure that they are measuring what they think they are measuring, and to provide other scientists with a replicable sequence of steps. Yet the progress of science is replete with examples in which *serendipity*—a totally unexpected occurrence—had a major effect on the course of the science. The findings of many organization theorists we discuss in this book, including Woodward and the Hawthorne researchers, are examples of this.

A FRAMEWORK
FOR ANALYZING ORGANIZATIONS

This book is concerned with *organization theory*, which we tentatively define as a framework for understanding, explaining, and predicting organizational effectiveness. We will approach our subject by reviewing the research findings on various topics, with an eye toward identifying, among other things:

The major determinants of organizational effectiveness

The relationships between these determinants

What makes one organization effective, and another ineffective

The applicability of this knowledge to practical problems

Why an organization that is effective in one situation may be ineffective in another

We assume in this book that organizations are systems—that they are purposeful social units and consist of people who carry out differentiated tasks which are coordinated to contribute to the organization's goals. This definition has several implications, including the fact that we need to view the topics in this book (division of work, leadership, groups, and so on) not as separate entities but in terms of their relation to each other, to the organization, and to the organization's effectiveness.

The topics in this book include the "context" of organizations, decision making, organization structure, motivation and compliance, leadership, groups, and change; they were chosen on the assumption that they all influence each other and organizational effectiveness. In analyzing these topics, it would therefore be useful to start with a hypothesis that tentatively explains *how* they relate to each other and to organizational effectiveness. Our hypothesized framework is presented in Figure 1-1. The rationale for this framework is as follows.

Context

First, as you can see, our framework assumes that the organization's "context"—its environment, technology, and size—influences how it is organized and managed. In Chapter 4, we explain how an organization's "strategy"— its basic long-term plan—answers the question, "What business are we in?" and thereby determines the environment in which the organization must compete, as well as its technology and size. In turn (as we'll also see in Chapter 4) the organization's context has a major influence on how the organization is structured and managed. For example, we'll see that in firms where efficiency is emphasized, effective organizations tend to be "mechanistic." They stress adherence to rules and to the chain of command, and they have a specialized division of work and directive leadership. At the other extreme, organizations like research labs may have unpredictable, nonroutine tasks. Here, creativity and entrepreneurial activities are emphasized, and to encourage such activities, these organizations tend to be "organic." They don't urge employees to "play it by the rules" or to abide closely by the chain of command. Similarly, jobs here tend to be less specialized, and leadership tends to be more "participative." The processes of decision making, communications, and information processing (discussed in Chapter 5) help explain the link between the organization and its context.

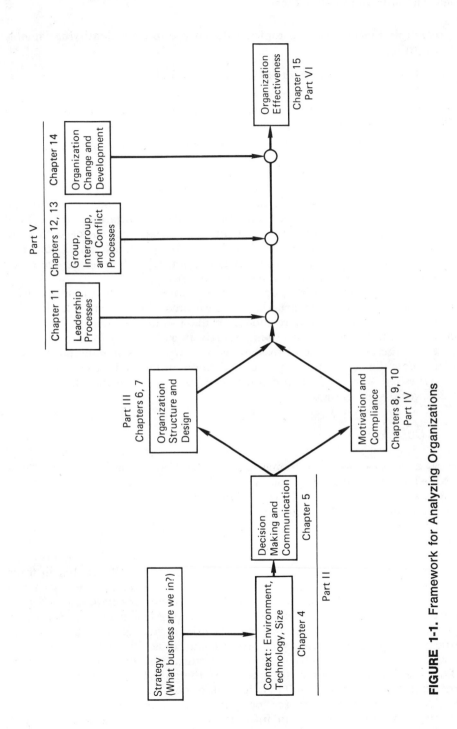

FIGURE 1-1. Framework for Analyzing Organizations

Structure and Compliance

Next—and this is very important—we assume that there are two basic aspects of organizations (their *structure,* and how *compliance* is ensured) that organization theorists have focused on and that we should therefore stress in this book. First, in Chapters 6 and 7, we address the question of *organization structure and design*—the question, in other words, of how to distribute specific tasks and responsibilities among the members of the organization. Here we discuss structural dimensions like departmentation, span of control, and coordination, and how context affects each dimension.

But from the point of view of an organization theorist (or manager), it is not enough to simply assign tasks to individuals; in addition, *you have to ensure that those tasks are in fact carried out*—that *compliance* takes place. For an organization to be able to function with any degree of effectiveness, each person must be able to assume that the people he or she directs will comply with orders and carry out their tasks. The president who directs the vice-president to increase efficiency, the shipping manager who directs the truckers to make certain deliveries, and the production foreman who directs an employee to tighten a bolt all issue orders on the assumption that those orders will be carried out. To the extent that orders are carried out, tasks can be accomplished in such a way that they contribute in an integrated manner to the organization's goals. To the extent that orders are not obeyed, there is no way to ensure that the logic of the organization's structure will function effectively. Therefore, we discuss motivation and compliance in Chapters 8, 9, and 10. We thus assume that *compliance* and *structure* are two major theoretical issues to be dealt with, and that both are influenced by the context of the organization.

Social Influences

However, although having an effective structure and ensuring compliance are important determinants of organization effectiveness, other factors also influence effectiveness (often through their effects on structure and compliance). In Chapters 11 through 14, we discuss four such influential factors —leadership, work groups, intergroup conflict, and organization change and development—with a particular focus on the question, "How does this particular factor influence organization structure and compliance?"

Effectiveness

Finally, in the last chapter, we focus on organization effectiveness and on answering the questions we raised above ("What are the major determinants of organizational effectiveness?" and so on).

But before proceeding to the first stage of our model on organizational context, we will discuss (in Chapters 2 and 3) the evolution of management and organization theory from preindustrial times to the present. This will help us put the various theories of organization into perspective as well as lay the groundwork for the chapters that follow.

FOOTNOTES

1 Paul Diederick, "Components of a Scientific Attitude," *The Science Teacher*, February 1967, pp. 23–24.

2 Quoted in Richard Haney, "The Development of Scientific Attitudes," *The Science Teacher*, December 1964, pp. 33–35.

Chapter 2

Classical

Organization Theories

CHAPTER OVERVIEW

In this and the following chapter, we discuss the evolution of management and organization theory from preindustrial times to the present. In keeping with our model, by the time you have finished reading this chapter, you should be able to answer the following questions:

1. What prescriptions did each theorist have for how organizations should be structured?
2. What prescriptions did each theorist have for how to best ensure compliance—that employees carry out their assigned tasks?
3. What was it about the work tasks each theorist focused on that influenced his or her prescriptions for how to structure organizations and obtain compliance?
4. What was it about the environment of the organizations each theorist focused on that influenced his or her prescriptions for how to structure organizations, and how to obtain compliance?

In this chapter, we will see that the organizations prescribed by classical theorists were generally highly centralized, and contained tasks that were quite specialized. These theorists generally prescribed close adherence to the "chain of command" and the use discipline, rules, and close supervision for ensuring compliance—prescriptions that were generally in keeping with the environments and tasks that these early theorists focused on. The pace of life was comparatively slow, organizations were seldom called upon to make high-speed decisions, and work tasks called for routine effort, not creativity. In this environment and with these kinds of tasks, the rigid "mechanistic" prescriptions of the classical theorists and their predecessors worked quite well.

The outline of this chapter is as follows:

I. Background: The Preindustrial Period
   A. Egypt, Greece, and Rome
   B. The Medieval Period
   C. The Capitalistic Ethic and Economic Individualism
   D. The Legacy
   E. The Industrial Revolution

II. Scientific Management
   A. Frederick Winslow Taylor

III. The Administrative Theorists
   A. Henri Fayol
   B. Urwick and Gulick; Mooney and Reilly
   C. Max Weber and Bureaucratic Organization Theory
   D. Criticism of Administrative and Bureaucratic Theories

IV. Summary

BACKGROUND:
THE PREINDUSTRIAL PERIOD

Many of the structures and assumptions of classical theory had their genesis in this early, preindustrial period, so an understanding of this background is important for putting the classical theories in perspective.

Egypt, Greece, and Rome

The first large-scale organizations were Egyptian state monopolies, used for carrying out such projects as irrigation, canal building, and the construction of pyramids. At the top of the organization was the pharaoh, who based his authority on divine right and delegated certain authority to his vizier. The vizier acted as prime minister, chief justice, and treasurer, and was directly responsible for an elaborate bureaucracy at the base of which were tens of thousands of slaves. The Egyptian economy was an almost totally agrarian one, and a major function of the bureaucracy was to forecast and utilize the rise and fall of the Nile River.

Although the Old Testament and Babylonian documents indicate that commerce existed during this period, it was not until the rise of ancient Greece that trade began to flourish. But ironically, as Tilgher points out, the aristocratic or philosophical Greek found that "any activity which brings the spirit into close contact with the material world . . . [was] a painful and humiliating necessity . . . truth alone being the only true concern."[1] Business in general, and money-lending in particular, were therefore carried out by slaves and less-than-respectable citizens; manual workers and merchants, in fact, were not permitted citizenship in the Greek democracy. To the high-placed Greek, commerce was necessary but distasteful.

The Romans inherited this disdain for business, and left these activities in the hands of Greek and Oriental freemen. Although the aristocracy entered into agreements with business in return for the provision of money for its wars, there was a persistent distrust of the merchant. Yet trade flourished, and the Roman state became increasingly involved in all aspects of economic life, largely because of the requirements for commercial standardization and a state-guaranteed system of weights, measures, and coins. In addition, the state levied tariffs and fines and regulated the guilds. Superimposed over these various state functions was the military autocracy, which, through the dual concepts of discipline and functionalism, ran the empire with an iron hand. Functionalism vested itself in a highly specialized division of work among the various military and governmental agencies, while discipline ensured the compliance that enabled a rigid, hierarchical, centralized structure to be utilized in carrying out the various functions.

As the autocratic Roman military organization reached its apex, the popularity of the Catholic Church began to spread. Church leaders found this popularity to be a two-edged sword, however, and in the second century A.D., they began to recognize that the growth of new sects was threatening the foundations of the Church. This concern manifested itself in a number of activities aimed at defining more rigorously the objectives, doctrine, and conditions for membership within the organization. The result was the development and establishment of scriptural canons, doctrine, and a centralized source of authority, all of which were aimed at ensuring the compliance of Church members and officers.

The Medieval Period

The period between the fall of Rome and the Renaissance was characterized by stagnation and a lack of economic and social development. The feudal system dominated the economic life of Europe, and the serf, who was legally free but almost entirely dependent on the manor lord, replaced the slave at the base of the economic social order. The Church was the dominant institution and prevailed over virtually all areas of human activity, both secular and spiritual. Salvation was stressed, and European man was taught to lead a subsistence, monastic life in return for an eternity in heaven.

With the Church as superstate, the warnings against lending for interest or desiring anything in this life perpetuated the idea of business as a necessary evil. But the Church, which Harbison describes as a paradox— "a divine church, with human worldly organization"[2]—became the largest landholder in Europe and employed thousands of serfs. There was a noticeable shift in Church views of business activities during the latter part of the medieval period, consistent with the growing commercialism. Even with these relaxations, however, the dominant view was that trade and commerce were to be tolerated as necessary evils. For example, Tawney describes the medieval period and its views of commerce as follows:

> At every turn, therefore, there are limits, restrictions, warnings against allowing economic interests to interfere with serious affairs. It is right for man to seek such wealth as is necessary for a livelihood in his station. To seek more is not enterprise, but avarice, and avarice is a deadly sin. Trade is legitimate; the different resources of different countries show that it was intended by Providence. But it is a dangerous business. A man must be sure that he carried it on for the public benefit, and the profits which he takes are no more than the wages of his labor. Private property is a necessary institution, at least in a fallen world; men work more and dispute less when goods are private than when they are common. But it is to be tolerated as a concession to frailty, not applauded as desirable in itself.[3]

This negative view had its origin in ancient Greece and still persists among certain groups and cultures. Before industrialization could take place, it had to be counterbalanced with a new view, that of the capitalistic ethic.

The Capitalistic Ethic and Economic Individualism

This new ethic had religious, political, and economic roots and had its origin in the Crusades, which were themselves a result of feudalism. The Crusades stimulated commerce by establishing new trade routes and exposing the parochial civilization of Europe to the wealth of the Orient. The first cracks began to appear in the Church's facade as the Crusaders, who had embarked on their journeys with unshakable religious conviction, were struck by the realization that the Middle Eastern culture was in many ways superior to theirs—particularly in trade and industry. In brief, the Crusades stimulated commerce by opening new trade routes, contributing to the rise of towns and a new middle class, and weakening the dominance of Christian belief.

Gradually, the spread of prosperity, the loosening of religious bonds by the Crusades, and the excesses of the Church resulted in the undermining of the Church's various secular duties. Slowly, throughout Europe, its three key powers of appointment, taxation and jurisdiction were circumscribed by monarchs. In Germany, which had the weakest of national governments, Martin Luther proclaimed his 95 theses and opened the first hole in the religious dike holding back individualism.

Economic individualism, which Harbison has described as "more a coincidence of the reformation than an effect of it," [4] would have its foundations in Luther's ideas of a *calling*. This idea discarded Catholic notions of subsistence living by urging the individual to fulfill the obligation imposed upon him in this world—that is, his calling. In addition, Luther's emphasis on the Bible (not the Church) as authority and on the whole community of Christ as the Church attracted wide acceptance. His ideas were espoused by workers, who felt they would be free of *both* Church and secular bonds; by the middle class, who saw in them the first visions of a religious rationale for trade and business; and by the governing class, who looked enviously at Church lands.

Whereas Luther's eyes were on the past, Calvin's were on the present, and he accepted the advanced commerce of his day. He developed the concept of the *elect*, who were those predestined to be saved. Each man must consider himself one of the elect; if he did not, his lack of self-confidence would be interpreted as a lack of faith. To attain this self-confidence, each man must engage intensely in work, for this activity could dispel religious doubts and give certainty of grace.

Although Protestantism did not condone the pursuit of wealth, it did encourage intense activity as the goal of the good life. Similarly, the wasting of time and unwillingness to work were the deadliest of sins, and the division and specialization of work was the result of a divine will, if it led to an increase in the quality and quantity of production. Furthermore, this division of work placed each man in his calling and required him to do his best; those workers who were nonspecialized demonstrated a lack of grace and therefore of predestination.

Religion, which once had a moderating effect on industry, now gradually took on a facilitative accelerative function. Unlike the Catholic of the Middle Ages, who was taught to strive for a subsistence, monastic existence while hoping for salvation, a Puritan was taught to believe that hard work reflected the fact that he was predestined. In particular:

> If an individual's destiny hangs on a private transaction between himself and his maker, what room is left for human intervention . . . the Puritan flings himself into practical activities with the daemonic energy of one who, all doubts allayed, is conscious that he is a sealed and chosen vessel.[5]

These were powerful ideas, and, as Tawney notes:

> Like traits of individual character which are suppressed until the approach of maturity releases them, the tendencies in Puritanism, which were to make it later a potent ally of the movement against the control of economic relations in the name either of social morality or of the public interest, did not reveal themselves till political and economic changes had prepared a congenial environment for their growth.[6]

Economically, the Middle Ages had been a sterile period, since the relatively simple, localized economies required no sophisticated theories of resource allocation. Toward the end of the Middle Ages, increased trade resulted in the growth of the domestic or "putting-out" system of production. Under this system, a merchant would act as a middleman in both procuring raw materials and selling the completed product. Upon obtaining the materials, he would allocate them to individual workers or families, who would use their own equipment in manufacturing the finished product for a wage. This system was well suited to the period: Trade was still in its infancy, a high-volume demand for goods had not yet been developed, and the nature of the domestic system itself militated against a standardization of either raw materials or the finished product. As the volume of trade grew, however, this system proved increasingly inefficient, and civilization moved inexorably toward the Industrial Revolution.

By the 16th century, international trade and the rise of centralized governments had resulted in the economic philosophy of mercantilism, which gave the government a strong central role in the financing and regulating of trade. In the 18th century, the Physiocratic School of economic thought, under François Quesnay, advocated laissez-faire capitalism, a philosophy that in turn influenced Adam Smith. In his *Wealth of Nations,* Smith called for the separation of government and economy, and described how the "invisible hand" of the market would ensure that resources flowed to the best consumption and their most efficient reward. The economic rationality and self-interest of each person and nation, acting in a fully competitive market, would bring about the greatest prosperity for all. For Smith, the division and specialization of work was a pillar of the free, competitive market mechanism and would lead to enormous increases in productivity and output. John Locke's essay, "Concerning Civil Government," was also published in this period; in it he attacked the divine right of kings and stated the principles of the English Bloodless Revolution of 1688. Justice, equality, and the rights of man became the prime movers of political action.

By about 1750, the ideological and cultural stage was set for the advent of the Industrial Revolution. Economic theory emphasized the utilitarian rationality and self-interest of man; *every man supposedly weighed the economic alternatives open to him and consistently chose the one that resulted in his highest net gain. For the worker, this was the highest possible wage.* Furthermore, the benefits of division of work were claimed as the economic rationale for the factory system. In conjunction with these two concepts, Protestantism—and particularly the later Puritanism—provided a religious rationale for hard work, specialization, and competition.

Ironically, though, the ideas of economic rationality, self-interest, and predestination acted in some respects as counteracting forces to the new ideas of political liberty. A legal–rational authority based on private property and technical competence was simply substituted for the traditional social-class authority founded on the divine right of kings. Leaders and entrepreneurs, who had previously based their autocratic treatment of workers on the concept of divine right and on philosophies like those of Machiavelli and Hobbes, now had the Protestant Ethic to guide them. The result was that many management writers in future years would continue to view the worker, as March and Simon put it, as an "inert instrument performing the task assigned him . . . as a given, rather than as a variable in the system." [7]

The Legacy

The major organizational legacy of this later preindustrial period reflected the traditional, social-class concept of authority, the Greek view of work, and the command philosophy of leadership reflected in the works of

Machiavelli and Hobbes. Historically, structures were highly centralized, the work tasks were specialized into functional units, and discipline, dogma, and fear were used to ensure the compliance of workers. A rigid, hierarchical chain of command was the norm, and authority and communications emanated from the top. In turn, these inflexible organizations largely reflected a stable, relatively unchanging environment. As Toffler has noted:

> Each age produces a form of organization appropriate to its own tempo. During the long epoch of agricultural civilization, societies were marked by low transience. Delays in communication and transportation slowed the rate at which information moved. The pace of individual life was comparatively slow. And organizations were seldom called upon to make what we would regard as high-speed decisions.[8]

The Industrial Revolution

The new economic, religious, and political ideas emerging at the time combined to produce a catalytic climate in which the scientific and technological discoveries of Galileo, Gilbert, Harvey, Watt, and others could contribute to industrialization. The Industrial Revolution, recognized as having centered in England around the 1780s, was characterized by a monumental event: the substitution of machine power for manpower. England during this period had a stable, constitutional government, a sensitivity to laissez-faire economics, and a strong spirit of self-reliance. It was therefore a logical epicenter for the industrial changes taking place.

Organizationally, industrialization resulted in an almost total emphasis on the strategy of resource accumulation and company growth. This was necessitated by the availability of capital and the widely recognized and accepted productivity advantages of division of work. Division of work and specialization require volume and stability, and growth therefore resulted in increasing returns; as sales, volume, and stability increased, unit costs decreased. In an age without mass communication or transportation, efficiency experts, research and development, or government interference, this strategy of resource accumulation was an effective one that helped protect the production facility from the vagaries of the marketplace.

Enlarged operations, however, created many problems for the entrepreneur. First, he found (as did managers before him) that he alone could not direct and control all the activities of his organizations; whereas the Church could resort to dogma, and the military to discipline, managers in the new factory system found themselves unable to properly monitor the work of submanagers and workers. In addition, there was a severe shortage of both managers and skilled labor, and the skilled labor that was available frequently resisted the standardization of parts, methods, and tools required by the interchangeable-parts method of production.

Management. These early entrepreneurs—faced with the dilemma of rigorous competition on the one hand, and an uncertain labor force on the other—quickly adopted the structures and principles of older organizations.

Such ideas as centralization, clear hierarchy, specialized division of work, and autocratic leadership were implemented as competitive pressures for size demanded increasingly predictable results from a frequently unwilling labor force. But it is important to remember that this emphasis on structure and imposed compliance also reflected the prevailing economic, religious, and political philosophies. Specifically—and this is important—these philosophies (particularly those of predestination, the religious benefits of division of work, and economic self-interest and rationality) combined to permit the entrepreneur to view his "human inputs" as little more than another tool, a view that would last through the first two decades of the present century. In addition, the competitive environment was one over which the entrepreneur had little control, except what he could exert through increased size. Therefore, the organizations of the period did not have to be structured for adapting to a rapidly changing and complex environment; instead, the entrepreneur had to exert all his energies and abilities toward the accumulation of more resources for the purpose of increasing the size and productivity of his manufacturing facility.

SCIENTIFIC MANAGEMENT

This race to accumulate resources and increase factory size was particularly pronounced in America. The War of 1812 had severed America economically from England and spurred the growth of manufacturing operations. Technological advances included the steamboat, the cotton gin, the iron plow, the telegraph, the electric motor, and the expansion of a railroad and canal network that opened new markets for producers. In turn, these new markets provided the volume that was a fundamental requirement for the division of work.

Chandler has pointed out that during the late 1800s, many new industries were completing the resource-accumulation stage of their existence and beginning to move into a "rationalization" stage.[9] The rationalization of the newly accumulated recources was necessary not only because of industry's pressing need for efficiency but also because of the crude forms of planning, organizing, controlling, and administering then in existence. Given the nature of the environment and of mass-production techniques, this rationalization was more crucial in the production shop than elsewhere in the organization. Production—and in particular, mass production—demanded, in addition to high volume, stability in raw materials, labor, and production techniques for its very existence. In total, therefore the stage was set for the American economy to move into its rationalization phase.

Frederick Winslow Taylor

Frederick Winslow Taylor was a mechanical engineer whose ideas were strongly influenced by a paper delivered in 1886 by Henry Towne to the Amercian Society of Mechanical Engineers. The paper, entitled, "The Engineer as Economist," asked engineers to build a management literature of "Science and Practice." Taylor had always shown an affinity for scientific investigation, research, and experimentation, and for improving things from a basis of fact; Towne's speech provided a direction for his energies.

The major theme of scientific management was that work, and especially blue-collar work, could be studied scientifically. Taylor believed that the objective analysis of data collected in the workplace could provide the basis for determining the "one best way" to organize work, and with his Quaker–Puritan background, he pursued this goal relentlessly.

In his two major works, *Shop Management* and *The Principles of Scientific Management*, Taylor proposed the framework for his new science of work. He suggested a system that can be summarized as consisting of four principles: [10]

1. *Finding the "one best way."* First, management—through observation and "the deliberate gathering in . . . of all the great mass of traditional knowledge, which in the past has been in the heads of the workmen . . . "—finds the "one best way" for performing each job.

2. *Scientific selection of personnel.* This next principle requires "the scientific selection and then the progressive development of the workmen." This involves finding each worker's limitations and "possibilities for development" and giving him the required training.

3. *Financial incentives.* Taylor knew that putting the right worker on the right job would not by itself ensure high productivity, and that some plan for motivating workers to do their best and to comply with their supervisor's instructions was necessary. He saw, in other words, that organization structure and division of work was only half the problem faced by an organization theorist: the other half involved finding some way to ensure that each worker performed his or her task effectively. Taylor, always the Puritan, proposed that a system of financial incentives be used, in which each worker was paid in direct proportion to how much he produced rather than simply according to a basic hourly wage. An incentive plan thus served much the same purpose in Taylor's organization theory as did the discipline, dogma, and threats of earlier military, religious, and feudal managers.

4. *Functional foremanship.* Finally, Taylor called for a division of work between manager and worker such that managers did all planning, preparing, and inspecting while the workers did the actual work. Taylor proposed using specialized experts ("functional foremen"), each of whom was to be responsible for some specific aspect of the worker's task, such as finding the best machine speed, deciding on job priorities, or inspecting the work. The worker was to take orders from each of these foremen, depending upon whether the matter concerned planning, machine speed, or inspecting, for example.

Taylor as an organization theorist. As a theorist Taylor dealt explicitly with both the structure and compliance questions of organization theory. With respect to structure, he focused not on questions of overall organization but rather on the best way for dividing the work at the workplace itself. Here, he prescribed functional foremanship and, more important, the scientific observation and analysis of each separate job in order to find the "one best way" for performing it.

The question of compliance—of how to get each worker to do his or her best—was probably Taylor's overriding concern, and it was one that manifested itself in both his incentive plan and his equating scientific management with a "mental revolution." Although Taylor was often criticized as the man who proposed a degrading, demoralizing, machinelike existence for the worker, his objectives were probably just the opposite. He said that scientific management was "not just an efficiency device, or a new scheme of paying men, or a bonus system," but instead:

> . . . involves a complete mental revolution on the part of the working man engaged in any particular establishment or industry—a complete mental revolution on the part of these men as to their duties toward their work, toward their fellow men, and toward their employees. And it involves the equally complete mental revolution on the part of those on the management side— the foreman, the superintendent, [etc.]. . . .

> The great revolution that takes place in the mental attitude of the two parties under scientific management is that both sides take their eyes off the division of the surplus as the all-important matter, and together turn their attention toward increasing the size of the surplus until the surplus becomes so large that it is unnecessary to quarrel over how it shall be divided. They come to see that when they stop pulling against one another and instead both turn and push shoulder to shoulder in the same direction, the size of the surplus created by their joint effort is truly astonishing.[11]

Taylor's ideas were firmly founded upon a desire for worker–management harmony and increased worker benefits. The problem lay not in Taylor's motives but in his assumptions, which were the prevailing utilitarian–rational assumptions of the day. The concepts of man as a rational being, and division of work as a manifestation of religious grace, allowed Taylor and his disciples to largely disregard the variables of human behavior in organizations. Furthermore, his idea of an increased surplus referred only to dollars, and he overestimated the extent to which wages were the sole concern of workers.

Scientific management was therefore a product of its times. Born and nurtured in an era of laissez-faire economics, the Protestant Ethic, and national optimism and dedication to efficiency, it was a reasonable and probably necessary method for rationalizing the recently accumulated resources of industry. Furthermore, the fact that the environment was still relatively stable, combined with Taylor's inherent production orientation, allowed him to largely disregard the environment as a vital force to which organizations must adapt.

As Thompson points out:

> Scientific management, focusing primarily on manufacturing or similar production activities, clearly employs economic efficiency as its ultimate criterion . . . and achieves conceptual closure of the organization by assuming that goals are known, tasks are repetitive, output of the production process somehow disappears, and resources in uniform qualities are available.[12]

THE ADMINISTRATIVE THEORISTS

The concepts and methods of scientific management were not generally applicable to the broader questions of organizational design. In fact, with the exception of planning and supervising, managerial functions like organizing, controlling, and staffing were not analyzed. These functions and questions were analyzed by subsequent theorists to whom we now turn.

Henri Fayol

Background. Henri Fayol was born and educated in France, and his working life (although spent entirely with the Commentry-Fourchambault Mining Company) fell into four periods.[13] From 1860 to 1872, he was a subordinate, working mainly on technical problems of mining engineering, such as the fire hazards of coal mining. From 1872 to 1888, he was the director of a group of mining pits, and his mind turned to the geographical problems of the area. From 1888 to 1918, he held the top position of managing director of the entire company, and he proved to be a remarkably effective chief executive. (When he was appointed in 1888, the company was on the verge of bankruptcy, and many of its divisions were showing heavy losses. Almost from the day he took charge, losses decreased, and by the time he retired at the age of 77, the firm's financial and managerial situation was unassailable.) Toward the end of this period, his work *General and Industrial Management* was first published in French. From 1918 until his death in 1925, he devoted himself to popularizing his theory of administration, which (unlike Taylor's production-shop orientation) viewed management from the general perspective of a chief executive. *General and Industrial Management* was first translated into English in 1929 but was apparently not published in the United States until the 1940s.

Fayol's definition of management. Fayol said that all industrial activities could be divided into one of six groups:

1. Technical activities (production, manufacturing, adaptation)
2. Commercial activities (buying, selling, exchange)
3. Financial activities (search for an optimum use of capital)
4. Security activities (protection of property and person)

5. Accounting activities (stock taking, balance sheets, costs, statistics)
6. Managerial activities (planning, organization, command, coordination, control)

Fayol felt that although management was only one of the six groups of activities necessary in companies, it was perhaps the most important one, and it was the only one he focused on in his writings. He also thought there was an absence of management teaching in schools and that this was due to the fact that there was "no generally accepted theory of management emanating from general discussion." He set out to present such a theory, based upon two concepts: principles of management, and elements of management.

Fayol's principles of management. Fayol prescribed fourteen principles of management, each of which, he emphasized, was "flexible and capable of adaptation to every need; it is a matter of knowing how to make use of them, which is a difficult art requiring intelligence, experience, decision and proportion." (Although he stressed that the principles should be applied flexibly, he also referred to them as "acknowledged truths regarded as proven on which to rely.") [14] He said these fourteen were the principles he most often used as a manager, but that many other principles could also be identified.

His fourteen principles (along with some of his comments on them) were as follows:

1. *Division of work.* The worker, always on the same part, and the manager, concerned always with the same matters, acquired ability, sureness, and accuracy, which increased their output.
2. *Authority and responsibility.* Authority is the right to give orders and the power to exact obedience. Distinction must be made between a manager's official authority, deriving from office, and personal authority, compounded of intelligence, experience, moral worth, and ability to lead.
3. *Discipline.* The best means of establishing and maintaining [discipline] are: good superiors at all levels; agreements as clear and fair as possible; sanctions [penalties] judiciously applied.
4. *Unity of command.* For any action whatsoever, an employee should receive orders from one superior only. . . .
5. *Unity of direction.* There should be one head and one plan for a group of activities serving the same objective.
6. *Subordination of individual interests to general interests.* This principle means that in a business, the interests of one employee or group of employees should not prevail over those of the concern. . . . Means of effecting it are: firmness and good example on the part of superiors; agreements as far as is possible; constant supervision.

7. *Remuneration of personnel.* Remuneration should be fair and as far as possible afford satisfaction to both personnel and firm.

8. *Centralization.* The question of centralization or decentralization is a simple question of proportion; it is a matter of finding the optimum degree for the particular concern. What appropriate share of initiative may be left to intermediaries depends on the personal character of the manager, on his moral worth, on the reliability of his subordinates, and also on the condition of the business. The degree of centralization must vary according to different cases.

9. *Scalar chain.* The scalar chain is the chain of superiors ranging from the ultimate authority to the lowest ranks. . . . It is an error to depart needlessly from the line of authority, but it is an even greater one to keep to it when detriment to the business ensues.

10. *Order.* For social order to prevail in a concern, there must be an appointed place for every employee and every employee must be in his appointed place.

11. *Equity.* For the personnel to be encouraged to carry out its duties with all the devotion and loyalty of which it is capable, it must be treated with kindliness, and equity results from the combination of kindness and justice. Equity excludes neither forcefulness nor sternness. . . .

12. *Stability of tenure of personnel.* Time is required for an employee to get used to new work and succeed in doing it well, always assuming that he possesses the requisite abilities. If, when he has gotten used to it, or before then, he is removed, he will not have had time to render worthwhile service.

13. *Initiative.* Thinking out a plan and ensuring its success is one of the keenest satisfactions for an intelligent man to experience. . . . This power of thinking out and executing is what is called initiative. . . . It . . . represents a great source of strength for business.

14. *Esprit de corps.* "Union is strength." Harmony, union among the personnel of a concern, is a great strength in that concern. Effort, then, should be made to establish it.

The elements of management. Fayol turned next to a discussion of his "elements" of management—planning, organizing, commanding, coordinating, and controlling—and for each he presented some prescriptions; for example:

1. *Planning.* The general features of a good plan of action include . . . unity, continuity, flexibility, precision.

2. *Organizing.* The general form of an organization depends almost solely on the number of its employees. . . . The personnel of

enterprises of all kinds is constituted in similar fashion to that of industrial concerns, so much so that all organizations at the same stage of expansion are alike. This likeness is explained by the fact of there being identity of functions in business of the same type.

3. *Command.* The organization, having been formed, must be set going, and this is the mission of command. . . . While it is taken for granted that every manager has authority to exact obedience, a business would be ill-served where obedience is obtained only by fear of oppression. . . . Some leaders get obedience, energy, zeal, and even loyalty without apparent effort; others never succeed at it . . . but managers should also conduct periodic audits of the organization, bring together their chief assistants by means of conferences, not become engrossed in detail, and aim at making unity, energy, initiative and loyalty prevail among the personnel. They can do this by allowing them the maximum share in activity consistent with their position and capability even at the cost of some mistakes, whose magnitude, however, may be circumscribed by means of watchful attention.[15]

4. *Coordination.* In a well-coordinated enterprise, each department works in harmony with the rest; and in each department, divisions and subdivisions are precisely informed as to the share they must take in the communal task. There is a weekly conference of department heads which has for its aim to inform management about the running of the concern. . . . If such meetings are impractical, the gap must be filled as far as possible by the use of liaison officers at meetings.

5. *Control.* In an undertaking, control consists in verifying whether everything occurs in conformity with the plan adopted, the instructions issued, and the principles established. It has for its object to point out weaknesses and errors in order to rectify them and prevent recurrences. It operates on everything—things, people, actions. . . .

Fayol as an organization theorist. As a theorist, Fayol dealt primarily with the question of organization structure, but his prescriptions touched on employee compliance as well. With respect to structure, he leaned toward recommending a more centralized, functionally specialized organization structure in which everyone and everything had a precisely defined place. (His narrative, however, contains frequent reference to his experience in his mining and steel firm, and you should keep in mind that to this day, most firms of this type will still reflect this "mechanistic" structure.) He concluded erroneously that all organizations at the same stage of development should have the same functional division of work and structure, and that number of employees was the main determinant of the "general form of organization."

When he did address the problem of compliance, he usually prescribed the use of "sanctions" (penalties), "constant supervision," and a subordination of individual interests to those of the firm. About the only explicit statement he makes in regard to using something other than sanctions or close supervision in motivating workers is his mention of managers' "setting a good example" and also letting subordinates make more decisions in order to tap their initiative.

Urwick and Gulick; Mooney and Reilly

During the 1920s and 1930s, a number of other theorists—primarily those engaged in management or consulting practices—set forth their views, following the concepts laid down by Fayol. Two of these, Luther Gulick and Lyndall Urwick, utilized their broad managerial experience in elaborating on Fayol's principles, and in 1937 they coedited *Papers on the Science of Administration*.[16] Their book included papers by Fayol, by Gulick (who was then a professor at Columbia University), by Urwick (then a management consultant), and by James D. Mooney (then a vice-president at General Motors Corporation).[17]

Gulick, Urwick, and organization theory. In their *Papers* Gulick and Urwick popularized principles governing *division of work, coordination, creating departments built around "purposes, process, persons, and place,"* and *the use of "staff."* [18] Their work emphasized questions of organization structure. For example, they explain the pros and cons of different ways of dividing and coordinating the work of the organization, how to make use of line and staff personnel, the best span of control, and the advantages of specialization. But while stressing structure, they at least make reference to the need for encouraging motivation and compliance; Gulick says, for example:

> Any large and complicated enterprise would be incapable of effective operation if reliance for coordination were placed in organization alone. Organization is necessary; in a large enterprise it is essential, but it does not take the place of a dominant central idea as the foundation of action and self-coordination in the daily operation of all the parts of the enterprise. Accordingly, the most difficult task of the chief executive is not command, it is leadership; that is, the development of the desire and will to work together for a purpose in the minds of those who are associated in any activity. Human beings are compounded of cogitation and emotion and do not function well when treated as though they were merely cogs in motion. Their capacity for great and productive labor, creative cooperative work, and loyal self-sacrifice knows no limits provided the whole man, body, mind, and spirit, is thrown into the program.[19]

Yet, having mentioned the idea that "the development of the desire" is important, they provide almost no guidelines for implementation. They simply suggest that "personnel administration"—selecting qualified employees—is important, that professionalism among workers should be encouraged, and that "dominant ideals" in which all organizational members can believe are crucial:

> Men of intelligence and goodwill will find little difficulty in working to-
> gether for a given purpose even without an organization. They do not need to
> be held in line or driven to do a specific task in a specific way at a specific time.
> They carry on because of their inner compulsion, and may in the end accom-
> plish a far better result for that very reason.[20]

Their statements (particularly the last one) stand as a brilliant insight into
the compliance problem of organization theory; yet their papers were devoted almost entirely to questions of organization structure.

Mooney and Reilly's principles of organization. In 1931, James
Mooney and Allen Reilly published their book, *Onward Industry*, which
had a major impact on management practice in America.[21] In it, they
stressed three principles of organization that they had found displayed in
governmental, religious, military, and business organizations. In their words:

1. *The coordinative principle.* Organization begins when people,
   even if they be only two or more, combine their efforts for a given
   purpose. A simple illustration is two people combining their
   strength to lift and move a weighty object. The efforts of these
   two lifters must be coordinated. If first one lifted and then the
   other, there would be no unity of action, and hence no true organization of effort. . . . Coordination expresses the principles of
   organization "in toto." . . .
2. *The scalar process.* It is essential to the very idea and concept of
   organization that there must be a process, formal in character,
   through which the supreme coordinating authority operates
   throughout the whole structure of the organized body. . . . The
   scalar process is the same form in organization which is sometimes
   called hierarchical. . . . It means the graduation of duties, not
   according to differentiated functions, for this involves another and
   different principle of organization, but simply according to degrees
   of authority and corresponding responsibility.
3. *The functional effect.* By the term functionalism, we mean the differentiation or distinction between kinds of duties.

Mooney, Reilly, and organization theory. Like Gulick and Urwick,
Mooney and Reilly emphasized organization structure. Mooney states, for
example:

> But what, in industrial organization, are the conditions necessary to the
> highest efficiency of considered effort? If we addressed this question to a score
> of representative executives, we would of course get many valuable and in-
> spirational answers. But I wonder how many of these answers would give the
> structural principles of organization the importance that I believe they
> deserve? [22]

Yet they too at least recognize the importance of the human element.
Mooney states, for example:

In this outline of the structural principles of organization I have done no more than expose the scaffolding, the framework out of which it is made. In stressing the importance of the framework, I hope no one will think I am overlooking the major importance of the human factor. Humanly speaking, the strength of any organization is simply the aggregate strength of the individuals who compose it.[23]

However, this "aggregate strength" is best tapped by designing an efficient organization structure:

We cannot forget, however, that the strength of the individual, whatever that strength may be, can only attain the highest measure of effectiveness through soundly adjusted relationships, and it is here that we see the fundamental importance of the structural principles. If we truly coordinate the jobs as such, we shall find that the more efficient and harmonious coordination of the people on the jobs is immensely facilitated.[24]

Max Weber and Bureaucratic Organization Theory

Background. Max Weber was a contemporary of both Taylor and Fayol, and his work, first published in Germany in 1921, bears remarkable similarity to that of Fayol, Urwick, and Gulick. However, it was not translated and published in America until 1947 and was apparently unknown to theorists of the 1930s.

Unlike most of these writers, Weber did not write from the vantage point of a manager, but from that of an intellectual. He had been born in 1864 to a well-to-do, cultured family and attended Heidelberg University, where he studied law, history, economics, and philosophy under a succession of eminent scholars. He served a year in the German army, and then resumed his university studies in Berlin and Goettingen; then, after practicing law, he accepted a chair as professor at Heidelberg.

Bureaucracy. Writing during the 1920s, Weber saw the growth of the large-scale organization and correctly predicted that this growth required a more formalized set of procedures for administrators. Today, he said,

it is primarily the capitalistic market economy which demands that the official business of the administration be discharged precisely, unambiguously, continuously, and with as much speed as possible.[25]

In line with this, Weber adopted the idea of an ideal or "pure form" of organization, which he called *bureaucracy*. This term, as developed by Weber and his followers, was not used in the now popularized sense of red tape and inefficiency. The bureaucratic model possesses certain structural characteristics that are found in every complex organization, and the model refers to these characteristics of organizational design. For Weber, bureaucracy was the most efficient form of organization, and could most effectively be used with the complex organizations that arose out of the needs of modern society. Weber described bureaucracy as having:

1. A well-defined hiearchy of authority
2. A clear division of work
3. A system of rules covering the rights and duties of position incumbents
4. A system of procedures for dealing with the work situation
5. Impersonality of interpersonal relationships
6. Selection for employment and promotion based on technical competence [26]

Such an organization was technically superior to any other form of organization:

> The fully developed bureaucratic mechanism compares with other organizations exactly as does the machine with the non-mechanical modes of production . . . precision, speed, unambiguity, continuity, discretion, unity, . . . these are raised to the optimum point in a strictly bureaucratic administration.[27]

Weber felt that these attributes were necessary because of the "extraordinary increase in the speed by which public announcements, as well as economic and political facts, are transmitted." He saw that the tempo of administrative action was increasing and concluded that "the optimum of such reaction time is normally obtained only by a strictly Bureaucratic organization." [28]

One of the ironies in the development of organization theory is that bureaucracy, which has come to mean a ponderous and unadaptive organization, was originally advocated as the best form for dealing with a changing environment. And yet, in the context of its time, the idea made a good deal of sense. The codified rules, predictable relationships, and clear job descriptions permitted these organizations to make faster decisions than before.

One of the work problems that the bureaucratic model was developed to deal with was what Bennis has described as:

> . . . the personal subjugation, nepotism, cruelty, emotional vicissitudes and subjective judgments which passed for managerial practices in the early days of the industrial revolution. . . .[29]

Bureaucracy, Weber points out,

> . . . is like a modern judge who is a vending machine into which the pleadings are inserted together with the fee and which then disgorges the judgment together with reasons mechanically derived from a code.[30]

Similarly, the individual bureaucrats or officeholders in this ideal organization are described as virtually mechanical objects:

> The individual bureaucrat cannot squirm out of the apparatus in which

he is harnessed . . . in a great majority of cases, he is only a single cog in an ever moving mechanism which prescribes to him an essentially fixed route of march. . . .[31]

Although the image of a mechanical organization, manned by automatons, has cast bureaucracy in an unfavorable light, remember that Weber's ideal model was usually very successful in dealing with the contemporary environment. As Bennis points out, there was a good reason for this:

> It was an ideal weapon to harness and routinize the human mechanical energy which fueled the industrial revolution. It can also function in a highly competitive, fairly undifferentiated and stable environment. The pyramid structure of bureaucracy where power was concentrated at the top—perhaps by one person or a group that had the knowledge and resources to control the entire enterprise—seemed perfect to "run a railroad." And undoubtedly for the routine tasks like building railroads, bureaucracy was and is an eminently suitable social arrangement.[32]

Weber and organization theory.   Weber's bureaucratic theory was primarily a theory of organization structure. In it, Weber tried to show how an ideal organization (one with clearly defined jobs, a stable hierarchy of authority, a system of written documents and procedures, and so on) was superior to less rationally conceived organizations.

Weber actually has very little to say about motivation or compliance in his essay, "Bureaucracy," but his thinking in this regard is made clear in another essay, "The Meaning of Discipline." [33] Discipline, Weber says,

> . . . is nothing but the consistently rationalized, methodically trained and exact execution of the received order, in which all personal criticism is unconditionally suspended and the actor is unswervingly and exclusively set for carrying out the command. . . .

From this essay, it is clear that Weber believed discipline to be a necessary prerequisite to bureaucracy, which he called discipline's "most rational offspring." [34] And discipline, he felt, grew out of workers' economic motives. On the one hand, he recognizes that leaders sometimes use "emotional means of all sorts," such as inspiration and reference to a comman cause, to evoke discipline. Yet, he says, even in war, *economic rationality* ensures the discipline of soldiers: "In the past the fully disciplined army has necessarily been a professional army, and therefore the basic problem has always been how to provide for the sustenance of the warriors." Similarly, he applies this thinking to industrial organizations:

> No special proof is necessary to show that military discipline is the ideal model for the modern capitalist factory. . . . Organizational discipline in the factory is founded upon a completely rational basis. With the help of appropriate methods of measurement, the optimum profitability of the individual worker is calculated like that of any material means of production. On the basis of this calculation, the American system of "scientific management" [35]

enjoys the greatest triumphs in the rational conditioning and training of work performances. The final consequences are drawn from the mechanization and discipline of the plant, and the psycho-physical apparatus of man is completely adjusted to the demands of the outer world, the tools, the machines—in short, to individual "function." . . .[36]

Criticism of Administrative and Bureaucratic Organization Theories

Fayol / Weber

Criticisms of these two theories, most of which also apply to scientific management, concern characteristics that fall into one of four categories:

1. Conflicting principles and lack of empirical validity
2. Inadequate assumptions about workers
3. Inadequate assumptions about the organization's tasks
4. Unanticipated consequences

Conflicting principles and lack of empirical validity. Prof. Herbert Simon has argued that the principles these theories embody are nothing more than proverbs that have neither empirical validation or universal application. Simon points out, for example:

> It is a fatal defect of the current principles of administration that, like proverbs, they occur in pairs. For almost every principle one can find an equally plausible and acceptable contradictory principle. Although the two principles of the pair will lead to exactly opposite organizational recommendations, there is nothing in the theory to indicate which is the proper one to apply.[37]

Inadequate assumptions about workers. Second, some say these theories tend to view workers as little more than machines. March and Simon say that they tend to view the employee as "an inert instrument performing the tasks assigned to him." These machine theories, they say, "have largely ignored factors associated with individual behavior and particularly its motivational basis." [38] Massie complains that these theories assume that people do not like to work, always act rationally, and require detailed guidance and clear job limits in order to perform adequately.[39] Another writer notes that "these are the implicit assumptions about man on which classical organizational theory seems to be based: he is lazy, short-sighted, selfish, liable to make mistakes, has poor judgment, and may even be a little dishonest." [40]

Although some of these allegations may be exaggerated, it does seem apparent that by assuming that man is primarily a rational, money-oriented decision maker, the "machine theorists" were able to relegate workers to a dependent, passive role in organizations. In other words, while clearly recognizing the importance of what Fayol called "keen" performance and "enthusiasm" on the part of the workers, these theorists *erroneously assumed that financial incentives combined with an efficient organization structure would result in optimal performance.* It is therefore not stretching the point too far to say that, despite their occasional disclaimers, these theorists tended to view organizations as something akin to machines—machines that could be laid out in blueprints (organization charts), designed to provide the most efficient service, and oiled periodically (with financial incentives) to keep all the human "parts" operating as they were designed to.

Inadequate assumptions about the organization's tasks.   Third, as Thompson has pointed out, these organizational theories invariably assume that goals are known, tasks are repetitive, production output somehow disappears from the factory, and the organization is a closed system and impervious to all but major changes in environment.[41] Similarly, others note that Taylor was most concerned with the kinds of tasks performed on the production floor or in clerical departments, and that these tasks are largely repetitive.[42] As a result, the tasks these theories (especially scientific management) were concerned with can usually be explained in terms of overt behavior like tightening a bolt or turning a screw, and the applicability of classical prescriptions to more creative tasks must be suspect.

Unanticipated consequences.   Finally, the classical theorists generally prescribed imposed controls (like rules and close supervision) for ensuring employee compliance, and one criticism of such controls is that they result in unanticipated consequences. Robert Merton, for example, says that in these theories, the techniques used to secure reliability include standard operating procedures and constant supervision. Consequences, he says, include a reduction in the amount of personalized relationships in the organization, and an internalization of the rules of the organization by participants whereby the rules, which are meant to be means to an end, become ends in themselves.[43]

Alvin Gouldner made a study of this phenomenon. He found that in practice, work rules provide cues for employees beyond those intended by the manager who developed the rules. Rules, for example, make it clear to employees what *un*acceptable behavior is, and the rules therefore become the minimum standards that employees know they can "get by" with.[44] (For example, the manager who tells his employees they can take only one hour for lunch may find that they rarely take more, but also never less.) The problem with this, of course, is that

> . . . for effective organizational functioning, many members must be willing on occasion to do *more* than their job prescriptions specify. If members of the system were to follow the precise letter of job descriptions and organizational protocol, things would soon grind to a halt. Many acts of spontaneous cooperation and many anticipations of organizational objectives are required to make the system viable. . . .[45]

Yet, such unanticipated consequences need not—in fact do not—always occur. Where jobs are in fact routine, where unexpected occurrences and atypical cases do not exist, and where creativity and initiative are not required of employees, unanticipated consequences would not be a serious problem. Such a description may fit the organizations that theorists like Fayol and Mooney were most familiar with, and to that extent, their prescriptions make a great deal of sense. However, we now recognize that even though people may be "rational," the "benefits" they try to maximize include things other than money, and so using rules, close supervision, and financial incentives to maintain compliance is bound to be inadequate.

More important, in the late 1920s organizations were moving into a new era, one in which the tempo of competition and change and the demand for organizational responsiveness increased. At the same time, as we will see in the next chapter, the tasks workers were called upon to do increasingly required a problem-solving ability and creativity not foreseen by early classical theorists. Man's values changed, the tempo of technological change increased, and the world moved toward what William Scott has called the period of collision.

SUMMARY

What can we conclude from this discussion of classical organization theories? Perhaps the best way to frame an answer to this is in terms of the four questions we listed in the overview to this chapter.

What prescriptions did each theorist have for how to best structure organizations? The highly centralized and mechanistic structures of classical theory had their genesis in the state monopolies of Egypt and the military empire of Rome. Faced with the need for structures through which to manage their new organizations, Industrial Revolution–era managers quickly adopted the structures and principles of the older, preindustrial organizations, and centralization, clear hierarchy of command, and specialized division of work soon became the norm. By and large, the classical theorists themselves—Taylor, Fayol, Urwick and Gulick, Mooney and Reilly, and Weber—generally focused on the question of organization structure, and their prescriptions tended to reflect the mechanistic structural prescriptions (for centralization, specialization of work, and so on) of preindustrial writers. This was due partly to the fairly routine tasks facing the classicists' organizations, and partly to the fact that Protestantism and the concept of economic individualism that prevailed in the early 1900s put great stress on the religious and economic advantages of highly specialized work.

What prescriptions did each theorist have for how to best ensure compliance—to ensure, in other words, that each worker carries out the task to which he or she is assigned? Preindustrial managers emphasized discipline, dogma, and fear in obtaining compliance, techniques that were probably effective where workers were slaves, serfs, or soldiers. But with the advent of the Industrial Revolution, scores of new workers had to be hired and controlled, and new techniques had to be developed to ensure employee compliance. Here, early managers and the later classical theorists found a rallying point in the economic individualism of Protestantism. Protestantism did not condone the pursuit of wealth but did encourage intense activity as the goal of the good life, and such activity was generally measured in economic terms. As a result, classical theorists were able to substitute a network of financial-incentives for the discipline and fear of earlier managers. Classical organization theory is thus replete with reference to the need for financial incentives and for close supervision for ensuring employee compliance.

What was it about the workers' tasks *each theorist focused on that influenced the prescriptions for how to structure organizations and obtain compliance?* During this period, the tasks facing workers were relatively routine and repetitive: Efficiency, rather than creativity or adaptability, was the rule. Jobs like these could be objectively measured and closely supervised, and so close supervision and financial incentives were useful techniques for ensuring compliance. Similarly, there was little or no need for workers to make problem-solving-type, creative decisions, and so most decisions could be made centrally and then enforced through the chain of command.

What was it about the environment *of the organizations each theorist focused on that influenced the prescriptions for how to structure organizations and gain compliance?* The answer to this was perhaps best summarized by Toffler, who said:

> Each age produces a form of organization appropriate to its own tempo. During the long epoch of agricultural civilization, societies were marked by low transience. Delays in communication and transportation slowed the rate at which information moved. The pace of individual life was comparatively slow. And organizations were seldom called upon to make what we would regard as high-speed decisions.

During this period, in other words, organizational environments (including competitors, customers, sources of labor, and so forth) were relatively simple and unchanging. Particularly during the early 1900s, most managers found a strong demand for their products and could focus attention on efficiency rather than on developing new products or adapting to a competitor's new product. And in this relatively undifferentiated and stable environment, an emphasis on efficiency (and therefore, centralized decision making, highly specialized jobs, financial incentives, and close supervision) made a good deal of sense. The most effective organizations, in fact, were those that could focus on efficiency and thus minimize their costs and selling prices.

Organizational environments and tasks thus emerge as important determinants of how an organization is structured and managed. How will the prescriptions of organization theorists change when the prevailing organizations must cope with complex, changing environments and creative, entrepreneurial tasks? This is a topic we turn to in the next chapter.

DISCUSSION QUESTIONS

1. Describe how developments during the preindustrial period contributed to later organization theory.
2. How did Protestantism influence classical organization theory?
3. Compare and contrast the organization theories of Taylor, Fayol, and Weber.
4. Discuss the criticisms of administrative and bureaucratic organizational theories. To what extent do you think these criticisms are valid?
5. What are the implicit assumptions of the classical organization theories?
6. "Organization theory and values tend to reflect the prevailing environment in which they develop." Discuss whether you agree or disagree with this statement. Include specific references to the various theories we discussed in this chapter.

FOOTNOTES

[1] Adriano Tilgher, *Work*, trans. Dorothy C. Fisher (New York: Harcourt, Brace, 1930), pp. 5–6, quoted in Richard Eells and Clarence Walton, *Conceptual Foundations of Business* (Homewood, Ill.: Richard D. Irwin, 1961), p. 21. For an excellent discussion of the evolution of management thought, see Daniel Wren, *The Evolution of Management Thought* (New York: Ronald, 1972). See also F. Kast and J. Rosenzweig, *Organization and Management* (New York: McGraw-Hill, 1974), 25-73.

[2] E. H. Harbison, *The Age of Reformation* (Ithaca, N.Y.: Cornell University Press, 1955).

[3] R. H. Tawney, *Religion and the Rise of Capitalism* (New York: New American Library, 1954), p. 35.

[4] Harbison, *The Age of Reformation*.

[5] Tawney, *Religion and the Rise of Capitalism*, p. 191.

[6] *Ibid.*, pp. 188–89.

[7] James G. March and Herbert A. Simon, *Organizations* (New York: John Wiley, 1958), p. 29.

[8] Alvin Toffler, *Future Shock* (New York: Bantam Books, 1971), p. 143.

[9] Alfred Chandler, *Strategy and Structure* (Cambridge, Mass.: M.I.T. Press, 1932).

[10] D. S. Pugh, *Organization Theory* (Baltimore: Penguin, 1971), pp. 126–27.

[11] Frederick W. Taylor, "What Is Scientific Management?" reprinted in Michael Matteson and John Ivancevich, *Management Classics* (Santa Monica: Goodyear, 1977), pp. 5–8.

[12] James D. Thompson, *Organizations in Action* (New York: McGraw-Hill, 1967), p. 5.

[13] Much of the information on Fayol was derived from Henri Fayol, *General and Industrial Management*, trans. Constance Storrs (London: Sir Isaac Pitman, 1949).

[14] *Ibid.*, p. 42.

[15] *Ibid.*, pp. 102–3.

[16] Luther Gulick and Lyndall Urwick, eds., *Papers on the Science of Administration* (Clifton, N.J.: A. M. Kelley, 1972).

[17] Also papers by, among others, Elton Mayo, Mary Parker Follett, and V. A. Graicunas.

[18] Gulick and Urwick, *Papers*, p. 3.

[19] *Ibid.*, p. 37.

[20] *Ibid.*, p. 38.

[21] James Mooney and Allen Reilly, *Onward Industry* (New York: Harper and Row, 1931).

[22] *Ibid.*, p. 92.

[23] *Ibid.*, p. 96.

[24] *Ibid.*, p. 96.

[25] Max Weber, "Bureaucracy," in *Essays in Sociology*, trans. and ed. H. H. Gerth and C. Wright Mills, copyright 1946 by Oxford University Press; reprinted in Joseph A. Litterer, *Organizations: Structure and Behavior* (New York: John Wiley, 1969), p. 34.

[26] Based on Richard D. Hall, "Intraorganizational Structure Variation: Application of the Bureaucratic Model," *Administrative Science Quarterly*, Vol. 7, No. 3 (December 1962), 295–308.

[27] Weber, "Bureaucracy."

[28] *Ibid.*

[29] Warren G. Bennis, "Organizational Development and the Fate of Bureaucracy," address to the Division of Industrial and Business Psychology, American Psychological Association, September 5, 1964. Reprinted in L. L. Cummings and W. E. Scott, Jr., *Organizational Behavior and Human Performance* (Homewood, Ill.: Richard D. Irwin and Dorsey, 1969), p. 436.

[30] R. Bendix, *Max Weber: An Intellectual Portrait* (New York: Doubleday, 1960), p. 421.

[31] Weber, "Bureaucracy," p. 37.

[32] Bennis, "Organizational Development," p. 443.

[33] In Weber, *Essays in Sociology*, pp. 253–64.

[34] *Ibid.*, p. 254.

[35] Weber had spent some time traveling in the United States.

[36] Weber, "The Meaning of Discipline," p. 261.

[37] Herbert A. Simon, *Administrative Behavior* (New York: Free Press, 1976), p. 20.

[38] March and Simon, *Organizations*, p. 29.

[39] J. L. Massie, "Management Theory," in *Handbook of Organizations*, ed. J. G. March (New York: Rand McNally, 1965).

[40] Mason Haire, "The Concept of Power and the Concept of Man," in *Social Science Approaches to Business Behavior*, ed. George B. Strother (Homewood, Ill.: Dorsey, 1962), p. 176.

[41] Thompson, *Organizations in Action*, p. 35.

[42] March and Simon, *Organizations*, p. 14.

[43] Robert Merton, *Social Theory and Social Structure*, rev. ed. (New York: Free Press, 1957).

[44] Alvin Gouldner, *Patterns of Industrial Bureaucracy* (New York: Free Press, 1954).

[45] Daniel Katz and Robert Kahn, *The Social Psychology of Organizations* (New York: John Wiley, 1966).

Chapter 3

Contemporary Organization Theories

CHAPTER OVERVIEW

In this chapter, we continue our discussion of the evolution of organization theory with a treatment of the period from roughly 1930 to the present. This period was marked by an increase in the rate of change facing organizations and with the emergence of work tasks that called for more creativity and problem solving on the part of employees. In this chapter we will see that these new environments and tasks influenced the prescriptions of contemporary organization theorists. Again, in order to understand the material in this chapter in relation to our model, please read it with the following four questions in mind:

1. What prescription did each theorist have for how organizations should be structured?
2. What prescriptions did each theorist have for how to best ensure compliance—that employees carry out their assigned tasks?
3. What was it about the work tasks each theorist focused on that influenced his or her prescription for how to structure organizations and obtain compliance?
4. What was it about the "environment" of the organizations each theorist focused on that influenced his or her prescription for how to structure organizations and obtain compliance?

The outline of this chapter is as follows:

I. Human-Relations Management: The Period of Collision

HUMAN-RELATIONS MANAGEMENT: THE PERIOD OF COLLISION

The Changing Environment

As early as 1900, events were occurring that, culminating in the late 1930s, would drastically alter man's view of himself, his organizations, and his environment. William Scott has proposed that the individualistic optimism of the 19th century slowly gave way to an era of conflict, which he called the Period of Collision.[1] The collision effect results from "environmental conditions which draw people into inescapable proximity and dependency on one another."[2] The factors leading to the dependency and proximity may be categorized as technology and population dynamics.

The technological factors were primarily products of the rapid industrialization of the period. Mechanization was rapidly replacing manpower, and standardization, division of work, and specialization were widely emphasized on both the production and organizational levels. In turn, such a division of work results in interdependency and a need for tight coordination. Furthermore, the nature of mass production and specialization necessitates a large number of functions, thus adding to worker proximity. The industrial factors were in turn compounded by the improving communications and transportation of the period. In addition to making the country "smaller," these factors contributed to expanded markets and therefore to increased industrialization. Dependency and proximity were also aggravated by the population trends of the early 1900s: The population in America doubled between 1890 and 1930, and the proportion of city dwellers rose from 20 percent in 1860 to over 50 percent by 1920.

These factors might not have added up to a "collision effect" had they not occurred simultaneously with the closing of the American frontier. The frontier, Scott says, had acted as a safety valve and contributed to a spirit of optimism and growth during the 19th century; with its closing, the proximity and dependency caused by technology and population growth resulted in conflict and collision:

> If left unharnessed, the collision effect would breed brutal competition, then conflict, to end in the degeneration of society.[3]

However, this did not occur, because the collision effect coincided with a change in societal values, characterized by a deemphasis on the individualistic ethic and a corresponding emphasis on a social ethic. This change manifested itself in a number of ways. Government became increasingly involved in economic matters, and a variety of suits based on the Sherman Act were initiated by President Theodore Roosevelt and his successors. The Progressives' movement became popular and with it their objectives of enfranchising women, electing senators by popular direct vote, establishing a minimum wage, and encouraging trade unions. The literature of the period became increasingly antiindividualistic and, as Allen has pointed out, "there was a continuing disposition among Americans, young and old, to look with a cynical eye upon the old Horatio Alger formula for success." [4] The factories poured forth products in abundance, and the fetish for efficiency was replaced by an emphasis on consumption. People craved security, and the need to belong became prevalent in American industrial life.

Hawthorne

In 1927, a series of studies was begun at the Chicago Hawthorne plant of the Western Electric Company that would eventually add an entirely new perspective to the analysis of organizations and management. We analyze these studies in detail in Chapter 12, but because of their importance to the present topic, we discuss them briefly at this point.

The original Hawthorne studies were based on a number of traditional scientific-management assumptions. In particular, the initial study was formulated to determine the relation of the level of illumination in the workplace to the efficiency of workers; but to the surprise of the researchers, their findings showed no consistent relation between these two factors. In fact, when the experiment was reversed and the illumination reduced, output actually continued to increase. These findings led to additional studies aimed at explaining the mysterious discrepancy between traditional assumptions about worker behavior and their actual behavior.

The Hawthorne results suggested that variables other than physical working conditions might be affecting worker behavior and output. Initially, this possibility was studied by examining the relationships between output and working conditions like length of the working day and rest periods. The researchers continued to find that regardless of how the physical conditions varied, production continued to increase. They finally hypothesized that the increases in output were not the result of physical job conditions but rather of the changed social situations of the workers—in particular, changes in their motivation, group norms, satisfaction, and patterns of supervision.[5] For the first time, the notion that workers' behavior depended on something more than just financial incentives and physical work conditions became popular.

The End of An Era

The Hawthorne experiments were ended in 1933 as the country fell deeper into the Great Depression. Between 1929 and 1933, the unemployment rate rose from 3.2 percent to 30 percent. Businesses were failing, unemployment was widespread, incomes were dropping, and national morale was low. The period of optimism and prosperity was gone; the old guideposts of individualism and self-help had failed, and the notion of the self-made man as a guarantee of economic order was rejected. Increasingly, the social ethic of the times played down achievement by individuals and emphasized the importance of the group and of getting along with others.

Changes were also occurring in economic theory. For years people had been taught to believe that saving money was a virtue, and that the "invisible hand" of the market would ensure that each person, working in his own self-interest, would unknowingly contribute to and ensure society's maximum welfare. British economist John Maynard Keynes attacked these assumptions, and showed in convincing terms that saving could actually diminish a nation's productive strength, and that government spending should be used—in fact *had* to be used—to breathe life back into the faltering economy.[6] His work provided a theoretical foundation for the new social ethic and cast doubts on the classical assumption of rationality as well.

As a result of the new social ethic, the depression, and the Hawthorne studies, a new set of assumptions about work and workers had to be formulated. Whereas leaders from the dawn of civilization to the classical organization theorists had viewed the worker as an inert tool, they would henceforth have to view him as a significant variable in the system. Organization theories would have to allow for interaction between the formal system and its human components. Furthermore, as we shall see, the environment in which organizations were operating was becoming increasingly complex, and this would result in a new emphasis on organizational adaptability and the fuller utilization of employee problem-solving potential. New techniques for eliciting creativity had to be developed.

BRIDGING THE ERAS:
FOLLETT, BARNARD, AND SIMON

The work of the writers described in this section does not fit neatly into any one school of organization theory. Although Follett wrote during the scientific-management era, her work pointed the way to human relations in management. Similarly, Barnard and Simon are often considered members of a "decision-theory" school, but their contributions actually spanned a number of schools and contributed to the development of an integrated theory of organizations.

Mary Parker Follett

Mary Parker Follett was trained in philosophy and political science and became interested in social psychology early in her career. She was an admirer of a philosophy in which the freedom of the individual was subordinated to that of the group. For Follett, democracy did not mean individualism, but rather the development of a social consciousness. The true democracy was to build from small neighborhood groups to community groups, and so on. She consistently stressed the need for "integration," which involved finding a solution that satisfied both sides without having one side dominate the other.

Integration as a principle, however, could not be implemented until a new concept of authority and power was developed. She sought to develop such a concept by advocating power *with* rather than power *over*, and by abolishing many aspects of the roles of boss and subordinate. "One person," she concluded, "should not give orders to another person, but both should agree to take their orders from the situation." [7]

Chester Barnard

Writing several years later, Chester Barnard used his experience as an executive to develop an important new organization theory. He was the president of New Jersey Bell Telephone Company and, at various times, president of the United Service Organization (the USO of World War II), president of the Rockefeller Foundation, and chairman of the National Science Foundation. His book, *The Functions of the Executive*, "is a direct outcome of Barnard's failure to find an adequate explanation of his own executive experience in classic organization or economic theory." [8]

Barnard's contributions lie in three areas: First, his was the first organization theory to attempt to explain the importance and variability of individual behavior at work. Second, he developed a classic explanation of compliance, an explanation that emphasized the importance of both financial and nonfinancial incentives. Third, he presented a new theory of organization structure, one that focused on the organization as a communication system. We will discuss each of these three contributions.

The importance of individual behavior. Classical organization theorists tended to focus on questions of organization structure. They largely neglected the question of compliance by assuming that workers were economically rational and would perform in direct relation to their financial incentives. People, in other words, were viewed as "givens" in the system, like the mechanical devices of an engineer.

Barnard was the first major theorist (after the Hawthorne studies) to emphasize the importance and variability of the individual in the work setting. He said, for example, that "an essential element of organizations is the willingness of persons to contribute their individual efforts to the cooperative system." And he added that "the individual is always the basic strategic factor in organization. Regardless of his history or his obligations, he must be induced to cooperate, or there can be no cooperation." Such remarks may seem obvious today, but when they were written in the mid 1930s, they represented a clear and important break with the classical theories.

Barnard's theory of compliance. Besides emphasizing the importance of individual behavior, Barnard developed a theory of motivation and compliance in organizations. It consisted of four basic elements:

1. *The willingness to cooperate is a basic requirement of organization.* First, Barnard states that compliance—the willingness of individuals to cooperate—is a basic element of organization.[9]

2. *In complying, the individual must "surrender" his personal preferences.* According to Barnard, an order has "authority"—it will be carried out—when it is such that the person getting the order is willing to surrender his own preferences and carry it out. Willingness, says Barnard, means "the surrender of control of personal conduct, the depersonalization of personal action."[10]

3. *The order must fall within the person's "zone of indifference."* Why should a person be willing to carry out his superior's orders? Because there exists, says Barnard, a "zone of indifference" in each individual in which orders are acceptable *without conscious questioning of their authority.*[11]

4. *The inducements and contributions determine how wide the zone of indifference is.* But why should a person be willing to unquestioningly suspend his own judgment? Incentives, says Barnard, provide the answer. He says that the willingness to cooperate is the expression of the net satisfactions or dissatisfactions experienced or anticipated by each person and that each, in effect, asks himself, "Is it to my advantage to carry out this order?"[12] Since orders must be "accepted" to be carried out, it behooves organizations to see to it that the advantages (of suspending judgment and carrying out the order) outweigh the disadvantages; for this, inducements (or incentives) must be used. Barnard, in a clear break with the classicists, states that material incentives by themselves

are not enough: "The unaided power of material incentives, when the minimum necessities are satisfied, in my opinion is exceedingly limited as to most men. . . ." [13] Instead, several other classes of incentives, including "the opportunities for distinction, prestige, personal power . . ." are also necessary. The extent to which the advantages outweigh the disadvantages (or the inducements outweigh the contributions) then determines the width of the zone of indifference: It will be "wider or narrower depending on the degree to which the inducement exceeds the burdens and sacrifices. . . ." [14] Finally, if an organization cannot provide adequate incentives, then coercion is sometimes used.

Barnard's theory of organization structure. Barnard also made contributions to the theory of organization structure. He stressed that the organization was a structure of decision makers and emphasized the importance of communications in organizations. He stressed the role of the informal organization and explained how it aids communication and cohesiveness. He was also probably the first to take a "systems" view of organizations, including in the latter investors, suppliers, and others whose actions contribute to the firm.

Herbert Simon

Barnard's view of the organization as a network of decision makers in which inducements play a major role was refined and developed by Herbert Simon.[15] Whereas Barnard wrote from the vantage point of an executive, Simon was a scholar who had a mastery of organization theory, economics, natural science, and political science.

Simon's theory of compliance. Like Barnard, Simon viewed developing and maintaining compliance as a major problem facing managers, and he said:

> Decisions reached in the higher ranks of the organization hierarchy will have no effect upon the activities of operative employees unless they are communicated downward. Consideration of the process requires an examination of the ways in which the behavior of the operative employee can be influenced. These influences fall roughly into two categories: (1) *establishing in the operative employee himself* attitudes, habits, and a state of mind which lead him to reach that decision which is advantageous to the organization and (2) *imposing on the operative employee* decisions reached elsewhere in the organization. The first type of influence operates by inculcating in the employee organizational loyalties and a concern with efficiency, and more generally by training him. The second type of influence depends primarily upon authority and upon advisory and informational services. It is not insisted that these categories are either exhaustive or mutually exclusive. . . .[16]

Thus, according to Simon, there are various types of influence an organization can use to ensure employee compliance, and to a large extent, these types are interchangeable. First, you can *impose authority* on an employee.[17] Here, a subordinate is said to accept authority whenever he permits his behavior to be guided by the decision of his superior, but . . . "if you attempt to carry authority beyond a certain point (the "zone of acceptance," which is equivalent to Barnard's zone of indifference) disobedience will follow."

What then determines the "width" of the person's zone of acceptance? Primarily, according to Simon, the nature and magnitude of the incentives the organization offers. These incentives include salary, status and prestige, opportunities for promotion, and other material and nonmaterial rewards.[18]

However, inducements are not the only methods of ensuring acceptance of authority. There are also sanctions (like the possibility of losing one's job) and the "social sanctions" that come from accepting the job in the first place. Specifically, joining the organization and accepting a "subordinate" role automatically "establishes an area of acceptance in behavior within which the subordinate is willing to accept the decisions made for him by his superior." [19]

But, according to Simon, there is an alternative to *imposed* authority. The organization can also establish in the employee *self-control*—the "attitudes, habits, and a state of mind which lead him to reach that decision which is advantageous to the organization." [20] Simon cites three factors contributing to the development of such self-control. One is *organizational loyalty* or identification. Here, the person identifies with the organization, and its goals become his own. The second is inculcation in employees of *the criterion of efficiency*. Here, the employee is motivated "to take the shortest path, the cheapest means, toward the attainment of the desired goals." [21] *Training* is a third method for developing self-control: It "prepares the organization member to reach satisfactory decisions himself, without the need for the constant exercise of authority or advice." [22]

Thus, according to Simon, managers can ensure that employees carry out their tasks in one of two ways: They can *impose* control (through the use of authority), or they can develop *self-control* (through training, the criterion of efficiency, and organizational identification or loyalty). And, in comparing these two Simon notes that

> Administrators have increasingly recognized in recent years [the early 1940s] that authority, unless buttressed by other forms of influence, is relatively impotent to control decision in any but a negative way. The elements entering into all but the most routine decisions are so numerous and so complex that it is impossible to control positively more than a few. Unless the subordinate is himself able to supply most of the premises of decision, and to synthesize them adequately, the task of supervision becomes hopelessly burdensome.[23]

Written when it was, this was a perceptive and useful insight. It helped to explain, for example, how the classical theories—dependent as they were on the exercise of authority, and on imposed control—had been so useful.

As long as tasks were simple, repetitive, and routine, no complex decision making was necessary. And where the rules always apply—where they cover every contingency, and the employee is never called upon to do more than what the rules tell him to—few controls beyond rules and close supervision are required.

However, and this is very important, few jobs can be laid out in advance with such perfect detail. Especially in the changing environment after World War II, employees have had to innovate—to do more than what is called for in the rules—to carry out their tasks satisfactorily. At the extreme, the job may depend so much on the employees' creativity and problem solving that relying on imposed authority for ensuring performance is virtually impossible. Here other modes of influence (like Simon's "organizational identification") that encourage self-control are necessary; and "the broader the sphere of discretion left to the subordinate, the more important become those types of influence which do not depend upon the exercise of formal authority." [24]

Simon's theory of organization structure. Simon also contributed to our understanding of organization structure by elaborating on Barnard's idea of an organization as a network of decision makers. For example, Simon and his associates classified decision making as routine versus creative, and then drew conclusions about what types of structures were best for facilitating each type of decision making. He was also one of the first to explain clearly why decentralized decision making is often preferable:

> It has been assumed that given ample time, the superior could make more accurate decisions than the subordinate and that centralization is therefore preferred. This will be true, however, only if the information upon which the decision is to be based is equally accessible to both. When decisions must be made against a deadline, or when the organization is characterized by geographical dispersion, this may be far from the case. [25]

Summary

The work of Follett, Barnard, and Simon, emerging as it did at about the time of the Hawthorne studies, resulted in a significant change in direction for organization theory. Up to this time, theorists were preoccupied with organization structure and with designing jobs as efficiently as possible. Employees were viewed as "givens," as little more than mechanical parts that could be expected to perform as ordered as long as financial incentives were adequate. There is little in the classicists' writing to indicate that they viewed man as worthless or lazy, and yet the ends were the same: By assuming that man was motivated by money alone, they were able to discount the variability in human behavior and instead devote their full energies to efficient organization design.

The work of the theorists we discussed in this section changed the course of organization theory. Most significantly, they introduced the idea that orders need not always be accepted, and that such acceptance was actually a function of a variety of material and nonmaterial inducements. Their work, in other words, turned the attention of theorists to the second major question of organization theory: the question of compliance—of how to ensure that employees carry out their assigned tasks. And whereas prior researchers had focused on organization structure and disregarded the question of compliance, later theorists would do the opposite: They focused almost entirely on questions of motivation, control, and compliance, often relegating questions of structure to a position of secondary importance.

THE BEHAVIORAL-SYSTEMS SCHOOL

The Environment: Increased Diversity and Change

Chandler has suggested that after accumulating and rationalizing resources, managers traditionally move into a third stage, in which organizations attempt to utilize these resources by developing new products and new markets. Movement into this third stage was hampered by the depression; but as Chandler points out, the presence of excess production capacity during the depression did stimulate research and development activities, which led to product diversification.[26] Furthermore, although World War II required industrial conversion to military production, the technological and managerial advancements of the war years resulted in a postwar reconversion that finally shifted most of American industry into Chandler's stage 3.

This period was characterized by product diversification and by increasingly differentiated, complex, and rapidly changing environments. Even before World War II, many companies had embarked upon extensive research and development activities, with the objective of developing new products and thereby better utilizing their resources. In fact, some companies, such as du Pont and General Electric, had already begun strategies of diversification, although these strategies generally did not become widespread until after the war. At General Electric and Westinghouse, research and development activities resulted in the manufacture of plastics and alloys, as well as a variety of other products based upon the science of electronics. And the automobile companies had already begun to produce airplane engines, electrical equipment, and household appliances before the war years. After the war, companies in the rubber industry—such as United States Rubber and B. F. Goodrich, which had concentrated on tire manufacturing—entered into systematic research and development and began to market latex, plastics, flooring, and so forth. Similarly, postwar gasoline companies began to diversify by developing a wide range of petrochemicals. Steel and aluminum companies also undertook strategies of diversification by developing more complete and wide-ranging product lines. Somewhat later, the large food-processing and -marketing organizations began to develop a wide variety of breakfast cereals, prepared foods, and other end products.[27]

These environmental changes were important for the development of organization theory for several reasons. First, as we will see, the increased rate of change and novelty meant that managers and management theorists could no longer view organizations as closed systems that were isolated from their environments.[28] Second, there was a corresponding shift in emphasis toward making organizations more adaptable, as evidenced by a trend toward decentralization.[29] Decentralization, however, required a new organizational philosophy. In particular, by placing a new emphasis upon the decision making and problem solving of people at all levels of the organization, it accentuated a number of the trends of this period. Managers increasingly found it necessary to elicit the self-control of their employees; and words such as *democratic* and *participative leadership* began to appear frequently in the management literature.

The first theorists who tried to deal with this new milieu may be called "behavioral-systems writers," since they focused on organization *behavior* and on the organization as a *system*. The classicists had designed the organization for efficiency and assumed that compliance would follow automatically through the use of financial incentives. The behavioral systems writers had the opposite point of view. Employees, they emphasized, are human beings who are motivated by a vast array of wants and needs. The main focus of organization theory should be on the question of motivation and compliance, and they, therefore, focused on developing theories and prescriptions for motivating employees. The classicists said, "Build the organization structure, and employees will comply." The theorists we discuss in this section said "Focus on motivating employees, and structure your organization to increase motivation and morale."

Kurt Lewin

Most behavioral-systems writers are primarily social psychologists, who look upon Kurt Lewin as the founder of their school. Lewin's major contributions were in the area of group dynamics; in this context he developed the idea of Field Theory, which holds that group behavior is an intricate set of interactions and forces that affect both group structure and individual behavior.[30]

Lewin's work, carried out in the late 1930s, was motivated by his desire to link human behavior and the environment. He developed a model describing the relationship between an individual and his environment:

$$B = f (P,E)$$

Lewin's model proposes that a worker's behavior in a factory (B) is a function of or is influenced significantly by the personality or personal characteristics of the worker (P) as well as the factory's environment or climate (E).

Although this model seems simple enough today, it is important to remember the conceptual jump it represented in the 1930s. What Lewin emphasized was that a person's behavior is not just some function of economic rewards. Instead, it is a complex product of the person's personality and the environment in which he works. Lewin's theory helped to emphasize that employee behavior was a *variable*, not a *given* in the organization.

Lewin's stress upon the relationship between the individual, group, organization, and environment was pursued by a number of researchers. At Yale, for example, a researcher studied the New England Telephone Company to determine how the company and the union were bound together in an integrated social system. His studies provided a new perspective that was a building block for later work carried out at the Tavistock Institute for Social Research in England.

Tavistock Studies

Researchers at the Tavistock Institute focused on the relationship between the technical and the social systems in organizations. In one study at the Glacier Metal Company, for example, researchers found that a technological change had drastically altered the organization's social system.[31] In another Tavistock study, Trist and his associates made an analysis of the British coal industry.[32] A new "long-wall" technology had been implemented that required the breakup of small, cohesive work groups and the substitution of specialized larger groups working in shifts. The logical efficiency of the long-wall method had resulted in severe emotional disturbances, low productivity, and an increasing sense of anomie. The conclusion in both cases was that the imperatives of efficiency had so disrupted the social organization that the hoped-for advantages of the new method never materialized.

Homans

Writing at about the same time, George Homans tried to conceptualize how an organization's social and technical systems are related. As seen in Figure 3-1, he divided the social system of a group into an internal and external system. The external system contained certain *required* actions, interactions, and sentiments, whereas the internal system was characterized by a number of *emergent* actions, interactions, and sentiments. Homans stressed that all the various elements in his model interacted with each other and that they all needed to be considered in the design of the organization.

Likert

The work of Rensis Likert is another example of the trends in organization theory during this period. Likert's thesis is that effective organizations differ markedly from ineffective ones in a number of ways. The effective organization encourages its supervisors to "focus their primary attention on endeavoring to build effective work groups with high performance goals." This can be contrasted with the less effective organization, which usually

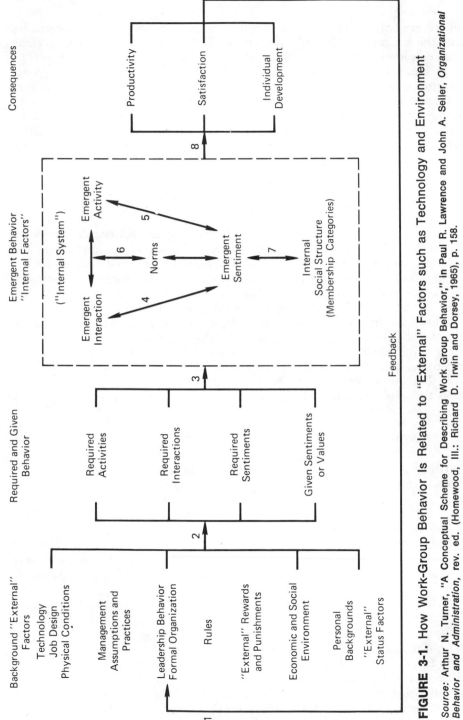

FIGURE 3-1. How Work-Group Behavior Is Related to "External" Factors such as Technology and Environment

Source: **Arthur N. Turner, "A Conceptual Scheme for Describing Work Group Behavior," in Paul R. Lawrence and John A. Seiler,** *Organizational Behavior and Administration,* **rev. ed. (Homewood, Ill.: Richard D. Irwin and Dorsey, 1965), p. 158.**

follows the prescriptions of classical organization theory. These less effective, "job-centered" organizations:

1. Break the total operation into simple component parts or tasks
2. Develop the best way to carry out each of the component parts
3. Hire people with appropriate aptitudes and skills to perform each of these tasks.
4. Train these people to do their respective tasks in the specified best way
5. Provide supervision to see that they perform their designated tasks, using the specified procedure and at an acceptable rate as determined by such procedures as timing the job
6. Use incentives, where feasible, in the form of individual or group wage rates [33]

For Likert, structure was only a means to an end, that end being the improved motivation and morale of employees. He says, for example:

> The leadership and other processes of the organization must be such as to insure a maximum probability that in all interactions and all relationships with the organization each member will, in the light of his background, values, and expectations, view the experience as supportive and one which builds and maintains his sense of personal worth and importance.[34]

In addition, he asserts that management will fully utilize its human resources only when each person in an organization is a member of one or more effectively functioning work groups that have a high degree of group loyalty.[35] And the most effective leaders in such groups are perceived as supportive, friendly, and helpful by their subordinates.

Notice the change that has taken place in organization theory between the classicists and Likert. Whereas the former stressed organization structure and assumed employee compliance, Likert stresses the importance of motivating employees and building a structure to serve that purpose. The classicists stressed efficiency, centralization, and narrow spans of control. Likert, seeking a structure to boost motivation, prescribes a flexible structure in which subordinates make important decisions and in which supervision is supportive and friendly. Thus compared with that of the classicists, Likert's approach formed a totally new theory, a theory in which questions of human motivation, self-control, and compliance were paramount.

McGregor

Working independently, Douglas McGregor arrived at conclusions concerning the interaction between the individual and the organization that were strikingly similar to those of Likert. According to McGregor, the traditional organization, with its highly specialized jobs, centralized decisionmaking, and top-down communications was not simply a product of economic necessity but rather a reflection of certain basic assumptions about human nature.[36] These assumptions, which McGregor somewhat arbitrarily classified as "Theory X," held that most people dislike work and responsibility and prefer to be directed; that people are motivated not by the desire to do a good job, but simply by financial incentives; and that therefore, most people must be closely supervised, controlled, and coerced into achieving organizational objectives.

McGregor questioned the truth of this view and, in doing so, naturally questioned whether such management practices as centralization and specialized division of work are appropriate for the sorts of tasks faced by many organizations today. He felt that management needed new organizations and practices, and that these in turn had to be based on a revised view of the nature of man. What emerged was an alternate set of assumptions, which McGregor called "Theory Y." Unlike the Theory X assumptions, these held that people could enjoy work and that, if the conditions were favorable, they would exercise substantial self-control over their performance. Implicit in these Theory Y assumptions is the belief that people are motivated by the desire to do a good job and by the opportunity to affiliate with their peers, rather than simply by financial rewards.

Based upon these theory Y assumptions, McGregor proposed a new approach to organization structure and compliance, one aimed at encouraging self-control.[37]

In order to develop such self-control, McGregor suggested several new techniques, some of which involved restructuring organizations. He said *decentralization* and *delegation* should be the norm in order to free people from the "too close control of conventional organization." *Job enlargement* (in which the variety of tasks an employee performed is increased) should be encouraged so that workers' jobs are made more challenging and interesting. *Participative management* (which he said would give employees "some voice in decisions that affect them") would similarly enhance self-control. Finally, he proposed using *management by objectives*; here, subordinates set goals jointly with their superiors and then are measured on the accomplishment of these goals, thus avoiding the need for day-to-day close supervision.

Argyris

Chris Argyris has reached similar conclusions, but he approaches the problem from a different perspective.[38] According to Argyris, the traditional highly structured organization inhibits people from maturing to the point where they can utilize their full potential. He said:

> The classical design for a formal organization has some very serious flaws. The nature of these flaws is apparent when we set side by side two pictures: first, a view of how human beings need to behave in our society in order to be healthy, productive, growing individuals; and second, how a

formal organization (a factory, business, or hospital) requires them to behave. Comparing these pictures, we see that the organization's requirements, as presented by "classical" descriptions, are sharply opposed to the individual's needs.[39]

Healthy people go through a maturation process says Argyris, one that involves seven changes in the personality of the individual. Specifically, as the person approaches adulthood, he moves to a state of increased activity, independence, and stronger interests. Furthermore, he becomes capable of behaving in a greater variety of ways and tends to have a much longer time perspective. Finally, he matures from the subordinate position of a child to one of an equal or superordinate position as an adult and, in addition, develops an increased awareness and control over himself. Argyris contends that in many instances, the formal structure, control, and other practices of the classical organizations inhibit these normal maturation changes by encouraging employees to be dependent, passive, and subordinate.

The most insidious aspect of classical organization theory, according to Argyris, is that the organization it prescribes is "rational"—"that is, it has been 'designed' and its parts are purposefully related within this design." [40] People, says Argyris, are forced to "stick to the rules," and the efficiency advantages of specialization force workers to perform increasingly specialized, routine, unchallenging jobs.

The total effect of applying these classical principles, Argyris says, is that employees work in an environment where they have little or no self-control and are encouraged to be dependent and passive. Thus, in the long run, the classicists' "efficient" organization is not really so efficient, since workers whose maturation is hampered become frustrated, apathetic, and less efficient. The classical assumptions, he implies, are not only incorrect but are actually unhealthy and harmful to employees. The solution is to decrease the dependency, subordination, and submissiveness of employees by developing (among other things) enlarged jobs and participative leaders. For Argyris (as for McGregor), organization structure is not something to be designed for efficiency without regard to employee behavior. Instead, structure is a vehicle for increasing the motivation and self-control of employees.

Katz and Kahn

The organization as an open system. Katz and Kahn are social psychologists who worked closely with Rensis Likert at the University of Michigan, and their backgrounds in social psychology help explain their unique approach to organization theory.[41] They believe that classical organization theories emphasized organization structure while overlooking the organization's people, whereas more recent behavioral approaches often focused on people while overlooking the organization structure existing around those people.[42] They sought therefore to more fully merge the "macro" subject of organization structure with the "micro" subject of individual behavior and to show the relations between the two.

Katz and Kahn's theory of motivation/compliance. Katz and Kahn say that because organizations are responsive, open systems, managers are constantly faced with the problem of somehow ensuring that the tasks they delegate are in fact carried out. The classicists' answer to this problem was to install a network of incentives, rules, and close supervision—to *impose* compliance. Yet such imposed or "legal" compliance has its shortcomings. For one thing, they say, "creativity is difficult to legislate," and so some jobs don't lend themselves to this type of compliance. Of even greater importance is the fact that:

> For effective organizational functioning many members must be willing, on occasion, to do more than their job description specifies. If members of the system were to follow their precise letter of job descriptions and organizational protocol, things would soon grind to a halt.[43]

The solution, say Katz and Kahn, is that managers can't just rely on *imposed compliance* like rules or close supervision; instead, three other "patterns of compliance" should also be used.

One involves the use of *rewards* for inducing the required behavior. Here, rewards are linked to desired behaviors, and the employee's actions thus supposedly become instrumental to his obtaining specific desired rewards. A second involves *job identification*. Here the job is challenging and the employee thus has opportunities for self-expression and achievement. He or she receives satisfaction from the job and so is motivated to perform it.[44]

Finally, at the opposite end of a continuum from *imposed* compliance is compliance based on the employee's *internalization* of the organization's goals. Here, employees adopt the organization's goals as their own, and they comply because by doing so, they are also contributing to their own goals.

Katz and Kahn's theory of organization structure. Katz and Kahn also dealt with the question of structure. Here they stressed that organizations were open systems that had to continually respond and adapt to their environments. And they elaborated on this idea by distinguishing among five types of formal organizational subsystems: production, maintenance, boundary, adaptive, and managerial. Members of the *production* subsystem are concerned with task accomplishment and may include employees in the production and distribution departments. The *maintenance* subsystem aims at maintaining stability and predictability in the organization. (Here, selection procedures are developed for screening employees, and raw materials are screened by quality control, for example.)

There are also *boundary* systems for procurement and disposal. These directly support the production system but, unlike the production system, necessarily carry on transactions with the environment. (Marketing and advertising influence the buying public, for example.)

Adaptive systems deal with the problems of planning. For example, there may be a long-range-planning committee, or a research and development group, to fill this role.

Finally, there is the *managerial* system, which "cuts across all of the operating structures of production, maintenance, environmental support, and adaptation." This subsystem coordinates the other subsystems, resolves conflicts between organizational levels, and coordinates external requirements with organizational resources.[45]

TOWARD A SITUATIONAL THEORY

The 20th century has been a period of diversity and change. Examples abound of swift changes and improvements in communication techniques, transportation, energy generation and consumption, economic growth, and knowledge accumulation.

Organizationally, this rapid change has manifested itself in more diverse, interwoven markets, the use of advanced technologies, the widespread use of specialists, and larger, more complex organizational structures, among other phenomena. In turn, these have resulted in an increasing concern for development of a general organization theory that the manager could use in dealing with the greater number of variables he must now take into account in his decision making.

This need for a general theory and a number of interrelated events beginning late in the 1950s combined to create a significant milestone in the evolution of organization theory. First, two reports—one commissioned by the Ford Foundation, one by the Carnegie Corporation—produced sharp indictments of the state of business education in the United States. They reported that business schools were adhering to worn-out precepts and were emphasizing "vocationalism." The reports stressed that problem solving, organization theory, management principles, and human relations should be integrated into business-school curricula. A second event was the publication in 1961 of a paper entitled, "The Management Theory Jungle," by Harold Koontz. In it, Koontz said that the variety of management schools, terminology, and assumptions had resulted in confusion and "jungle warfare" between the various groups.[46] The direct result of this article was a symposium in California, attended by a group of eminent scholars and practitioners with diverse research and analytical approaches to management. These incidents encouraged a renewed interest in principles, giving rise to questions about the universality of the classical principles and the tackling of other pressing problems—all in the search for a unified organization theory.

Finally, along with these developments, a number of organizational-research studies were being carried out in England and America. Their combined effect was to underscore the need for a "situational" view of organization theory—one in which the appropriateness of the organization and management system was contingent upon the rate of change in organizational environment and technology. In one such study, Burns and Stalker carried out an analysis of a number of industrial firms in England and concluded that whether a "mechanistic" or an "organic" management system was appropriate depended upon the nature of the organization's environment. They wrote:

> We have endeavored to stress the appropriateness of each system to its own specific set of conditions. Equally, we desire to avoid the suggestion that either system is superior under all circumstances to the other. In particular, nothing in our experience justifies the assumption that the mechanistic systems should be superseded by organic in conditions of stability. The beginning of administrative wisdom is the awareness that there is no one optimum type of management system.[47]

Also in England, Joan Woodward and a group of researchers from the Tavistock Institute analyzed the relationship between the organization and the technology of a group of firms in the South Essex area. The organic, flexible system described by Burns and Stalker appeared to be more appropriate in firms with either small-batch or continuous-process production systems, whereas the mechanistic, classical system was appropriate where mass-production technology was utilized.[48]

These findings and others like them have culminated in what can be called a situational approach to organization theory. As Lawrence and Lorsch, two of the original investigators in this area, put it:

> During the past few years there has been evident a new trend in the study of organizational phenomena. Underlying this new approach is the idea that the internal functioning of organizations must be consistent with the demands of the organization's task, technology, or external environment, and the need of its members if the organization is to be effective. Rather than searching for the panacea of the one best way to organize under all conditions, investigators have more and more tended to examine the functioning of organizations in relation to the needs of their particular members and the external pressures facing them. Basically, this approach seems to be leading to the development of a "contingency" theory of organization with the appropriate internal states and processes of the organization contingent upon external requirements and member needs.[49]

The implications of this new "situational" theory of organizations will be pursued in the following chapter.

SUMMARY

The period from roughly 1925 to the present saw a drastic change in organization theory. To fully appreciate these changes, we can answer the questions posed at the beginning of this chapter and compare our answers with those of the preceding chapter.

What prescriptions did each theorist have for how organizations should be structured? The behavioral-systems writers prescribed a radically different form of organization from that of classical theorists. The structure of the classicists was a "mechanistic" one in which decision making was centralized, there was close adherence to the chain of command, employees were told to "stick to the rules," jobs were highly specialized, and employees were rarely asked to participate in decision making. In contrast, writers like Likert, Argyris, and McGregor were more concerned with the mental health and motivation of employees, and they saw organization structure as a means toward improving that health and motivation. They therefore prescribed structures in which decision making was pushed to the lowest level possible, jobs were varied and unspecialized, and managers were not preoccupied with adherence to the chain of command or enforcing rules; the organization, in other words, was more "organic." The efficiency-oriented, machine-like structure of the classicists was thus replaced by the adaptive, relatively open structure of the behavioralists.

What prescriptions did each theorist have for how to best ensure compliance—that employees carry out their assigned tasks? It was on the question of compliance that the writers we discussed in this chapter differed most markedly from the classicists. The latter emphasized the use of rules, close supervision, and financial incentives for ensuring that workers accomplished their tasks. The writers discussed in this chapter, on the other hand, emphasized gaining the self-control of employees, rather than imposing controls on them. Barnard, for example, said that the power of material incentives, when the minimum necessities are satisfied, "is exceedingly limited as to most men," and he prescribed nonmaterial inducements like prestige for ensuring compliance. Simon made a similar distinction and said that through training, organizational loyalty, and instilling the "criterion of efficiency," managers can elicit self-control. Behavioral-systems writers like Likert, McGregor, and Argyris built upon these ideas and prescribed specific techniques, like management by objectives, participative leadership, job enlargement, and delegation, for building self-control.

What was it about the workers' tasks these theorists focused on that influenced their prescriptions for how to structure organizations and obtain compliance? Tasks studied by the classical theorists tended to be routine, repetitive, and easily measured. Taylor, for example, focused almost entirely on jobs in the production shop, where jobs tended to be routine and mechanical. By the mid-1900s, however, employees' tasks were no longer uniformly routine. Several things, including product research and development and the growth and size of organizations, resulted in more jobs of a problem-solving, creative nature; in many industries, the emphasis on efficiency thus gave way to an emphasis on adaptability and creativity.

What was it about the environment of the organizations each theorist focused on that influenced his or her prescriptions for how to structure and obtain compliance? The environment faced by classicists was relatively simple and unchanging, and prevailing values emphasized economic individualism and hard work. But by the 1930s, various factors had combined to drastically alter the environment faced by organization theorists. The depression forced many to question the underlying values of economic individualism and resulted in a partial replacement of the work ethic with a social ethic. More important, perhaps, World War II had stimulated research and development activities, and by the end of the war, many firms had embarked on strategies of diversification. Gradually, the environments of organizations became increasingly complex as firms found themselves more and more dependent upon the actions of previously unrelated firms. Change and novelty became the rule, and managers soon found themselves flooded with information—on new products, competitors, new technologies, and so forth—from their environments.

To understand an organization theory, one must understand the milieu in which it evolved; this seems especially true when viewed in the light of our discussions from this and the preceding chapter. Scientific management, bureaucracy, and administrative theory are all appropriate responses to the problems classicists faced—problems centering on efficiency, on environments that were relatively unchanging, on tasks that were simple, and on organizations of limited size. In such situations, it would seem, prescribing centralized decision making, specialized jobs, rules, incentives, and close supervision made sense.

The writers we discussed in this chapter, on the other hand, faced very different situations. New-product development, technological advances, increased competition, diversity, and increased organization size required that companys change their strategys from *efficiency* to *diversification and adaptability*. Environments were no longer simple and unchanging and, related to this fact, an increasing number of work tasks required initiative, creativity, and problem solving. The new organization theories we discussed in this chapter were aimed at dealing with these new conditions. In the next chapter, we pursue this line of thought and turn our attention to a more detailed analysis of the relationships between environment, task, and organization.

DISCUSSION QUESTIONS

1. What are some of the fundamental trends that have been leading to increasing complexity in the environments of organizations? What impact do you think this complexity is having for organization theory and values?

2. How would you account for the emergence of a contingency or situational approach to organizations and management?

3. What are the implicit assumptions of the behavioral systems writers' organization theory? How do these compare with the assumptions of the classical organization theorists?

4. What role did financial incentives play in Barnard's theory of compliance? How did they relate to his "zone of indifference"?

5. What specific techniques did McGregor prescribe for developing self-

control? Why didn't the classical organization theorists prescribe such techniques?

FOOTNOTES

1 William Scott, *Organization Theory* (Homewood, Ill.: Irwin, 1967). For an excellent discussion of the evolution of management thought, see Daniel Wren, *The Evolution of Management Thought* (New York: Ronald, 1972).

2 Scott, *Organization Theory*, p. 48.

3 *Ibid.*, p. 52.

4 Frederick Lewis Allen, *The Big Change* (New York: Harper & Row, 1952), p. 132.

5 F. J. Roethlisberger and William J. Dickson, *Management and the Worker* (New York: John Wiley, 1964).

6 John Maynard Keynes, *The General Theory of Employment, Interest and Money* (New York: Harcourt, Brace, 1964).

7 Mary Parker Follett, *Creative Experience* (London: Longmans, Green, 1924), p. 59.

8 Chester Barnard, *The Functions of the Executive* (Cambridge: Harvard University Press, 1968).

9 *Ibid.*, p. 83.

10 *Ibid.*, p. 84.

11 *Ibid.*, p. 167.

12 *Ibid.*, p. 85.

13 *Ibid.*, p. 143.

14 *Ibid.*, p. 169.

15 Herbert A. Simon, *Administrative Behavior* (New York: Free Press, 1976).

16 *Ibid.*, p. 11.

17 *Ibid.*, p. 226.

18 *Ibid.*, pp. 116–17.

19 *Ibid.*, p. 133.

20 *Ibid.*, p. 11.

21 *Ibid.*, p. 14.

22 *Ibid.*, p. 15.

23 *Ibid.*, p. 227.

24 *Ibid.*, p. 225.

25 *Ibid.*, p. 238.

26 Alfred Chandler, *Strategy and Structure* (Cambridge, Mass.: M.I.T. Press, 1932), pp. 19–51.

27 See also F. E. Emery and E. C. Trist, "The Causal Texture of Organizational Environments," *Human Relations*, Vol. 18 (August 1963), 20–26.

28 Warren G. Bennis, "Organizational Development and the Fate of Bureaucracy," address to the Division of Industrial and Business Psychology, American Psychological Association, September 5, 1964. Reprinted in L. L. Cummings and W. E. Scott, Jr., *Organizational Behavior and Human Performance* (Homewood, Ill.: Richard D. Irwin and Dorsey, 1969), p. 436.

29 Alvin Toffler, *Future Shock* (New York: Bantam Books, 1971), pp. 124–51.

30 Kurt Lewin, *Field Theory and Social Science* (New York: Harper & Row, 1951), p. 241.

31 W. B. D. Brown and E. Jaques, *The Glacier Project Papers* (London: Heineman, 1965).

[32] E. Trist and K. Bamforth, "Some Social and Psychological Consequences of the Long Wall Method of Coal-Getting," *Human Relations*, Vol. 4, No. 1 (1951).

[33] Rensis Likert, *New Patterns of Management* (New York: McGraw-Hill, 1961), p. 6.

[34] *Ibid.*, p. 103.

[35] *Ibid.*, p. 104.

[36] Douglas McGregor, *The Human Side of Enterprise* (New York: McGraw-Hill, 1960). See also Byron G. Firman, "An Investigation of the Relationships among Supervisory Attitudes, Behaviors, and Outputs: An Examination of McGregor's Theory Y," *Personnel Psychology*, Vol. 26 (Spring 1973), 95–105.

[37] Douglas McGregor, "The Human Side of Enterprise," in Edward Deci, B. von Haller Gilmer, and Harry Karn, *Readings in Industrial and Organizational Psychology* (New York: McGraw-Hill, 1972), p. 123.

[38] Chris Argyris, *Integrating the Individual and the Organization* (New York: John Wiley, 1964).

[39] Chris Argyris, "Being Human and Being Organized," *Transaction*, Vol. 1 (1964), 3–6. Reprinted in Deci et al., *Readings*, pp. 68–73.

[40] *Ibid.*, p. 69.

[41] Daniel Katz and Robert Kahn, *The Social Psychology of Organization* (New York: John Wiley, 1966).

[42] *Ibid.*, p. 336.

[43] *Ibid.*, p. 340.

[44] *Ibid.*, p. 345.

[45] *Ibid.*, p. 94.

[46] Not everyone agreed with this conclusion. Simon, for example, stated that there was no confusion and that he was "exhilarated by the progress we have made." See Harold Koontz, ed., *Toward a Unified Theory of Management* (New York: McGraw-Hill, 1964), p. 79.

[47] Tom Burns and G. M. Stalker, *The Management of Innovation* (London: Tavistock Publications Ltd., 1961), p. 125.

[48] Joan Woodward, *Industrial Organization: Theory and Practice* (London: Oxford University Press, 1965), pp. 64–65.

[49] Jay W. Lorsch and Paul R. Lawrence, eds., *Studies in Organization Design* (Homewood, Ill.: Richard D. Irwin and Dorsey, 1970), p. 1.

PART II

THE CONTEXT
OF ORGANIZATIONS

In this section of the book we will discuss environment, technology, and organizational size and the ways in which these "contextual" factors influence and determine an organization's structure and processes. And, we discuss the intermediaries (decision making and communications) through which these factors influence the organization.

The idea that contextual factors like environment influence organization is in keeping with the points we made in the last few chapters. In the last two chapters, for example, we traced the evolution of organization theory and saw that each theory seemed to reflect the "situation" with which each theorist was faced. In particular, the environment, task, and size of the organization prevailing during each period seemed to influence the type of organization prescribed. Thus, the highly centralized structure, with its specialized jobs and rules, incentives, and close supervision, seemed to largely reflect the emphasis on efficiency, stability, and repetitiveness that prevailed at the time.

What are the contextual determinants of organization? What are the mechanisms through which these determinants influence organization? These are the two main questions we address in this section.

Chapter 4

The Context of Organizations: Environment, Technology, Size

CHAPTER OVERVIEW

In the last two chapters we saw that to understand how an organization is structured, and how the compliance of its workers is ensured, it is necessary to understand that organization's *context*: its environment, technology, and size. In this chapter we turn to a detailed look at how organizations and their contexts are related, and we focus on three main questions:

How do contextual factors like environment, technology, and size influence organization structure?

How do these contextual factors influence organizational compliance?

What mechanisms seem to account for the effects these contextual factors have on organization structure and compliance?

We begin with a discussion of how an organization's *strategy*—its basic long-term plan—determines the environment in which it will operate. We next discuss a case study by Emery and Trist of the *environments* of organization and how they progress from simple and predictable to complex and uncertain. The studies by Burns and Stalker and by Lawrence and Lorsch show how these different types of environments *in turn affect the organization* and how it is managed. The Woodward and New Jersey studies show that *technology*—the means an organization employs to produce its goods or services—also affects the organization and its management. We will see that complexity, uncertainty, and diversity emerge as important determinants of organizational design. These determinants, in turn, mirror the type of task the organization must perform, with entrepreneurial, creative tasks resulting in greater uncertainty, complexity, and diversity for the organization.

The outline of this chapter is as follows:

I. Organizational Environments
   A. Strategy and Environment
   B. The Emery and Trist Studies

II. Environment and Organization
   A. Introduction: The Impact of Information
   B. The Burns and Stalker Studies
   C. The Lawrence and Lorsch Studies

III. Technology and Organization
   A. The Woodward Studies
   B. The Aston Studies
   C. The New Jersey Studies

IV. Organization Size and Structure
   A. Positive Findings
   B. Negative Findings
   C. Research Problems

V. Summary

ORGANIZATIONAL ENVIRONMENTS

Strategy and Environment

A *strategy* is a type of plan. It specifies the central concept or purpose of the organization in terms of the service it will render to society, and usually the means by which it intends to create and distribute these services. It describes the basic mission of the enterprise, the objectives and goals it seeks to achieve, and the ways in which the resources of the enterprise will be used in order to achieve its goals.

The strategy gives the enterprise its basic direction. It answers the question, "What business are we in?" That is, it provides the firm (and its managers) with basic guidelines for the nature and scope of its business commitment and specifies what business or businesses the firm will engage in, thus determining the environment in which the firm chooses to compete. (Henry Ford's decision in the early 1900s to define his business as providing and supplying low-priced autos for the mass market is a succinct example of such a strategy.)

The Emery and Trist study we discuss next helps show how a firm's strategy determines the environment in which it must compete. In this case, the firm's strategy included installing inflexible, automated machinery, and this strategy locked it into a particular high-volume mass market for its products. When that market—and the rest of the firm's environment—began to change, the firm found its competitive posture threatened.

The Emery and Trist Studies

Organizational environments are becoming more complex, diverse, and unpredictable. A major contribution of the Emery and Trist case studies is that they help illustrate how environments evolve from simplicity and stability to complexity and change.

Emery and Trist distinguish between four "ideal types" of environments, each of which differs in the complexity, "relevant uncertainty," relatedness, and overall "causal texture" with which constituent organizations must cope.[1] These may be summarized as follows:

Type 1, placid, randomized. This type of environment is the simplest and corresponds to the economist's classical market. The organization, unable to predict what its environment will do, can operate independently of it. Therefore, "the best tactic . . . can be learned only by trial and error."

Type 2, placid, clustered. Here, it is possible to make probability estimates of the relation between causes and effects of events, although the environment is still not changing rapidly. Unlike the case with the first type, "survival becomes critically linked with what an organization knows of its environment." To gather and adapt to environmental information, the organization must now construct a master plan and see to it that resources are appropriately allocated.

Type 3, disturbed, reactive. The significant difference between this and the preceding type is the existence of a number of similar organizations, a fact that becomes the dominant characteristic of this environment. In addition to considering its counterparts, which it meets at random, the organization must now consider that what it knows can also be known by the others. "This type is comparable to the economist's oligopolistic market." Here, strategies must be worked out that take into consideration not only the reaction of the market and the long-run goals of the organization, but also the probable reactions of competitors. Therefore, the relatively simple cause–effect relations of the type 2 environment give way in type 3 to a more complex, uncertain situation in which reactions of competitors must be considered. The organization must decide not only where it is going but how to get there "while insuring that others . . . do not." Adapting to the reactions of others requires greater flexibility, however; and "the flexibility required encourages a certain decentralization and also puts a premium on quality and speed of decision. . . ."

Type 4, turbulent field. In this type of environment, dynamic processes "arise from the field itself" and not merely from the interactions of components. "The turbulance results from the complexity and multiple character of the causal interconnections." This is the most complex, rapidly changing environment and arises as a result of three interrelated trends. First, in order to adapt to the demands of the type 3 environment, organizations grow and become linked until they begin to alter the nature of their environment. Second, there is "a deepening interdependence between the economic and the other facets of the society." Finally, and perhaps most important, "the increasing reliance on research and development . . . leads to a situation in which a change gradient is continuously present in the environmental field."

Emery and Trist present a case history that, along with others not described in their paper, led them to develop their ideas about types of environments. The case history involved a British food-canning company that decided to install highly automated machinery, only to find the markets for its goods rapidly changed. The changes were wrought by a number of seemingly unrelated factors in the firm's environment, such as the emergence of the quick-freezing process, a decrease in the price of tin for cans, and an increase in competition. Thus the "causal texture" of the environment had changed, resulting in new complexities and uncertainties for the firm.

ENVIRONMENT AND ORGANIZATION

Introduction: The Impact of Information

Theorists like Simon view organizations as structures of decision makers, and this focus on decision making helps explain how the organization and its environment are related. Decisions require information, and so a firm's environment can be thought of in terms of the *information* it provides to the firm, information concerning competitors, suppliers, and so forth.[2] This information triggers action on the part of the firm—actions regarding what its goals should be, the means it uses to accomplish these goals, its constraints, and how it evaluates its performance, for example. In turn, we will see in this section that the uncertainty and complexity of the information inherent in a firm's environment influence how the firm is structured and managed.

The Burns and Stalker Studies

Burns and Stalker examined some twenty industrial firms in the United Kingdom. Their work focused on how the management processes in these companies were related to certain facets of their environments, and in particular to the rates of change in scientific techniques and markets of the selected industries. Although they did not utilize quantitative measures, their evidence was collected by extensive interviewing of key people in all twenty companies and provided a useful picture of the relationship between environment and organization. They found that:

> When novelty and unfamiliarity in both market situations and technical information become the accepted order of things, a fundamentally dif-

ferent kind of management system becomes appropriate from that which applies to a relatively stable commercial and technical environment.[3]

The companies studied, drawn from a variety of industries, included a rayon manufacturer, a large engineering concern, a number of diverse electronics firms, and eight firms operating within different segments of the electronics industry. Early in the field work, the authors were struck with the distinctly different types of management methods in the different industries, as well as with the fact that these industries' environments differed markedly in terms of their rates of technological and market change. They found, as we will see, that these different rates of change had influenced the management practices in each firm, having forced each management to deal with different degrees of uncertainty and change.[4] As a first step, the researchers distinguished between five different kinds of environments, ranging from "stable" to "least predictable." They then related each to different organization practices and structures.

Findings. The environment of the rayon mill was the most stable, primarily because of the nature of the production process, which required stability and long runs. In this organization, everything was explicitly devised to keep production stable:

> At all levels, decision making occurred within the framework of familiar expectations and beliefs, many of which could be formulated numerically as a program. Fluctuations in demand did occur, but these were treated as deviations from normality, and part of the task of management was to urge the sales office in London to avoid such deviation.[5]

The organization was a "pyramid of knowledge," which was run on the basis of standing plans; succeedingly lower levels in the hierarchy had more limited information, authority, and responsibility. Roles were carefully defined, with "the normative character of everybody's work quite explicit." Roles and tasks also became increasingly well defined lower in the hierarchy, so the employee "is capable of not only knowing what to do in normal circumstances without consulting anyone else, but also knows just how far he may allow a situation to depart from the normal" before he had to report to his superior. Even the top manager's task was carried out within the framework of a well defined program, "with uncertainties and expectations, so far as demand is concerned, ironed out for him beforehand." [6]

The organization studied in the second type of environment was in the electrical engineering industry and produced switchgears. In this firm, every contract required some special units, and there was a constant flow of design improvements. Furthermore, "the rate of technical development was significantly faster" than in the rayon firm.[7]

This changing environment manifested itself in a more flexible organization structure. A number of plans were devised specifically to meet contingencies, and there was a deliberate avoidance of clearly defined functions and lines of responsibility in the firm. Tasks were less clearly defined, even at the lower levels, and the personnel tended to regard their work as a contribution to the overall task of the firm. Communications, aided by committee meetings, tended to flow easily outside the formal organization structure.

The firm's environment was stable, however, compared with that of the radio- and television-manufacturing firms. These were undergoing much faster rates of technical change. And they had relatively adaptable organization structures. For example, there was a greater emphasis on committee meetings for coordinating projects, and even at lower levels, jobs were not highly defined and specialized. No organization chart existed, and in all their interviews, Burns and Stalker found that managers had great difficulty in saying who was at their own level in the firm.

Most of the other electronics firms were operating in an even more uncertain environment. Consequently, there was often a "deliberate attempt to avoid specifying individual tasks and to forbid any dependency on the management hierarchy as a structure of defined functions and authority." [8] Individual jobs, therefore, were defined as ambiguously as possible, so that they could develop to fit the changing needs of a task. Relatedly, the head of one firm considered "the utilization of employees' capabilities" as his primary requirement. This ambiguity was not without its drawbacks, however, and some people were uncomfortable with it. For example, one product engineer noted, "One of the troubles here is that nobody is very clear about his title or status, or even his function." On the whole, though, the drawbacks were more than compensated for by "a general awareness of the common purpose of the concern." [9]

The organization in the least predictable environment was a newly created electronics-development firm. Individual tasks here "were defined almost exclusively as the consequence of interaction with superiors, colleagues, and subordinates; there was no specification by the head of the concern." [10] Everyone here recognized the need for common beliefs and goals, and these common goals helped ensure that all could work together with little or no guidance. In turn, this pervasive self-control helped the firm adapt quickly and "unbureaucratically" to its rapidly changing environment. This firm—like the others previously described—had an organizational structure that was contingent upon and appropriate for the nature of its environment.

Conclusions. From findings like these, Burns and Stalker concluded that an organization's structure and management system depended upon certain extrinsic factors, and that:

> These extrinsic factors are all, in our view, identifiable as different rates of technical or market change. By change we mean the appearance of novelties; i.e., new scientific discoveries or technical inventions, and requirements for products of a kind not previously available or demanded.[11]

This realization led Burns and Stalker to distinguish between two divergent systems of management practice, which they called *mechanistic* and *organic*: [12]

CHARACTERISTICS OF
ORGANIC SYSTEMS OF MANAGEMENT

The contributive nature of special knowledge and experience to the common task of the concern

The "realistic" nature of the individual task, which is seen as set by the total situation of the concern

The adjustment and continual redefinition of individual tasks through interaction with others

The shedding of "responsibility" as a limited field of rights, obligations, and methods

The growth of commitment to the concern beyond any technical definition

A network structure of control, authority, and communication

Omniscience no longer imputed to the head of the concern; location of knowledge about the technical or commercial nature of the present task located anywhere in the network

A lateral rather than a vertical direction of communication through the organization; also, a communication between people of different rank, resembling consultation rather than command

Content of communication consisting of information and advice rather than instructions and decisions

Commitment to the concern's task and to the "technological ethos" of material progress and expansion more highly valued than loyalty and obedience

Importance and prestige attached to affiliations and expertise valid in the industrial, technical, and commercial environments outside the firm

CHARACTERISTICS OF
MECHANISTIC SYSTEMS OF MANAGEMENT

The specialized differentiation of functions, to which the problems and tasks facing the concern as a whole are broken down

The abstract nature of each task, which is pursued with techniques and purposes more or less distinct from those of the concern as a whole

The use of the formal hierarchy for coordination

The precise definition of rights, obligations, and technical methods attached to each functional role

The translation of rights, obligations, and methods into the responsibilities of a functional position

Hierarchic structure of control, authority, and communication

A reinforcement of the hierarchic structure by the location of knowledge of actualities exclusively at the top of the hierarchy

A tendency for interaction between members of the concern to be vertical; i.e., between superior and subordinate

A tendency for operations and working behavior to be governed by the instructions and decisions issued by superiors

Insistence on loyalty to the concern and obedience to superiors as a condition of membership

A greater importance and prestige attaching to internal (local) than to general (cosmopolitan) knowledge, experience, and skill

As the displayed lists show, efficiency-oriented *mechanistic* systems are characterized by highly specialized jobs, centralization, and vertical communications. *Organic* systems are adapted to unstable conditions, "when problems and requirements for action arise which cannot be broken down and distributed . . . within a clearly defined hierarchy." There is a great need here for all employees to identify with the goals of the firm and to exercise self-control. Jobs tend to lose much of their formal definition, and communications and interaction run laterally as well as vertically.

In summary, Burns and Stalker distinguish between mechanistic and organic management systems, and conclude that the rate of change of a firm's environment determines which system is most appropriate.

The Lawrence and Lorsch Studies

Paul Lawrence and Jay Lorsch have carried out studies to determine "What kind of organization does it take to deal with various economic and market conditions?" [13] Their research was carried out in two steps. In the first, six firms in the plastics industry were analyzed: This analysis provided a qualitative understanding of how environment and organizational structure are related. Second, an effective organization and an ineffective one in each of the plastics, food, and container industries were studied and compared. These three industries were chosen because they displayed important differences in environmental uncertainty and diversity. For example, the industries had a "different rate of technological change in both products and processes."

Lawrence and Lorsch focused on two questions. First (in line with the Burns and Stalker findings), they sought to analyze the relationship between the uncertainty of an organization's environment and its internal structure. To do this, they distinguished between three main "subsystems" of an organization—marketing, economic–technical, and scientific—and hypothesized that the structure of *each* subsystem or department would depend on how predictable its own environment was. Their hypothesis was that "the greater the degree of certainty of the relevant subenvironment, the more formalized the structure of the subsystem." [14]

The second, related question focused on what they called "differentiation and integration." They said that since the environments of the departments differed, the departments themselves—how they were structured, and managed—might differ as well. In other words, the organization would be *differentiated*. By *differentiation*, Lawrence and Lorsch mean the "state of segmentation of the organization into subsystems, each of which tends to develop particular attributes in relation to the requirements posed by its relevant external environment." This differentiation, in turn, necessitates "integration," or the "process of achieving unity of effort among the various subsystems in the accomplishment of the organization's task." [15] Specifically, they expected the departments or subsystems to differ in terms of attributes like:

1. Structure (use of rules, chain of command, etc.)
2. Member's orientation toward time
3. Member's orientation toward goals

Data about the environments of each department were collected in interviews with the top executives in each organization. From these interviews, Lawrence and Lorsch concluded that the uncertainty of an environment reflected three things:

1. The rate of change in environmental conditions
2. The certainty of information at a given time about environmental conditions
3. The time span—how long it took to get feedback.[16]

Findings. As Table 4-1 shows, Lawrence and Lorsch found that subsystems within each organization tended to "develop a degree of formalized

TABLE 4-1

Subsystem Structure Scores Ranked from Low to High

Subsystem	Firm I	Firm II	Firm III	Firm IV	Firm V	Firm VI
Fundamental research (most *uncertain* environment)	1	1.5	1	1	1.5	1
Applied research	2.5	1.5	2	2	1.5	2
Sales	2.5	3	3	4	3	3.5
Production (most *predictable* environment)	4	4	4	3	4	3.5

Numbers are rank orders: 1 = Low Structure, 4 = High Structure. Fundamental research units usually had the most *uncertain* environments. Production units usually had the most *predictable* environments.
Source: Paul R. Lawrence and Jay W. Lorsch, "Differentiation and Integration in Complex Organizations," *Administrative Science Quarterly*, Vol. 12, No. 1 (June 1967).

structure related to the certainty of their relevant environment." For example:

> Production, with [a] more certain subenvironment, tended to have the highest structure in all but one organization, while fundamental research subsystems tended to have the least structure. Sales subsystems with moderately certain tasks tended to be more structural than research subsystems, but usually less structured than production.[17]

Furthermore, certain behavioral characteristics of the employees in each department were related to the nature of its environment. For example, employees' time orientation (short-run, medium, long-run) reflected how long it tended to take to get feedback in their environment: Production employees tended to have short-run orientations, since they were used to getting daily feedback concerning their decisions. Fundamental-research scientists tended to have long-run perspectives, since it often took them years to get feedback. As expected, employees also tended to be most oriented toward the goals of their own, rather than some other, department.

Summary. The studies by Lawrence and Lorsch and Burns and Stalker help illustrate how environment and organization are related. Organizations in stable, unchanging environments tend to develop structures that are mechanistic and formal. Those that must deal with more uncertain environments develop more organic, adaptive structures. Since different departments within organizations usually have their own "subenvironments" to deal with, organizations are *differentiated*, with each department having its own degree of structure and its own behavioral characteristics.

TECHNOLOGY AND ORGANIZATION

Environment is one important determinant of organizational form; the firm's technology—the processes it uses to produce its products or services—is another.

The Woodward Studies

The studies by Joan Woodward and her research team began in 1953 as an attempt to survey the organizational practices of local firms and to develop research hypotheses.[18] The researchers selected the geographical area of South Essex, England, which surrounded their college, and studied virtually all the firms in that area that employed at least 100 people. They thereby secured a sample of 100 firms in widely diverse lines of business.

In each of these firms, the team spent up to a week collecting data on various aspects of the organization and its management. Through interviews, observation, and analysis of company records, they obtained information from each firm on the following subjects:

1. History, background, and objectives.
2. Description of the manufacturing processes and methods, and organization structure.
3. Forms and routines through which the firm was organized and operated.
4. Facts and figures that could be used to assess the firm's commercial success. These included factual material from annual reports, the fluctuation of shares on the stock exchange, changes in share of the market, and the general state of the industry of which the firm was a part (for example, some industries were expanding, while some were stable or contracting).
5. Based upon the information above, the team also obtained general impressions of two other factors. The first was the degree of "organization consciousness" the firm exhibited. This measured the extent to which a formal organizational structure was understood to exist by the personnel. Second, a firm was evaluated as organic or mechanistic, in line with the Burns and Stalker findings. High organizational consciousness was usually associated with a mechanistic system, whereas "in most cases, lack of organizational consciousness—inability to produce an organization chart or to state precisely who is responsible to whom in the hierarchy—indicated an organic management system." [19]

Initial findings. The research team used this information to identify interorganizational differences in structure and management practices. At the outset, some obvious differences in structure were identified. For example, the number of managerial levels varied from two to twelve, and the spans of control (the number of persons reporting to a manager) of the chief executives varied from two to eighteen. Furthermore, the ratio of production workers to staff personnel varied from less than 1:1 to more han 10:1.

These variations in structure stimulated the research team to seek the causes of the differences, but a review of their data led to some disconcerting discoveries. First, contrary to expectations, they found that the differences did not relate to the size of the firm or to its general industrial category. On the average, for example, large companies weren't any more "formalized" than small companies. Furthermore, the twenty firms assessed "above average" in success had little in common organizationally, nor did the twenty firms assessed as "below average." [20]

Therefore, the Woodward team had reached an impasse. The "principles of organization" that were often stressed by classical theorists appeared to be unrelated to success. Over half the successful firms, in fact, were low in organizational consciousness and tended to operate under the relatively free-wheeling organic system of management.

Relating technology to organization. The researchers then sought some way to explain these findings. The final unused data the team had consisted of information relating to technology—"the methods and processes

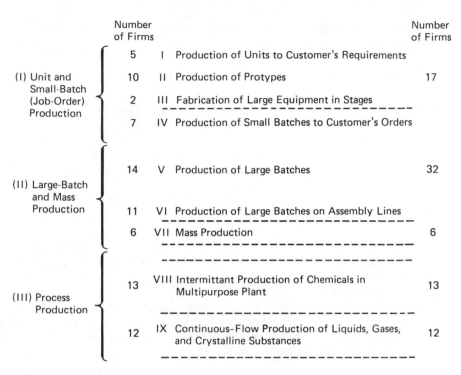

	Number of Firms			Number of Firms
(I) Unit and Small-Batch (Job-Order) Production	5	I	Production of Units to Customer's Requirements	17
	10	II	Production of Protypes	
	2	III	Fabrication of Large Equipment in Stages	
	7	IV	Production of Small Batches to Customer's Orders	
(II) Large-Batch and Mass Production	14	V	Production of Large Batches	32
	11	VI	Production of Large Batches on Assembly Lines	
	6	VII	Mass Production	6
(III) Process Production	13	VIII	Intermittant Production of Chemicals in Multipurpose Plant	13
	12	IX	Continuous-Flow Production of Liquids, Gases, and Crystalline Substances	12

FIGURE 4-1. Woodward's Technology Classifications

Source: Joan Woodward, *Industrial Organization: Theory and Practice* (London: Oxford University Press, 1965), p. 39.

of manufacture." As Figure 4-1 shows, the researchers hit upon the idea of classifying the firms into three main groups and nine subgroups, according to complexity of technology:

1. Unit and small-batch production, such as custom built cars
2. Large-batch and mass production, such as mass produced cars
3. Long-run process production of the same product, such as chemicals

Woodward described some of the differences between these production systems as follows:

Moving along the scale from system One to Nine, it becomes increasingly possible to exercise control over manufacturing operations, the physical limitations of production becoming better known and understood. Targets can be set and reached more effectively in continuous flow production plants than they can in the most up-to-date and efficient batch production firms and the factors likely to limit performance can be allowed for. However well developed production procedures may be in batch production firms, there will be a degree of uncertainty in prediction of results.[21]

Therefore, these classifications formed a rough scale of the predictability and degree of control over the production process. In job-order manufacturing, each unit is made to the customer's specifications, and the operations performed on each unit tend not to be repeated; the movement of material from one machine to the next depends mostly on the unique nature of the customer's specification. On the other hand, mass-produced articles are usually more standardized and the production steps more predictable. However, product variations still remain and create some unpredictability in production sequencing. The most standardized and predictable production sequence is represented by Woodward's process technology. Here, the product is standardized and is locked into a predictable, repetitive sequence from one step to the next.

Once the firms were classified by technology, it became apparent that different organization structures seemed to be appropriate for different technologies. For example, as summarized in Table 4-2, the number of organizational levels varied among the three groups, with process manufacturing having the largest number of levels (or longest chain of command). The chief executives' span of control also varied with technology, with managers in process-manufacturing facilities having the widest span. Job-order and process manufacturing supervisors tended to have narrower spans of control, and those in the mass-production plants had wider ones. The more advanced technologies utilized proportionately more clerical, administrative, and staff personnel. There also seemed to be a clear relationship between structure and success within each technology classification. In particular, the successful unit-production firms had characteristics in common, as did the above-average mass-production firms and above-average process-production firms (see Table 4-2).

In addition, the research team found other differences that seemed due to technology. First,

> There was a tendency for organic management systems to predominate in the production categories at the extremes of the technical scale, while mechanistic systems dominated in the middle ranges. Clear-cut definition of duties and responsibilities was a characteristic of firms in the middle ranges, while flexible organization with a high degree of delegation both of authority and of the responsibility for decision making, and with permissive and participating management, was characteristic of firms at the extremes.[22]

They also found that the organizations at each extreme made greater use of verbal communications, whereas mass-production organizations tended to use written communications. Furthermore, jobs tended to be more specialized in mass-production firms than in either job-order or process firms. And, the mass-production firms relied heavily on the traditional line–staff type of organization. Line managers in these firms engaged primarily in direct supervision, while technical decisions were made by staff

TABLE 4-2

Summary of Woodward's Research Findings on the Organizational Structures of Successful Firms

Technological Characteristics	Unit and Small-Batch Production	Large-Batch and Mass Production	Process Production
Lower levels	Informally organized narrow spans of control	Organized by formal process; wide spans	Organized by technological task demands; narrow spans of control
Higher levels	Informally organized; no distinction between line and staff	Organized by administrative processes with line-staff separation	Informally organized; no distinction between line and staff
General characteristics	Few levels; narrow spans of control; low "organizational consciousness"; no clear chain of command; low ratio of administrative to nonadministrative personnel	More "organizational consciousness"; more clearly defined positions; clear chain of command	Many levels; less "organizational consciousness"; high ratio of administrative to nonadministrative personnel

personnel. On the other hand, line managers in job-order and process firms were expected to have greater technical expertise, and to make technical decisions themselves. Finally, there were more skilled workers in job and process firms and fewer ones in the mass production firms.

Interpretations. Woodward's own explanation for these findings is that the firms differed in the degree of coordination they required. In unit-production firms, for example:

> Direct and speedy channels of communication between one department and another were essential at every level of the hierarchy. Bridge communications were important, for a crisis occurring at any stage in the manufacturing sequence could quickly involve all departments.[23]

On the other hand, in the mass-production firms, the functions were more independent of each other and more self-contained. This, in turn, meant that the end result "did not depend on the establishment of a close operational relationship between the people responsible for development, production, and sales. . . ." [24] Research and development, marketing, and production are even more independent of each other in the process firms, says Woodward.

Alternatively, we can interpret her findings by focusing on the importance and number of contingencies—unexpected events—to which each firm had to adapt. For example, unit firms probably face the greatest number of contingencies, but the nature of their flexible production technologies are such that they can readily adapt to most. At the other extreme, in the process firms, contingencies arise only occasionally, but when they do, they are of major importance. Since these highly automated, continuous-flow facilities depend upon predetermined work flows, exceptions or breakdowns may be quite serious. Therefore, the structure of these organizations remains organic, with highly skilled maintenance specialists standing ready to respond to emergencies, or contingencies when they arise.

There is an underlying question that can help put the Woodward findings and interpretations into perspective. It is, "how much uncertainty or how many contingencies must each organization cope with?" The idea that emerges from the Woodward findings, and from those of the other researchers described in this chapter, is that two different kinds of organizations can be conceived of. One is geared chiefly to performance and one to problem solving, and the appropriateness of each is tied to the number of contingencies to which it must adapt. This possibility was predicted by a number of theorists, including March and Simon; [25] however, it has been only in the past few years that empirical support has been obtained and some of the specific relationships discovered.

The Aston Studies

For several years, the research evidence generally supported Woodward's findings.[26] Within a few years, however, members of the Industrial Administration Research Unit at the University of Aston in Birmingham, England, obtained findings that were strikingly at odds with those of the Woodward team. Specifically, the Aston findings seemed to suggest that an organization's size—not its technology—was the main determinent of its organization structure. Their data came from 52 organizations, 31 of which were manufacturing firms. The Aston team initially presented its research findings in two papers, one relating a number of "contextual" variables (like technology and location) to organization structure, and the second focusing on the relation between technology and organization structure. We'll discuss the findings of each paper in turn, but we should first show what these researchers meant by "contextual variables" and "structure."

The Aston "contextual variables." [27]   Theorists like Burns and Stalker and Woodward focused on one contextual factor (environment or technology) and described its relation to organizational structure. The Aston group began by assuming that there might be *many* factors that could influence structure, and they defined some of these as follows:

1. *Origin and history.* For example, was the firm started by an entrepreneur, or by an existing organization? How old was the firm?
2. *Ownership and control.* For example, how much public accountability was the firm responsible for? What was the relation of the ownership to the management of the firm?

3. *Size.* In terms of the number of employees and amount of net assets of the firm.
4. *Charter.* "Charter" meant the purpose and goals of the firm, and particularly the multiplicity and diversity of its products and services.
5. *Technology.* This basically related to how rigid and automated the work flow was, and how interdependent its segments were.
6. *Location.* Primarily, the number of operating sites the firm had. (The last three contextual variables—charter/technology/location —were found to be highly interrelated.)
7. *Dependence.* For example, how dependent was the firm on a parent firm for its resources, or on a particular supplier?

The Aston definition of organization structure.   To the Aston group, *organization structure* had three components:

1. *Structuring of activities.* This reflected things like the degree to which jobs were specified in detail, and the degree to which rules and procedures were formalized and documented.
2. *Concentration of authority.* This reflected three factors: the overall degree to which decisions in the organization were centralized, how much autonomy the organization had in relation to its parent firm, and the degree to which selection and promotion procedures were standardized.
3. *Line control of work flow.* This reflected the degree to which supervisors (rather than impersonal rules) controlled the work flow in the firm.

Findings: How context influenced structure.   Table 4-3 summarizes how the Aston group found context and structure to be related. Their findings suggest that as organization size increases, there is more structuring of activities in terms of documentation of rules, functional specialization, and specification of jobs. Furthermore, the more dependent is the organization on some outside organization (a parent firm or large supplier) the more authority tends to be concentrated at the top of the hierarchy. Operating variability—the extent to which nonstandard products must be produced—is related to "line control of work flow": Here it would seem that the more "nonstandard" the firm's products are, the more it has to depend on direct supervisory control rather than formal rules and procedures.

In summary, size, dependence, and the interrelated charter/technology/location factors largely determine organization structure, according to this study. These findings contradict Woodward's, since she found little or no relation between size and structure and found that technology was the dominant determinant of structure. The Aston group's second paper therefore turns specifically to the question of the technology–structure relationship.

TABLE 4-3

Salient Elements of Context *

Elements of Context	Structuring of Activities	Concentration of Authority	Line Control of Workflow
Age	—	−0.38	—
Size of organization †	0.69	—	—
Size of parent organization †	0.39	0.39	—
Operating variability	—	—	0.57
Diversity of products	—	−0.30	—
Workflow integration (technology)	0.34	−0.30	−0.46
Number of operating sites	—	0.39	0.39
Dependence	—	0.66	—

* Significant product-moment correlations.

† Logarithm of number of employees.

Source: Pugh, et al., "The Context of Organization Structures," Administrative Science Quarterly, Vol. 14 (1969), 110.

Measuring technology. In their research, the Aston group focused on what they called *operations* technology, which consisted of four factors: [28]

1. *Automaticity,* the degree to which the production process is automated.
2. *Work-flow rigidity,* how rigid (versus adaptable) the work-flow process is. For example, in the event of a breakdown, does all work flow stop immediately?
3. *Specificity of evaluations,* or how precisely performance could be measured against formal criteria.
4. Finally, the Aston group also measured technology using a production "continuity" scale similar to Woodward's unit-mass-process production continuum.

Findings: Technology and structure. Findings of this follow-up study again suggested that organizational size, not technology, is a main determinant of organizational structure.[29] In 46 randomly selected firms, for example, technology correlated slightly with structure, but its effects were usually overwhelmed by those of organization size. Similar results were obtained with a separate test on the 31 manufacturing firms.

The New Jersey Studies

How could the Aston group's findings be so different from those of Woodward (who found that technology, not size, determined structure)? [30] A recent study of production plants in New Jersey by sociologist Peter Blau and his associates provides the latest and perhaps clearest answers to this question.[31]

This study consisted of interviews with the "chief executive," plant managers, and so on in 110 New Jersey manufacturing plants. Blau and his associates sought to determine, among other things, how technology (as measured by both the Aston and Woodward groups) influenced organization structure.

Initial findings.   Blau and his team first measured the degree of relationship between technology and organization structure in a manner similar to that used by the Aston group. Specifically, they computed "correlation coefficients" in order to test the degree of (linear) relationship between technology and each dimension of organization structure. Here they found that Woodward's conclusion concerning a broad "technological imperative" was not confirmed. For example, little or no relationship was found between technology and various structural features like number of levels, span of control, and the proportion of management and supervisory personnel. On the other hand, *organization size* seemed to influence organization structure, as the Aston group had found. And, the Blau group found that technology had no stronger relation to structure in those departments that were closer to the production floor or in smaller-sized firms in general.

The Blau group's additional findings.   The researchers thought it was odd that technology seemed to have so little effect on the structures of the manufacturing plants. They, therefore, carried out an additional study. Here, they categorized firms into Woodward's three production categories —unit, mass and process. They also statistically tested the degree of *curvilinear* relation between technology and organization structure.

Now their findings were much closer to Woodward's. They found curvilinear (∩ shaped) relationships between technology and dimensions of structure like number of levels and supervisory spans of control, for instance. (In other words, the average span of control increases as we move from unit to mass production firms, and decreases as we move on from mass to process firms.) Apparently, testing for the *linear* relationship between technology and structure (as the Aston and Blau groups had done initially) hid these Woodward-like curvilinear results.

Interpretations.   Therefore, both Woodward and Blau found that structures in unit- and process-production firms were similar, and that they differed from those in the middle, mass-production firms. According to Blau and his assoicates, this is because

> As one moves from small batch to mass production, the nature of manufacturing tasks becomes more uniform, which is reflected in an increase in routine work, a lower skill level of the labor force, and reductions in support components. The data indicate that these trends are reversed in advanced production technologies (process firms). Thus, production jobs are least standardized in process plants, since they generally involve maintenance of complex equipment or responsible monitoring functions there. Process plants usually have not only the most highly skilled blue collar work force,

but also the largest proportion of white collar jobs requiring specialized skills.[32]

In summary, the New Jersey studies thus help explain the Woodward and Aston findings, and put them in perspective. Woodward's initial conclusion that technology and structure are linearly related is invalidated by the Blau findings, as it was by those of the Aston group. However, both the Woodward and Aston groups found certain curvilinear relations between technology and strutcure that they generally did not emphasize in their reports. (Woodward, for example, found that organic management systems predominated in unit and process firms, and both groups found the narrowest first line supervisor spans of control in unit and process firms.) The Blau findings explicitly tested for curvilinear relations between technology and structure. They suggest that technology and structure are curvilinearly related, and that structures at the extremes—unit and process —tend to be more organic.[33] On the other hand, it is the firm in the middle— the mass production firm that the classicists studied—that is organized mechanistically along the lines of the classical management principles. Thus, a firm's technology, like its environment, influences its structure.

ORGANIZATION SIZE AND STRUCTURE

The proposition that size is related to structure seems plausible. For example, imagine how your organization would evolve as it grew from a handful of employees to 50, 100, or more. At the beginning, you probably wouldn't need an organization structure and could simply have all employees reporting directly to you. But as the number of employees increased, this "structure" would become unwieldy. Eventually you would have to delegate authority to certain of your subordinates, establish separate departments (like production and marketing), and develop more elaborate control systems for monitoring performance and taking corrective action. Although such a scenario seems reasonable, the research findings on the relationship between size and structure are actually quite inconsistent. Few researchers would argue that the two are unrelated, but the prevailing evidence suggests that the effects of size on structure are unclear and are moderated by factors like technology.

Positive Findings

In a study carried out for the American Management Association, Ernest Dale used a questionnaire to survey 100 large (5,000 or more employees) and 66 medium-sized (500 to 5,000 employees) firms.[34] The questionnaire was used to obtain information on topics like type of division of labor, degree of centralization, and number of levels in the company.

Dale found a tendency for organizational size and decentralization to be related. However, he found that certain large corporations retained their functional, centralized organizational structures. His findings support those of Alfred Chandler, who found that even the largest companies in the steel, mining, and paper industries retain the functional, centralized organization structure.[35] Other researchers have come to similar conclusions. The Aston group for example, concluded that:

> The correlation between [size] and structuring of activities lends strong support to descriptive studies of the effects of size on bureaucratization. . . . Larger organizations tend to have more specialization, more standardization and more formalization than smaller organizations. . . .

In a replication of the Aston study, John Child came to similar conclusions. His data were based on 82 British organizations, and he found that for those firms, size "remains the major predictor of decentralization." [36] In their study, the Blau group found that size (in terms of number of employees) was related to some organization-structure features, including the number of levels and divisions.

Negative Findings

On the other hand, Woodward found little or no relationship between organization size and structure. And in a major study of the influence of organizational size, a group of researchers concluded that:

> In general, the findings of this study in regard to size are similar to those in previous research which utilize size as a major variable; that is, the relationships between size and other structural components are inconsistent. . . . There is a slight tendency for larger organizations to be both more complex and more formalized, but only on a few variables does the relationship prove to be strong. On others, there is little, if any, established relationship.

Research Problems

Kimberly, in a recent review of some 80 empirical studies of size and organization structure, identified several problems that may help to explain the inconsistent findings concerning size and structure.[37] First, he says, researchers have generally not provided any theoretical explanations for the proposed relationship between size and structure; in other words, why should size affect organization structure at all? Second, his review suggests that there is little agreement on what "size" is, or on how to measure it. For example, some researchers use number of employees; other use the logarithm of number of employees; some use total net assets; and some include part-time and volunteer help, while others do not. Third, Kimberly says, there is not enough evidence concerning the effects (if any) of size on different types of organizations—those in different industries, with different technologies, and so on.

Finally, he says, it is difficult to ascertain whether size "causes" structure, or structure "causes" size. Most studies of size and structure have focused on one or more organizations at one point in time, rather than on several organizations over time. Thus it is difficult to determine whether size has influenced structure, or whether, for example, a manager's decision to structure his firm in a particular way (say, to decentralize it) has resulted in duplication of certain services and an increase in number of employees.

Discussion

Given these inconsistent findings, what can we conclude about the size/structure relation? First, certain structural features—like number of levels, number of divisions, and number of job titles—generally *do* increase with organization size. This seems to make sense, since the larger the "task," the more levels, divisions, and job titles you would expect to have.

On the other hand, conclusions concerning the relation between organizational size and *decentralization* apparently cannot be made without considering the technology of the organization. Process-production firms (such as paper) and those in industries where production efficiency is traditionally paramount (such as steel) seem to maintain centralized structures even though they are quite large. In other industries where competition is more keen (electrical appliances, autos), increased size generally results in increased decentralization and a pushing down of decision making to the lowest level possible.

SUMMARY

In this chapter we have discussed the effect of three contextual factors —environment, technology, and size—on organizations. *How do these influence organization structure?* We found that a more uncertain, complex environment was usually related to a more decentralized, organic structure. Similarly, unit- and process-production firms (where jobs are less routine and employees more highly skilled) also have more organic structures. Size and structure were also related: Division of work (number of divisions, number of levels) proceeds further in larger organizations, and size results in more decentralization, at least in industries where competition and innovation, rather than efficiency, are paramount.

How do these contextual factors influence organizational compliance? Although most of the studies focus on the context–structure relationship, some of the findings relate, at least implicitly, to how contextual factors influence organizational compliance. For example, Burns and Stalker found a more formal hierarchical structure of control to be the norm in mechanistic organizations, whereas a "network" structure of control and more reliance on professionalism and self-control were the norm in organic systems. The findings of Blau and Woodward similarly suggest that in mass-production firms, work is more routine and more closely monitored than in unit- or process-production firms.

What mechanisms seem to account for the effects of context on structure and compliance? Let us assume, as do theorists like Simon, that organizations are structures of decision makers. These decisions require information—information on new products being introduced by competitors, new machines for producing these products, and supplies of raw materials, for example. And, let us further assume that, other things equal, uncertain environments, unit or process technologies, and large size all force decision makers to cope with more information—or to stand ready to cope with more information—than would unchanging environments, mass-production technologies, or smaller-sized organizations.

By this interpretation, decision making, communication, and information emerge as crucial intermediaries for explaining the relation between (1) environment, technology, or size, and (2) organization. In the next chapter, therefore, we will turn to a discussion of decision making, communication, and information, and their role in organization design.

DISCUSSION QUESTIONS

1. Discuss the relationship between environment, technology, size, and organization.
2. What are some of the basic differences and similarities between mechanistic and organic organizations?
3. As a short project, choose one very familiar organization that you feel is either organic or mechanistic. Look closely at the management functions in this organization, paying particular attention to such things as adherence to rules and procedures, adherence to chain of command, and the type of leadership style. What makes this organization particularly appropriate for dealing with the type of tasks that it has? If you chose a mechanistic organization, what is it about this organization that you think would make it particularly inappropriate for dealing with entrepreneurial, creative, rapidly changing tasks? If you chose an organic organization, why do you think it would be inappropriate for routine tasks?

FOOTNOTES

1 F. E. Emery and E. C. Trist, "The Causal Texture of Organizational Environments," *Human Relations*, Vol. 18 (August 1965), 20–26.

2 William R. Dill, "The Impact of Environment on Organizational Development," in Sidney Mailick and Edward H. Van Ness, eds., *Concepts and Issues in Administrative Behavior* (Englewood Cliffs, N.J.: Prentice-Hall, 1962).

3 Tom Burns and G. M. Stalker, *The Management of Innovation* (London: Tavistock Publications, 1961), p. vii. © Tavistock Publications (1959) Ltd, 1961.

4 *Ibid.*, p. 78.

5 *Ibid.*, p. 83.

6 *Ibid.*, p. 82.

7 *Ibid.*, p. 89.

8 *Ibid.*, p. 92.

9 *Ibid.*, p. 93.

10 *Ibid.*, p. 94.

11 *Ibid.*, p. 96.

12 Based on Burns and Stalker, *The Management of Innovation*, pp. 120–22.

13 Paul R. Lawrence and Jay W. Lorsch, *Organization and Environment* (Boston: Division of Research, Graduate School of Business Administration, Harvard University, 1967), p. 1.

14 Paul R. Lawrence and Jay W. Lorsch, "Differentiation and Integration in Complex Organizations," *Administrative Science Quarterly*, Vol. 12, No. 1 (June 1967), 1–47.

15 *Ibid.*

16 Although this conclusion is intuitively attractive, there is debate over (1) how to operationally define "environment," and (2) how adequate the Lawrence and Lorsch environmental-uncertainty questionnaire was. See, for example, Henri Tosi, Ramon Aldag, and Ronald Storey, "On the Measurement of the Environment: An Assessment of the Lawrence and Lorsch Environmental Uncertainty Scale," *Administrative Science Quarterly*, March 1973, pp. 27–36; Robert B. Duncan, "Characteristics of Organizational Environments and Perceived Environmental Uncertainty," *Administrative Science Quarterly*, September 1972, pp. 313–36; Richard N. Osborn and James G. Hunt, "Environment and Organizational Effectiveness," *Administrative Science Quarterly*, June 1974, pp. 231–46.

17 Lawrence and Lorsch, "Differentiation and Integration."

18 Joan Woodward, *Industrial Organization: Theory and Practice* (London: Oxford University Press, 1965).

19 *Ibid.*, p. 24.

20 *Ibid.*, p. 33.

21 *Ibid.*, p. 40.

22 *Ibid.*, p. 64. Some more recent findings provide support for this assertion. See Robert T. Keller, John W. Slocum, Jr., and Gerald I. Susman, "Management System, Uncertainty, and Continuous Process Technology," Proceedings of the Academy of Management Thirty-third Annual Meeting, August 1973, Thad Green and Dennis Ray, eds., pp. 507–8.

23 Woodward, *Industrial Organization*, p. 134.

24 *Ibid.*, p. 137.

25 James March and Herbert Simon, *Organizations* (New York: John Wiley, 1958).

26 W. H. Zwerman, *New Perspectives on Organization Theory* (Westport, Conn.: Greenwood Press, 1970).

27 D. S. Pugh, D. J. Hickson, C. R. Hinings, and C. Turner, "The Context of Organizations," *Administrative Science Quarterly*, Vol. 14 (1969), 91–114.

28 The Aston researchers actually distinguish between three kinds of technology: *operations* (the techniques used in its work flow activities); *materials* (the actions a person performs on an object); and *knowledge* (how many exceptional cases are there).

29 The Aston group's findings concerning the dominance of size (as opposed to technology) as a determinant of structure were later confirmed in a study by Child and Mansfield on the "national" group of British firms, and by a study by Hickson et al. of U. S. firms. See John Child and Roger Mansfield, "Technology, Size, and Organization Structure," *Sociology*, Vol. 6 (1972), 369–93; David Hickson, C. R. Hinings, C. J. McMillan, and J. P.

Schwitter, "The Culture-Free Context of Organization Structure: A Trinational Comparison," *Sociology*, Vol. 8 (1974), 59–80.

[30] See, for example, Martin Evans and Will McQuillan, "A Longitudinal Analysis of the Context and Structure of a Large British Financial Institution," *The Journal of Management Studies*, May 1977 for one of a number of studies that suggested that the Aston findings refute those of Woodward.

[31] Peter M. Blau, Cecilia McHugh Falbe, William McKinley, and Phelps K. Tracy, "Technology and Organization in Manufacturing," *Administrative Science Quarterly*, Vol. 21 (March 1976), 20–40.

[32] Blau et al., "Technology and Organization," p. 30.

[33] The Blau group also found that "a process technology in production and the automation of the support functions by on-site computers also exert numerous parallel influences on the administrative structure."

[34] This section, except as noted, is based on Richard Hall, *Organizations: Structure and Process* (Englewood Cliffs, N.J.: Prentice-Hall, 1972), pp. 112–39; and Gary Dessler, *Organization and Management: A Contingency Approach* (Englewood Cliffs, N.J.: Prentice-Hall, 1976), p. 111.

[35] Ernest Dale, *Organization* (New York: American Management Association, 1967), p. 110; Alfred Chandler, *Strategy and Structure* (Cambridge, Mass.: M.I.T. Press, 1962).

[36] John Child, "Predicting and Understanding Organization Structure," *Administrative Science Quarterly*, June 1973, pp. 168–85.

[37] John R. Kimberly, "Organizational Size and the Structuralist Perspective: A Review, Critique, and Proposal," *Administrative Science Quarterly*, Vol. 21 (December 1976), 571.

ADDITIONAL REFERENCES

CHILD, J., "Managerial and Organizational Factors Associated with Company Performance—Part I," *The Journal of Management Studies*, Vol. 11, No. 3 (October 1974).

DUNCAN, ROBERT B., "Characteristics of Organizational Environments and Perceived Environmental Uncertainty," *Administrative Science Quarterly*, September 1972.

EVANS, MARTIN G., and WILL McQUILLAN, "A Longitudinal Analysis of the Context and Structure of a Large British Financial Institution," *The Journal of Management Studies*, May 1977.

HININGS, C. R., D. S. PUGH, D. J. HICKSON, and C. TURNER, "An Approach to the Study of Bureaucracy," *Sociology*, January 1967, pp. 62–72.

LYNCH, BEVERLY P., "An Empirical Assessment of Perrow's Technology Construct," *Administrative Science Quarterly*, September 1974.

OSBORN, RICHARD N., and JAMES G. HUNT, "Environment and Organizational Effectiveness," *Administrative Science Quarterly*, June 1974.

PUGH, D. S., D. J. HICKSON, and C. R. HININGS, "An Empirical Taxonomy of Work Organization Structures," *Administrative Science Quarterly*, 1969, pp. 115–26.

PUGH, D. S., D. J. HICKSON, C. R. HININGS, K. M. MacDONALD, C. TURNER, and R. LUPTON, "A Conceptual Scheme for Organizational Analysis," *Administrative Science Quarterly*, 1963, pp. 289–315.

TOSI, HENRY, RAMON ALDAG, and RONALD STOREY, "On the Measurement of the Environment: An Assessment of the Lawrence and Lorsch Environmental Uncertainty Subscale," *Administrative Science Quarterly*, March 1973.

Chapter 5

Decision Making and Communication

CHAPTER OVERVIEW

The three topics we discuss in this chapter—decision making, communication, and information—are clearly interrelated. Managers are, first and foremost, decision makers, and decision making requires information, information which is useless unless communicated to the decision maker. This is one reason for studying these three topics together.

But there is also a second reason: an understanding of these three processes can contribute to what we know about how to design organizations. Organizations are systems composed of decision makers, and they, therefore, run on information—information on competitors' actions, new products, price levels, and so forth. And, to follow up on the idea we developed in the last chapter, factors like environment, technology, and size seem to influence an organization's structure and processes primarily through the kinds of information they force managers to cope with. For example, unpredictable situations in which unforeseen emergencies are likely to develop are most often associated with adaptable, organic structures. Predictable, unchanging conditions tend to result in mechanistic structures.

This being the case, we should expect that the research findings on decision making, communication, and information processing would help to explain and illustrate how "information" influences organization. For example, from the research on human information processing, we might expect to find that people have limited processing capabilities, and that when the information load becomes excessive, breakdowns—or some sort of adjustments—occur. Similarly, from the research on communication we might expect that some small-group communications networks are more effective at handling uncertain, ambiguous situations than are others.

In this chapter we, therefore, turn to a discussion of decision making, communication, and information processing. And, as illustrated in our framework, we will try to show how these processes explain the link between an organization's environment, technology, and size, and its internal structure and practices. Three of the questions we focus on are:

1. What implications do the findings on decision making have for organization structure and compliance?
2. What implications do the findings on communication have for organization structure and compliance?
3. What implications do the findings on information processing have for organization structure and compliance?

The outline of this chapter is as follows:

I. Types of Decision Makers
   A. Economic Man
   B. Administrative Man
   C. Decision Making and Organization: Implications

II. Communication
   A. What Is Communication?
   B. Characteristics of Communications
   C. Communications Networks

III. Human Information Processing
   A. The Iota Research
   B. The Schroder, Driver, Streufert Research
   C. Causes of Information Overload
   D. Summary: Information Processing and Organization

IV. Organizational Methods for Handling Information
   A. Information Processing in "Mechanistic" Organizations
   B. Adapting to Increased Information

V. Summary

TYPES OF DECISION MAKERS

Organization theorists must necessarily make some assumptions about how managers make decisions and these assumptions then influence the theorists' prescriptions. Thus, classical theorists assumed that decision makers were rational "economic men," always seeking to maximize their utility and maintain efficiency; centralized mechanistic structures and the use of incentives flowed logically from such assumptions. Simon's "Administrative

Man," unlike "Economic Man," does not have complete knowledge, nor does he seek to maximize; the need for managers making nonroutine decisions, for adaptive organizations, and for an emphasis on nonmaterial rewards flow from such assumptions. What assumptions have been made about how managers make decisions? Which assumptions are correct, given the research findings? What implications do these findings have for organization theory? We turn to these questions in this section.

Economic Man

Most classical theorists assumed that the decision maker was operating in a routine, predictable environment in which all possible alternatives, and the outcome for each, were known with certainty. This decision maker, who has come to be known as Economic Man, has complete information on all matters pertaining to his consumption decisions. He knows the full range of goods and services available on the market, and the capacity of each good or service to satisfy his wants. He or she also knows the exact price of each good or service, and that these prices will not be changed by his actions in the market, since (it is assumed) he has an inconsequentially small part of that market. This person also knows precisely what his monthly income will be during the planning period and is able to order his preferences for different bundles (or budgets) of products or services. He can thus choose whichever combination best satisfies his needs (or "maximizes his utility"). Under this theory, businessmen were concerned only with profits, and employees only with maximizing their wages.

As we discussed in Chapter 2, this theory can be traced back at least as far as the writings of Luther and Calvin. By 1750, economic theory—developing in an era of Industrial Revolution and under the guidance of theorists like Adam Smith—emphasized the utilitarian rationality and self-interest of man. The model of Economic Man was based on the assumption that every man weighed the economic alternatives open to him and consistently chose an alternative that resulted in his highest net gain or utility. We saw that with spreading industrialization, this theory provided a rationale for industry's embracing of the centralized, specialized, and autocratic structures of the military and religious organizations of previous centuries, and their emphasis on financial incentives. It was out of such an environment that classical organization theory and the scientific-management movement grew.

Administrative Man

In contrast to this somewhat mechanical Economic Man, Herbert Simon and his associates propose an alternate type of decision maker: Administrative Man. Administrative Man, they say, does not have complete knowledge, and although his decisions may be "rational," they are only so given the person's unique values, needs, and aspirations. Simon and his associates therefore substitute the concept of *subjective rationality* for that of objective rationality. The behavior of any single individual, they say, cannot reach any high degree of rationality because:

> The number of alternatives he must explore is so great, the information he would need to evaluate them so vast that even an approximation to objective rationality is hard to conceive. Individual choice takes place in an environment of "givens"—premises that are accepted by the subject as bases for his choice; and behavior is adaptive only within the limits set by these "givens." [1]

Because of these "cognitive limits on rationality," Administrative Man "satisfices" rather than maximizes. According to March and Simon, "Most human decision making, whether individual or organizational, is concerned with the discovery and selection of satisfactory alternatives; only in exceptional cases is it concerned with the discovery and selection of optimal alternatives." [2] If Simon is correct, then in most instances a centralized, mechanistic structure with one all-knowing chief would be unrealistic, as would a preoccupation with maximizing incentives.

Many studies have been carried out to determine if classical-man or administrative-man assumptions are accurate, but the findings are somewhat inconsistent. In one study, Clarkson developed a computer program that successfully duplicated the investment decisions of a bank investment trust officer.[3] The program, which Clarkson developed based on his observations of the officer, rather consistently developed the same portfolio of stock-market investments as did the officer when provided with the same inputs in terms of total value of the portfolio and level of risk. The study seems to support some of the assumptions underlying the administrative-man proposition, particularly in regard to the satisficing assumption.

The Soelberg study. On the other hand, a study by Soelberg resulted in findings that lead one to question administrative-man assumptions; they also provide a vivid picture of decision making in action.[4] Soelberg's subjects were business school graduate students who were making their postgraduate job decisions. Soelberg and his colleagues carried out a series of open-ended interviews with the students, and the following picture of the students' decision making process developed: First, each student decided on an "ideal" job, and then laid out a set of operational criteria for evaluating specific job alternatives. Second, the person began sifting through several alternatives, screening each against the operational criteria established. But, contrary to administrative-man assumptions, the students did *not* necessarily halt their search once they had identified acceptable alternatives. And when they did finally end their search for new alternatives, they usually had more than a single acceptable alternative in their "active rosters." Third, after actually ceasing the search, each person usually refused to admit that his or her choice had already been made. Instead, before recognizing this choice explicitly, the person often engaged in perhaps a two- or three-month "confirmation" process, in which, for the first time, all alternatives were compared to each other, criterion by criterion. These alternatives were generally reduced to two—the choice candidate, and a "confirmation" candidate. This confirmation process apparently helped resolve any residual uncertainties or problems connected with the choice candidate, and helped arrive at a decision that convinced the student that the choice candidate was best. In a follow up study Soelberg found that almost 90 percent of the students had actually made up their minds ten days or more before the date on which they reported having made their decisions.

Soelberg's findings suggest that decision makers do not "satisfice" in any easily discernible way. On the other hand, they also suggest that decision making is not quite as "rational" as envisioned by classical theorists, since decision makers were not found to rationally (or in any way) order their preferences for various alternatives during the search process.

The findings from other studies further cloud the issue of whether the assumptions of Economic Man, Administrative Man, or "Soelberg's man" are correct. Some evidence suggests that perhaps *several* types of decision makers exist. Glueck, for example, obtained data from 30 students on how they chose an employer. He found that 14 followed a decision pattern called "economic maximizer," 9 followed the Soelberg "confirmation" pattern, and 7 followed the "satisficer" pattern. Satisficing may also depend on the number of available alternatives, being less likely to occur when a set of acceptable alternatives is small, and where evaluating alternatives is inexpensive.[5]

Systematic vs. intuitive decision makers.   In a similar line of research, McKenney and Keen distinguish between systematic and intuitive decision makers.[6] At one extreme, *systematic* people "tend to approach a problem by structuring it in terms of some method which, if followed through, leads to a likely solution." At the other extreme, *intuitive* decision makers use more of a trial-and-error approach to solving problems. "They are much more willing to jump from one method to another, to disregard information, and to be sensitive to cues that they may not be able to identify verbally."

In their study, twenty subjects (MBA students) whose test results clearly classify them as either systematic or intuitive were presented with a set of 16 problems from which they had to choose any five to answer. Subjects were invited to talk aloud as they dealt with each problem. The "systematics" preferred programmed-type problems, whereas the "intuitives" liked open-ended ones, especially those that required ingenuity or opinion. The systematic subjects tended to be very concerned with getting into a problem by defining how to solve it. "In contrast, the intuitive subjects tended to jump in, try something, and see where it led them. They generally showed a pattern of rapid solution testing, abandoning lines of exploration that did not seem profitable."

Each of the two types of decision makers were found to be more appropriate for different types of problems. For example, one problem required decoding of a coded message; intuitive subjects excelled, but none of the systematics was able to solve it. In this case, finding a solution seemed to require more of an intuitive decision-making approach, including "a random testing of ideas, followed by a necessary incubation period in which the implications of these tests were assimilated, and then a sudden jump to the answer."

Decision Making and Organization: Implications

The findings on decision making provide some important implications for organizations and organization theory. We began this section by noting that organization theorists necessarily make some assumptions about how managers make decisions and that these assumptions then influence the theorists' prescriptions. Thus, classical theorists assumed that decision makers were rational "economic men," always seeking to maximize their utility and maintain efficiency; centralized, mechanistic structures and the use of incentives flowed logically from such assumptions. If Simon's "Administrative Man" is valid, this fact would tend to suggest the need for more adaptive organizations and for more emphasis on nonmaterial rewards.

Which set of assumptions is correct? Based on our review of research findings in this section, it appears that several types of decision makers exist. And at the risk of oversimplifying a complicated subject, we will classify these decision makers as economic-man/systematic, and administrative-man/intuitive. The former tends to take a more "rational" approach to decision making and to solve problems in a formal, step-by-step manner while trying to maximize some goal. On the other hand, our more intuitive decision maker doesn't take a "locked-in" approach to decision making; instead, he or she randomly tests ideas and then jumps to answers. Classical man excels at "programmed-type" problems, the kind that might be faced by financial analysts. The more intuitive decision maker excels at open-ended, "unprogrammed" decisions, especially those requiring ingenuity (as in architecture).

In summary, both the economic man and administrative man assumptions make sense, and to that extent, so do their organizational analogues—mechanistic and organic structures. And, related to this, each type of decision making unit seems most appropriate to a particular type of problem. Programmed, routine decisions are generally associated with mechanistic structures, as we saw in Chapter 4. Similarly, according to Burns and Stalker:

> There are industrial concerns for which nonprogrammed decision making is a normal function; [for which] indeed this kind of activity takes up most management time, and is the most important function. Such firms, insofar as they are successful, have either spontaneously or deliberately worked out a kind of management system which will facilitate nonprogrammed decision making. . . . [This] organic form is appropriate to changing conditions which give rise constantly to fresh problems and unforeseen requirements for action which cannot be broken down nor distributed automatically.[7]

Therefore:

1. The different assumptions about how man makes decisions parallel the different approaches to organization theory that have evolved—such as classical versus behavioral.
2. Different models of decision making—that is, economic man, administrative man, and so on, are viable.
3. Systematic decision makers and mechanistic structures seem best suited for each other, and for programmed, routine decisions, while intuitive decision makers and organic structures seem best suited for each other, and for nonprogrammed, entrepreneurial decisions.

COMMUNICATION

What Is Communication?

Communication defined. Katz and Kahn say that communication is the exchange of information and the transmission of meaning, and that it is the very essence of an organization.[8] Managers operate on the basis of information—on, say, competitors' tactics, the supply of labor and raw materials, or delays on assembly lines. And, say Katz and Kahn, it is not the *actions* themselves (of competitors, of supplies decreasing, or of delays) that prompt managerial action, but rather the *information* about these things.

A communications model. The basic model depicting the communication process was developed by Shannon and Weaver [9] and is presented in Figure 5-1. According to this model, any communication has four basic components: There is an *information source*, which provides the "raw material" for the message—for example, a machine breakdown on a production

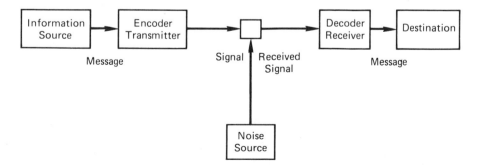

FIGURE 5-1. Symbolic Representation of Communication Process

Source: Claude E. Shannon and Warren Weaver, *The Mathematical Theory of Communication* (Urbana, Il.: University of Illinois Press, 1949), p. 98.

line. Next, there is a *transmitter* (or what some writers call an "encoder"). This monitors the information source and changes or encodes the information into a form (language, a production report, telegram, or other) that can then be transmitted to the receiver. The plant manager who discovers the machine breakdown and telegraphs a report to company headquarters is an example of a transmitter. There is also a communication *receiver* or "decoder." The receiver (for example, the company's head of production) decodes the message and then transmits it in a more useful form (perhaps with a list of production delay implications) to the *ultimate destination*, which might be the company president. (Note from the model that the message received may also be filtered or distorted by "noise" from outside the system.)

This model can be used to depict any communications system. We could, for example, use it to represent two people holding a phone conversation. The information source is the person speaking into the telephone's mouthpiece. The phone then acts as transmitter/encoder, transforming speech vibrations into electrical impulses that are transmitted along the phone lines. At the other end of the line, the receiver/decoder takes these electrical impulses and transforms (decodes) them into vibrations, which are transmitted through the earpiece to the other person on the line, the destination. Electrical storms, faulty cables, and the like are potential sources of noise that could filter and distort the message between transmitter and receiver.[10]

One reason this model is useful is because it emphasizes the fact that a communications system can be no stronger than its weakest link. If there is too much "noise" between transmitter and receiver, if the receiver does not properly decode the message or the decoder does not properly interpret the information, an accurate message will not reach the destination, and to that extent effective communication will not take place.[11] In practice there are many barriers to organizational communication, including not only distortion and filtering of information, but also breakdowns caused by time pressure or an overload of information.

Communication directions.   Organizational communications can flow downward, laterally, and upward. Downward communications are transmitted from superior to subordinate and generally consist of any of five types of messages: job instructions (what the job entails); job rationale (explaining the purpose of the job); procedures and practices to be followed; feedback on performance; and the indoctrination of subordinates on organization goals.

Lateral or horizontal communications, essential in many organizations, involve communications across the organizational hierarchy, generally between people at about the same level but in different departments. Classical management theorists generally viewed lateral communications with caution and prescribed restricting them as much as possible.[12]

Organizational communications can also flow upward. Upward communication can provide top management with valuable information concerning organizational functioning. It can take various forms, including budget reports, morale surveys, and grievance procedures, through which employees are permitted to appeal disciplinary actions to higher organizational levels.

Characteristics of Communications

According to Katz and Kahn, communications systems have five basic characteristics: the size of the communications loop; the repetitiveness of the system; whether the system is open or closed; the efficiency of the system for its task; and the "fit" between the system and the function it serves.[13]

Size of loop. First, communications systems can be characterized in terms of their size, and specifically in terms of the numbers and types of employees they interconnect. For example, some systems may be confined to only the top echelons of the organization, such as the board of directors and executive staff. Others, such as organizationwide "newsletters," might include everyone from president to janitor.

The matter of system size is important for several reasons. The larger the communications system, the more apt it is to face breakdowns, distortion, and other types of "noise." Also, managers often misjudge the size of their communications systems, sometimes overestimating the number of people their communications reach, and sometimes overestimating their own needs for information.

Repetitiveness. Communications systems can also be characterized in terms of their repetitiveness. For example, in some systems, a communication (say, an order) is transmitted downward virtually without modification, with each management "transmitter" simply echoing the message he or she has received. Other systems are characterized by modified messages, with interpretation occurring at each step in the system.

Feedback. Communications systems also differ in the extent to which their feedback is open to change or modification. In a completely "closed" system, feedback (in the form of directives) flows back to the information source and must be implemented without modification; there is no provision for admitting new information. In an open system, new information is encouraged (perhaps by welcoming feedback from lower-level employees), and information oscillates back and forth across the communications network until a preferred solution is reached.

The fit between a communications system and its purpose. We can also characterize communications systems in terms of their appropriateness to the purpose for which they are established. For example, a "closed" communications system may be appropriate for taking action under emergency situations but inappropriate for solving complex planning problems where time is not of the essence.

The efficiency of communications networks. Finally, we can categorize communications systems in terms of the "networks" they form, specifically in terms of how communications in these networks are restricted.
This is the subject of the next section.

Communications Networks

Small-group experiments. Much of what we know about the relative
efficiency of different communications networks derives from a series of
studies carried out in the 1950s. In an early study, subjects were 100 male
undergraduates. They were divided into 20 groups of five men each, and
each group was structured in one of the four types of networks shown in
Figure 5-2.

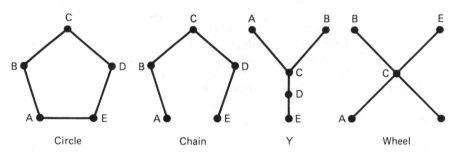

Circle   Chain   Y   Wheel

FIGURE 5-2. Experimental Communication Networks

Source: Harold J. Leavitt, "Some Effects of Certain Communication Patterns on Group Performance," *Journal of Abnormal and Social Psychology,* Vol. 46 (1951), 38-50.

Each subject was placed in a compartment at a table in such a way
that his communication was restricted. For example, each subject in the
"circle" network could communicate only with subjects to his left and to
his right. Subjects in the "wheel" network could communicate only with
the subject in the central position in the network, but this "central person"
could communicate with the four remaining subjects in his network. The
lines in the networks (Figure 5-2) show two-way linkages. In the study, the
overall structure of the network for any group was unknown to the subjects. All a person knew was to whom he could send messages and from
whom he could receive them.

These early studies generally involved having the groups solve simple,
uncomplicated problems. In one study, for example, each network member
held a card bearing five symbols, only one of which was common to the
cards of all members. Their objective was to discover what symbol they all
had in common, and they could communicate only by passing notes through
partitions. When a group member thought he knew what the symbol was,

he could signal the researchers; when all five members had signaled, the trial was ended.

The wheel network usually solved this straightforward problem most efficiently. It minimized the number of communication links and so arrived at a decision on the common symbol more quickly than did the other networks. The circle and chain groups were generally the slowest to solve the problem. The wheel groups are viewed by most writers as "centralized," because there is one person in a central position with whom everyone must communicate. On the other hand, the circle network is viewed as "decentralized," since there is no single dominant decision maker.

A follow-up study in which networks had to solve a more complex problem resulted in rather different findings.[14] In the earlier studies, the problem facing each group member was straightforward: He had to identify which symbols he had and impart this information to those group members he was permitted to communicate with. In later studies, the problem was made more complex by, for example, giving group members a set of marbles that were difficult to describe. Two people looking at identical marbles could describe them quite differently; for instance, what one might view as "greenish-yellow," another might call "aqua."

In this case it was the more "decentralized" circle network that solved the problems the fastest. One reason seems to be the relatively free-flowing communications in the circle networks, which were able to send many more messages than did the wheel networks. Additional findings suggest that leaders emerge more quickly in wheel networks, that group members are more satisfied in circle networks, and that decentralized (circle) networks may be as efficient as centralized (wheel) networks even for routine problems, if given the opportunity to discover their structure and organize themselves.

Organizational communications networks. A few studies of communications networks have been carried out in large organizations. One such study involved groups of systems and procedure personnel from divisions in a large aerospace firm, and took place in connection with a reorganization.[15] The initial organization is presented in Figure 5-3. According to the researcher, the communications system of this group "was primarily a free circle network. Everyone in the group was free to utilize whatever channels of communication he desired, with the result that most of the group's time was spent in discussion, and very little work was accomplished." The morale of this group was high, each person's advice was appreciated and carefully evaluated, and individual group members were therefore very involved in their tasks.

The group was reorganized by management into a wheel network (see Figure 5-4). Whereas communications were formerly unrestricted, they were now very restricted, and this restriction (concerning who could communicate with whom) was formalized by a strongly worded directive from management. Employees eventually reacted by following this directive completely, and by protecting their own interests by commenting only on what affected them; as a result, the number of errors grew tremendously.

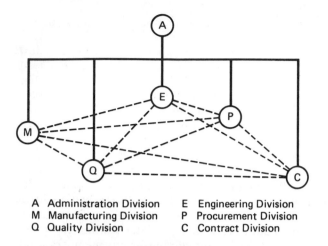

A Administration Division E Engineering Division
M Manufacturing Division P Procurement Division
Q Quality Division C Contract Division

FIGURE 5-3. The Initial Organization: A Circle Network

Source: Peter Mears, "Structuring Communication in a Working Group," *The Journal of Communication,* Vol. 24, No. 1 (1975), 73.

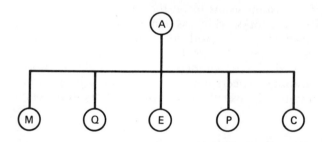

FIGURE 5-4. New "Wheel Network" Organization

Source: Peter Mears, "Structuring Communication in a Working Group," *The Journal of Communication,* Vol. 24, No. 1 (1975), 74.

The researcher found that part of the reason for the breakdown in the wheel network was the "overload" on the central, coordinating group member:

> The task was complex, and the individuals refused to accept the dictates of the central person without sufficient information. This forced the central person to handle more and more messages until he could do only one of two things: either state that he could not handle the job, or try to circumvent the group entirely by pointing out to management that the group was uncooperative. Management ultimately allowed the structure to return to a network somewhat closer to what it had been originally. Morale in this group even after several months had not returned to its previous levels. These findings may support the notion that more decentralized free-flowing communications networks are appropriate for solving complex problems

where employee participation is required, and also that such networks, on the whole, are associated with higher employee morale.

Implications. Findings like these suggest several implications for organization theory. Communications systems can be characterized in terms of repetitiveness, efficiency, and how they fit their purpose. And, the results of studies suggest that more centralized and directive "wheel" networks are especially efficient at solving straightforward, clear-cut problems. The organizational analogue to such a network is a centralized structure with one chief issuing downward orders and all subordinates communicating only with this chief.

On the other hand, wheel networks were not so effective where problems were more complex and ambiguous. Here, the amount of information the chief had to handle often proved so excessive that the network became "overloaded" and activities ground to a halt. In these situations, a more "decentralized," circle network solved the problems fastest. Here, communications were also relatively free-flowing and subordinates could communicate upward, downward, and laterally.

In addition to their implications for structure, these findings also suggest some implications for the question of compliance. Most important, morale was consistently higher in the circle networks, and employees seemed to want to do that "little bit extra" that was required to get their work done effectively. In the centralized wheel network, on the other hand, employees reacted more "bureaucratically" and seemed to refuse to exhibit the self-control necessary for effective organizational functioning.

HUMAN INFORMATION PROCESSING

Human information processing refers to the cognitive processes and techniques through which people assimilate information and make decisions. It is the third and perhaps most basic of our links between context and organization, since the "bottom line" of both decision making and communication is the processing of information.

Our main point in this section is that both individuals and organizations can effectively process information only up to a point; beyond this point, "information overload" occurs, and some modification of the system's method of handling information (its structure) is required.

The Iota Research

Research findings suggest that the ability of individuals and organizations to process information—to assimilate it and make decisions on it—increases until some "optimum" amount of information must be processed, and thereafter it declines quickly.[16]

One representative group of studies was carried out by James Miller and his associates, using specially built equipment known as the Iota (information overload testing aid). This equipment consists of a ground-glass screen about three feet by four feet on which various visual stimuli can be projected, and contains a number of buttons and pedals through which subjects can react to the stimuli and slow down the rate at which the stimuli are projected on the screen. Based on a series of experiments with this apparatus, Miller and his associates have been able to develop a clear picture of how people adjust to overloads of information and of what the "optimum" amount of information is.

These researchers say there are eight means by which people can adjust to overloads of information:

Omission—not processing some of the information

Errors—incorrectly identifying some of the information

Queuing—delaying a response during heavy loads, and then catching up during slack periods

Filtering—a systematic omission of certain types of information, usually by some priority system

Approximation—less precise response is given

Multiple Channels—the use of parallel subsystems for processing information—for example, using both audio and visual cues, if available

Escape—leaving the situation or cutting off the input of information

Miller's subjects were able to use all these adjustment processes; his findings may be summarized as follows: At slow rates of transmission (very little information projected on the screen), subjects used few adjustments. At medium rates, most subjects attempted to use all adjustment processes at one time or another. At higher rates of transmission, subjects switched to filtering—systematically omitting certain types of information, usually using some priority system. Finally, as Miller's subjects reached their "maximum channel capacity"—the absolute limit of their ability to assimilate and process information—they began adjusting primarily by using omission; they simply ceased processing much of the information, omitting information in some random pattern.

The researchers found that subjects' ability to process information reflected a " ∩ curve" pattern. Specifically, the subjects' ability to process information actually increased somewhat as the amount of information they had to process increased. It reached a maximum level at some "optimum" amount of information, and then diminished quickly.

The Schroder, Driver, Streufert Research

These researchers' findings complement Miller's, and focus on two variables: the *level of information processing* by individuals, and the *amount of information* the individual is confronted with.[17]

One series of studies involved "the tactical game task."[18] A group of four subjects was given a list of military resources and confronted with a model of a volcanic island, which was described as being held by an enemy. The group members were told they were military commanders of equal status aboard a fleet sailing toward the island and 50 miles from it.[19] They were to find out what the situation was on the island and take appropriate action. In the beginning, they had no information about the "enemy" (which was actually played by the experimenters). The only way each group could obtain information was by "probing" the island by air, sea, or land reconnaissance or attack. Whatever their action, the group was presented with the feedback they would have received if they had actually made a particular decision (such as to land men for reconnaissance). Teams had to specify decisions in great detail, thus permitting the experimenters to determine what feedback to provide.

The objectives of the group were to arrive at assumptions or hypotheses about the strength and deployment of the enemy on the island, to test these assumptions, and to make decisions about future action. The game was played for six half-hour periods. The researchers found that the level of information processing of subjects, in terms of quality of decisions, gradually increased as information load (feedback about the "enemy" and results of various tactical decisions by the "commanders") increased. However, when the amount of information (feedback) confronting subjects increased beyond some optimal point, the subjects' level of information processing diminished as "overload" occurred.[20]

Causes of Information Overload

Does this kind of information overload occur in real organizations? Katz and Kahn point out that for managers working in real situations, information overload is a very real problem.[21] Managers, they say, are decision makers and coordinators and thus occupy spots in the organization that require them to assimilate information from sources like subordinates, peers, superiors, and outside vendors. They must then interpret this information and make decisions that result in a coordinated effort, while meeting some "deadline."

The problem of overload arises because organizations do not exist in a constant, unchanging environment. Potential sources of supply may diminish and require additional search for new ones. Markets for products grow and decline. Competitors introduce new products, initiate advertising campaigns, change pricing strategies, and buy new, more efficient equipment. The labor market fluctuates, and personnel leave the organization. Thus, managers are almost continually faced with the dilemma of (1) having to coordinate activities within a given time period, while at the same time (2) having to deal with unpredictable, changing environments and frequent floods of information.

Summary: Information Processing
and Organization

There is little reason to believe that a manager's reactions to this dilemma are very different from those of the Miller or Schroder teams' subjects. As managers are faced with more and more information—with more uncertain information, more complex information, or more types of information—they reach their capacity for processing it and making decisions, and information overload occurs. And, one would assume, it is at this point that the manager ends up using some adjustment mechanism like filtering or omitting information, and making poorer decisions. In any event, it seems likely that effective managers must take some action before such relatively imperfect adjustments are necessary, and these actions generally involve redesigning the organization so it can handle more information.

ORGANIZATIONAL METHODS FOR HANDLING INFORMATION

Jay Galbraith has developed a useful theory for explaining how managers redesign their organizations in order to avoid overloading themselves with information and thus having to adjust through errors or omission.[22] For Galbraith, "uncertainty"—the difference between the amount of information needed to perform the task and the amount already possessed by the organization—is a main factor in overloading managers with information, since:

> The greater the task uncertainty, the greater the amount of information that must be processed among decision makers during task execution to achieve a given level of performance.

Information Processing in "Mechanistic" Organizations

To understand Galbraith's theory, imagine you are company president. Some time ago, you established a relatively "mechanistic" organization structure: Subordinates were given clear job descriptions and specialized jobs; there was a "functional" division of work, in that separate departments, each with its own manager, were established for finance, production, and sales. These three officers report to you.

In this situation, there are, according to Galbraith, three techniques you can use to ensure that the amount of information you have to deal with is kept within reasonable limits while at the same time you effectively coordinate your subordinates' tasks.

1. *Coordination by rules or programs.* If the work that needs to be done is predictable and you are able to plan for it in advance, you can specify ahead of time what actions your subordinates should take under the various circumstances that might crop up. Rules and programs are useful (and are used by all organizations) for dealing with routine, recurring problems or tasks. They specify in detail, ahead of time, what course of action a subordinate is to take if some predictable situation should arise.

2. *Coordination by targets or goals.* As the number of unforeseen occurrences (the amount of uncertainty) increases, it becomes impossible to plan for all contingencies—to make decisions in advance for them. In our example, you would find yourself having to make more and more decisions. To cope with this, you could increase the discretion of your subordinates, allowing them to make more of the necessary decisions themselves. At the same time, you have to be sure that the decisions each subordinate makes "makes sense"—is coordinated with—those of your other subordinates. And to do this, you specify targets that each must shoot for. For example, to decrease the burden on you, you might allow your sales manager to make virtually all sales decisions himself, as long as he increases sales this year by 10,000 units and in all advertising and sales efforts emphasizes the high quality of your firm's products. Similarly, your production manager could make all production-related decisions—what machines to buy, how to schedule the work, etc.—subject to two constraints (or targets): that he be prepared to produce 10,000 more units of your product, and that he maintain very high quality-control standards. You would no longer be involved in day-to-day production or sales decisions—which advertising media to use, how to schedule production, what machines to buy, etc.—and you could be fairly sure that the work of the two departments would be coordinated, since their targets make them so.

3. *Using the hierarchy.* In addition to using rules, and targets and goals, you would use the organizational hierarchy, on an "exception" basis: When situations occur that are not covered by rules or for which targets do not apply, subordinates are trained to bring to you requests for decisions. For example, should a situation arise that requires a change in targets—perhaps a competitor has introduced an all-new product—subordinates would come to you for a decision as to how to proceed.[23]

But according to Galbraith, many (but not all) organizations eventually face a situation in which relying on rules, targets, and the hierarchy is no longer effective. As the "environment" in which the manager operates —sources of labor, his competitors, sources of raw material, production technology, and so on—becomes more differentiated and/or less predictable, he soon finds subordinates referring more and more decisions to him. Rules are no longer useful, since one cannot predict what situations need to be covered by the rules. The targets previously used to ensure coordinated effort become outdated as competitors introduce a stream of innovative products. The manager again finds himself about to become overloaded; his capacity for processing the information that's essential for making decisions is on the verge of being exceeded. Now, Galbraith says, there are five organization-design adjustments the manager can make to avoid becoming overloaded. He calls these environmental management, creation of slack resources, creation of self-contained tasks, investment in vertical information systems, and creation of lateral relationships. The first three reduce the information with which the firm must cope; the last two increase its information-processing capacity.

Adapting to Increased Information

Environmental management. First, the manager could take steps to reduce the need for processing information, through what Galbraith calls environmental management. "Vertical integration" is one familiar example of this. For example, an automobile manufacturer might try to decrease the uncertainties and fluctuations in his sources of supply by buying a steel manufacturer and a tire manufacturer. A clothing manufacturer might try to smooth out his sales demand by buying a chain of retail clothing stores.

Creation of slack resources. The manager could also reduce the need for information processing by creating "slack resources," and there are several ways to do this. Perhaps the most familiar is by establishing inventories. One could, for example, establish inventories of raw materials and thus become less susceptible to fluctuations in raw-material supplies, or inventories of finished goods so as to buffer the firm from sales fluctuations. With such slack resources, exceptions are less likely to occur, and uncertainties are in effect reduced.

Creation of self-contained tasks. The third way to reduce the need for processing information is to create self-contained tasks. One way to do this is to set up self-contained product divisions. Now each product or product line has its own product manager, and its own finance, production, and sales managers. According to Galbraith, such product groups reduce the amount of information processing facing a particular manager by reducing the diversity of products he needs to make decisions on.

Investment in vertical information systems. Managers can increase the information-processing capacity of their organizations by investing in what Galbraith calls vertical information systems. One way to do this is with computerized information systems that accumulate information from various sources inside and outside the organization, quickly compile it, and present it to a manager on, say, a daily basis. Use of staff personnel like an "assistant-to" is another "vertical" way to increase the information-processing capacity of the manager and organization. The staff person can compile information for the manager, research the problem, and advise on what alternatives are available, thus effectively increasing the manager's information processing ability.

Creation of lateral relationships. Finally, the manager can increase the organization's ability to process information by creating one or more special lateral relationships. For example, he could encourage direct contact between managers of the production and sales departments so that decisions are made at their level instead of being referred up the hierarchy. Or he could create special liaison positions for people who act as go-betweens, facilitating the flow of information between two or more departments. Interdepartmental committees could be set up to meet periodically to discuss and iron out schedules and problems, or a special task force of personnel could be drawn from various departments working on a special project.

SUMMARY

The concepts of communication, decision making, and information processing are crucial ones in organization theory, since (as illustrated in our model) they help to explain how and why contextual factors like environment, technology, and size have the impact they do on organizations.

What implications do the findings on decision making have for organization structure and compliance? We saw that both the economic man and administrative man assumptions make sense; and to that extent, so do the organizational forms theorists have built on them—mechanistic and organic. And, related to this, each type of decision making unit seems most appropriate to a particular type of problem. Programmed, routine decisions are generally associated with mechanistic structures, as we saw in Chapter 4. Similarly, unprogrammed decisions are generally associated with organic structures.

The decision making findings also have some implications for organizational compliance, although the link here is more indirect. First, (as we discussed in Chapter 3) economic man and administrative man assumptions each are associated with a particular approach to compliance: the former with an emphasis on financial incentives for gaining compliance, and the latter with organizational loyalty and satisfying nonmaterial needs. Second, from the research findings we know that "intuitive" decision makers seem to need a more unstructured environment in which to make decisions, and we might assume that rules and close supervision inhibit this sort of decision making. An emphasis on self-control would seem more appropriate here.

What implications do the findings on communications have for organization structure and compliance? The centralized, mechanistic wheel structures were best at solving simple, repetitive problems. The more unstructured circle networks did best at solving ambiguous, nonroutine problems. Thus, the communications networks findings generally support, by analogy, the findings of researchers like Burns and Stalker.

In terms of compliance, the communications findings suggest that circle networks (and, perhaps, their organizational analogues, organic structures) contribute to the emergence of self-control. In the centralized wheel networks employees tended to be more resistant and buraucratic, and one might assume that here rules and close supervision would be more necessary for maintaining control.

What implications do the findings on information processing have for organization structure and compliance? These findings suggest that the ability of individuals and organizations to process information—to assimilate it and make decisions on it—increases until some optimal amount of information must be processed, and thereafter declines quickly. At this point, some adjustment (like omission) or redesign (like establishing self-contained tasks) is required.

We can infer from these findings that human information processing may also influence compliance. As the amount of information to be processed increases, a manager's ability to closely supervise the work of subordinates diminishes. Similarly, uncertainty makes the use of predetermined rules and policies impractical. In such situations, then, one would expect more reliance on self-control, and on monitoring overall goals or ends, rather than means.

In summary, we view organizations as structures of decision makers. They are composed of people, and we have seen that people have limited information-processing capabilities. When the information with which the manager must cope becomes too great, "overload" occurs, communication diminishes, and poor decisions are made. In turn, it is contextual factors like environment, technology, and size that largely determine the predictability and quantity of information with which managers must cope.

According to Galbraith, there are several strategies managers can use in reacting to information overload. They can redesign the organization so it has to *handle less information*. Techniques here include environmental management, creating slack resources, and forming self-contained departments. Or the manager can increase the organization's *capacity for handling information*. Techniques here include investing in vertical information systems and creating lateral relationships. In the next two chapters, we discuss these design strategies more completely.

DISCUSSION QUESTIONS

1. Compare and contrast the economic man, the administrative man, and the satisficer decision making theories.

2. In what way is a "systematic" decision maker like our mechanistic organization? An "intuitive" decision maker like our organic organization?

3. In this book we assume that "information" is the link that helps explain how an organization and its environment, technology, and size are related. What other explanations could you propose for findings like those of Burns and Stalker and Woodward?

4. "In terms of Galbraith's design theory, environmental management is conceptually different from the other design strategies since the others assume that the organization primarily reacts to its environment, while environmental management assumes that the organization takes more of an offensive posture in trying to change its environment." Explain whether you agree or disagree with this statement and why.

FOOTNOTES

1 Herbert Simon, *Administrative Behavior* (New York: Free Press, 1976).

2 James March and Herbert Simon, *Organizations* (New York: John Wiley, 1958), pp. 140–41.

3 G. P. E. Clarkson, "A Model of Trust Investment Behavior," in R. M. Cyert and J. G. March, *A Behavioral Theory of the Firm* (Englewood Cliffs, N.J.: Prentice-Hall, 1963), pp. 265–66.

4 Peer Soelberg, "Unprogrammed Decision Making," *Papers and Proceedings*, 26th Annual Meeting, The Academy of Management, December 1966, pp. 3–16.

5 John E. Sheridan, Max Richards, and John W. Slocum, Jr., "The Descriptive Power of Vroom's Expectancy Model of Motivation," *Proceedings*, Academy of Management National Meeting, Boston, 1973, eds. Thad Green and Dennis F. Ray; William F. Glueck, "Decision Making: Organization Choice," *Personnel Psychology*, Vol. 27 (1974), 77–93; David Rados, "Selection and Evaluation of Alternatives and Repetitive Decision Making," *Administrative Science Quarterly*, June 1972; Ronald Taylor and Marvin D. Dunnette, "Influence of Dogmatism, Risk Taking Propensity, and Intelligence on Decision Making Strategies for a Sample of Industrial Managers," *Journal of Applied Psychology*, Vol. 59, No. 4 (1974), 420–23; Harvey Brightman and Thomas Urban, "The Influence of the Dogmatic Personality upon Information Processing: A Comparison with a Bayesian Information Processor," *Organizational Behavior and Human Performance*, Vol. 11 (1974), 266–76.

6 James McKenney and Peter Keen, "How Managers' Minds Work," *Harvard Business Review*, May–June 1974, pp. 74–90.

7 Tom Burns and G. M. Stalker, *The Management of Innovation* (London: Tavistock, 1961), p. 119; also see William McWhinney, "Organizational Form, Decision Modalities, and the Environment," *Human Relations*, Vol. 21 (August 1968), 269–81; and John Maurer, *Readings in Organization Theory: Open System Approaches* (New York: Random House, 1971), pp. 435–47.

8 Daniel Katz and Robert Kahn, *The Social Psychology of Organizations* (New York: John Wiley, 1966).

9 Claude Shannon and Warren Weaver, *The Mathematical Theory of Communications* (Urbana: University of Illinois Press, 1949).

10 Richard Johnson, Fremont Kast, and James Rosenzweig, *The Theory and Management of Systems* (New York: McGraw-Hill, 1973), p. 98.

11 *Ibid.*, p. 97.

12 We will see that minimizing lateral communications generally assumes that the tasks can be so completely routinized that coordination can be carried out almost entirely via rules and the organization's hierarchy. Where rules and reliance on hierarchy are not sufficient, lateral-communication links, including, for example, interdepartmental committees, need to be established.

13 This section is based on Katz and Kahn, *The Social Psychology of Organizations*, pp. 235–47.

14 Harold J. Leavitt, "Some Effects of Certain Communication Patterns on Group Performance," *Journal of Abnormal and Social Psychology*, Vol. 46 (1951), 38–50.

15 Peter Mears, "Structuring Communication in a Working Group," *The Journal of Communication*, Vol. 24, No. 1 (1975), 71–79; Keith Davis, *Organizational Behavior: A Book of Readings* (New York: McGraw-Hill, 1977).

16 Information in this section is based on James G. Miller, "Adjusting to Overloads of Information," in Joseph A. Litterer, *Organizations: Structure and Behavior* (New York: John Wiley, 1969), pp. 313–22.

17 Harold Schroder, Michael Driver, and Siegfried Streufert, *Human Information Processing* (New York: Holt, Rinehart & Winston, 1967).

18 *Ibid.*, p. 5.

19 *Ibid.*, pp. 54–55.

20 *Ibid.*, p. 61.

21 Katz and Kahn, *The Social Psychology of Organizations*, pp. 230–34.

22 Except as noted, this section is based on Jay Galbraith, "Organizational Design: An Information Processing View," *Interfaces*, Vol. 4, No. 3 (May 1974), 28–36; reprinted in J. Richard Hackman, Edward Lawler, and Lyman Porter, *Perspective on Behavior in Organizations* (New York: McGraw-Hill, 1977), pp. 207–14. For a more extensive treatment see Jay Galbraith, *Organization Design* (Addison-Wesley, 1977).

23 Coordination by rules and targets is similar to what March and Simon refer to as coordination by plan; coordination through the hierarchy is similar to what they refer to as coordination by feedback. See March and Simon, *Organizations*, p. 160.

case for part II:
the food canning company

The following case history helps illustrate several important features of organizational environments. It shows for example, how such environments evolve and become complex, and how these complexities influence the organization's functioning. This actual example is excerpted from a paper by British researchers Emery and Trist: [1]

The company concerned was the foremost in its particular market in the food-canning industry in the U.K. and belonged to a large parent group. Its main product—a canned vegetable—had some 65 percent of this market, a situation which had been relatively stable since before the war. Believing it would continue to hold this position, the company persuaded the group board to invest several million pounds sterling in erecting a new, automated factory, which, however, based its economies on an inbuilt rigidity—it was set up exclusively for the long runs expected from the traditional market.

The character of the environment, however, began to change while the factory was being built. A number of small canning firms appeared, not dealing with this product nor indeed with others in the company's range, but with imported fruits. These firms arose because the last of the postwar controls had been removed from steel strip and tin, and cheaper cans could now be obtained in any numbers—while at the same time a larger market was developing in imported fruits. This trade being seasonal, these firms were anxious to find a way of using their machinery and retaining their labor in winter. They became able to do so through a curious side effect of the development of quick-frozen foods.

The quick-freezing process demanded great constancy at the growing end. It was not possible to control this beyond a certain point, so that quite large crops unsuitable for quick freezing but suitable for canning became available—originally from another country (the United States) where a large market for quick-frozen foods had been established. These surplus crops had been sold at a very low price for animal feed. They were now imported by the small canners, at a better but still comparatively low price, and additional cheap supplies soon began to be procurable from underdeveloped countries.

Before the introduction of the quick-freezing form, the company's own canned product—whose raw material had been specially grown at additional cost—had been the premier brand, superior to other varieties and charged at a higher price. But its position in the product spectrum now changed. With the increasing affluence of the society, more people were able to afford the quick-frozen form. Moreover, there was competition from a great many other vegetable products which could substitute for the staple, and people preferred this greater variety. The advantage of being the premier line among canned forms diminished, and demand increased both for the not-so-expensive varieties among them and for the quick-frozen forms. At the same time, major changes were taking place in retailing; supermarkets were developing, and more and more large grocery chains were coming into existence. These establishments wanted to sell certain types of goods under their own house names, and began to place bulk orders with the small canners for their own varieties of the company's staple that fell within this class. As the small canners provided an extremely cheap article (having no marketing expenses and a cheaper raw material), they could undercut the manufacturers' branded product, and within three years they captured over 50 percent of the market. Previously, retailers' varieties had accounted for less than 1 percent.

The new automatic factory could not be adapted to the new situation until alternative products with a big sales volume could be developed, and the scale of research and development, based on the type of market analysis required to identify these, was beyond the scope of the existing resources of the company either in people or in funds.

The changed texture of the environment was not recognized by an able but traditional management until it was too late. They failed entirely to appreciate that a number of outside events were becoming connected with each other in a way that was leading up to irreversible general change. Their first reaction was to make a herculean effort to defend the traditional product, then the board split on whether or not to make entry into the cheaper unbranded market in a supplier role. Group H.Q. now felt they had no option but to step in, and many upheavals and changes in management took place until a "redefinition of mission" was agreed, and slowly and painfully the company reemerged with a very much altered product mix and something of a new identity.

QUESTIONS

1. Emery and Trist entitle their paper "The Causal Texture of Organizational Environments." What do they mean by the term "causal texture"?

2. How, based on this case history, are a company's strategy and its environment related?

3. In what way was this company's problem a result of a poorly chosen strategy?

4. In what way did the firm's technology become part of its "context"?

5. How did an evolving environment create new uncertainties and unpredictable contingencies for this company? What were some of these new unpredictable events?

FOOTNOTE

1 F. E. Emery and E. C. Trist, "The Causal Texture of Organizational Environments," *Human Relations*, Vol. 18, No. 1 (February 1965), 21–32; reprinted in John Maurer, ed., *Readings in Organization Theory* (New York: Random House, 1971), pp. 46–57.

PART III

ORGANIZATION STRUCTURE AND DESIGN

In the last section, we discussed how environment, technology, and size influence organization structure and compliance. In this section, we turn to a more detailed discussion of organization structure and design. In Chapter 6, we discuss departmentation and coordination, and the use of line and staff units. In Chapter 7, we discuss organizational levels and the span of control, the organizational hierarchy, and delegation and decentralization. Thus we focus here almost exclusively on the question of organization structure and design before turning, in Part IV, to a discussion of motivation and compliance.

Chapter 6

Departmentation

and Coordination

CHAPTER OVERVIEW

What is organization structure? Given the amount of effort that has gone into studying the subject, one might imagine that the concept of organization structure would be easily defined, but this is not the case. Different writers define it differently and so determining what exactly is meant by "organization structure" is therefore not an easy matter.

Because there is no unanimous agreement as to how to define or measure organization structure, we will define it as consisting of the following dimensions:

1. Departmentation
2. Line and staff
3. Coordination
4. Levels and span of control
5. Authority hierarchy
6. Delegation

In this first chapter, we will focus on the first three of these dimensions: departmentation, line and staff, and coordination. These make up the "horizontal" or lateral aspect of organization structure, since they involve dividing the work of the organization, assigning tasks to departments, and coordinating these departments. In Chapter 7, we will focus on the last three dimensions—on the "vertical" aspect of structure—and specifically on how authority is delegated or "pushed down" vertically in the organization.

Following our model, in this chapter we will be especially interested in answering these questions:

1. How do contextual factors like environment affect each dimension of structure?
2. How is the effectiveness of a structure determined by its appropriateness to its "situation"?

The outline of this chapter is as follows:

DEPARTMENTATION

Purpose versus Process Departmentation

Every organization has to carry out certain activities such as manufacturing, selling, and accounting. *Departmentation* is the process through which these activities are grouped logically into distinct areas and assigned to managers: it is the organization-wide division of work. It results in "departments"—logical groupings of activities—that also often go by the name divisions, branches, units, groups, or sections.

How can an organization's work be divided? These are numerous [1] but most bases of departmentation conveniently fall into one of two categories, which March and Simon refer to as *purpose departmentation* and *process departmentation*.[2] The former encompasses work arrangements built around specific products, customers, or geographic locations—specific, *self-contained* purposes or outputs. This type of departmentation emphasizes an external, "market" orientation. On the other hand, departmentation by process is more internally or "production"-oriented and focuses upon building departments around such functions as sales, manufacturing, or planning. As a result,

> Process departmentalization generally takes greater advantage of the potentialities for economy of specialization than does purpose departmentalization: purpose departmentalization lends to greater self-containment and lower coordination costs than process departmentalization. . . .[3]

In other words, departmentation by purpose results in departments that are self-contained in that there are separate sales, promotion, personnel, and finance units for *each* product, customer, or location. This mode of departmentation therefore facilitates coordination, adaptation, and information processing.

Process departmentation tends to isolate functions like manufacturing and marketing into specialized departments, which serve *all* products, customers, or markets, and this specialization frequently results in increased efficiencies. As March and Simon stress, choosing between purpose and process departmentation is largely a trade-off. They note that a major problem of departmentation is that "the forms of departmentation that are advantageous in terms of one of these outcomes [self-containment versus skill specialization] are often costly in terms of the other."[4]

Specific Bases of Departmentation— Their Advantages and Disadvantages

Departmentation by purpose. There are three basic ways in which work can be departmentized by *purpose*:

1. By product
2. By customer
3. By location

Departmentation by *product* is depicted in Figure 6-1. Examples would be the Buick Division of General Motors, which is concerned with the many activities in producing a Buick, and a city's police department.

Departmentation by *customer* reflects the arrangement of work around particular customers or markets. An example of this would be a chemical company that establishes separate departments to serve its industrial and its consumer markets. This method is also depicted in Figure 6-1.

Finally, work may be arranged into departments that serve particular *locations,* as in Figure 6-2. A hotel chain, for example, might decide to establish geographical divisions and make one officer responsible for the operation of all the hotels within his district.

There are a number of advantages associated with the purpose form of departmentation, mostly because these departments, as mentioned above,

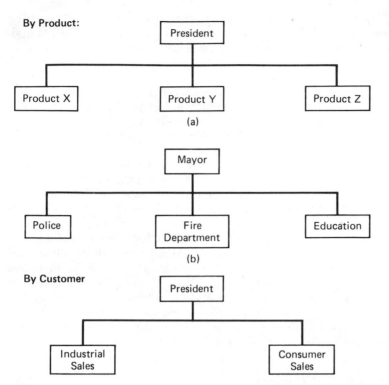

FIGURE 6-1. Division of Work by Products and by Customer

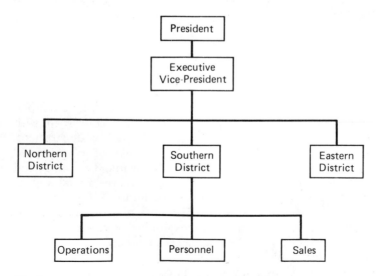

FIGURE 6-2. Dividing Work by Area or Location

tend to be relatively self-contained and easier to coordinate internally. Bringing together under a single head all the work on a project or purpose leads to continuous and undivided attention to the product, customer, or location; also, the department tends to be somewhat more adaptive to the needs of its "purpose." Since the department can operate with some autonomy, its work can be more clearly recognized and evaluated; it does not become lost in the activities of other units. Finally, the greater autonomy frequently given the department head, along with the clearer recognition of performance standards, may motivate him to better performance.

On the other hand, there are a number of frequently mentioned drawbacks to this type of division of work. The implicit autonomy frequently leads to an attitude of independence, which can result in a sub-unit's drifting away from the overall organizational goal. (This is one reason that some writers emphasize the importance of establishing control systems in conjunction with "decentralizing authority").[5] A second disadvantage is that it frequently results in duplication of effort. For example, each of the product divisions may establish planning and sales departments of its own; or a company may decide to organize into product divisions, only to find that its customers are annoyed by being visited by different salesmen representing different divisions.

Departmentation by process. Departmentation by *process*, on the other hand, avoids this sort of duplication and therefore tends to be relatively efficient in many instances. There are two widely used arrangements for dividing work by process.[6] Probably the more familiar is by business function, which is depicted in Figure 6-3. In this type of depart-

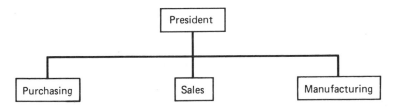

FIGURE 6-3. Dividing Work according to Business Function

mentation, units are established around such functions as sales, manufacturing, finance, and personnel. In turn, each of the departments makes its unique, specialized contribution to every product the company produces and sells. A second basic way in which process departmentation can be used is by dividing work into managerial functions, such as planning, organizing, and controlling. Similarly, work may be divided on the basis of technology, perhaps with separate departments arranged around welding, painting, and assembling.

There are a number of advantages to process departmentation.[7] One is that placing a major emphasis on a particular task or function frequently leads to increased proficiency and technical competence and therefore to improved efficiency. Also, this type of division of work facilitates centralized control, since the separate, specialized functional heads are inherently more dependent upon a central unit for coordinating their work.

However, there are also a number of significant disadvantages. For one, employees in each specialized department may become more involved with their own specialty than with the end purpose of the organization. As a result, interdepartmental communications may be hampered while the need for coordination between the specialized units is increasing. Finally, an employee who has risen through the hierarchy in his own specialized department is frequently not as fit for assuming a companywide managerial post as is his counterpart who has risen in a product-oriented division.

Before turning to some of the research findings on purpose versus process departmentation, we should emphasize that most large organizations utilize a combination of these two structures. For example, as shown in Figure 6-4, we may find that, at the top of the organization, departmenta-

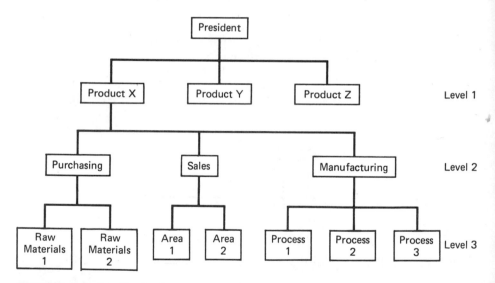

FIGURE 6-4. An Illustration of Multiple Ways of Departmentalizing

tion by purpose is utilized, and separate product divisions are established. However, the fact that each product division is relatively self-contained implies that beneath this top level, there may be departmentation by function, and that for each product, there are therefore separate purchasing, manufacturing, and sales departments. Many arrangements are possible, and even at particular organizational levels, there is no reason to expect the basis of departmentation to be uniform. For example, a president may have vice-presidents for products A and B reporting to him (purpose), as well as vice-presidents for long-range planning and sales (process).

Research Findings: Purpose versus Process Departmentation

Although there has been little empirical research devoted to studying the relative merits of purpose versus process departmentation, the existing studies confirm the advantages and disadvantages discussed above. Furthermore, as might be expected, the research evidence suggests that process departmentation, with its emphasis on specialization, is more appropriate in relatively stable situations. On the other hand, departmentation by purpose, with its lower efficiency but advantages of self-containment, is more appropriate where the situation is rapidly changing or unpredictable.

For example, Chandler found that the industries that opted for the decentralized, product-division structure were those that had followed a strategy of diversification. Their environments were thus more complex and changing. He says:

> [T]he dominant centralized (process-oriented) structure had one basic weakness. A very few men were still entrusted with a great number of complex decisions. . . . As long as an enterprise belonged in an industry whose market, sources of raw materials, and production processes remained relatively unchanged, few entrepreneurial decisions had to be reached. In that situation, such a weakness was not critical, but where technology, market, and sources of supplies were changing rapidly, the defect of such a structure became more obvious.[8]

Similar conclusions were reached by Burns and Stalker, who found that as the rate of change and appearance of "novelties" increased, firms tended to organize more around products and projects and less around functions like sales and production.[9]

The Walker and Lorsch study. Walker and Lorsch have analyzed the relative merits of purpose versus process departmentation.[10] Two manufacturing plants were used—one ("F") organized by process (function), and the other ("P") organized by purpose (product). Although they had different organizational structures, the two plants were otherwise similar. Both were making the same product, and their markets, technology, and raw materials were identical. Furthermore, the parent companies were similar, in that both were large, national corporations that developed, manufactured, and marketed many consumer products. Management philosophies were also similar; they stressed a desire to foster employee initiative and autonomy, and placed great reliance on selection of well-qualified heads. The organization structures of the plants are depicted in Figures 6-5 and 6-6.

As we can see from the organization charts, there were identical functional specialists for manufacturing, packing, quality control, planning and

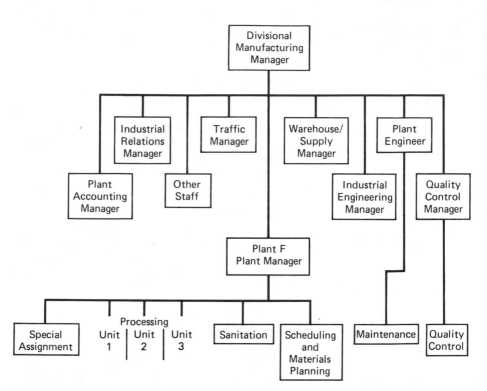

FIGURE 6-5. Organization Chart of Plant F

Note: Notice how, from the point of view of the division manufacturing manager, this is a *functional* departmentation. Basically, the plant manager is in charge of only a specialized manufacturing function.

Source: Arthur H. Walker and Jay W. Lorsch, "Organizational Choice: Product vs. Function," *Harvard Business Review*, Vol. 46, No. 6 (1968), 133-34.

scheduling, warehousing, industrial engineering, and plant engineering in each plant. However in plant F, with the functional basis of division of work:

> Only the manufacturing departments and the planning and scheduling function reported to the plant manager responsible for the product. All other functional specialists reported to the staff of the divisional manufacturing manager, who is also responsible for plants manufacturing other products. At plant P (with the product basis of organization), all functional specialists with the exception of plant engineering reported to the plant manager.[11]

Plant F, therefore, was considered functionally organized, since the plant manager was primarily responsible for manufacturing and reported to the divisional manufacturing manager. The latter also had the other functional managers for maintenance, quality control, warehousing, and

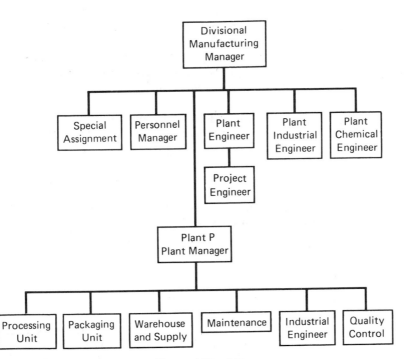

FIGURE 6-6. Organization Chart of Plant P

Note: Notice how, from the point of view of the division manufacturing manager, this is a more product (purpose) oriented departmentation. The plant manager is in charge, basically, of a more complete, self-contained unit: Unlike at plant F, he has managers for packaging, warehouse and supply, maintenance, industrial engineering, and quality control reporting to him.

Source: Arthur H. Walker and Jay W. Lorsch, "Organizational Choice: Product vs. Function," *Harvard Business Review,* Vol. 46, No. 6 (1968), 133-34.

industrial engineering, reporting to him. On the other hand, plant P was considered to be organized by product, since the *plant manager* had most of the functional managers (such as the industrial engineer and the maintenance manager) reporting directly to *him.* Plant P was more self-contained and autonomous, whereas plant F depended on the coordinative efforts of the divisional manufacturing manager for supplying necessary maintenance, quality control, warehousing, industrial engineering, and other advice and resources.

Walker and Lorsch found that plant P was better coordinated than plant F. In plant F, for example, "collaboration between maintenance and production personnel and between production and scheduling was a problem." On the other hand, the only coordination problem in plant P was between production and quality control. Furthermore, communication among employees in plant P was more frequent, less formal, and more often of a face-to-face nature than in plant F.

In terms of performance, the management of both plants had the same two objectives:

1. Maximizing current output within existing capabilities
2. Improving the capabilities of the plant

Walker and Lorsch found that plant F met the first objective more effectively than plant P did. Specifically, the former was achieving a higher production rate with greater efficiency and at less cost. In terms of the second objective, however—which Walker and Lorsch felt was more of a "problem-solving" task—plant P was superior. For example, the productivity of plant P had increased by 23 percent from 1963 to 1966, as compared with an increment of only 3 percent for plant F. In concluding, they point out that "the functional organization seems to lead to better results in situations where the task is more routine and requires less innovative problem solving." [12]

Summary. Purpose-oriented departmentation results in units that are relatively self-contained, and in a structure in which authority for more decisions and for a wider range of decisions rests in the departments. This arrangement should reduce the quantity of information a chief executive would be faced with, and should therefore be an appropriate structure in uncertain, diverse environments. This in fact seems to be the case: The research findings suggest that where uncertain, diverse conditions prevail, effective firms have opted for purpose-oriented departments, and this has made these firms more adaptable. Conversely, process-based structures seem more appropriate in routine situations where efficiency is paramount.

LINE–STAFF STRUCTURE

Introduction

Another familiar way to distinguish between departments is to view them as either *line* or *staff* units. Most writers consider *line functions* to be those that have direct responsibility for accomplishing the objectives of the enterprise, and *staff functions* as those that assist and advise the line manager in accomplishing these objectives. However, keep in mind that staff is not necessarily "less important" than line, and that many essential activities—including personnel, purchasing, quality control, and plant maintenance—would fall into the staff category.

Frederick Taylor was one of the first organization theorists to see the need for distinguishing between "line," and "staff" (or advisory) functions. His solution was a "functional organization" (Figure 6-7), in which each employee reports to *a number of* formal supervisors, each of whom is a specialist in one area. For example, an assembly-line employee might have

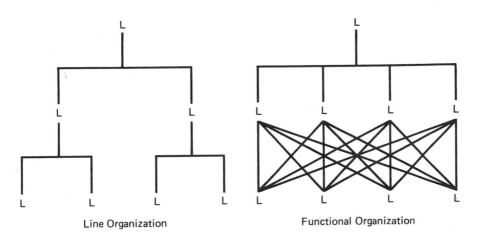

Line Organization Functional Organization

FIGURE 6-7. Line vs. Functional Organization

four bosses, one each for planning, production control, quality control, and inspection.

One of the problems with this type of organization is that the employees are frequently put in a position in which the orders of one boss conflict with those of another. Because of this problem and others, few organizations have adopted the functional form of organization.[13]

The line and staff organization is the more usual way of obtaining the specialized advice that Taylor accurately saw was necessary, while avoiding the disadvantages of having an employee with more than one boss. Using *staff* has also been proposed as one means by which a manager can increase his information-handling capacity. The staff unit can compile, analyze, and advise on various matters, so that the manager's ability to process information is, in effect, extended.

Types of Staff

We can distinguish between two basic types of staff: general staff and specialist staff. The former, frequently described as part of the "office" of an executive, reports to the executive it serves. One familiar example of *general staff* is the "assistant-to" position, in which the person's primary responsibility is to assist his superior in a variety of problems.

A second type of general staff is frequently found in the home office of a decentralized, divisionalized organization. In this type of organization, the actual line responsibility for manufacturing and marketing decisions has been delegated to the division managers. However, the home office frequently has a number of staff units titled "Manufacturing," "Marketing," and so forth. The executives of these units often serve as the policy-making and advisory bodies in their specialized areas, although they do not have line authority in their specialized areas over the division managers.

119

Examples of *specialist staffs* would include quality control, production control, and industrial engineering. These units advise all the other staff managers in the organization. For example, the Personnel staff helps all managers recruit, train, and discipline employees.

Factors Determining the Use of Staff

The Woodward studies: technology and staff. Under what conditions is the use of "staff" appropriate? Technology is one of the factors that have been found to influence the appropriateness of the line–staff structure. Woodward and her team carried out an analysis of the relationship between technology and the use of staff in various English manufacturing firms. They concluded that the line–staff structure was particularly appropriate in large-batch and mass-production firms.[14]

The Woodward Team found the simple line organization depicted in Figure 6-8 to be characteristic of successful firms at the extremes of her

FIGURE 6-8. Line Specialization

Source: Joan Woodward, *Industrial Organization* (London: Oxford University Press, 1965), p. 101.

technological scale—"either small unit production firms or large process production firms of a single-purpose plant type."[15]

If these firms did not have formal staff units, how were the specialized staff functions—such as production control—carried out? The answer apparently is that in the unit-production firms, the necessary technical expertise was held by the line managers themselves. In the process firms, on the other hand, the line–staff distinction had become so blurred that it had simply ceased to exist. Specifically, the highly automated and complex nature of the production process in these firms led to a situation in which units that have normally been considered "staff"—such as plant maintenance —had in fact taken on direct-command authority over the line manager in some areas.

While the line–staff structure did not exist at the extremes of Woodward's technological scale, it predominated in the middle. In the mass-production firms, "line managers were held accountable for end results, while staff managers were formally responsible for giving advice and guidance to line managers." [16]

Woodward found that three main types of line-staff structures had emerged. The first of these is depicted in Figure 6-9. In these firms, the only

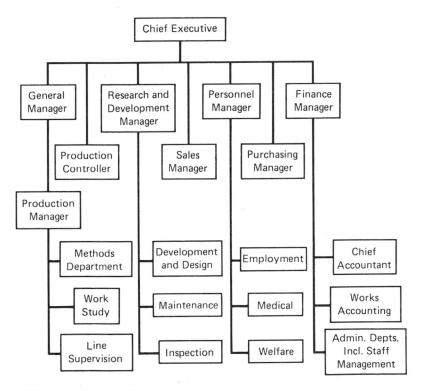

FIGURE 6-9. Line–Staff Organization

Note: Only the production-related managers were considered line managers.

Source: Joan Woodward, *Industrial Organization* (London: Oxford University Press, 1965), p. 105.

managers recognized to have line authority were those with direct responsibility for the production operations. All the other managers, including personnel, sales, research and development, and finance, were considered staff, and advisory to the chief executive.

The second type of line–staff organization is illustrated in Figure 6-10. In this type of organization extensive staff specialization had been carried out within the production department, which had its own personnel, accounting, and purchasing units. These staff units, however, had no responsibility for anything outside production management. For example, the personnel manager was not responsible for the personnel function in either the research or sales department.

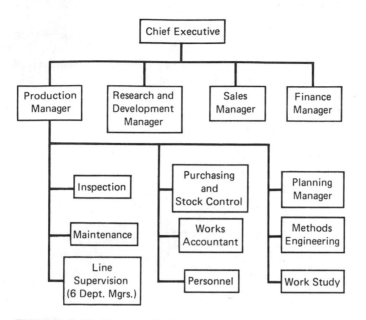

FIGURE 6-10. Line–Staff Organization Inside Production

Note: Extensive staff specialization existed within the production department.

Source: Joan Woodward, *Industrial Organization* (London: Oxford University Press, 1965), p. 106.

The third kind of organization is illustrated in Figure 6-11. This kind was referred to by those interviewed as "divisionalized organization," and is a good example of an application of the general-staff concept, which we discussed above. The organization was divisionalized to the extent that separate production divisions were established for each product. Each of these product divisions had, in addition to its own line manager, a variety of staff specialists, including those for personnel, accounting, and inspection. In addition however, a "general staff," a small group of specialists of senior status, had been appointed to advise the chief executive and board on the formulation of policy relating to their own areas of specialization. These included quality control, personnel, and research and development. These staff specialists, however, had no line authority over the managers of the production divisions.

Staff and organization size. The *size* of an organization also influences the extent to which it uses staff units.[17] In one representative study researchers found that staff employment represented a consistent 75 percent of line employment at all size levels.[18] A similar study focused on line–staff ratios in 155 automotive-parts manufacturers. Here it was found that staff as a percentage of line increased rapidly until the firm had about 550 direct-

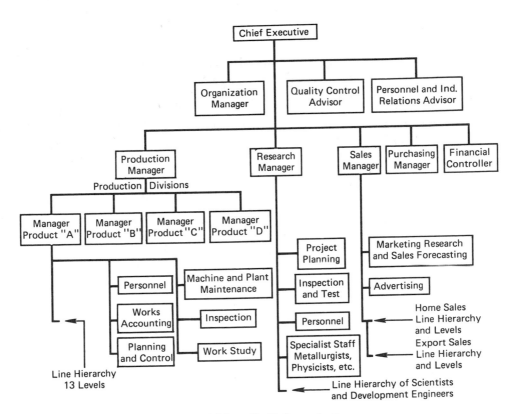

FIGURE 6-11. Product-Centered Line–Staff Organization

Note: This shows the "general staff" concept. The head office has senior staff managers for advising the chief executive and board in the areas of research, quality control, and personnel.

Source: Joan Woodward, *Industrial Organization* (London: Oxford University Press, 1965), p. 108.

production employees. Beyond this point, the ratio declined slowly from about 57 to 51 percent.[19]

Haire studied the relative growth of staff employment in four firms and at four levels of employment: 200, 275, 300, and 2,000 employees. His results indicate that the utilization of staff increased rapidly during the early growth of all firms, and then stabilized at about 25 percent of total employment in two firms and at about 50 percent in the other two.[20] Filley used a similar approach to determine the increase in staff in five firms with total employments of 37, 59, 70, 378, and 450 employees. He found that in three of the firms, staff increased quickly, with two stabilizing at about 20 percent of total employment and the third at 40 percent. In the other two firms, however, the ratio of staff to total employment remained relatively constant at about 20 and 10 percent.[21]

Based on this information, it appears that the proportion of staff usually increases relatively quickly in the earlier stages of an organization's growth, then stabilizes at a certain proportion of total employment. In addition, the proportion of staff, once the organization has reached a certain size, does not increase any more rapidly than total employment in general. Finally, the stabilized ratio between staff and total employment seems to vary markedly between different organizations. In the examples above, for instance, the ratio of staff to total employment ranged from about 10 percent to as high as 75 percent. This, in turn, is compatible with Woodward's findings. If, as Woodward found, technology is an important determinant of the use of staff, then we would expect to find a wide variation in staff utilization where the studies focus only upon the relation between organizational size and the use of staff, and do not "control" for technology.

COORDINATION

Departmentation and Coordination

Departmentation (especially by *function*) results in units that are interdependent, since the output of each unit is relatively useless to the organization by itself. Sales are of little use, for example, if production cannot supply the finished products, and the auto assembly line would grind to a halt if each door installer were not kept supplied with doors. Yet while these departments are often *interdependent*, they are, at the same time, highly *differentiated* in that they develop different goals, points of view, and organization structures, for example. Some process must therefore integrate these interdependent but differentiated units, and that process is coordination.

Coordination in Classical Organization Theory

Classical organization theorists recognized the importance of coordination and considered it one of the primary functions of management. Fayol viewed it as the binding together of individual efforts to accomplish a common objective, and identified coordination as one of the five major management functions.[22] Mooney and Reilly defined coordination as "the orderly arrangement of group effort, to provide unity of action in the pursuit of a common purpose" and called it the "first principle of management in that it expresses the principles of organization in toto: nothing less."[23]

As we discussed in the last chapter, the mechanistic organizations of the classicists generally relied on *rule, plans,* and the *organizational hierarchy* for achieving coordination. Rules—decisions made in advance to guide execution—were used to show employees what behaviors were appropriate to different situations. Employees could then supposedly be depended upon to behave in the appropriate way, and the resulting aggregate response was a coordinated one.[24] As situations arose that were not predictable enough to be covered by rules, managers could give subordinates more discretion, and try to ensure coordination by developing *plans* in which subordinates all had targets to achieve. As long as these targets were reached, the separate activities were automatically coordinated. Finally, when situations changed so rapidly that neither rules nor plans were of use, coordination could be achieved through the *organizational hierarchy*, with subordinates bringing "exceptions" (to the rules and plans) to their superior. The use of rules, plans, and the hierarchy was viewed by classicists as the "standard" technique for achieving coordination. These are still used in virtually all organizations today and are thus the most basic coordination techniques.

Of course, the classicists—most of whom were managers or consultants —were experienced enough to know that there are times when techniques other than rules, plans, and the hierarchy are necessary for achieving coordination. But although they recognized the need for other techniques, they generally viewed them as aberrations and as indications of a poorly designed organization. Gulick pointed out, for example:

> In discussions thus far, it has been assumed that the normal method of interdepartmental coordination is hierarchical in its operation . . . in actual practice there are also other means of interdepartmental coordination which must be regarded as part of the organization as such. Among these must be included planning boards and committees, interdepartmental committees, coordinators, and officially arranged regional meetings, etc. . . . Coordination of this type is essential. It greatly lessens the military stiffness and red tape of the strictly hierarchical structure. It greatly increases the consultative process in administration. It must be recognized, however, that it is to be used only to deal with abnormal situations or where matters of policy are involved, as in planning. The organization itself should be set up so that it can dispose of the routine work without such devices, because these devices are too dilatory, irresponsible, and time consuming for normal administration. Whenever an organization needs continual resort to special coordinating devices in the discharge of its regular work, this is proof that the organization is bad. . . .[25]

Prescriptions like these worked fairly well, of course, as long as "abnormal situations" were not the rule. As long as an organization could be viewed as operating in a stable environment in which novel, unexpected occurrences were at a minimum, hierarchic coordination (through the chain of command) and coordination through rules and plans did not cause many problems, and was probably an efficient way of doing things. But as the amount of information to be processed becomes unmanageable, systems become overloaded and errors begin to mount.

Coordination in Contemporary Organization Theory

As we discussed in the last chapter, there are several alternatives managers can pursue at this point to reduce or better handle the information. They can engage in *environmental management*—for example, by buying suppliers. They can create *slack resources*—for example, by building inventories of raw materials. They can create *self-contained tasks*—for example, by creating *purpose-oriented departments*. They can also invest in *vertical information systems*—for example, by hiring a staff assistant who analyzes situations and advises on alternative courses of action.

Finally, our overloaded manager can *create lateral relations*. He or she can, in other words, redesign the organization so as to use special coordination mechanisms. These include *liaison* personnel, special *committees* and teams, *matrix* organizations, and *integrators*.

Liaison roles. Jay Galbraith suggests that "When the volume of contacts between any two departments grows, it becomes economical to set up a specialized job to handle this communication." For example, an engineering liaison person may be part of the engineering department but be physically located in the production plant. In that way, he or she can advise production personnel concerning what product decisions are feasible, and also ensure that all items produced meet the engineering department's specifications.

Committees and task forces. Liaison personnel are effective when just two or three managers or functions are involved. But when problems arise that involve perhaps seven or eight departments, direct contacts and liaison roles won't suffice. Increasingly, problems are referred upward, and the more unpredictable the organization's tasks, the more acute the situation becomes.

It is at this point that managers create interdepartmental committees, task forces, or teams. These are usually composed of representatives of the seven or eight interdependent departments, and they meet periodically to discuss common problems and ensure interdepartmental coordination.

Matrix organizations.[26] Many companies, such as those in the aerospace industry, find it necessary from time to time to organize around a series of one-time projects, and these projects often call for more full-time attention than can be provided by a task force or committee. In this case, the solution may be a "matrix organization." In the example in Figure 6-12, the company's aerospace projects division is functionally (process) oriented —production, engineering, and so forth. Notice, though, that there is also a purpose-oriented departmentation superimposed over this functional organization. There are three purpose-oriented groupings—for the Venus project, Mars project, and Saturn project.

This is a typical matrix organization. A manager is put in charge of each project and given the authority and responsibility for completing the project. He is assigned a number of personnel from the various functional departments (production, engineering, and so on). He has the authority for relieving his personnel from their "regular" functional group assignments and for rewarding them with promotions, salary increases, and the like. This is a temporary kind of departmentation, and on completion of the project, the personnel return to their functional departments for reassign-

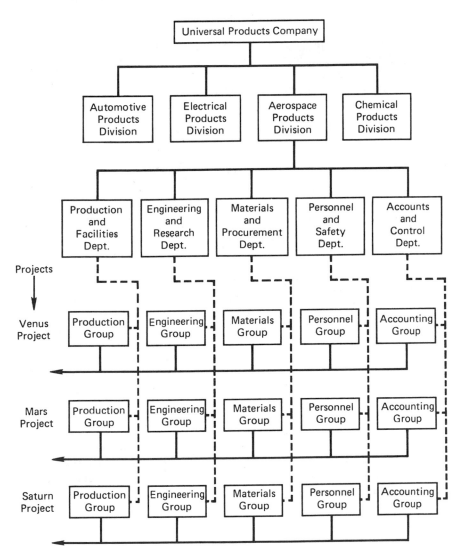

FIGURE 6-12. Matrix Departmentation

Source: Adapted from John Mee, "Matrix Organizations," *Business Horizons,* Vol. VII, No. 2 Summer (1964), 70-72; reprinted in David Hampton, *Modern Management Issues and Ideas* (Belmont: Dickerson, 1969), pp. 92-95.

ment. While they exist, the matrix groupings ensure a self-contained department for each project, one that can devote its continuous and undivided attention to the needs of its own project.

Independent "integrators." Lawrence and Lorsch found that many organizations create special independent "integrators," which may be either individuals or departments. In either case, their entire role is to coordinate the activities of several departments. They differ from liaison personnel in that the integrators are independent of (not attached to) the departments they are coordinating. Instead, they might report to the manager that the departments they must coordinate report to.

Research Findings:
Achieving Effective Coordination

How do effective organizations achieve coordination? What determines whether liaison personnel, committees, or integrators are appropriate? We turn to these questions in this section.

The Lawrence and Lorsch studies. We discussed some of Lawrence and Lorsch's general findings in Chapter 4. Now let us review these findings in more detail, focusing especially on their "coordination" findings.[27]

As you may recall Lawrence and Lorsch's main objective was to answer the question, "What kind of organization does it take to deal with various economic and market conditions?" The researchers pursued this question by focusing upon two basic concepts, which they called differentiation and integration. *Differentiation* was defined as the "segmentation of the organizational system into subsystems, each of which tends to develop particular attributes in relation to the requirements posed by its relevant external environment." They expected to find interdepartmental differences in the formal structure of the departments, in the interpersonal orientations of department members, and in the goal and time orientations of department members.

Lawrence and Lorsch used the term *integration* synonymously with *coordination,* and defined it as the process of achieving unity of effort among the various subsystems in accomplishing the organization's tasks.[28] They predicted that seven factors would influence whether coordination (integration) was effectively achieved:

1. the type of coordinating unit used;
2. whether the unit was "intermediate" between the units it was coordinating;
3. the influence the coordinator had;
4. how the coordinator was rewarded;
5. the total level of influence in the organization;
6. whether most influence was centered at the right organizational level; and
7. how conflicts were resolved.

Lawrence and Lorsch studied effective and ineffective firms in the plastics, food, and container industries. They obtained three basic sets of findings, concerning (1) uncertainty, (2) differentiation, and (3) integration (coordination).

Their findings concerning the uncertainty facing each department were as follows. The total level of uncertainty—in terms of how clear job requirements are, how long it takes to get results on job performance, and so on—was considerably higher in the plastics and food firms than in the container firms. Furthermore, as shown in Figure 6-13, virtually every de-

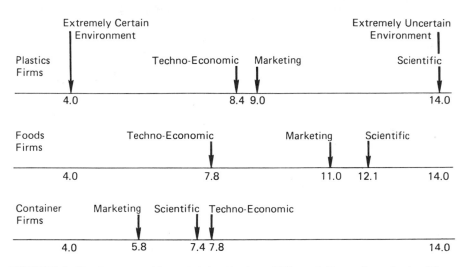

FIGURE 6-13. Average Uncertainty Facing Different Departments in Three Industries

Source: Adapted from Paul R. Lawrence and Jay W. Lorsch, *Organization and Environment* (Boston: Division of Research, Graduate School of Business Administration, Harvard University, 1967), p. 95.

partment within the plastics and foods firms had to cope with more uncertainty than any of the three departments in the container industry. And in the container firms, all the departments faced about the same level of uncertainty. In the plastics and foods firms, the research departments faced highly uncertain environments, while the other departments faced predictable environments.[29]

In turn, the departments in the plastics and foods industries were more differentiated than those in the container firms in terms of how structured they were, and in their goal, time, and interpersonal orientations.

In terms of how the firms achieved integration or coordination, Lawrence and Lorsch found the following.[30] First (see table 6-1) there were some striking differences in the methods used by each of the firms to achieve coordination. Both successful firms in the relatively uncertain plastics and foods industries utilized special integrating units. In the plastics firm, a special integrating department had been established, as well as permanent cross-functional committees at various managerial levels. The successful foods company utilized one person as an integrator and maintained temporary cross-functional teams.

TABLE 6-1

How High- and Low-Performing Firms in Three Industries
Achieved Integration and Conflict Resolution

	Average Level of Differen- tiation *	Average Level of Integration **	Integrating Device	Intermediate Position of Integrators
PLASTICS				
High Perf.	10.7	5.6	Special department	Yes
Low Perf.	9.0	5.1	Special department	Sometimes
FOODS				
High Perf.	8.0	5.3	Special individuals	Yes
Low Perf.	6.5	5.0	Special departments	No
CONTAINERS				
High Perf.	5.7	5.7	Hierarchy	N.A.
Low Perf.	5.7	4.8	Special department	N.A.

* Reflects how different departments were from each other in terms of such factors as formality of structure, time and goal orientation, and interpersonal relationships. Higher number reflects greater differentiation between departments.

** Reflects such factors as the quality of relations between departments. Higher number reflects higher integration.

Source: Gary Dessler, *Organization and Management* (Englewood Cliffs: Prentice-Hall, 1976), pp. 146-47.

The high-performing container firm, which was operating in a more stable environment, achieved coordination through the organizational hierarchy.[31]

On the other hand, managers in the *low*-performing container firm were trying to achieve coordination through a formal integrating department. This department, which reported to the general manager of the firm, had the assigned function of integrating sales requirements and production capacity. However, such a special integrating unit, which had worked so successfully in the more uncertain and rapidly changing plastics and foods industries, seemed inappropriate and ineffective in the more stable container

TABLE 6-1

How High- and Low-Performing Firms in Three Industries
Achieved Integration and Conflict Resolution (*cont.*)

Influence of Integrating Departments	Reward System for Integrators	Total Level of Organizational Influence	Influence At Required Level	Mode of Conflict Resolution
Integrators very high	Overall product group stressed	High	Yes Decentralized	Almost all confrontation; problem-solving
Integrators very high	Integrators' solo performance in functional area stressed	Low	No Centralized	Little confrontation; some forcing and smoothing
Integrators high	Overall product group stressed	High	Yes Decentralized	Confrontation; problem-solving
All units about the same	Overall product group stressed	Low	No Centralized	Confrontation; problem-solving
All functional departments about same	N.A.	Low	Yes Centralized	Confrontation; problem-solving
Sales high	N.A.	High	No Decentralized	Less confrontation

environment. As a matter of fact, it led to "considerable confusion about where conflicts were to be resolved," and this contributed to the poor performance of this firm.

Finally, as shown in Table 6-1, the six other "coordination" factors also influenced whether coordination was achieved, and whether conflicts were dealt with effectively. Coordination was more effective when:

1. The integrating person or group was hierarchically about midway between the departments being coordinated.
2. The integrator had a good deal of influence
3. The integrators were rewarded for doing a good job of coordinating
4. The amount of authority or influence lower level employees had was high (plastics and food firms) or low (container firms)
5. The firm was centralized (container firms) or decentralized (plastics and food firms).[32]

In addition, all the successful firms utilized open confrontation and a problem-solving approach to resolving conflicts to a much greater extent than did the low-performing firms.

The Vandeven, Delbecq, Koenig studies.[33] Subjects here included supervisors and personnel in offices of the administrative headquarters of a large state employment agency. The sample consisted of 197 formal work units, with each work unit "consisting of a supervisor and all nonsupervisory personnel immediately reporting to a supervisor."

As one aspect of their study, the researchers sought to determine what relationship there was between the "task uncertainty" facing a work unit and how the unit achieved coordination. Six methods for achieving coordination were considered: rules; plans; "vertical channels" (referral of problems by the subordinates to their supervisor); "horizontal channels" (designated work coordinators or informal contact between unit members); unscheduled meetings; and scheduled meetings.

Research findings, presented in Figure 6-14, suggest the following: As the uncertainty of the tasks undertaken by a work unit increases, the use of *impersonal* coordination techniques like rules and plans decreases significantly, while the use of personal and group coordination increases significantly. According to the researchers, as task uncertainty increased from low to high, there were substantial decreases in the use of impersonal rules and

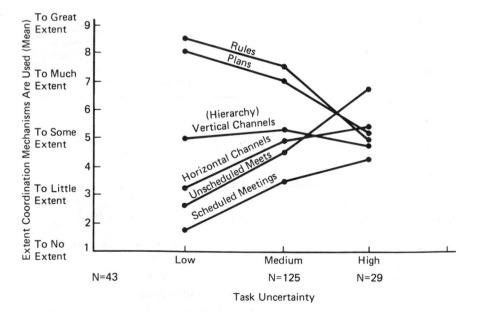

FIGURE 6-14. Coordination Mechanisms Used by Level of Task Uncertainty

Source: Andrew H. Van De Ven, Andre L. Delbecq, and Richard Koenig, Jr., "Determinants of Coordination Modes within Organizations," *American Sociological Association,* Vol. 41 (April 1976), 330.

plans for work coordination, and large increases in the use of horizontal communication channels and both scheduled and unscheduled group meetings. However, the use of "vertical channels"—the hierarchy, where the supervisor is used to coordinate work activities within the unit—remained quite stable regardless of how uncertain the task. The researchers conclude that as task uncertainty increases, horizontal channels and group meetings are substituted for and replace impersonal modes of coordination like rules and plans, and the hierarchy.

Determinants of coordination: summary. Departmentation results in tasks that are interdependent and therefore must be coordinated. All organizations use rules, plans, and the hierarchy to coordinate work units, but as the number of problems referred up the hierarchy increases, the manager's capacity for making required decisions—for processing information—may be insufficient.

Before this happens managers usually react by redesigning their organizations. Environmental management, creation of slack resources and self-contained tasks, and investment in vertical information systems (such as a staff assistant) can be used to reduce the number of problems and extend a manager's information handling capacity. Beyond this, the manager can create *lateral relationships*—special coordinating mechanisms aimed at reducing the problems he must deal with personally.

In this section we discussed four examples of such mechanisms: liaison roles, committees, matrix organizations, and independent integrators. Research findings suggest that as the uncertainties facing a manager increase and as the amount of information he must process increases, he or she tends to rely less on rules, plans, and the hierarchy for coordination, and more on "personal" lateral coordination mechanisms like committee meetings. Under very unpredictable conditions, the organization may develop independent integrating departments whose sole purpose is to coordinate the work of other departments.

SUMMARY

How does the organization's context influence organization structure? How is the effectiveness of structure tied to its appropriateness to the "situation"? These were the important questions we set out to answer in this chapter.

The findings on departmentation suggest that departmentation by purpose, with its lower efficiency but advantage of self-containment, is more appropriate where the situation is rapidly changing or unpredictable. On the other hand, process departmentation, with its high degree of specialization, is more appropriate in relatively stable situations.

We said that use of staff (like an "assistant-to") reflects an investment in vertical information systems, and to the extent that a staff assistant analyzes, digests, and synthesizes information for the boss, he or she can increase the information-processing capacity of the manager and organization. The findings we reviewed suggested that the line–staff structure was especially predominant in mass-production-type firms and that the use of staff increased rapidly with increased organization size.

Coordination refers to the integration of the organization's separate functions or departments. The findings here suggest that as the tasks an organization must cope with become more uncertain managers rely less on "mechanistic" coordination techniques like rules, plans, and the hierarchy, and more on special mechanisms like liaison roles, committees, matrix organizations and independent integrators.

DISCUSSION QUESTIONS

1. What are the differences between departmentation by purpose and by process? What attributes make each appropriate for a different type of task?
2. Discuss the factors that should be considered before implementing a line-staff organization.
3. What was the classicists' approach to coordination? Why do you think they took this approach?
4. What do Lawrence and Lorsch mean by differentiation and integration? What was the main objective of their study?
5. Based on any information you have, rank from high to low the environmental uncertainty and diversity of the following organizations: a college of education; a college of engineering; the university police department; a college of arts and sciences; a college bookstore. What type of integration techniques do you think would be appropriate in each organization?
6. Under what conditions did Lawrence and Lorsch find that special integrating departments or individuals were appropriate? What relationship does this have to what we discuss about departmentation by purpose?

FOOTNOTES

[1] See, for example, Ernest Dale, *Planning and Developing the Company Organization Structure* (New York: American Management Association, 1952).

[2] James March and Herbert Simon, *Organizations* (New York: John Wiley, 1958), pp. 24–25.

[3] *Ibid.*, p. 29.

[4] *Ibid.,*.p. 29.

[5] Peter F. Drucker, *The Practice of Management* (New York: Harper, 1954); Harold Koontz and Cyril O'Donnell, *Principles of Management* (New York: McGraw-Hill, 1964), pp. 326–35.

[6] Ernest Dale, *Organization* (New York: American Management Association, 1967), pp. 104–30.

[7] See, for example, March and Simon, *Organizations,* pp. 22–30.

[8] *Ibid.,* p. 41.

[9] Burns and Stalker, *The Management of Innovation,* p. 125.

[10] Arthur H. Walker and Jay W. Lorsch, "Organizational Choice: Product vs. Function," *Harvard Business Review,* Vol. 46, No. 6 (1968), 133–34.

[11] *Ibid.*

[12] *Ibid.*

[13] Some researchers have found organizations that successfully implemented the functional organization. For an example of this, see Woodward, *Industrial Organization.* Woodward discovered two firms in the process industry with such an organization.

[14] Woodward, *Industrial Organization.*

[15] *Ibid.,* p. 101.

[16] *Ibid.,* pp. 102–3.

[17] Woodward, however, found that size and use of staff were *not* related. See *Ibid.,* p. 31.

[18] A. W. Baker and R. C. Davis, "Ratios of Staff to Line Employees and Stages of Differentiation of Staff Functions," *Research Monograph No. 72,* Bureau of Business Research. The Ohio State University, 1954. Also, see John Child, "Parkinson's Progress: Accounting for the Number of Specialists in Organizations," *Administrative Science Quarterly,* September 1973, pp. 328–48.

[19] B. DeSpelder, "Ratios of Staff to Line Personnel," *Research Monograph No. 106,* Bureau of Business Research, The Ohio State University, 1962.

[20] Mason Haire, "Biological Models and Empirical Histories of the Growth of Organizations," in *Modern Organization Theory,* ed. Mason Haire (New York: John Wiley, 1959), pp. 272–306.

[21] Allen C. Filley, "Decisions and Research in Staff Utilizations," *Academy of Management Journal,* September 1963, pp. 220–31.

[22] Henri Fayol, *General and Industrial Management,* trans. Constance Storrs (London: Sir Isaac Pitman, 1949).

[23] James Mooney and Allen Reilly, *Onward Industry* (New York: Harper and Row, 1931).

[24] Jay Galbraith, "Organizational Design: An Information Processing View," *Interfaces,* Vol. 4, No. 3 (May 1974).

[25] Luther Gulick, "Notes on the Theory of Organization," in Luther Gulick and Lyndall Urwick, eds., *Papers on the Science of Administration* (Clifton, N.J.: A. M. Kelley, 1972).

[26] Gary Dessler, *Management Fundamentals* (Reston, Va., Reston, 1977), pp. 131–32; John Mee, "Matrix Organization," *Business Horizons,* Vol. 7, No. 2 (Summer 1964), 70–72. Stanley Davis and Paul Lawrence, *Matrix* (Reading: Addison-Wesley, 1977).

[27] Paul R. Lawrence and Jay W. Lorsch, *Organization and Environment* (Boston: Division of Research, Graduate School of Business Administration, Harvard University, 1967), p. 1.

[28] Paul R. Lawrence and Jay W. Lorsch, "Differentiation and Integration in Complex Organizations," *Administrative Science Quarterly,* Vol. 12, No. 1 (June 1967), 1–47.

[29] Lawrence and Lorsch, *Organization and Environment,* p. 93.

[30] *Ibid.,* pp. 95–96.

[31] *Ibid.,* p. 138.

[32] *Ibid.,* pp. 140–51.

[33] Andrew H. Vandeven, Andre L. Delbecq, and Richard Koenig, Jr., "Determinants of Coordination Modes within Organizations," *American Sociological Review,* Vol. 41 (April 1976), 322–38.

Chapter 7

Organizational Hierarchy and Delegation

CHAPTER OVERVIEW

In Chapter 6, we focused primarily on the "lateral" aspects of organization structure, and on the differentiation and integration that results from departmentation, creation of line and staff units, and coordination. In Chapter 7, we will focus on the more "vertical" aspects of organization structure, and on the structural dimensions of delegation, decentralization, and span of control. Again, as you read this chapter, ask, "How do contextual factors influence these structural dimensions?" and, "How does the appropriateness of each dimension for the 'situation' affect organizational effectiveness?"

The outline of this chapter is as follows:

I. Delegation and Decentralization
   A. The Process of Delegation
   B. Decentralization Defined
   C. Decentralization and Departmentation
   D. Situational Determinants of Decentralization

II. Hierarchical Levels and the Span of Control
   A. Flat versus Tall Organizations
   B. Span of Control

III. Summary

DELEGATION AND DECENTRALIZATION

The Process of Delegation

Organizing departments and jobs would be impossible without delegation, which we define as the pushing down of authority from superior to subordinate. This is because the assignment of responsibility for some department or job usually goes hand in hand with the delegation of adequate authority to get the task done. For example, it would be inappropriate to assign a subordinate the responsibility for designing a new product, and then tell him he hasn't the authority to hire designers or choose the best design.

The process of delegation can be traced back as far as ancient Egypt, and the advisability of delegating has been recognized by writers representing virtually all schools of organization theory. Even the classical theorists, who have advocated hierarchical, centralized organizations, recognized that organizational responsibilities should be assigned to the lowest level in the organization at which sufficient competence and information for effective task performance exists.

Decentralization Defined

The way many people use the term, decentralization means about the same thing as "delegation"—simply pushing authority down to subordinates. Decentralization, according to them, is the opposite of "centralization" in which all, or nearly all, of the authority to make decisions and take action is retained by top management.[1]

But decentralization is and was always meant to be much more than simply delegation. Decentralization is a philosophy of organization and management, one that implies both selective disbursal *and* concentration of authority.[2] It involves selectively determining what authority to push down into the organization; developing standing plans (such as policies) to guide subordinates who have this authority delegated to them; and implementing selective but adequate controls for monitoring performance. Thus: Decentralization is a philosophy of organization and management that involves both selective delegation of authority, as well as concentration of authority through the imposition of policies and selective but adequate controls.

Example: The organization of the General Motors Corporation provides a good example of "decentralization in practice."

When former President Alfred Sloan first developed G.M.'s decentralized structure his approach was based on two principles: [3]

1. First, he said that the responsibility attached to the top manager of each division should in no way be limited. Each division was to be headed by a top manager and be complete "in every necessary function" so that it could exercise "its full initiative and logical development."

2. However, "certain central organizational functions are absolutely essential for the logical development and proper control of the corporation's activities."

In other words, Sloan believed that each of his division managers (like those for the Buick, Chevrolet, and Cadillac divisions) should head complete, self-contained divisions. Each of these divisions would be "self-contained" in that they would do their own manufacturing, marketing, hiring, and so forth.

But Sloan knew that delegating this much authority to his top managers could result in matters getting "out of control." He, therefore, said that certain "organization functions" would have to be controlled *centrally*. To implement this Sloan expanded the company's central office and created (or expanded) many special staff functions for monitoring and controlling the firm's operating divisions. For example, he expanded the "finance committee" and made them responsible for authorizing dividend rates, top management salaries, and major appropriations. In this way, G.M.'s central-office staff groups ended up controlling things like:

> *Capital appropriations.* For example, all projects requiring capital expenditures had to be submitted to an appropriations committee functioning under the finance and executive committees. Each request was given uniform treatment and funds were approved for projects on the basis of their relative value to the corporation.
>
> *Cash.* A system was set up whereby all incoming cash receipts were deposited in certain specified banks. The operating divisions (Buick, Cadillac, etc.) had no control over cash withdrawals or transfers, and all accounts were administered by the headquarters's financial staff.
>
> *Inventory.* A new inventory control system was established that was tied to division managers' forecasts of the number of cars and trucks to be produced. These forecasts were submitted to corporate headquarters for approval on a monthly basis and inventory levels had to be kept within the quantities required by the approved forecasts.
>
> *Division profitability.* A system of interlocking financial ratios was established whereby each division was measured in terms of profits relative to invested capital. Each division, in other words, was evaluated in terms of its overall profitability on the assumption that ". . . If we had the means to review and judge the effectiveness of operations, we could safely leave the prosecution of those operations to the men in charge of them."

Decentralization at G.M., therefore, represented a shrewd balance between decentralized autonomy and centralized control. On the one hand, division managers had considerable autonomy and the means for designing, producing, and marketing their cars. On the other hand, Alfred Sloan was able to maintain control of this far-flung company by centralizing—retaining control over—such things as capital appropriations, cash allocations, and inventory levels. This is why we call decentralization "a philosophy of orga-

nization and management that involves both selective delegation of authority, as well as concentration of authority through the imposition of policies
and selective but adequate controls."

Decentralization and Departmentation

Although they are related, decentralization and departmentation are two
different things. The former involves delegating authority and imposing
selected controls; the latter refers to dividing the work of the organization
into logical groupings of activities. The two, however, are sometimes con-
fused. This is because the term "decentralization" is also used to describe
an organization that has been departmentalized in a certain way—usually
around product divisions.

The reason for this—and this is extremely important—*is that the authority for making a decision can and should be delegated to the level at
which the impact of the decision is local.*[4] In an organization departmentalized by business functions (such as that depicted in Figure 7-1) the president

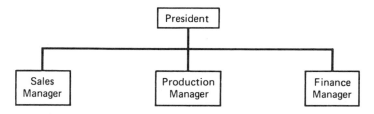

FIGURE 7-1. Departmentation by Business Function

Note: Each manager could only be delegated authority to make
decisions involving his own department. Decisions having com-
pany-wide impact would have to be centralized in the president's
office.

could delegate sales-related decisions to the sales manager, and production-
related decisions to the production manager. For each of these managers,
the decisions they would be making would be localized to their own departments. On the other hand, decisions having *companywide* impact—
such as those concerning companywide union agreements—would have to
be centralized in the president's office.[5]

This is where product departmentation (sometimes called "divisionalization") comes in. As in Figure 7-2, the managers of product-oriented divisions are often in charge of what amount to their own miniature companies.
All or most of the decisions that have anything to do with their product
(whether production, sales, design, or personnel) are "local"—concerned only
with their own unit—as far as these product managers are concerned.

Therefore, what happens when a company opts for product departmentation? It is automatically establishing a situation in which the president can delegate authority for a wider range of decisions to his product
managers than he could if each was responsible for only one specific func-

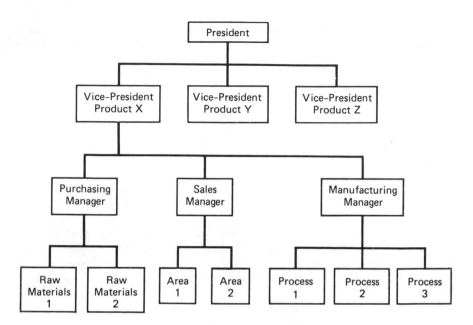

FIGURE 7-2. The "Self-Contained" Aspect of Product-Oriented Departments

Note: Notice how the vice president for product X (and for Y, and Z, although not shown) has managers for purchasing, sales, and manufacturing reporting to him. His division is "self-contained" in that it can manufacture and sell product X with little or no help from other divisions.

tion, such as production, sales, or personnel. It is because one can delegate *more* decisions, and a *wider range* of decisions to subordinates that this type of departmentation has become so closely associated with decentralization. In summary:

1. One can and should delegate authority for a decision to the level where the impact of that decision is local.
2. With product departmentation, each manager is in charge of his own self-contained unit. Thus a wider range of decisions (for production, sales, personnel, etc.) are localized to and pertain to his division only.
3. Because of this, delegation and decentralization usually proceed further in companies departmentalized by product (or perhaps some other "purpose") than by process.

Situational Determinants of Decentralization

Practicing managers and management consultants are usually in agreement about the advantages of decentralization. Drucker, in an early analysis of decentralization at the General Motors Corporation, found that decentralization led to speedier, more responsive decisions, improved management development, and increased motivation on the part of the managers to do a good job and be rewarded for it.[6] Similarly, Stieglitz states that the advantages of decentralization include quicker and better decisions, better manager development, fewer levels of organization, and the freeing of supervisors to concentrate on broader responsibilities.[7]

Furthermore, decentralization is usually associated with purpose-oriented units. Such units are more self-contained, and their managers can more completely focus on the problems of their "purposes." Also decentralization usually results in "enlarged," more meaningful (and motivating) jobs for managers.

In summary, decentralization can be effective. By giving subordinates wide-ranging authority while still centrally controlling certain specific activities you help ensure a more responsive, adaptive organization.

Yet we know that in many cases decentralization has failed. Decentralization, to be effective, has to be appropriate, and there are many situations and conditions that simply do not lend themselves to the increased autonomy and duplication of effort that are usually associated with decentralization. With this in mind, let us review some of the research studies concerning the situational determinants of decentralization.

The influence of diversity: The Chandler study. Historian Alfred Chandler studied the relationship between a firm's strategy, its environment, and its structure, and he has concluded that "structure follows strategy." Specifically, his findings suggest that a strategy of diversification typically leads to the need for a firm to decentralize. Chandler investigated this thesis by analyzing the administrative histories of about 100 of America's largest industrial enterprises. Information was obtained from such sources as annual reports, articles, and government publications, as well as selected interviews with senior executives.

He found that a changing economic environment in America led companies to develop new strategies, which in turn necessitated new organizational structures:

> The prospect of a new market or the threatened loss of a current one stimulated (the strategies of) *geographical expansion, vertical integration,* and *product diversification.* Moreover, once a firm had accumulated large resources, the need to keep its men, money, and materials steadily employed provided a constant stimulus to look for new markets by moving into new areas, by taking on new functions, or by developing new product lines.[8]

Eventually, the linking together of these three basic strategies ultimately resulted in the need for the decentralized, divisionalized structure:

> Expansion of volume, . . . [g]rowth through geographical dispersion, . . . [and finally] the developing of new lines of products . . . brought the formation of the multi-divisional structure. . . .[9]

Among the industries that widely accepted the new, decentralized structure were the electrical and electronics, power-machinery (including automobiles), and chemical industries, with all but two of the twenty leading companies in these industries managed in 1960 through a multidivisional administrative structure.[10]

What is it about these three industries that made them choose this form of organization? Chandler found that companies in these three industries all placed an emphasis upon research and development and on a strategy of expansion through diversification. The two giants of the electronics industry, Westinghouse and General Electric, had specialized before World War II in producing and marketing equipment for providing electric power and light. The majority of these products went directly to other industrial firms, the one exception being the marketing of light bulbs directly to mass consumers. This latter market, however, was highly differentiated from the companies' industrial markets. Furthermore the complexities of designing and producing electrical and electronic components created an atmosphere in which research and development activities thrived.

The ensuing rapid rate of new-product development and further differentiation of markets rendered ineffective the centralized organizational structure in these two firms. As a Westinghouse executive pointed out:

> All of the activities of the company were divided into production, engineering, and sales, each of which was the responsibility of a vice president. The domain of each vice president covered the whole diversified and far flung operations of the corporation. Such an organization of the corporation's management lacks responsiveness. There was too much delay in the recognition of problems and in the solution of problems after they were recognized.[11]

In other words, because these firms' products were so diverse, and because new products were introduced so often, an organization in which the *same* production department, sales department, and so on served *all* products became unresponsive. As a result, these firms *decentralized* by setting up self-contained product divisions. At Westinghouse, merchandise divisions were established for various electric appliances. These allowed division executives to make most of the sales, engineering, and manufacturing decisions for products in their divisions. Similarly, General Electric established a decentralized organization with vice-presidents for such divisional groups as consumer products, aerospace, and construction materials.

On the other hand, Chandler found that the trend in other industries, such as steel, was toward increased centralization of operations. The differences between the steel and electrical industries are informative. Whereas the demands facing the latter could be described as diverse, differentiated, and rapidly changing, the demands of the steel industry could best be described as routine, undifferentiated, and stable. These differences reflect similar differences in the strategic issues facing the two industries. For example, research, development, and engineering seem consistently paramount in the electrical industry. However, the strategic issue facing steel firms has historically been production efficiency. In turn, this emphasis was closely associated with a need for a high-volume output and predictable demand.

This stress on production and the closely associated need for maintaining stable and predictable markets led to centralized organizations in the steel industry. For example, the organizational structure of the United States Steel Company evolved from a relatively decentralized one in the early 1900s to a centralized one today. In fact, by 1950, two-thirds of the corporation's steelmaking activities were consolidated into "central" operations:

> [A] single set of executive vice presidents became to a large extent responsible for the administration of their different functions in every part of the corporation. The executive vice president in charge of production had under him vice presidents for coal, steel, and fabricating.[12]

Thus, structure followed strategy. A strategy aimed at increasing volume and production efficiency led to an environment that was relatively stable and undifferentiated. A strategy of diversification led to an environment in which technology, markets, and sources of supply were rapidly changing; and in such a situation, the defects of the centralized organization structure became obvious. Organizational adaptation and effectiveness were impaired, and firms faced with such environments found it necessary to take on the new decentralized form.

Similar findings have been obtained in a developing country. Researchers collected data from 30 manufacturing firms in India, a variety of industries that included chemicals, pharmaceuticals, cosmetics, machine tools, and soft drinks.[13]

The researchers used "degree of market competition" (degree of price competition, number of alternatives available to consumer, and so on) as their measure of environmental predictability. They found that the results of their study "provide further evidence in support of a contingency theory of organizations." They could not conclude that dynamic, competitive market conditions necessitated decentralization, whereas stable conditions necessitated centralization. However, they did find that the decentralized structure was "more important" for a firm's effectiveness when the environment was dynamic than when it was stable.

The influence of organization size. In a study carried out for the American Management Association, Dale utilized a questionnaire survey of 100 large (5,000 or more employees) and 66 medium-sized (500 to 5,000 employees) companies. The questionnaire was used to obtain information on such topics as type of division of labor, degree of centralization, and number of levels in the company.

Dale found a tendency for organization size and decentralization to be related. However, he found (as did Chandler) that certain large corporations retain their functional, centralized organization structures.[14] His findings support those of Chandler, in that even the largest companies in the steel, mining, and paper industries retained the functional, centralized organization structure.

Dale's findings on the relation between size and decentralization were supported in a later study by Child.[15] His main source of data was 82

British business organizations, and he found that for those firms, size "remains the major predictor of decentralization."

The influence of technology and environment. In her study, Woodward found that centralization was most evident in the mass-production firms. At the extremes of her technological scale (where production was either unit or continuous), she found that a more decentralized, organic structure was closely related to success. The Aston researchers found that production technology was related to decentralization in small firms (where the technology impinged on most managerial activities), but that other factors appeared to be more closely related to decentralization in larger firms.[16] These factors included the size of the organization, and whether it was highly dependent on other organizations in its environment for survival. Where a company was dependent on a single environmental force—such as a large purchaser or a powerful corporate headquarters—it tended to retain a highly centralized structure. On the other hand, where a company was less dependent upon such stable outside forces, and where the environment was therefore less predictable, the company was likely to be more decentralized. These findings are summarized in Table 7-1.

TABLE 7-1

Situational Factors That Influence Decentralization

Factor Influencing Degree of Decentralization	Tendency toward Centralization	Tendency toward Decentralization
Uncertainty; rate of change; appearance of novelties (Chandler, Lawrence and Lorsch, Burns and Stalker, Hall)	Low Uncertainty	High Uncertainty
Differentiation of customers, etc.; diversity (Dill, Chandler)	Little Differentiation	Much Differentiation
Organizational size (Dale, Child, Woodward, Pugh et al., Hall)	Small Size	Large Size
Dependence on stable outside factor— large purchaser, etc. (Pugh et al., Dill)	Much Dependence	Little Dependence
Production technology (Woodward, Pugh et al.)	Mass Production	Unit or Continuous Production

Interpretation. We will interpret these findings to mean that decentralization is a good method for handling a great deal of information. Katz and Kahn, for example, point out that "decentralization . . . is the deliberate restructuring of an organization to handle [information] overload." [17]

Viewed in this light, the five factors summarized above can be viewed in terms of the problem solving, decision making, and overall information processing they require management to carry out. A more changing or diverse environment, or a relatively large organization, would necessarily give rise to the need for upper-level managers to handle greater quantities of information and problems. There is a limit, however, to how much information a person can effectively handle; beyond some point, he has to delegate some of that problem solving and decision making to subordinates. Similarly, an organization that is highly dependent on a stable external factor, such as a large purchaser, may tend to have stable demands and fewer unique, diverse problems to solve. Overall, its top management would (as the Aston team found) be able to maintain centralized decision making.[18]

HIERARCHICAL LEVELS AND THE SPAN OF CONTROL

The number of hierarchical levels and the span of control are two other dimensions of organization structure. We discuss these dimensions in this section.[19]

There is a close relationship between the number of people reporting to a manager and the number of management *levels* in an organization. For example, if an organization with 64 workers to be supervised contains a span of control of 8, there will be 8 supervisors directing the workers and 1 manager directing the supervisors (a "flat" organization). If, on the other hand, the span of control were 4, the same number of workers would require 16 supervisors, who would in turn be directed by 4 managers. These 4 managers would in turn be directed by 1 manager (a "tall" organization).

Classical theorists such as Graicunas and Fayol felt that tall organizational structures improved performance by requiring small spans and close supervision.[20] The superiority of tall organizations has not been supported by researchers, however.

Flat versus Tall Organizations

There are two related categories of findings concerning flat versus tall organizations. One involves the impact of each type of organization on the morale of the employees. The second concerns the relative efficiency of each type of organization.

Effects on morale. One of the first and most extensive empirical studies on the effect of flat and tall organizations on morale was carried out by Worthy in the Sears, Roebuck company.[21] He found that the merchandising vice-president and store managers each had over 40 managers reporting directly to them. Because of this wide span, managers "cannot be running constantly to superiors for approval of their actions," so that this broad, flat type of structure encouraged manager development and increased employee morale.

Worthy's views have gained wide acceptance, but findings of a number of other studies cast some doubt on their validity. Two researchers surveyed over 700 scientists working in organizations in the United States to determine what if any relationship existed between their satisfaction with their jobs and the tallness or flatness of the organizations in which they were working.[22] Most of the organizations they studied were quite small; yet the fact that they found generally insignificant relationships between tallness or flatness and satisfaction cast some doubt on the generality of the Worthy findings. Porter and Lawler surveyed over 1,500 managers in an effort to determine the nature of the relationship between tall or flat organizations and manager satisfaction.[23] Although they did not find any clear general superiority of flat over tall organizations, they did find that in companies employing fewer than 5,000 people, managerial satisfaction was greater in flat than in tall organizations. On the other hand, in companies with 5,000 or more employees, the tall type of organization seemed related to greater satisfaction. In one recent study of nearly 300 salesmen in three organizations, salesmen whose managers had wide spans reported that they were more satisfied, under less stress, and also performed better than salesmen whose managers had narrow spans.[24]

On the whole, the findings suggest that employees whose managers have wide spans of control (which would be associated with flat organizations) tend to have higher morale. However, this is not always the case, and several factors including the size of the organization and personality of the employee help determine the emergent morale.[25]

Which is more efficient? Carzo and Yanouzas set up a laboratory experiment to test the relative efficiency of flat and tall structures under controlled conditions.[26] Their two experimental organizations are shown in Figure 7-3. Each organization had 15 members, with the tall structure having four levels and the flat having two. Each position had a specialized task and title, and a definite hierarchy existed, with the president's office as the central position at the top of it. Each president was responsible for coordinating all tasks and for making final decisions on the assigned problem, and each of the subordinates to the president was responsible for decision making in particular market areas.

The experimental task was for each organization to arrive at decisions about the quantity of goods to order from its suppliers. To do this, organization members had to estimate demand, analyze inventories from the previous period, and consider back orders from the previous period and restrictions on the amounts that could be ordered.

Although experience at the task improved performance, "organization structure had no significant effect on the time taken to make decisions or on the pattern of improvement." Carzo and Yanouzas suggest:

> This may be partly because coordination time in the flat structure offset the greater time required for decisions to pass through several levels of a tall structure.[27]

The researchers found that the tall structure was associated with

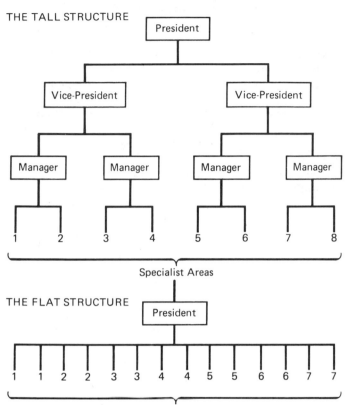

FIGURE 7-3. Tall and Flat Structures

Source: Rocco Carzo, Jr., and John N. Yanouzas, "Effects of Flat and Tall Organization Structure," *Administrative Science Quarterly*, Vol. 14, No. 2 (June 1969), 181.

higher profits and rate of return—at least, once the groups had learned their tasks.

> [This] seemed to be partly because in these organizations decisions were subjected to more analysis, and because the narrow span of supervision in a tall structure permitted a more orderly decision and communication process.[28]

Span of Control

Early theorists favored a narrow span of control. Fayol, for example, stated:

> Whatever his rank, a man has only to command a very small number of direct subordinates, usually less than 6, except that a foreman, who is

dealing with quite a simple operation, is in direct command of 20 or 30 men.[29]

However, most of these writers were experienced enough to know that the span of control at any level could deviate from these optimums in response to factors such as interdependence of subordinates and the company's rate of growth.

In 1933, Graicunas made an interesting attempt at explaining the disadvantages of large spans of control.[30] He pointed out that arithmetical increases in the number of subordinates reporting directly to a manager are accompanied by potentially geometric increases in the number of possible contacts within the manager's work group. Graicunas expressed this relationship in the formula:

$$C = N \left(2N/2 + N - 1\right)$$

where C represents the total possible contacts and N the number of subordinates reporting directly to the manager. His formula assumes that all possible relationships are used and that the manager must be involved in supervising all his subordinates. In practice, however, many interrelationships never take place, and many subordinates need little or no supervision from their managers. Furthermore, his formula does not consider such factors as interdependence of subordinates or the nature of their jobs, and the research evidence indicates that these have an important influence on the span of control.

It is therefore not surprising that spans that deviate considerably from those recommended by the classicists are found in current practice. Dale, for example, found that in 100 companies with more than 5,000 employees, the number of executives reporting to the chief executive varied from 1 to 24, with a median of 9. In fact, as seen in Table 7-2, there were only 26 companies in which the span was as narrow as 6. In 46 companies with fewer than 5,000 employees, the chief executives had from 1 to 17 immediate subordinates, and the median was about 7.

Determinants of span: research findings. Research attempts to account for these variations in spans provide some useful insights.[31] They indicate that factors such as *technology, task routineness,* and *employee professionalism* influence what is an "optimal" span for a situation. Woodward presents evidence (Table 7-3) that indicates three things: First, supervisory spans varied widely. Second, both unit (span = 23) and process (span = 13) firms had smaller supervisory spans than mass-production firms (span = 49). Finally, within each type of technology, successful firms had spans at or near the median, while those which were less successful had spans that were either too low or too high for their production systems.

Lawrence and Lorsch measured average span of control as one dimension of their measure of organizational structure. They considered spans of 10 to 11 persons as indicative of low structure, and spans of 3 to 5

TABLE 7-2

Number of Executives Reporting to the President in 100 Large Companies

Number of Executives Reporting to the President	Number of Companies
1	6
2	—
3	1
4	3
5	7
6	9
7	11
8	8
	Median
9	8
10	6
11	7
12	10
13	8
14	4
15	1
16	5
17	—
18	1
19	—
20	1
21	1
22	—
23	2
24	1
	Total 100

as indicative of high structure. Their findings suggest that spans tend to increase with increasing task uncertainty.[32]

The Lockheed Company has developed a weighted-index system as an aid in organization design and planning.[33] Based upon experience and the prescriptions of classical theory, Lockheed pinpointed several factors that it felt should be weighed in determining the span of control.

Similarity of subordinates' functions

Geographic closeness of subordinates

Complexity of subordinates' functions

Direction and control required by subordinates

Coordination of subordinates required

Planning importance, complexity, and time required

TABLE 7-3

Average Span of Control of First-Line Supervisors,
Analyzed by Level of Success

	Span of Control					
Production System	Up to 20	21 to 40	41 to 60	61 to 80	81 to 90	Median
Unit and Small-Batch						
All firms	7	12	4			23
Above-average success		5				
Below-average success	2		3			
Large-Batch and Mass						
All firms	1	7	13	6	3	49
Above-average success			5			
Below-average success	1	2		1	2	
Process						
All firms	18	7				13
Above-average success	6					
Below-average success	1	3				

Source: Adapted from Joan Woodward, *Industrial Organization: Theory and Practice* (London: Oxford University Press, 1965), p. 69.

The Lockheed weighting system is shown in Table 7-4. Each management position is evaluated for each of the six span factors (such as similarity of functions and coordination). Then the point values for each manager's position are added up to provide a "supervisory index," which reflects how much difficulty he should have managing the work of his subordinates. As shown in Table 7-5, the higher the supervisory index, the lower the suggested span of control.

The company had some success with this approach. One of its units expanded its average span from 3.8 to 4.2, and thus reduced supervisory levels from 5 to 4. Another unit extended the average span of managers from 3.0 to 4.2 and thus cut levels from 6 to 5. All told, the savings in managerial and supervisory payrolls were reported as "substantial."

How valid is the Lockheed system? Udell carried out a study to determine whether the Lockheed span factors corresponded to differences in span of control for marketing and sales executives in 67 Midwest manufacturing companies.[34] He found a positive relation between span of control and geographical separation of subordinates. He also found positive (but not very significant) relations between span and:

1. Similarity of functions supervised
2. Subordinate's experience on the job
3. The use of personal assistants by the supervisor
4. The amount of supervision subordinates received from others in the firm.

TABLE 7-4

The Lockheed Weighting System

Span Factor	Point Value for Each Factor				
Similarity of functions	Identical 1	Essentially alike 2	Similar 3	Inherently different 4	Fundamentally distinct 5
Geographic closeness	All together 1	All in one building 2	Separate building, 1 plant location 3	Separate locations, 1 geographic area 4	Dispersed geographic areas 5
Complexity of functions	Simple, repetitive 2	Routine 4	Some complexity 6	Complex, varied 8	Highly complex, varied 10
Direction and control	Minimum supervision and training 3	Limited supervision 6	Moderate, periodic supervision 9	Frequent, continuing supervision 12	Constant, close supervision 15
Coordination	Minimum relationships with others 2	Relationships limited to defined courses 4	Moderate relationships easily controlled 6	Considerable close relationships 8	Extensive mutual nonrecruiting relationships 10
Planning	Minimum scope and complexity 2	Limited scope and complexity 4	Moderate scope and complexity 6	Considerable effort required; guided only by broad policies 8	Extensive effort required; areas and policies not chartered 10

Source: Harold Stieglitz, "Optimizing Span of Control," *Management Record*, Vol. 24 (September 1962), 27. © 1962 National Industrial Conference Board.

TABLE 7-5

Middle-Management Index and
Suggested Span of Control

Supervisory Index	Suggested Standard Span
40-42	4-5
37-39	4-6
34-36	4-7
31-33	5-8
28-30	6-9
25-27	7-10
22-24	8-11

Source: Harold Stieglitz, "Optimizing Span of Control," Management Record, Vol. 24 (September 1962), 29. © 1962 National Industrial Conference Board.

Determinants of span of control: Summary. What contextual factors determine span of control? In what way is organizational effectiveness determined by the appropriateness of the span of control to the situation? These questions can now be addressed.

The evidence concerning appropriate spans of control is conflicting. On the one hand, the prescriptions of classical theorists and the work done by Lockheed suggest that the more complicated subordinates' jobs are, the narrower must be the manager's span of control. Intuitively this makes sense, since it should be more difficult for a manager to supervise the work of subordinates whose jobs are complex than of subordinates whose jobs are simple.

Yet the research findings (of Woodward, for example) suggest that this "common-sense" solution doesn't always apply. Generally, as a matter of fact, where subordinates' jobs are complex and unpredictable, we often find wider— not narrower—spans of control.

There are probably several reasons for this. We know, for example, that where a person's task is non-routine, that person is usually given more autonomy;[35] and such increased autonomy would seem to be related to wider rather than narrower spans of control. Furthermore, it seems likely that complex, unpredictable work tasks are associated with people who have more experience and professionalism and who can therefore be expected to exhibit a greater degree of self-control. In conclusion, it appears that complex, uncertain tasks are usually associated with wide spans of control but that this probably assumes a high degree of professionalism and self-control on the part of subordinates.

SUMMARY

How do contextual factors like environment and technology influence "vertical" dimensions of structure like delegation, decentralization, and span of control? How does the appropriateness of each dimension for the "situation" affect organizational effectiveness? In the last chapter, we answered these questions with reference to the structural dimensions of departmentation and coordination. In the present chapter, following our model, we try to answer them for our remaining structural dimensions.

With respect to delegation and decentralization, we concluded that in effective organizations, both decentralization and span usually increase as the requirements for information processing increase. We noted, for example, that determinants of degree of decentralization include uncertainty and rate of change, differentiation of customers and diversity, organization size, dependence on a stable outside factor, and production technology. Generally, high uncertainty, much diversity, large size, little dependence, and unit or continuous technologies are associated with more decentralization. On the other hand, low uncertainty, little differentiation, small size, much dependence, and mass-production technology are associated with centralization. We viewed these situational factors or determinants in terms of the problem solving, decision making, and overall information processing that they require management to engage in. For example, a more changing or diverse environment, or a relatively large organization, would necessarily give rise to the need for upper-level managers to handle greater quantities of information and problems. Since there is a limit to how much information a person can effectively handle, beyond some point that manager must transfer some of the problem solving and decision making to subordinates, by delegating more decision making to them or by setting up self-contained "decentralized" divisions.

We also concluded that more complex, unpredictable tasks are associated with wider spans of control, assuming the subordinates have sufficient experience and professionalism to exhibit self-control.

Up to this point, we have focused on structure, and on its contextual determinants—determinants like environment, technology, and size. Some of our conclusions, however (especially those with respect to span of control), suggest that we can't develop any prescriptions or hypotheses about organization structure without reference to the people who make up that structure. For example, the width of the span of control depends partly on the extent to which the workers in question are capable of exhibiting self-control. As Simon has pointed out:

> Problems of organization cannot be considered apart from the specifications of the employees who are to fill the positions established by the organization. The whole subject of job classification needs to be brought into closer coordination with the theory of organization. The optimum organizational structure is a variable, depending for its form upon the staffing of the agency. Conversely, the classification of the position is a variable depending upon the degree of centralization or decentralization which is desired or anticipated in the operation. . . .[36]

Keeping this in mind, we turn in the next section to a discussion of compliance, motivation, and control in organizations.

DISCUSSION QUESTIONS

1. Discuss the relationships between delegation, decentralization, and centralization. Why are decentralization, divisionalization, and departmentation by purpose closely associated?
2. What were the factors that Chandler found had led many organizations to adopt the divisionalized organization structure? What is some of the other evidence in support of Chandler's findings?
3. What are some of the advantages and disadvantages of flat and tall organizations? What are some of the factors that influence what span of control is most appropriate?
4. What do we mean when we say "the authority for making a decision can and should be delegated to the level at which the impact of the decision is local"?

FOOTNOTES

1 Joseph Litterer, *The Analysis of Organizations* (New York: John Wiley, 1965), p. 379.

2 Harold Koontz and Cyril O'Donnell, *Management* (New York: McGraw-Hill, 1976), p. 375.

3 This section is based on Thomas J. McNichols, *Executive Policy and Strategic Planning* (New York: McGraw-Hill, 1977), pp. 38–43.

4 See Harold Stieglitz, *Organizational Planning* (New York: The National Industrial Conference Board, Inc., 1962); Harold Lazarus and E. Kirby Warren, *The Progress of Management* (Englewood Cliffs, N.J.: Prentice-Hall, 1968), p. 72.

5 Gary Dessler, *Organization and Management* (Englewood Cliffs, N.J.: Prentice-Hall, 1976), pp. 107–8.

6 Peter Drucker, *Concept of the Corporation* (New York: John Day, 1946), pp. 47–48.

7 Harold Stieglitz, *Organizational Planning* (New York: The National Industrial Conference Board, Inc., 1962).

8 Alfred Chandler, Jr., *Strategy and Structure* (Cambridge, Mass.: The M.I.T. Press, 1962), p. 15.

9 *Ibid.*, p. 14. Franko obtained similar findings in a study of 127 European companies. He found that approximately one-half had changed to the divisionalized structure. However, the changes seemed more in response to "specific changes in the competitive environment . . . than as a result of changes in product diversification strategies." Lawrence G. Franko, "The Move toward a Multidivisional Structure in European Organizations," *Administrative Science Quarterly*, December 1974, pp. 493–505. See also Robert J. Pavan, "Diversification and the Division Structure in Italy," paper presented at the 34th annual meeting, Academy of Management, Seattle, Washington, August 18–21, 1974.

10 Chandler, *Strategy and Structure*, p. 362.

11 *Ibid.*, p. 366.

12 *Ibid.*, p. 335.

13 Anant R. Negandhi and Bernard C. Reimann, "A Contingency Theory of Organization in the Context of a Developing Country," *Academy of Management Journal*, Vol. 15, No. 2 (June 1972), 137–46.

14 Dale, *Organization*, p. 110.

15 John Child, "Predicting and Understanding Organization Structure," *Administra-*

tive Science Quarterly, June 1973, pp. 168–85. Also see Daniel Robey, M. M. Bakr, and Thomas S. Miller, "Organizational Size and Management Autonomy: Some Structural Discontinuities," *Academy of Management Journal*, Vol. 20, No. 3 (1977), 378–97.

16 D. S. Pugh, D. J. Hickson, C. R. Hinings, and C. Turner, "Dimensions of Organization Structure," *Administrative Science Quarterly*, Vol. 13 (1968), 65–105; see also "The Context of Organization Structures," *Administrative Science Quarterly*, Vol. 14 (1969), 91–114. Sergio Mindlin and Howard Albrich present a good review of this in "Interorganizational Dependence: A Review of the Concept and a Re-Examination of the Findings of the Aston Group," *Administrative Science Quarterly*, Vol. 20 (September 1975), pp. 382–91.

17 Daniel Katz and Robert L. Kahn, *The Social Psychology of Organizations* (New York: John Wiley, 1966), p. 233.

18 This tentative interpretation receives some support from a variety of theoretical and empirical findings. Thompson and Perrow suggest, for example, that the task of decision making, problem solving, and overall information processing is a basic dimension underlying why factors such as uncertainty, diversity, and some technologies require decentralization. Driver and Schroeder et al., suggest that three factors—amount of information, diversity of information, and rate of information change—are roughly equivalent in the way they affect individual problem solving and decision making. Finally, there is, as we have seen, considerable evidence (Schroeder et al.) to support the idea that individual (and group) information processing decreases in effectiveness once the amount of information to be processed becomes too great.

19 Robert L. Kahn and Daniel Katz, "Leadership Practices in Relation to Productivity and Morale," in D. Cartwright and A. Zander, *Group Dynamics, Research and Theory* (Evanston, Ill.: Row, Peterson and Company, 1960), pp. 554–70.

20 A. Graicunas, "Relationship in Organization," in Luther Gulick and L. Urwick, *Papers on the Science of Administration* (New York: Institute of Public Administration, 1937), pp. 181–88; Henri Fayol, *General and Industrial Management*, trans. Constance Storrs (London: Sir Isaac Pittman, 1949).

21 James Worthy, "Organization Structures and Employee Morale," *American Sociological Review*, Vol. 15 (1950), 169–79.

22 L. Meltzer and Jay Salter, "Organizational Structure and the Performance of Job Satisfaction of Physiologists," *American Sociological Review*, Vol. 27 (1962), 351–62.

23 Lyman W. Porter and Edward E. Lawler III, "The Effects of Tall versus Flat Organizaiton Structures on Managerial Job Satisfaction," *Personnel Psychology*, Vol. 17 (1964), 135–48; Lyman Porter and Jay Siegel, "The Effects of Tall versus Flat Organization Structures on Managerial Satisfactions in Foreign Countries," unpublished manuscript, University of California, Berkeley, 1964.

24 John Ivancevich and James Donnelly, Jr., "Relation of Organizational Structure to Job Satisfaction, Anxiety, Stress, and Performance," *Administrative Science Quarterly* (June 1975), 272–80.

25 Edwin E. Ghiselli and Jacob P. Siegel, "Leadership and Managerial Success in Tall and Flat Organization Structures," *Personnel Psychology*, Vol. 25 (September 1972), 617–24.

26 Rocco Carzo, Jr., and John N. Yanouzas, "Effects of Flat and Tall Organization Structure," *Administrative Science Quarterly*, Vol. 14, No. 2 (June 1969), 178–91.

27 *Ibid.*, p. 189.

28 *Ibid.*, p. 190. The experimental control and statistical analyses of the Carzo-Yanouzas experiment have been criticized by Hummon and justified by Carzo and Yanouzas. See Norman P. Hummon, "Criticism of Effects of Flat and Tall Organization Structure," *Administrative Science Quarterly*, Vol. 15, No. 2 (June 1970), 230–40; and Rocco Carzo, Jr., and John Yanouzas, "Justification for the Carzo-Yanouzas Experiment on Flat and Tall Structures," *Administrative Science Quarterly*, Vol. 15, No. 2 (June 1970).

29 Fayol, *General and Industrial Management;* see also R. C. Davis, *Fundamentals of Top Management* (New York: Harper & Row, 1951).

30 Graicunas, "Relationship in Organization."

31 Some writers have noted that the problem of measuring the span of control is more complicated than it might first appear. They say that while most researchers use "raw span"—total subordinates divided by total superiors—other, adjusted measures, including such factors as the number of "helpers" the supervisor has, may better reflect span of control and total supervisory effort. See, for example, William G. Ouchi and John B. Dowling, "Defining the Span of Control," *Administrative Science Quarterly*, September 1974, 357–65. For a second view of this problem, see Kenneth D. MacKenzie, "Measuring a Person's Capacity for Interaction in a Problem Solving Group," *Organizational Behavior and Human Performance*, Vol. 12 (1974), 149–69.

32 Joan Woodward, *Industrial Organization: Theory and Practice* (Oxford: Oxford University Press, 1965), p. 69. Copyright Oxford University Press, 1965. See also Paul K. Lawrence and Jay W. Lorsch, *Organization and Environment* (Boston: Division of Research, Graduate School of Business Administration, Harvard University, 1967), p. 32.

33 Reported by Harold Stieglitz, "Optimizing Span of Control," *Management Record*, Vol. 24 (September 1962), 25–29. See also James Gibson, John Ivancevich, and James Donnelly, Jr., *Organizations* (Dallas: B.P.J., 1973), pp. 133–35.

34 J. G. Udell, "An Empirical Test of Hypotheses Relating to Span of Control," *Administrative Science Quarterly*, Vol. 12 (1967), 420–39.

35 See Gerald Bell, "The Influence of Technological Components of Work upon Management Control," *Journal of the Academy of Management*, Vol. 8, No. 2 (1965), 127–32.

36 Herbert Simon, *Administrative Behavior* (New York: The Free Press, 1976), p. 228.

case for part III:
prebuilt, inc.

SITUATION

Prebuilt, Inc., supplies large-scale prefabricated shelters to customers for whom time is of the essence, and the firm's reputation for meeting deadlines is therefore critical to its survival. The need to respond quickly to the client's needs necessarily results in a number of daily crises, but at Prebuilt, the number and severity of these crises seem to be aggravated by several internal organizational problems that are most likely the result of the rapid growth the firm has had in the past two years. Prebuilt currently meets its deadlines, a fact that seems primarily due to the extraordinary efforts of a group of highly motivated and committed managers. However, the firm does little or no long-range planning, managers are "utility infielders" without the time to give proper attention to their own departments, and profitability is probably affected adversely by the need for rework and by the errors that eventually occur. Furthermore, the firm apparently can't handle as much business as it might otherwise, and it may be approaching its capacity for handling additional projects, deadlines, and crises.

BACKGROUND

Prebuilt, founded twenty years ago by William Ross, originally manufactured a patented construction panel consisting of a honeycomb core to which two steel faces were laminated. The firm's first customers were door manufacturers, who used the sturdy, lightweight panels to manufacture their products.

Since that time, however, the range of products and services offered by Prebuilt has expanded considerably, and especially rapidly during the last four years. Expansion of the product line began fifteen years ago, when the firm developed the capability to manufacture doors. In addition, at about that time, an engineer named Bob Roan became affiliated with the firm and developed a system whereby Prebuilt's panels could be structurally connected into complete shelters (houses and the like).

About four years ago, the firm was approached by a representative of the Egyptian government who asked if Prebuilt could provide his government with what amounted to a complete town—1,000 homes, a commissary, a small hospital, a school building, and other structures. Prebuilt took the contract and, in doing so, had to add a variety of new services to those already offered, including "buy outs" (buying and providing the electrical equipment, washing machines, and air conditioners needed to complete the houses), transportation of all goods and materials from the United States to Egypt, and on-site supervision and construction (laborers were recruited from Taiwan). Numerous problems, most of which are still in the process of being worked out, were incurred on this project, and whether the firm can win a new, larger contract of the same type is now the question.

Over the past twenty years, the firm has gone through a series of expansions and contractions, but none as drastic as in the past four years. Prior to being awarded the Egyptian contract, the firm had fewer than fifty employees. It now employs almost 600 people, and this rapid growth has amplified the "growing pains" the company might normally be expected to experience. In addition, the nature of its current business—which management defines as "providing 'turnkey,' fully complete and operational towns for foreign governments"—makes meeting deadlines (rather than costs) the primary consideration, and these time pressures have compounded Prebuilt's problems. The difficulty of constructing shelters thousands of miles away from the company's home base (which is Atlanta) and the communication problem involved in doing business in the Middle East (management can plan on making only one phone call per day out of Egypt) has aggravated even further the normal problems that might be expected to arise in the manufacture and distribution of this product.

As a result of the many problems and daily crises that have surfaced over the past four years, Mr. Ross called in a group of consultants to analyze the firm and make recommendations for improving the organization's responsiveness and overall effectiveness. Most of the following has been excerpted from the consultant's report:

Engineering. From our preliminary investigation, the main problem is probably a lack of effective project design input at the sales presentation stage and thereafter. A common occurrence is apparently for Sales and the client to meet and develop a project based on a set of "standard" designs with little or no input from Engineering, and for the Sales Department to then estimate the project's cost. Engineering is brought in after the fact to develop the project, a situation that seems to put them on the defensive and generally results in their identifying required project modifications. Engineering sends a list of required material to Purchasing, often making assumptions about quality of components, etc., without input from Sales. Someone in Engineering finds a mistake (or Sales stumbles on one), and orders have to be changed. This entire process is additionally hampered by the fact that Engineering is inadequately staffed. For example, it appears that the lack of sufficient in-house structural and mechanical engineers frequently results in a bottleneck, since it makes the firm more dependent on the schedule of its outside consultants.

Organizational structure and coordination. Inadequate and informal interdepartmental project coordination is a major problem at Prebuilt, and the lack of effective coordination may in fact lie at the root of many of the firm's other problems. At the present time, there is no formal organization chart. In interviews, we found constant reference to the need for improved coordination between Sales and Engineering, between Engineering and Purchasing, and between Shipping and Purchasing, for example. As a larger issue, it appears that projects are often sold, engineered, purchased, and shipped without any one identifiable person or group of people having both the authority and responsibility for managing them from start to finish. There also appear to be no regularly scheduled meetings of the department heads to monitor the progress of projects. Formal project schedules that could aid the coordination are apparently inadequate. In addition to the fact that there is no organization chart, there are also no job descriptions or clear lines of authority at Prebuilt, and actions are often seen as "violations of the chain of command," with many managers complaining that they don't know who reports to them. To some extent, this lack of structure may be beneficial: In a firm where responsiveness is essential, a preoccupation with adhering to the chain of command could be deadly. And in the absence of formal coordination devices, such as effective schedules, project managers, and schedules of meetings, top managers must often inject themselves into all departments and at all levels in order to handle crises and perform the missing coordination function. The problem is that at Prebuilt, the organization is not formally structured to be flexible—there is instead no structure at all. Everyone is a "utility infielder"; no one "minds the store"; more crises erupt; formal coordination is adequate; and everyone again becomes a "utility infielder." This cycle is in turn aggravated by the firm's engineering, documentation, and communications problems. In addition, several key jobs apparently must be staffed, or restaffed.

Procedures/documentation/scheduling. Prebuilt needs to thoroughly reevaluate its procedures and documentation on a department-by-department basis. References were constantly made, for example, to material that is "lost in corners" in the warehouse, and to unverifiable "short-shipping" claims by clients. Paperwork, particularly bills of material, sometimes get mislaid, and there is a need for a more complete documentation (an "archive") of past products for sales presentation purposes. Personnel policies and procedures are needed covering basic areas such as job descriptions, performance appraisal, and compensation management. A more effective project scheduling and reporting system for planning, controlling, and coordinating projects is also needed; projects that management thought were on time have been found to be as much as two months late.

Communications. Vertical and horizontal communications throughout the organization are inadequate. For example, there is often inadequate communication between Sales and Engineering. The result is that projects can be designed and engineered that don't entirely meet the expectations of the client, since specific requirements (such as what quality floors to use), while known by Sales, often never reach Engineering, who in turn make erroneous assumptions about these factors. For their part, the sales group apparently often gets little feedback on the final prices until purchase orders are already filled, and so their input often surfaces too late. In terms of vertical communications, managers refer to the fact that they often "just hear rumors" about what is going on at the corporate level; one such rumor concerned the possible purchase of a construction firm, and another concerned the hiring of a personnel manager.

PROBLEMS

These various problems have manifested themselves in what can only be described as an ongoing series of crises. A great deal of the work has to be redone when, for example, it is determined that ceilings don't conform to the customer's specifications, or electrical equipment is not compatible with the voltage available in the client country. Much of the incoming material gets lost in the company's warehouse, with no record kept of its location. No clear records are kept of exactly how much material (how many panels, say) is shipped to the customer, and the firm usually cannot prove its case when the customer complains that it hasn't received all the necessary material. In order to fight these ongoing crises, middle- and top-level managers often find themselves in the shipping area in the dead of night, loading trucks to expedite orders. The net effect is that costs are so much higher than anticipated that the profitability of the project (and the firm's cash-flow position) is much lower than it should be. In addition, the firm now finds itself unable to bid for new, larger projects from a position of strength. Unless its major customers are shown that

Prebuilt is eliminating its organizational and managerial problems and can successfully complete its current project, it is doubtful that any additional major contracts will be forthcoming. Without new contracts, the firm would have to lay off virtually all the employees who were hired in the past four years and, in addition, would be left with so much indebtedness that the viability of the firm would be in danger.

DISCUSSION QUESTIONS

In the last four chapters, we discussed the context of organizations and the way this context influences organization structure and design. We discussed several organization-design strategies and the fact that under uncertain conditions, mechanistic methods for structuring and coordinating organizations are insufficient. Here, instead, other strategies—like environmental management, or the creation of self-contained tasks—become necessary.

Prebuilt is a good example of a company that operates in a fairly uncertain and unpredictable environment. Customer specifications often change overnight; problems can occur during transportation and in Egypt that require quick, effective reaction; and the firm is constantly working against what often seem impossible deadlines in a situation where meeting deadlines is by far the main criterion of effectiveness.

Given these facts, which of the following organization-design strategies would you suggest if you were Prebuilt's consultants?

Mechanistic (hierarchy, rules and procedures, planning, and goal setting). These are "basic" strategies for ensuring that the work of the different units or departments in the organization is coordinated. Rules, for example, are predetermined decisions that are aimed at ensuring that decisions made in each unit contribute in a coordinated way to the organization's goals; managers in the hierarchy are then supposedly left free to handle only "exceptions." We saw that as situations become more unpredictable, organizations and their managers have to process more information, and these mechanistic devices become inadequate. It is at this point that one or more of the following design strategies become necessary.

Environmental management. The organization can attempt to "manage" its environment—for example, by purchasing suppliers or entering cartels.

Creation of slack resources. The organization can attempt to reduce the number and severity of exceptions by introducing "slack resources" like inventories. Thus, a sudden, rush job doesn't create the additional problem of having to find the necessary raw materials.

Creation of self-contained tasks. We also know that creating self-contained departments that can focus all their attention on, say, one specific project facilitates coordination.

Invest in vertical information systems. Another technique the organization can use to handle overloads of information is the establishment of "vertical information systems," like staff assistants who analyze and summarize problems for line managers, thereby, in effect, increasing the managers' ability to process information and make decisions.

Create lateral relations. Finally, the organization can encourage "lateral relations" in order to reduce the information that must be relayed up the chain of command. This might involve simply direct contact between lower-level managers, or the creation of committees, integrators, or special liaison personnel.

Which of these design strategies would you recommend if you were Prebuilt's consultant? At a minimum, your recommendation should make provision for the following departments: Marketing/Sales; Accounting/Finance; Engineering; Manufacturing; Purchasing; and Shipping, Warehousing, Receiving. Develop an organization structure, and present *specific* examples of how you would implement the other design strategies you choose to recommend. (Please do not read any further until you have completed this project.)

RECOMMENDATIONS

The actual recommendations made by the consultants in this case and implemented by Prebuilt utilized all the design strategies we discussed.

Mechanistic. First, an organization structure was designed (see Figure 1). This clarified responsibilities and reporting relationships; provided a chain of command through which decisions could be made; and furnished job descriptions that answered the question, "Who does what?" In order to provide for more effective project coordination, a matrix structure was implemented in which a project manager was identified and project teams developed for each of the company's major projects. The organization structure, in other words, provided for the self-containment of tasks (projects).

In addition, all procedures, documentation, and forms were evaluated department by department, and the flow of written information between departments was tracked to determine what changes in procedures were necessary. A policy and procedures manual was developed that specified, for example, the procedure to be used in determining customer requirements and communicating these requirements between the Sales and Engineering departments. A more effective project scheduling and reporting system was set up to indicate planned milestones and provide for daily feedback to top management as to the status of each component of each project. Every department (Production, Sales, Purchasing, and so on) involved in a project participated in developing the project's schedule and then concentrated on meeting its deadlines (as detailed in the schedule) and thereby the overall project deadline.

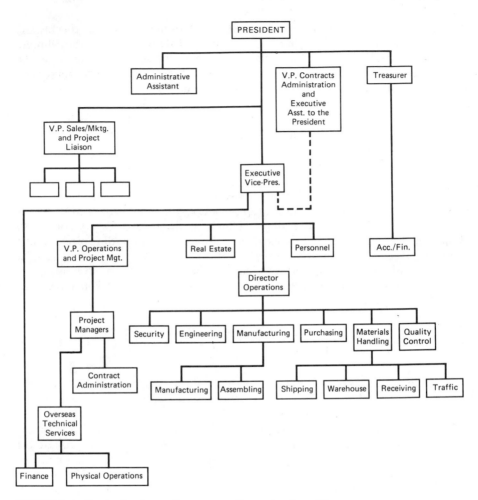

FIGURE 1. Prebuilt, Inc., Corporate Organization Chart

Environmental management. Environmental management was a second design strategy used. Long-term contracts were entered into between the company and a construction firm in Taiwan to reduce the uncertainties involved in recruiting, hiring, and supervising the construction teams in Egypt. The company also began manufacturing more of the basic components of its products: For example, whereas it had formerly purchased the honeycomb cores for its panels, it now set up assembly lines for manufacturing its own cores. A set of "standard" shelters was designed from which the sales team developed orders; this further reduced the number of "exceptions" the firm had to deal with. A long-range-planning committee was established, to determine what markets the firm should pursue over the next five to ten years. It was felt that this type of planning would reduce the "knee-jerk" reactions the firm was currently making to new and unexpected market possibilities.

Create slack resources. Several specific actions that were undertaken to reduce the number of exceptions that could arise might be considered creation of slack resources. The company's basic "house" was redesigned so that more of the actual assembly could take place at the Atlanta factory. For example, roof trusses that were formerly shipped in pieces to the foreign country and then constructed on the site were now bolted together at the factory. The net result was a reduction in the number of separate parts that had to be transported, warehoused in Egypt, and constructed on-site. Furthermore (particularly since costs were of secondary importance to the customer), substantial increases were made in inventory levels, and intentional overshipping of parts to Egypt was begun in order to ensure that no part shortages occurred there. To further reduce uncertainties, full prototypes of each house and shelter to be built overseas were first constructed at the firm's Atlanta facility, in order to ensure that the "bugs" were designed out of each before the materials for thousands of them were shipped overseas.

Create self-contained tasks. As noted above, a matrix structure was developed for each project. A manager and team for each project were assigned, thus ensuring that each project received the continuous and undivided attention of one group.

Create vertical information system. Several vertical information systems were also developed: A computer system was installed that provided project managers and top managers with "on-line" feedback concerning the progress of each project, inventory levels, and so on. Each project manager was assigned a "project control officer" whose function was to carefully monitor each step of each project and keep the manager advised of project progress.

Create lateral relations. Finally, several steps were taken in the way of lateral relations to reduce the number of exceptions and amount of information being channeled up the chain of command: An "engineering liaison officer" was assigned to the Sales Department. His function was to attend sales presentations and generally ensure (1) that customer requirements were communicated to the Engineering Department, and (2) that Engineering had an opportunity to provide early input in the early stages of the development of the project. Project teams met weekly to discuss problems, and the president, executive vice-president, and director of operations met weekly with the managers for Engineering, Manufacturing, Purchasing, Material Handling, Sales, and Project Management to discuss matters of concern.

PART IV

MOTIVATION
AND COMPLIANCE
IN ORGANIZATIONS

In the preceding section of this book, we discussed organization structure and design, but we have seen that providing an organization structure is only half the problem facing the organization theorist or manager. The basic assumption one makes in structuring an organization and giving each worker a task is that those tasks *will in fact be carried out* in some dependable, predictable fashion; in this section, therefore, we shift our focus to *motivation and compliance* in organizations.

Unfortunately, the problem of ensuring compliance is not as simple as it might seem, and there are several reasons for this. First, as we will see, employees have many ingenious ways of circumventing the sorts of control systems often used to ensure compliance. Beyond this, the problem of ensuring that each member of the organization carries out his task in such a way that the organization successfully accomplishes its goals is complicated by the fact that for all but the most routine tasks, simple compliance with the "letter of the law" is insufficient; employees must also be *"motivated."* For organizations to function effectively, in other words, it is usually not enough for employees to simply meet their minimum standards of performance. Instead, these standards should be exceeded, and in addition, innovative, creative, and spontaneous behavior must take place.

Examples abound of what happens when such "extra effort" is not made. One familiar example is the group of dissatisfied unionized city workers who, barred from striking (as are many public employees), decide to take a "job action" by following the precise letter of the law as contained in their job descriptions and their organization's procedures. The myriad informal communications and contacts that normally expedite solutions and handle exceptions no longer take place, and the city finds itself slowly smothering under a mountain of overdue requests for services.

In summary, we will see in the next three chapters that imposing compliance—through rules, formal control systems, and close supervision—is probably a fairly effective technique for ensuring that the most routine of tasks (as might be found on an assembly line) are accomplished. However, organizations cannot legislate creativity, and the manager who wants to ensure that standards are not only met but exceeded, and that innovative, creative, spontaneous behavior takes place, must make provisions for *motivating* his employees to exhibit such behavior. We will discuss these ideas in more detail.

Chapter 8

Motivation and Organization Theory

CHAPTER OVERVIEW

In the next two chapters (9 and 10), we will describe some techniques for eliciting imposed and self-control respectively. First, however, we discuss in this chapter some theories of motivation, since a knowledge of the foundations of motivation is required for understanding those techniques. For example, the effective use of incentives is based on the psychology of motivation, as are "self-control" techniques like job enrichment and management by objectives. We will survey the following motivation theories: Reinforcement, Maslow's Hierarchy of Needs, the Herzberg Motivator-Hygiene Theory, achievement motivation, and expectancy theory. As you read this material, keep the following questions in mind:

1. Does the context of the organization affect whether that organization should use imposed or self-control?
2. How do the concepts of imposed and self-control relate to the motivation theories we discuss in this chapter?
3. Are some motivation theories more appropriate in different "situations" than others?

The outline of this chapter is as follows:

I. Imposed vs. Self-Control in Organization Theory
   A. Katz and Kahn's Theory
   B. Imposed vs. Self-Control: Other Views
   C. Situational Determinants of Imposed vs. Self-Control

IMPOSED VS. SELF-CONTROL IN ORGANIZATION THEORY

We have already touched on the distinction between imposed control and self-control—for example, in Chapters 2 and 3. Now we address this subject more completely, beginning with a discussion of how theorists have distinguished between imposed and self-control.

Katz and Kahn's Theory

According to Katz and Kahn, there are at least three categories of behaviors that organizations must elicit to survive—*attracting* employees, ensuring *dependable* behavior, and evoking *innovative* behavior—and different "motivational patterns" are required for producing these behaviors.[1] They say there are four such "motivational patterns" (see Table 8-1), and that these can be viewed as forming a continuum from imposed, legal compliance through self-control.

Type A is legal or imposed compliance. Here, employees comply with rules or directives because they consider them legitimate job demands, or because of a fear of sanctions. This, according to Katz and Kahn, is the basic pattern of motivation in classical organization theory. Motivation and the desire to comply bear no relation to the task itself; instead, any rule or directive from the proper authority must be obeyed because it is the law of the organization, and acceptance of these laws is part of the "contract" the employee enters into when he joins the organization. Katz and Kahn say the problem with legal compliance "lies in its inability to motivate people for anything but routine compliance with role requirements." The classicists' solution to this problem was the use of rewards.

Katz and Kahn's second (type B) pattern involves the use of rewards for inducing required behavior. Here, rewards are linked to desired behaviors. In other words, the employees' actions become *instrumental* in the achieving of specific desired rewards. Such rewards include pay, promotion, benefits, achievement, and approval from supervisors or from one's own group.

Katz and Kahn's third and fourth types differ conceptually from these

TABLE 8-1

Motivational Patterns for Producing Various Types of Required Behaviors

A. *Legal compliance.* Securing acceptance of role prescriptions and organizational controls on the basis of their legitimacy. The rule enforcement approach of simple machine theory. Controlling production through the speed of the assembly line.

B. *The use of rewards* or instrumental satisfactions for inducing required behaviors. The approach of modified machine theory.
   (1) System rewards earned through membership or seniority in system such as fringe benefits, cost-of-living raises, or other benefits across the board.
   (2) Individual rewards such as pay incentives and promotion on the basis of individual merit.
   (3) Instrumental identification with organizational leaders in which followers are motivated to secure the approval of leaders.
   (4) Affiliation with peers to secure social approval from own group.

C. *Internalized pattern of self-determination* and self-expression. The satisfactions from accomplishment and the expressions of talents and abilities.

D. *Internalized values and the self-concept.* The incorporation of organizational goals or subgoals as reflecting values or self-concept.

Source: Daniel Katz and Robert L. Kahn, *The Social Psychology of Organizations* (New York: John Wiley, 1966), p. 341.

first two. Both A and B rely on the use of *external* reminders, like rules and rewards. Types C and D, on the other hand, are aimed at encouraging *self-control*, and in both types, the employee derives gratification directly from the nature of the job itself. Here, "motivation is so *internalized* that performance is autonomous. The supervisor does not have to be present to wave a stick or offer candy. The activities carry their own rewards. . . ."[2]

Type C involves job identification. Here, the job is sufficiently challenging and interesting that it provides an opportunity for self-expression and achievement for the employee. He or she thus derives satisfaction directly from performing the task, just as a scientist does from scientific inquiry, and a composer from creating a symphony. The employee complies —carries out the job assigned—not because rules or supervision is imposed on him, but because he identifies with the job and receives satisfaction from accomplishing it.

Katz and Kahn's final type, D, is based on the employee internalizing the organization's goals. Here, the goals of the group actually become identical with those of the employee as he adopts the organization's goals as his own. The person complies or is motivated to accomplish a task because by doing so and contributing to the organization's goals, he is also contributing to his own. The wave of nationalism that compelled young men to join the army during World War II is one example of this. Some firm's "profit-sharing" plans are another.

According to Katz and Kahn, each of these four patterns is appropriate for tapping a different type of behavior. For example, *legal compliance* (type A) is usually not effective for attracting people into a system or holding them there, except in such instances as military service. However, it *can* bring about acceptable levels of individual performance both in quantity and quality, and the more routine the activity, the more likely this is to be true.

Classical theorists recognized this and added *rewards* (type B) to ensure compliance above minimum standards. But although organizationwide and individual rewards can be useful for attracting people to the organization and ensuring dependable behavior, they are not as useful for invoking the strong motivation necessary for ensuring innovative and spontaneous behavior.

For evoking innovative behavior, managers have to depend more on the employee's *self-control*. Katz and Kahn say that type C (job identification) is an excellent device for ensuring dependable and innovative behavior, since it affords intrinsic job satisfaction. Type D (the *internalization of organizational goals*) is also useful for ensuring both dependable and innovative behavior, since here, various techniques are used to synchronize organizational and individual goals. In both cases, employees perform their jobs because they *want* to.

Imposed vs. Self-Control: Other Views

Other theorists have also distinguished between imposed and self-control. For example, McGregor's Theory X, which we discussed in Chapter 3, seems to emphasize control of people by rewards and punishments. His Theory Y "emphasizes the ability of people to exercise self-control and their desire to perform effectively." [3] Similarly, Blau distinguishes between "behavior control" and "output control' and says that evaluating a person on the basis of his *output* makes him want to discipline himself, and renders close, imposed supervision of the person's day to day *behavior* superfluous.[4]

Another writer says that in controlling the work of people there are only two phenomena that can be observed, monitored, and counted—*behavior,* and the *outputs* that result from behavior.[5] He says that in order to apply behavior control, the organization must possess at least agreement, if not true knowledge, about means and relationships. In other words, to control behavior, one must understand how that behavior is related to the actual output—the product or service—that the organization is ultimately interested in. Whether control is based on monitoring *behavior* or *output,* he says, thus depends upon the accuracy with which each can be measured, and the technological or task characteristics of the work will play an important role in this determination. For example:

> Except at the extremes, the dean of the school of business cannot control his faculty research by observing the behavior of faculty members. At best, he can control the quantity of output, but certainly not the quality through these means. On the other hand, the manager of a tin can plant can observe the behavior of his employees, and, if they behave as he knows they should, he can be certain that the expected tin cans are being produced. . . .
> The business school dean, wanting the research produced by his faculty to

be well regarded by their peer group, can simply survey that peer group for their evaluations.[6]

Situational Determinants of Imposed vs. Self-Control

Is imposed "behavior" control more appropriate where tasks are routine? Is self-control (where just "output" is monitored) more appropriate where tasks are unpredictable?

There has not been a great deal of research on these questions. In their study, Lawrence and Lorsch found that in the more uncertain plastics firms even low level managers made many important decisions. In the more predictable container firms, decision making was centralized, and so lower level managers had their behavior more circumscribed than did those in the plastic firms.[7] (This is illustrated in Figure 8-1.) However, perhaps a better illustration of when imposed (versus self) control is appropriate is contained in a study by Bell, to which we now turn.

The Bell studies. Bell [8] carried out a study to test the following hypothesis:

> The more unpredictable the work demands of a subordinate's job, the more distant the supervision will be . . . the more predictable the work demands, the closer the supervision.

To test this hypothesis, Bell developed questions for measuring task predictability and closeness of supervision. Predictability was measured by asking respondents two questions:

1. If you listed the exact activities you would be confronted with on an average workday, what percentage of these activities do you think would be interrupted by unexpected events?
2. Everyone is confronted with certain routine and repetitive activities. What percentage of the activities or work demands connected with your job would you consider to be of a routine nature?

Closeness of supervision was measured by asking the respondents the following two questions:

1. How often does your supervisor keep a close check on what you are doing and closely observe your work?
2. To what extent does your immediate supervisor influence what you do in a particular workweek?

The findings supported Bell's hypothesis. In those jobs in which the work tasks were very predictable, the supervisors exerted relatively close control over the subordinates. Jobs containing unpredictable activities evidenced a lack of close supervision. Bell also found that worker discretion (the extent to which he exercised self-control), as measured by questions

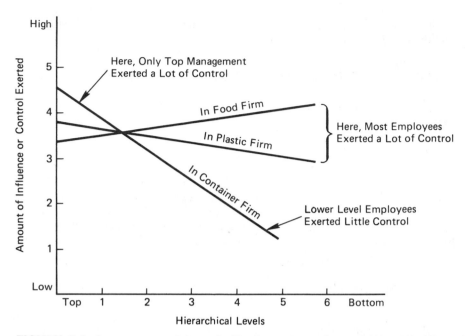

FIGURE 8-1. Lawrence and Lorsch Findings: How Control Was Distributed in Three Organizations

Note: In the more entrepreneurial, uncertain food and plastics firms, total control was high and people at *all* levels exerted high control. In the more mechanistic container firm, employees at lower levels had little autonomy, people at higher levels exerted most of the control, and those at lower levels simply followed orders.

Source: Paul R. Lawrence and Jay W. Lorsch, *Organization and Environment* (Boston: Harvard University Press, 1967), p. 143. Reprinted by permission of Harvard University Press from *Organization and Environment* by Paul R. Lawrence and Jay Lorsch, Boston, Mass.: Division of Research, Graduate School of Business Administration, Harvard University, copyright © 1967 by the President and Fellows of Harvard College.

such as, "To what extent do you control your job and the general pace of your work?" was related to the predictability of work demands. The more unpredictable the work demands confronting the employee, the greater the likelihood that he will exert a high degree of discretion. Bell also obtained findings suggesting that the more professional training an employee has, the more self-control he exerts in carrying out his duties.

A SURVEY OF MOTIVATION THEORIES

Why Study Motivation Theory?

How does one ensure that employees carry out the tasks they have been assigned? We assumed that two basic approaches—imposed control and self-control—could be distinguished, and in the next two chapters we will discuss some specific techniques for implementing each of these. In Chapter 9, for example, we discuss authority, formal control systems such as budgets, and incentives; these are *extrinsic* methods aimed at imposing compliance. In Chapter 10, we discuss techniques like job enrichment and management by objectives, which are intrinsic techniques aimed at evoking self-control.

But before proceeding, we should discuss some basic theories of motivation, in order that we may better understand these techniques. The effective use of incentives is based on the psychology of motivation, for example, as are techniques for eliciting self-control, techniques like job enrichment and management by objectives.

Reinforcement

Introduction.   The use of reinforcement (also known as "operant conditioning" or "behavior modification") is a powerful motivation tool. It is based on the work of B. F. Skinner and is built on two principles: (1) Behavior that appears to lead to a positive consequence (a "reward") tends to be repeated, whereas behavior that appears to lead to a negative consequence tends not to be repeated; [9] and (2) therefore, by providing the properly scheduled rewards, it is possible to influence people's behavior.

Operant conditioning is similar in some respects to the "classical conditioning" made famous by Pavlov. Pavlov had carried out experiments on the digestive systems of dogs in the early 1900s. During one of these experiments, he noticed that the dog salivated not only when food was placed in its mouth but also when other, associated stimuli were presented. For example, Pavlov found that if he presented a "neutral" stimulus (ringing a bell) every time food was presented to the dog, the dog eventually salivated in response to the bell alone.

In classical conditioning, the sequence of events (ringing bell leads to salivation) is *independent* of the subject's behavior. The response is simply a reflex action and the subject (in this case, the dog) is at the mercy of his environment and past conditioning history.[10]

Operant conditioning is different. Here, the "consequences" (rewards or punishments) are made to occur *as a consequence of the subject's response* (or lack of response). Thus, whether or not rewards (or punishments) are forthcoming is *dependent* on the subject's *voluntary* behavior. His or her behavior is thus said to "operate" on the environment (in such a way as to elicit the reward or punishment). With Pavlov's classical conditioning, the subject's behavior is simply respondent to the stimuli.

Both classical and operant conditioning are basically learning theories. They both explain how learning takes place and habits are formed.

Types of reinforcement.   Assume you are a manager, and your employees are chronically late for work. You want to use operant conditioning to train them to come in on time. There are four types of reinforcement you could use: positive reinforcement, negative reinforcement, extinction, and punishment.

First, you could focus on reinforcing the desired behavior—in this case, coming to work on time. Here, you could use either positive or negative reinforcement. *Positive* reinforcement would include rewards like praise or raises. *Negative* reinforcement also focuses on reinforcing the desired behavior. But instead of providing a positive reward, the "reward" is that the employee avoids some negative consequence; for example, the employee is not harassed or is not reprimanded for coming in late. Thus the reward is a "negative" one—employees come in on time to avoid some negative consequence like harassment, a reprimand, or a pay cut.

Alternatively, you might focus, as many managers seem to, on reducing the *undesired* behavior (coming in late) rather than on rewarding the desired behavior. With operant conditioning, there are two types of reinforcement you can use to reduce undesired behavior: extinction and punishment. (These are all summarized in Table 8-2.) People tend to repeat behavior that they have learned leads to positive consequences. With *extinction*, positive reinforcement is withheld, so that over time, the undesired behavior (com-

TABLE 8-2

Types of Reinforcements

Stimulus	Work Behavior	Possible Supervisory Action	Type of Reinforcement
	1. Consistently records intake correctly	1. Praise employee and recommend a high increase in pay	Positive Reinforcement
		2. Avoid harassing the employee and do not reprimand	Negative Reinforcement (Avoidance)
Nursing supervisor's instructions to record fluid intake on patient record			
	2. Consistently fails to record intake correctly	3. Withhold praise and merit pay increase	Extinction
		4. Reprimand and harass employee	Punishment

Source: John Ivancevich, Andrew Szilagyi, Jr., and Marc Wallace, Jr., *Organizational Behavior and Performance* (Santa Monica: Goodyear, 1977), p. 84.

ing in late) disappears. For example, suppose your employees learned from experience that lateness seemed to be unrelated to their merit raises—that despite being late, employees still received such raises. Extinction would involve withholding merit raises from chronically late employees to make them unlearn their "bad habits." *Punishment* is a second method of reducing the frequency of undesired behavior. Here, for example, you might reprimand or harass late employees. Punishment is the most controversial method of modifying behavior, and this is one reason why Skinner recommends extinction rather than punishment for decreasing the frequency of undesired behaviors.[11]

We have discussed four types of reinforcement: positive reinforcement, negative reinforcement (avoidance), extinction, and punishment. Positive and negative reinforcement are conceptually quite different from extinction and punishment, since the first two focus on getting employees to learn the *desired* behavior. Extinction and punishment, on the other hand, focus on unlearning the *undesired* behavior and can't be of much use in teaching people the correct, desired behavior.

Schedules of positive reinforcement. The schedule with which you apply positive reinforcement is as important as the type of reinforcement you decide to use. Basically (as you can see in Table 8-3) there are two basic

TABLE 8-3

Schedules of Reinforcement

Type of Reinforcement:	Explanation
I. Continuous (or "mass")	Reward each and every time desired performance occurs
II. Partial	Reward part of the time
1. Fixed interval	According to fixed *time* periods
2. Variable interval	According to variable *time* periods
3. Fixed ratio	After fixed numbers of desired responses
4. Variable ratio	After varying number of responses

schedules you could adhere to. First, there is continuous (or "mass") reinforcement. Here (to use our example), you might praise or otherwise reward an employee *each and every time* that person arrives for work on time. Second, you could follow a "partial" reinforcement schedule and provide positive reinforcement only *part* of the time, according to some schedule. If you opt for such a schedule, there are four specific schedules you could follow: fixed interval, variable interval, fixed ratio, and variable ratio.

A fixed-interval schedule is based on time. Here, a reinforcer (reward) is administered only when the desired response occurs *and only after the passage of a specified fixed period of time* since the previous reinforcement.

Variable-interval schedules are also based on time. However, reinforcement is administered at some *variable* interval, around some average.

A fixed-ratio schedule is based on units of *output* rather than on time. With a fixed-ratio schedule, rewards are delivered only when a fixed number of desired responses occurs. Most "piecework" incentive pay plans are on a fixed-ratio schedule. The worker is "rewarded" every time he or she produces a *fixed number* of pieces. Variable-ratio schedules are also based on units of output, but the number of desired outcomes necessary to elicit a reward changes from time to time, around some average. The Las Vegas-type slot machines are probably the best examples of rewards administered according to variable-ratio schedules. The number of times you can expect to hit a jackpot with such machines *on the average* over the long term is predictable; yet the jackpots come randomly, on a variable-interval schedule.

Which ratio schedule is most effective? Several conclusions can be drawn from research into the effectiveness of different reinforcement schedules:

1. Continuous (or "mass") reinforcement schedules seem to result in the *fastest* learning. In other words, the way to get someone to learn quickly is to reinforce desired outcomes continuously, each and every time they occur. The drawback is that the desired behavior also diminishes very rapidly once you stop reinforcing it.

2. Partial reinforcement schedules (any of the four we discussed) lead to slower learning but stronger retention. In other words, learning is more permanent when you reward correct behavior only part of the time.

3. The two reinforcement schedules based on output (fixed ratio and variable ratio) are both more effective than are those schedules based on time (fixed interval and variable interval).[12]

4. Of the four partial reinforcement schedules we discussed (fixed and variable interval, and fixed and variable ratio), variable-ratio reinforcement is the most powerful at *sustaining* behavior.[13]

Applications.   Operant conditioning has been successfully used in industry. As an example, it has been used effectively to control employee absenteeism.[14] An electronics manufacturer found that it had an acute absenteeism problem and that tardiness was a problem as well. Management initiated a program to reward the desired behavior, prompt and regular attendance. Under this program, described in a company bulletin, employees could qualify for a monthly drawing of a prize only if they had perfect attendance and punctuality records for the month. All absences of any kind precluded eligibility. A drawing was held on the last workday of each month, and a winner was selected at random from a basket containing the names of all employees who had maintained perfect attendance and punctuality records for that month. A $10 cash prize was awarded to the winner of each monthly lottery. In addition, the names of all employees who qualified were listed on the plant bulletin board. (Note that this was

TABLE 8-4

Composite of Sick-Leave Expenditures
Before and After Positive Reinforcement System

Months	"Prior" Monthly Costs ($)	"Post" Monthly Costs($)	Prior Costs Minus Post Costs
September	553.17	935.25	−382.08
October	755.16	561.78	193.38
November	1,087.62	314.51	773.11
December	563.26	575.61	−12.35
January	1,209.02	736.81	472.21
February	1,075.37	584.50	490.87
March	1,136.31	745.64	390.67
April	1,394.29	774.82	619.47
May	826.42	595.54	230.88
June	814.36	767.26	47.10
July	754.60	468.75	285.85
TOTAL	$10,169.58	$7,060.47	$3,109.11

Source: "The Positive Reinforcement Approach to Controlling Employee Absenteeism," by Ronald D. Johnson and Jerry A. Wallin. Reprinted with permission Personnel Journal, copyright August 1976.

an example of variable-ratio scheduling, since the "jackpot'—the $10 prize —was awarded based on randomly drawing names out of a basket.)

The results of this program, presented in Table 8-4, are fairly impressive. The average monthly savings amounted to about $282. The total yearly savings was over $3,000.

Reinforcement: conclusions. Research on the effectiveness of reinforcement in organizational settings has been very limited, but several conclusions seem warranted. First, it *can* be effective; positive reinforcement in particular has been used successfully for years (for example, as part of the programmed learning devices often used for training). Second, the employee must clearly understand that rewards are contingent on good performance; therefore, emphasizing the relation between performance and rewards is very important. Third, it is clear that when people are continually *not* rewarded for good performance, decreased motivation and performance (extinction) may result. Fourth, if you must "punish" an employee for doing something wrong, at least take the opportunity to explain carefully what was done wrong, what results were desired, and how positive rewards will result from those desired outcomes. Finally, remember that variable-ratio schedules of reinforcement are the most powerful for sustaining motivated behavior in people. This schedule may not be practical for salary, but it can certainly be used for praise, financial incentive plans, promotion, and other positive reinforcements (rewards). Most important, though, remember that regardless of the schedule, employees should always be rewarded *contingent on their performance*; rewards (where you can control them) should not be non-performance-based.[15]

But keep in mind that operant conditioning (as applied to people) has some powerful detractors, who have criticized it on several grounds. It is said that this technique is inhumane and that it restricts freedom of choice. (Visions of a laboratory pigeon dutifully ringing a bell each time it wants a peanut help lay the groundwork for such criticisms.) Others say that operant conditioning ignores the individuality of man, and the fact that a person can be motivated by the job itself. Its focus on external rewards, like money and praise, is an attempt by management, some say, to control employees' behavior so they will "do what they're told." Yet all these criticisms have been themselves criticized, and the debate between advocates and detractors of reinforcement is both lively and ongoing.[16]

Maslow's Hierarchy of Needs

One of the most widely discussed theories of motivation was developed by Abraham Maslow.[17] His *Needs-Hierarchy Theory* assumes that man's needs can be visualized in a hierarchy, with each correspondingly higher-level need becoming a motivator as the next lower need is fulfilled. The theory postulates that people are continuously in a motivational state, and that as one desire becomes satisfied, another arises to take its place. These needs are as follows:

The physiological needs. The lowest level of needs on the hierarchy and the ones people try to satisfy first are those that sustain life. These include needs for nourishment, oxygen, rest, and protection from the elements. Unless the circumstances are unusual, needs for status or recognition are inoperative as long as the physiological needs are unfulfilled. As Maslow facetiously puts it, "It is quite true that man lives by bread alone—when there is no bread."

The safety and security needs. When the physiological needs are reasonably satisfied, needs at the next hierarchical level—those for safety and security—begin to dominate man's behavior; in other words, to motivate him. These needs are concerned with protection from danger, deprivation, and threat. Whereas protection from physical dangers is of less consequence today, the nature of industrialization makes economic security a strong need, and it is especially important when considering the dependent relationship between employee and employer.

Social needs. After the physiological and safety-and-security needs have been satisfied, the social needs become important motivators of behavior. These include giving and receiving affection, associating with and being accepted by others, and feeling oneself a part of social groups.

Esteem or ego needs. The fourth level of needs are those for self-esteem and esteem from others. The former refers to needs for achievement, competence, self-confidence, and knowledge. The latter relates to such needs as status, appreciation, and recognition. McGregor has suggested that these needs are rarely fully satisfied, and that they usually do not become dominant until the physiological, safety, and social needs are well fulfilled.

Self-actualization needs. The highest level of needs in the hierarchy is for fulfillment, self-realization, and self-actualization. These are the needs for realizing one's potentialities and for fully utilizing abilities, thereby accomplishing all that one is capable of accomplishing.

Maslow recognized that the order in which man seeks to satisfy these needs may change and that on occasion even basic needs will be ignored in an attempt to satisfy some higher goal. Both he and McGregor have also emphasized that the various levels are interdependent and overlapping, so a higher-level need can be expected to emerge before the lower-level need has been completely satisfied.

Research findings. Maslow's original papers presented almost no empirical evidence in support of the theory and no research at all that tested the model in its entirety. In fact, Maslow argued that the theory was primarily useful as a framework for future research, and he pointed out the limitations of his model—noting, for example, that the needs may be unconscious rather than conscious. Unfortunately, others were not quite so careful, and a widely publicized paper by McGregor left the impression that the model could be accepted without question and was fairly easy to apply.[18] (Maslow said, however, "I'm a little worried about this stuff which I consider to be tentative being swallowed whole by all sorts of enthusiastic people, who really should be a little more tentative in the way that I am.")[19]

Although the Maslow theory is widely discussed, it is extremely difficult to test, and there are few empirical studies that either prove or refute it. The research there is suggests that needs fall into a two-level hierarchy, with "lower level-security needs" on the bottom and "higher needs" on the top.[20] In one relevant study, the researchers used a questionnaire to measure a set of needs slightly modified from Maslow's. The needs categories, along with examples of items on their questionnaire, were these:

Security needs ("the feeling of insecurity associated with one's position")

Social needs ("the opportunity to give help to other people")

Esteem needs ("the feeling of self-esteem a person gets in his position")

Autonomy needs ("the opportunity for independent thought and action")

Self-fulfillment or self-actualization needs ("the opportunity for personal growth and development")

To obtain the data for their study, the researchers mailed a questionnaire to Canadian accountants, engineers, and scientists. The results suggest that the needs form a two-level hierarchy as described above.[21]

Herzberg's Two-Factor Theory

The theory that has probably stimulated the most interest in recent years was developed by Frederick Herzberg and is sometimes described as the *Motivator-Hygiene Theory*. It is similar in several respects to Maslow's Needs-Hierarchy Theory, and postulates two classes of factors that roughly coincide with the lower- and higher-level categories of the Maslow framework. The first, or *hygiene* factors, include such things as company policy and administration, technical supervision, and working conditions. The second, or *motivator* factors, include such intrinsic job-content items as achievement, recognition, and advancement. The theory states that only the motivators can motivate behavior; fulfillment of the hygiene factors simply prevents an employee from becoming dissatisfied, but it cannot contribute to positive satisfaction. The theory is the basis for the job-enrichment program Herzberg espouses; and before proceeding, we should summarize the foundation study on which the theory has been built.

The nature of the study.[22] During a series of interviews, 200 engineers and accountants in nine companies were asked to describe several previous job experiences in which they had felt "exceptionally good" or "exceptionally bad" about their jobs. In addition, they were asked to indicate the *degree* to which their feelings had been influenced positively or negatively by each experience they had described.

The researchers then took these interview data and broke them down into "thought units," such as, "I feel fresh and eager, ready to come to work," or, "I like to know there is a reason for doing the job." Five thousand such statements were then classified (Figure 8-2) into categories such as "achievement," "working conditions," and "work itself." In addition, the events or thought units were compared, to determine whether they were associated with "high" or "low" job-attitude events (essentially, whether they resulted in motivation).

As a result of this analysis, the researchers concluded that certain job events—the "motivator" factors—lead to job satisfaction if they are present, but do not cause dissatisfaction if they are absent; other job events—the "hygiene" factors—lead to job dissatisfaction if they are absent, but will not add to employee satisfaction if they are present.

The theory. Results such as these have led Herzberg to conclude that only the fulfillment of the motivator factors can lead to positive satisfaction on the job. Fulfilling the hygiene factors can prevent an employee from being dissatisfied, but cannot contribute to positive satisfaction. In this view, job satisfaction and dissatisfaction are considered not as opposite ends of the same continuum, but rather as different factors. The opposite of *satisfaction* is *no satisfaction*; the opposite of *dissatisfaction* is *no dissatisfaction*.

Supporting studies. One study widely viewed as supporting Herzberg's two-factor theory was carried out at the Texas Instruments Com-

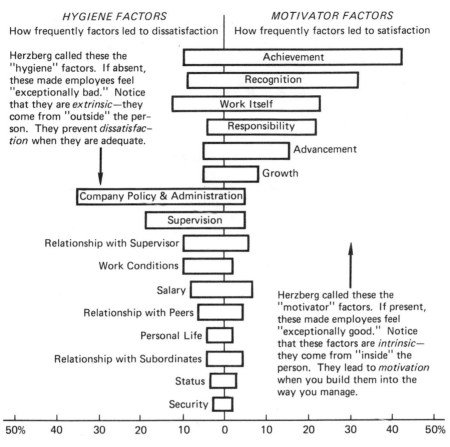

HYGIENE FACTORS
How frequently factors led to dissatisfaction

MOTIVATOR FACTORS
How frequently factors led to satisfaction

Herzberg called these the "hygiene" factors. If absent, these made employees feel "exceptionally bad." Notice that they are *extrinsic*—they come from "outside" the person. They prevent *dissatisfaction* when they are adequate.

Achievement

Recognition

Work Itself

Responsibility

Advancement

Growth

Company Policy & Administration

Supervision

Relationship with Supervisor

Work Conditions

Salary

Relationship with Peers

Personal Life

Relationship with Subordinates

Status

Security

Herzberg called these the "motivator" factors. If present, these made employees feel "exceptionally good." Notice that these factors are *intrinsic*—they come from "inside" the person. They lead to *motivation* when you build them into the way you manage.

50%   40   30   20   10   0   10   20   30   40   50%

FIGURE 8-2. Summary of Herzberg's Motivator-Hygiene Findings

Source: Adapted from Frederick Herzberg, "One More Time: How Do You Motivate Employees?" *Harvard Business Review,* January-February 1968.

pany.[23] The method was similar to that followed by Herzberg and included intensive interviewing of 282 employees, 52 of them females, in various occupational groups. Although the results were generally supportive of the Herzberg theory, there were some differences in that some occupational groups seemed to be more motivated by "hygienes" like pay than by "motivators" like recognition.

Similar support for the theory was found by Soliman.[24] He reviewed the literature and found that only three of twenty studies that used the Herzberg technique failed to support the theory.

Criticism of the theory. Many of the recent criticisms of the Herzberg theory concern his reliance on the recall of critical incidents. In essence, critics suggest that this methodology introduces a bias that restricts employees' "opportunities to register negative reactions to motivators and positive reactions to hygienes." [25] In one study, researchers asked more than 500 people to describe both a previously dissatisfying and a previously satisfying job situation by choosing from among 36 preselected and scaled statements.[26] These statements were worded in such a way that they could describe *either* a satisfying or a dissatisfying job event. For example, two of the statements were:

> I felt a great deal of satisfaction because of doing a job well.
> I felt a great deal of dissatisfaction because of doing a job poorly.

The statements were then analyzed to derive "scores" on each of twelve Herzberg-type factors. Certain motivator factors, such as achievement and responsibility, and certain hygiene factors, such as supervision, were associated with *both* satisfying and dissatisfying situations. In other words, some of the hygiene factors were associated with satisfying situations, while some of the motivator factors were associated with dissatisfying situations. Such results are inconsistent with Herzberg's theory. Similarly, House and Wigdor found that all the motivator and hygiene factors have been reported as *both* satisfiers and dissatisfiers.[27] (See Table 8-5.) Vroom points out that Herzberg's method may bias the result because the person may be more likely to attribute his satisfaction to his own job accomplishments and his dissatisfaction to factors in the work environment,[28] a contention that has been supported.[29] Other findings not supporting the theory have been obtained in a sample of blue- and white-collar workers,[30] and among solid-waste-management employees.[31]

TABLE 8-5

Frequency of Reports for Satisfiers and Dissatisfiers
out of Total Number of 1,220 People in Six Studies
Reported by Herzberg (1966)

Factor	Reported as Satisfier	Reported as Dissatisfier
Achievement	440	122
Recognition	309	110
Advancement	126	48
Responsibility	168	35
Work itself	175	75
Policy and administration	55	337
Supervision	22	182
Work conditions	20	108
Relations with superior	15	59
Relations with peers	9	57

Source: Robert J. House and Lawrence J. Wigdor, "Herzberg's Dual Factor Theory of Job Satisfaction and Motivation: A Review of the Evidence and a Criticism," *Personnel Psychology*, Vol. 20, No. 4 (1967), p. 375.

Others have questioned whether the Herzberg factors are mutually exclusive.[32] In one study the researchers surveyed 1,099 salaried employees from five operating companies of a midwestern corporation. They concluded that Herzberg's two-factor explanation of satisfaction was not adequate. Instead, "A Four-Factor Theory (satisfaction with personal progress and development, with compensation, with the organizational context, and with superior–subordinate relationships) is more comprehensive." [33]

In response ot such criticisms, the theory's defenders charge that the critics have misinterpreted the theory, engaged in weak methods of investigation, and misinterpreted results.[34] Recent studies [35] suggest that Herzberg's theory is, in fact, viable.[36]

Discussion. The controversy is an ongoing one, and it is doubtful whether the fate of the theory will be sealed for some time.[37] There is some support for the argument that the two-factor theory is an oversimplified model of the mechanism by which job satisfaction comes about.[38] However, although it is easy to question the *general* applicability of the theory, it may be more applicable with certain groups or classes of people—such as engineers.[39]

Achievement Motivation

Both McClelland and Atkinson have focused their efforts on studying achievement-oriented behavior. Based upon his work with the personality test known as the "Thematic Apperception Test" (TAT), Atkinson formulated the concept of the need to achieve and argued that it was a relatively stable personality trait that was rooted in childhood experiences.[40] Although most of McClelland's interest has been in the association between achievement motivation and entrepreneurial activities in developing countries, the possible implications actually cover a variety of applications in organizations.[41]

Achievement-motivation theory. In its simplest form, this theory aims at predicting the behavior of those who rank high or low in achievement motivation, which one writer defines as ". . . the disposition to strive for satisfaction derived from success in competition with some standard of excellence." [42] High-achievement people have an affinity for tasks for which there is a reasonable chance for success, avoiding those that are either too easy or too difficult. Relatedly, such people prefer taking personal responsibility for accomplishing tasks and obtaining specific criticism and feedback about how they are doing at their tasks.

Discussion and research findings. The studies—most of which have been carried out by McClelland and his colleagues—confirm the existence of a strong relationship between achievement motivation and both economic and entrepreneurial success.[43] McClelland has found, for example, that societies high in achievement motivation had relatively high economic growth rates, and those low in achievement motivation had lower rates. He also found that over a fourteen-year period, the proportion of students entering entrepreneurial occupations was greater among those with high achievement motivation than among those with low achievement needs. McClelland and Winter found that achievement-motivation training produced significant increases in business activity.[44] Most evidence indicates that achievement motivation can be increased through training procedures.[45]

A recent study by Durand provides a good illustration of the research on achievement motivation, as well as on the applicability of achievement motivation theory in organizations.[46] Subjects were twenty-seven male and eight female participants from the black community of a large midwestern metropolitan area. All thirty-five subjects were either owners or operators of businesses or were seriously considering entering into business at the conclusion of the researchers' achievement-motivation training course.

The training was conducted in two parts over a three-month period. The first part consisted of achievement-motivation sessions and lasted six days. Then, after this motivation training, two and one half hour (2.5 hours) management development sessions were held weekly for eight weeks. In these sessions, introductory concepts in marketing, finance, accounting, and management were presented and discussed. This second phase was attended by not only the thirty-five subjects who had already gone through achievement-motivation training, but also ten other people who had not.

Durand found that the achievement-motivation-trained participants increased their achievement-motivation test scores after taking the management-development training, and that they also became "significantly more active (in terms of hours worked, new investments, employees hired, etc.) than did the group receiving only management-development training." The results suggest that management-development training may enhance the impact of motivation training, since businessmen who received both "engaged in more entrepreneurial activities than persons who received motivation training alone."

In summary, most of the research supports the hypothesis that need for achievement motivation contributes to economic and entrepreneurial success.

Some questions have been raised about the theory, however. For example, there is a question as to what effects (if any) "fear of failure" has on the need to achieve. Researchers once assumed that fear of failure was an integral part of the need to achieve, and that the fear of failure augmented the need to achieve. Today, however, we believe that fear of failure detracts from the motivation that the need to achieve would normally generate, and that for a person to be effective, his need to achieve has to exceed his fear of failure. In addition, motivation theories like those of McClelland, Maslow and Herzberg address only the question of what needs motivate behavior; they do not fully address the question of the process of motivation—of how it comes about. For this, "process" theories of motivation are necessary, such as reinforcement theory and expectancy theory.

Vroom's Expectancy Theory of Motivation

A number of theories of work motivation that have been considered in recent years are sometimes referred to as expectancy, or instrumentality, theories. Vroom has formulated one of the more popular versions of expectancy theory; his interpretation is based upon three concepts—valence, instrumentality, and expectancy.[47]

Valence represents the value or importance that a particular outcome has for a person. It reflects the strength of a person's desire for or attraction toward the outcomes of particular courses of action. *Instrumentality* reflects the person's perception of the relation between a "first-level outcome" (such as high performance) and a "second-level outcome" (such as a promotion). For example, it might reflect the extent to which a person feels that performance will be instrumental in getting him a promotion. *Expectancy* refers to the extent to which he feels that his efforts will lead to the first-level outcome—in this case, performance.

In sum, Vroom feels that motivation involves a conscious or unconscious three-step thought process:

1. Does the person feel that the second-level goal, such as promotion, is important to him, or high in *valence*?
2. Does he feel that high performance—the first-level outcome in this case—will be instrumental in getting him his promotion?
3. Does he feel that exerting effort will in fact result in increased performance?

Research findings and discussion. Many of the research findings tend to support Vroom's expectancy theory of motivation. In one such study, Vroom found that 76 percent of the students he studied chose to go to work for employers whom they ranked as being the most instrumental in fulfilling their goals.[48] In a study carried out among factory workers, it was similarly found that productivity was directly related to the extent to which workers felt that high productivity was instrumental in satisfying important goals.[49] Two researchers surveyed a group of government workers and found that the expectancy model predicted the employee's self-reported effort fairly well, but not to the same extent superiors' ratings of employee effort.[50] However, not all the findings have been supporting.[51] For example, expectancy theory assumes that people can rank order their preferences for different rewards, and there is debate as to whether people can do so in the manner suggested by expectancy theory.[52]

Motivation Theory: Summary

Summarizing all this work on motivation is difficult, for at least two reasons. First, the results concerning the effectiveness of each theory (with the possible exception of reinforcement theory) are inconsistent. Second, motivation is a function of a person's needs, and since needs are highly individualized, so are the things that motivate them.

Yet we believe it is still useful to attempt to summarize and integrate these theories, and the model shown in Figure 8-3 serves this purpose. As you can see, we view motivation within an *expectancy-theory framework*. Expectancy theory, you will recall, states that motivation will be aroused if:

1. The incentive is of value or importance to the person.
2. The person is reasonably sure that effort on his or her part will result in accomplishing the task and attaining the incentive.

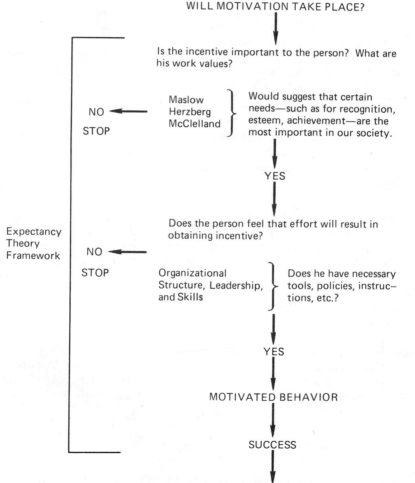

FIGURE 8-3. A Model of Motivation

Some motivation theories, such as those of Maslow and McClelland, deal primarily with identifying important needs. Others, including reinforcement and expectancy theory, deal with the process through which motivation is aroused. As you can see from our model, for motivation to take place, two things must occur. First, the incentive must be important to the person. Here, theorists like Maslow, Herzberg, and McClelland would suggest that certain needs—such as for recognition, esteem, and achievement—are the most important in our society. Second, the person must feel that effort will result in attaining the incentives. Here, as you can see, other, "nonmotivational" matters must be addressed, including the appropriateness of the person for the job, and the effectiveness of the organization's structure.

SUMMARY

We have seen that providing an organization structure is only half the problem facing the organization theorist or manager. The basic assumption one makes in structuring an organization and giving each worker a task is that those tasks will in fact be (at least) carried out in some dependable, predictable fashion. In this chapter, therefore, we began our discussion of compliance, and for simplicity, we distinguished between two basic types of compliance: imposed and self-control.

Does the context of the organization affect whether that organization should use imposed or self-control? The research findings suggest that unpredictable work demands tend to be associated with more reliance on self-control. For example, Lawrence and Lorsch found that lower-level managers in more "uncertain" environments felt they had relatively more influence in decision making. Bell found that employees with more unpredictable work demands usually exercised more self-control. These findings complement those of others we have discussed (like those of Burns and Stalker, and Woodward), in which an emphasis on imposed control and extrinsic rewards characterized predictable environments and mechanistic systems, while self-control characterized uncertain environments and organic systems.

How do the concepts of imposed and self-control relate to the motivation theories we discussed in this chapter? We discussed two categories of motivation theories in this chapter, *process* and *content* theories. The latter, we will assume, relate most clearly to the concepts of imposed and self-control.

The various content theories of motivation focus on important human needs. These theories (those of Maslow, Herzberg, and McClelland) are actually quite similar. For example, Maslow's "lower-level" needs (for security and so on) and Herzberg's "hygiene" factors (pay, security, supervision, and the like) are comparable, as are Maslow's "higher-level" needs (achievement, self-actualization) and Herzberg's "motivator" factors (challenge, achievement). McClelland's achievement needs would of course fall in the "high-level needs" category. We will assume that the higher-level needs are the ones that are usually tapped when self-control is the goal, and that lower-level needs are usually relied on when aiming for extrinsic, imposed control. For example, Herzberg says that only by appealing to higher-level needs for achievement and so forth can managers make employees "self-starters" and get them to exhibit self-control.[53] Similarly, Katz and Kahn refer to higher level needs like "challenge," "self-expression," and "achievement" when discussing self-control.

Are some motivation theories more appropriate in different situations (and tasks) than others? Assume the process theories apply as well to mechanistic situations as organic ones. With respect to the content theories, however, we will assume that appealing to higher level needs is generally more necessary and appropriate when tasks demand innovation, creativity, and self-control. Perhaps this is why, as we saw in Chapters 2 and 3, the emerging emphasis on higher-level needs and social relationships tended to parallel an increase in creative, innovative jobs (as well as other changes). Similarly, Katz and Kahn say that eliciting self-control by appealing to higher level needs for achievement is especially necessary where innovative behavior (as opposed to just dependable behavior) is required.

DISCUSSION QUESTIONS

1. Compare and contrast the Maslow and Herzberg motivation theories.
2. Compare and contrast the Herzberg and Vroom theories of motivation. Are they compatible?
3. "With today's complex organizations and emphasis on productivity, it is more important than ever to appeal to the higher level motives of employees." Discuss why you agree or disagree with this statement.
4. Compare and contrast reinforcement theory with Vroom's expectancy theory of motivation.
5. Compare and contrast (1) behavior control and output control with (2) imposed and self-control respectively.
6. Why would we expect to find an emphasis on self-control in organic organizations and an emphasis on imposed control in mechanistic ones?

FOOTNOTES

[1] Daniel Katz and Robert L. Kahn, *The Social Psychology of Organizations* (New York: John Wiley, 1966), p. 336.

[2] *Ibid.*, p. 345.

[3] Edward Lawler III and John Grant Rhode, *Information and Control in Organizations* (Pacific Palisades, Calif.: Goodyear, 1976).

[4] Peter Blau, *Bureaucracy in Modern Society* (New York: Random House, 1956), p. 82. See also Peter Blau and W. Richard Scott, *Formal Organizations* (San Francisco: Chandler, 1962).

5 William G. Ouchi, "The Relationship between Organizational Structure and Organizational Control," *Administrative Science Quarterly*, March 1977, p. 99.

6 *Ibid.*, p. 97.

7 Paul R. Lawrence and Jay W. Lorsch, *Organization and Environment* (Boston: Division of Research, Graduate School of Business Administration, Harvard University, 1967).

8 Gerald D. Bell, "The Influence of Technological Components of Work upon Management Control," *Journal of the Academy of Management*, Vol. 8, No. 2 (1965), 127–32. See also Bell, "Predictability of Work Demands and Professionalism as Determinants of Worker's Discretion," *Journal of the Academy of Management*, Vol. 9, No. 1 (March 1966), 20–28.

9 W. Clay Hamner, "Reinforcement Theory and Contingency Management in Organization Settings," in Henry Tosi and W. Clay Hamner, *Organizational Behavior and Management: A Contingency Approach* (Chicago: St. Clair, 1974), pp. 86–112. This principle is also known as "The Law of Effect."

10 *Ibid.*, p. 89.

11 *Ibid.*, p. 95.

12 Gary Latham and Gary Yukl, "Assigned versus Participative Goal Setting with Educated and Uneducated Woodworkers," *Journal of Applied Psychology*, Vol. 60 (1975), 299–302; also, Gary Yukl, Gary Latham, and Elliot Pursell, "The Effectiveness of Performance Incentives under Continuous and Variable Ratio Schedules of Reinforcement," *Personnel Psychology*, Vol. 29 (Summer 1976), 221–33; and Robert Pritchard, Dale Leonard, Clarence Von Bergen, Jr., and Raymond Kirk, "The Effects of Varying Schedules of Reinforcement on Human Task Performance," *Organizational Behavior and Human Performance*, Vol. 16, No. 2 (August 1976), 205–30.

13 See, for example, Robert Pritchard, Dale Leonard, Clarence Von Bergen, Jr., and Raymond Kirk, "The Effects of Varying Schedules of Reinforcement on Human Task Performance," *Organizational Behavior and Human Performance*, Vol. 16, No. 2 (August 1976), 205–30; Brian Deslauriers and Peter Everett, "Effective Intermittent and Continuous Token Reinforcement on Bus Ridership," *Journal of Applied Psychology*, Vol. 62, No. 4 (1977), 369–75. For a contrasting view, Yukl and his associates have found that continuous reinforcement—at least in their studies—is superior. See, for example, Gary Yukl and Gary Latham, "Consequences of Reinforcement Schedules and Incentive Magnitudes for Employee Performance: Problems Encountered in an Industrial Setting," *Journal of Applied Psychology*, Vol. 60, No. 3 (June 1975); Gary Yukl, Gary Latham, Elliot Pursell, "The Effectiveness of Performance Incentives under Continuous and Variable Ratio Schedules of Reinforcement," *Personnel Psychology*, Vol. 29, No. 2 (Summer 1976).

14 This is based on Jerry Wallin and Ronald Johnson, "The Positive Reinforcement Approach to Controlling Employee Absenteeism," *Personnel Journal*, August 1976, 390–92.

15 John Ivancevich, Andrew Szilagyi, and Marc Wallace, *Organizational Behavior and Performance* (Santa Monica, Calif.: Goodyear, 1977), p. 124.

16 See also, for example, W. C. Hamner and L. W. Foster, "Are Intrinsic and Extrinsic Rewards Additive? A Test of Deci's Cognitive Evaluation Theory of Task Motivation," *Organizational Behavior and Human Performance*, Vol. 14 (December 1975); W. E. Scott, Jr., "The Effects of Extrinsic Rewards on 'Intrinsic' Motivation," *Organizational Behavior and Human Performance*, Vol. 15 (February 1976); Robert D. Pritchard, Kathleen Campbell, and Donald Campbell, "The Effects of Extrinsic Financial Rewards on Intrinsic Motivation," *Journal of Applied Psychology*, Vol. 62 (1977), 9–15; Graig C. Pinder, "Additivity versus Nonadditivity of Intrinsic and Extrinsic Incentives: Implications for Work Motivation, Performance and Attitude," *Journal of Applied Psychology*, Vol. 61 (December 1976); William H. Whyte, "Pigeons, Persons, and Piece Rates," *Psychology Today*, April 1972, 67–68, 96, 98, 100; reprinted in Jerry Gron and Frederick Storke, *Readings in Organizational Behavior* (Columbus, O.: Merrill, 1977), pp. 18–56.

17 Abraham H. Maslow, *Motivation and Personality*, 2nd ed. (New York: Harper & Row, 1970).

[18] Douglas McGregor, "Adventure in Thought and Action," Proceedings of the Fifth Anniversary Convocation of the School of Industrial Management, Massachusetts Institute of Technology (Cambridge: Massachusetts Institute of Technology, 1957), pp. 23–30.

[19] A. Maslow, *Eupsychian Management* (Homewood, Ill.: Dorsey, 1965), pp. 55–56.

[20] Mahmoud Wahba and Lawrence Bridwell, "Maslow Reconsidered: A Review of Research on the Need Hierarchy Theory," *Organizational Behavior and Human Performance*, Vol. 15, No. 2 (April 1976). This is based on Vance Mitchell and Pravin Moudgil, "Measurement of Maslow's Need Hierarchy," *Organizational Behavior and Human Performance*, Vol. 16 (August 1976), 334–49. For other studies that provide both modest support and lack of support, see Lyman W. Porter, "A Study of Perceived Job Satisfactions in Bottom and Middle Management Jobs," *Journal of Applied Psychology*, Vol. 45 (1961), 232–36; "Job Attitudes in Management: Perceived Deficiencies in Need Fulfillment as a Function of Job Level," *Journal of Applied Psychology*, Vol. 36 (1962), 1–10; and "Job Attitudes in Management: Perceived Importance of Needs as a Function of Job Level," *Journal of Applied Psychology*, Vol. 47 (1963), 141–48; R. Payne, "Factor Analysis of a Maslow-Type Needs Satisfaction Questionnaire," *Personnel Psychology*, Vol. 23 (1970), 251–68; K. H. Roberts, G. A. Walter, and M. E. Miles, "A Factor-Analytic Study of Job Satisfaction Items Designed to Measure Maslow Need Categories," *Personnel Psychology*, Vol. 24 (1971), 205–20.

[21] The researchers note that this finding was partly the result of how they carried out their analysis and does not obviate the possibility that the needs can in fact also form a five-level hierarchy at the same time.

[22] F. Herzberg, B. Mausner, and D. B. Snyderman, *The Motivation to Work* (New York: John Wiley, 1959). See also Frederick Herzberg, *Work and the Nature of Man* (New York: World Publishing Co., 1966).

[23] M. Scott Myers, "Who Are Your Motivated Workers?" *Harvard Business Review*, Vol. 42 (January–February 1964), 73–88.

[24] H. M. Soliman, "Motivator-Hygiene Theory of Job Attitudes," *Journal of Applied Psychology*, Vol. 54 (1970), 452–61.

[25] Michael E. Gordon and Norman M. Pryor, "An Examination of Scaling Bias in Herzberg's Theory of Job Satisfaction," *Organizational Behavior and Human Performance*, Vol. 11 (1974), 106–21.

[26] M. D. Dunnette, J. P. Campbell, and M. D. Hakel, "Factors Contributing to Job Satisfaction and Job Dissatisfaction in Six Occupational Groups," *Organizational Behavior and Human Performance*, Vol. 2 (1967), 143–74.

[27] Robert J. House and Lawrence J. Wigdor, "Herzberg's Dual Factor Theory of Job Satisfaction and Motivation: A Review of the Evidence and a Criticism," *Personnel Psychology*, Vol. 20, No. 4 (1967), 369–90.

[28] Victor H. Vroom, "Some Observations Regarding Herzberg's Two-Factor Theory," paper presented at the American Psychological Association Convention, New York, September 1966.

[29] D. A. Ondrack, "Defense Mechanisms and the Herzberg Theory: An Alternate Test," *Academy of Management Journal*, Vol. 17, No. 1 (March 1974).

[30] Edwin A. Locke, "Satisfiers and Dissatisfiers among White Collar and Blue Collar Workers," *Journal of Applied Psychology*, Vol. 58, No. 1 (1973), 67–76.

[31] Edwin Locke and Roman J. Whiting, "Sources of Satisfaction and Dissatisfaction among Solid Waste Management Employees," *Journal of Applied Psychology*, Vol. 59, No. 2 (1974), 145–56.

[32] See, for example, M. R. Malinovsky and J. R. Barry, "Determinants of Work Attitude," *Journal of Applied Psychology*, 1965, 446–51.

[33] William Weitzel, Patrick R. Pinto, Rene V. Dauts, and Philip A. Jury, "The Impact of the Organization on the Structure of Job Satisfaction: Some Factor Analytic Findings," *Personnel Psychology*, Vol. 26 (1973), 545–57.

[34] D. A. Whitsett and E. K. Winslow, "An Analysis of Studies Critical of the Motivator-Hygiene Theory," *Personnel Psychology*, Vol. 20, No. 4 (1967), 391–415.

35 Steven Kerr, Anne Harlan, and Ralph M. Stogdill, "Preference for Motivator and Hygiene Factors in a Hypothetical Interview Situation," *Personnel Psychology*, Vol. 27 (1974), 109–24.

36 Earl B. French, Morton L. Metersky, David S. Thaler, and Jerome T. Tresler, "Herzberg's Two Factor Theory: Consistency versus Method Dependency," *Personnel Psychology*, Vol. 26 (1973), 369–75.

37 H. B. Karp and Jack W. Nickson, Jr., "Motivator-Hygiene Deprivation as a Predictor of Job Turnover," *Personnel Psychology*, Vol. 26 (1973), 377–84.

38 Dunnette, Campbell and Hakel, "Factors Contributing to Job Satisfaction and Job Dissatisfaction in Six Occupational Groups."

39 In line with this, some writers have noted that the Herzberg Theory may contain a "middle-class bias." Specifically, it seems to assume that certain needs often identified with middle-class, white-collar workers are important motivators for all classes of workers. As we will see below, people in different geographical and occupational groups do have somewhat different values and needs, and this criticism is therefore a serious one. See, for example, Locke, "Satisfiers and Dissatisfiers among White Collar and Blue Collar Workers," and Locke and Whiting, "Sources of Satisfaction and Dissatisfaction among Solid Waste Management Employees."

40 D. C. McClelland, *The Achieving Society* (Princeton, N.J.: Van Nostrand, 1961). Also, D. C. McClelland and D. G. Winter, *Motivating Economic Achievement* (New York: Free Press, 1969).

41 J. W. Atkinson, "Motivational Determinants of Risk Taking Behavior," *Psychological Review*, Vol. 64 (1957), 359–72.

42 R. deCharms, *Personal Causation and Internal Effective Determinants of Behavior* (New York: Academic Press, 1968).

43 McClelland, *The Achieving Society.*

44 McClelland and Winter, *Motivating Economic Achievement;* and Douglas Durand, "Effect of Achievement Motivation and Skill Training on the Entrepreneurial Behavior of Black Businessmen," *Organizational Behavior and Human Performance*, Vol. 14 (1975), 76–90.

45 J. Arnoff and G. H. Litwin, "Achievement Motivation Training and Executive Advancement," *Journal of Applied Behavioral Science*, Vol. 7 (1971), 215–29; Carl Jackson and Dennis Jay, "Motivation Training and Perspective," in W. Nort, ed., *Concepts and Controversy in Organizational Behavior* (Pacific Palisades, Calif.: Goodyear, 1972), pp. 100–118; D. A. Colb, "Achievement Motivation Training for Underachieving High School Boys," *Journal of Personality and Social Psychology*, Vol. 2 (1965), 783–92.

46 Duran, "Effects of Achievement Motivation."

47 Victor H. Vroom, *Work and Motivation* (New York: John Wiley, 1964).

48 Victor H. Vroom, "Organizational Choice: A Study of Pre and Post Decision Processes," *Organizational Behavior and Human Performance*, Vol. 1 (1966), 212–25.

49 J. Galbraith and L. L. Cummings, "An Empirical Investigation of the Motivational Determinants of Task Performance: Interactive Effects between Instrumentality-Valence and Motivation-Ability," *Organizational Behavior and Human Performance*, Vol. 2 (1967), 237–57.

50 Robert Pritchard and Mark S. Sanders, "The Influence of Valence, Instrumentality, and Expectancy on Effort and Performance," *Journal of Applied Psychology*, Vol. 57, No. 1 (1973), 55–60. See also John Sheridan, John W. Slocum, Jr., and Byung Min, "Motivational Determinants of Job Performance," *Journal of Applied Psychology*, Vol. 60, No. 1 (February 1975); and Donald F. Parker and Lee Dyer, "Expectancy Theory as a Within Person Behavioral Choice Model: An Empirical Test of Some Conceptual and Methodological Refinements," *Organizational Behavior and Human Performance*, Vol. 17, No. 1 (October 1976), 97–117. Expectance theory has also been supported in a cross-cultural study of Japanese workers; see, for example, Tamao Matsui and Toshitake Terai, "A Cross Cultural Study of the Validity of the Expectancy Theory of Work Motivation," *Journal of Applied Psychology*, Vol. 60, No. 2 (April 1975).

[51] J. B. Miner and H. P. Dachler, "Personnel Attitudes and Motivation," *Annual Review of Psychology,* Vol. 24 (1973), 379–402. See also Leon Reinharth and Mahmoud Wahba, "Expectancy Theory as a Predictor of Work Motivation, Effort Expenditure, and Job Performance," *Academy of Management Journal,* Vol. 18, No. 3 (September 1975); and Orlando Behling and Frederick A. Starke, "The Postulates of Expectancy Theory," *Academy of Management Journal,* Vol. 16, No. 3 (September 1973).

[52] See Frederick Starke and Orlando Behling, "A Test of Two Postulates Underlying Expectancy Theory," *Academy of Management Journal,* Vol. 18, No. 4 (December 1975); and William Liddell and Robert Solomon, "A Total and Stochastic Test of the Transitivity Postulate Underlying Expectancy Theory," *Organizational Behavior and Human Performance,* Vol. 19 (1977), 311–24.

[53] Frederick Herzberg, "One More Time: How Do You Motivate Employees?" *Harvard Business Review,* January–February 1968.

Chapter 9

Authority, Control, and Reward Systems

CHAPTER OVERVIEW

In the last chapter, we distinguished between two basic ways for ensuring compliance—for ensuring, in other words, that employees effectively carry out their assigned tasks. In one, compliance results from formal controls, or from extrinsically supplied rewards and punishments. In the other, employees comply because they are intrinsically motivated—because they identify with their jobs or are committed to the organization's goals, for example.

In this chapter, we discuss the first set of techniques, those concerned with *formal, imposed controls and extrinsically supplied rewards.* These include the use of *authority, control systems,* and *reward systems. Intrinsic* techniques for eliciting self-control will be treated in the next chapter.

The outline of this chapter is as follows:

I. Power and Authority in Organizations
   A. Power and Authority Defined
   B. The Sources of Power and Authority
   C. Obedience to Authority: Why People Comply

II. Control Systems
   A. Process of Control
   B. Specific Human Problems of Controls
   C. How Employees Evade Controls
   D. The Effectiveness of "Legal Compliance"

POWER AND AUTHORITY IN ORGANIZATIONS

Power and Authority Defined

Authority may be thought of as the "fuel" of organization, since without a distribution of authority, the organization structure is merely a shell. Authority is the right each position holder has to influence or command thought, opinion, or behavior. It gives managers the right to carry out their tasks by giving orders to their subordinates, and it gives them the right to expect compliance.

The words *authority, power,* and *influence* are interrelated. *Influence* is usually defined as the act of producing an effect—of somehow getting someone or something to take some action. *Power,* on the other hand, is usually viewed as the possession of the *potential* for influencing others, or the *ability* to act or produce some effect. To Weber, "Power is the probability that one actor within a social relationship will be in a position to carry out his own will despite resistance, regardless of the basis on which this probability rests." [1]

Similarly, Etzioni defines power as "an actor's ability to induce or influence another actor to carry out his directives or any other norms he supports." [2] He distinguishes among three types of power, which he calls coercive, remunerative, and normative. Coercive power involves the application (or threat of application) of physical sanctions. Remunerative power is control over incentives and rewards. A person's normative power derives from his esteem or prestige. Thiebault and Kelley say that all types of power derive from one person's dependence on another: "The power of A over B is equal to, and based upon, the dependence of B on A." [3]

A person's power can (but need not) stem from "illegitimate" sources, sources that violate prevailing norms of acceptability. For example, a thief might have power over a victim because of the gun he holds.

Authority, like power, refers to a person's potential for influencing others, but the word *authority* "has implicit in it the notion of legitimacy or ethical sanctification." [4] In line with this, Weber says there are three legitimate bases of authority: charismatic, traditional, and legal. [5] *Charismatic* authority derives from some "extraordinary" quality of the person that makes others wish to do his bidding. *Traditional* authority is based on "piety for what actually, allegedly, or personally has always existed"; the authority of a monarch would be one example. With *legal* authority, submission does not rest upon devotion to charismatic persons, or upon some sacred tradition:

> Rather, submission under legal authority is based upon an *impersonal* bond to the generally defined and functional "duty of office." The official duty—like the corresponding right to exercise authority . . . is fixed by *rationally established* norms, by enactments, decrees, and regulations, in such a manner that the legitimacy of the authority becomes the legality of the general rule, which is purposely thought out, enacted, and announced with formal correctness.[6]

In modern organizations, what Weber calls "legal authority" is probably most widely used for exacting obedience. Each person in the organizational hierarchy is delegated authority to make certain decisions and take certain actions. *Subordinates who are hired and who elect to remain with the organization generally do so with the understanding that they accept this authority as legal*; as Simon points out, "The most striking characteristic of the 'subordinate' role is that it establishes an area of acceptance in behavior within which the subordinate is willing to accept the decisions made for him by his superior." [7] Simon views authority not from the point of view of the authority holder, but from the point of view of the subordinate. He says:

> An individual accepts authority when he sets himself a general rule that permits the communicated decision of another to guide his own choice (i.e. to serve as a premise of that choice) independently of his judgment of the correctness or acceptability of the premise.[8]

In other words, according to Simon, for authority (as he defines it) to be exercised, each subordinate must obey almost mechanically, without particularly examining the merits of the order and carrying it out on its merits. To the extent that a subordinate *does* examine the merits of each order and carry it out on its merits, types of influence other than authority (such as persuasion) must have been used. According to Simon, therefore, authority strictly speaking is exercised only when an order is carried out and the subordinate does not examine its merits (or hardly does so), or when he carries it out even though he thinks it is wrong.

The Sources of Power and Authority

In investigating the sources of power and authority, we will see that two basic factors—dependence, and the acceptance of legal authority that is a natural consequence of the subordinate's role—together help explain the sources of power and authority in organizations.

The bases of social power.[9] French and Raven distinguish among five bases of power that to them "seem especially common and important."

They call these reward power, coercive power, legitimate power, referent power, and expert power.

Reward power is defined as power whose basis is the ability to reward. According to French and Raven, the strength of the reward power one person holds over another increases with the magnitude of the rewards the latter perceives the former can mediate for him. A person has power over another to the extent that he or she can significantly influence the positive rewards (such as money) accruing to the other person and can significantly reduce the "negative" rewards (such as poor working conditions) the other person might otherwise have to endure.

Coercive power is similar to reward power in that it also involves one person's ability to manipulate the attainment by another of positive (or negative) rewards. The coercive power of one person over another stems from the real or imagined expectation on the part of the latter that he will be punished if he fails to conform to the influence attempt. In organizations, coercive power is a familiar ingredient in group pressure. Groups are famous, for example, for keeping "rate busters" in line by coercing them with fears of ostracism or physical violence.

French and Raven's *legitimate power* is similar to Weber's "legitimate authority" (which, remember, may be based on charisma, tradition, or legality) and is characterized by the feeling of "oughtness" on the part of a person. Legitimate power is defined as stemming from internalized values in a person that dictate that another has a legitimate right to influence him and that he has an obligation to accept this influence. The actual source of this legitimate power, and the reason subordinates feel they ought to obey, might be tradition (as in the case of a monarch) or may derive from the office the superior holds. For example, on agreeing to join an organization, its salesmen accept the right of the sales manager to assign them work, since this is a legitimate right of the office of "sales manager" in the organization structure. Similarly, "a judge has a right to levy fines, a foreman should assign work, a priest is justified in prescribing religious beliefs, and it is the management's prerogative to make certain decisions."[10]

The *referent power* one person has over another is similar to Weber's "charismatic authority" (which is based on the "extraordinary" characteristics of the person in power) but goes a step further: Referent power is based on the fact that one person identifies with and is highly attracted to another. A verbalization of such power might be, "I want to be like that person, and therefore I shall behave or believe as he does."

Finally, *expert power* derives from the fact that one person is viewed as an expert in some area and others must therefore depend on him for advice and counsel. Expert power in an organization often stems from a person's position in the communications network and from that person's ability to control access to coveted information. Thus, even an organization's president may find herself deferring to one of her firm's research scientists in those cases where the scientist has the knowledge and expertise to solve some critical problem with one of the firm's products.

Sources of power of lower participants in organizations. David Mechanic points out that it is not unusual for lower participants "to assume and wield considerable power and influence not associated with their formally defined positions." He says that the source of this power is other people's dependence on these "lower participants." [11] In essence, he says, these low-ranking employees have a considerable personal power but no delegated authority, and this power stems not so much from their personal traits as from particular aspects of their location within their organizations.

Mechanic says that power stems from dependence, and that when a person is dependent on another, he or she is potentially subject to the other person's power. Within organizations, he says, one makes others dependent by controlling access to *information, persons,* or *instrumentalities.* Thus, a scientist might have power because others depend on the information she has about an important production process. The president's secretary might have power because she controls access to an important person—the president. An air-base commander may find himself partly at the mercy of the maintenance clerk whose years of experience have given him access to and control over sources of airplane parts.

Several factors contribute to such dependence, and therefore to the power of lower participants. One is their expertise—the knowledge they have for which others must depend on them. Another is the person's effort and interest—his or her willingness to take on a task that others are unwilling to do. Another attribute is attractiveness, charisma, or "personality." The person's location in the organization is also important, as exemplified by the president's secretary. Other "participants" have power that derives from coalitions they have formed—for example, with suppliers, allowing them to control access to critical supplies.

Conclusion. We will assume that there are two basic sources of power and authority in organizations. One stems from dependence. This can result from the power holder's access to people, information, or instrumentalities, or, to use French and Raven's terms, from his ability to reward, coerce, or act as referent or expert to another.

The second source of power and authority might be termed *legality.* It derives from the feeling of a person that another person has a legitimate right to command obedience. Traditional authority (like that of a monarch) is one example of this. In organizations, one familiar example is the acceptance by a subordinate of the authority of a superior, an authority legally sanctioned by the organization and accepted by the subordinate as one of the conditions of continued employment. This is the "legitimate" base of French and Raven's analysis of social power, and it manifests itself in (in Simon's words, quoted earlier) "an area of acceptance and behavior within which the subordinate is willing to accept the decisions made for him by his superior."

Obedience to Authority: Why People Comply

Predictability is an essential ingredient of organizations. For an organization to be able to function with any degree of effectiveness, each position holder must be able to assume that the people he or she directs will comply with orders and carry out their tasks. The president who directs the vice-presidents to increase efficiency, the shipping manager who directs the truckers to make certain deliveries, and the production foreman who directs an employee to tighten a bolt all issue orders on the assumption that these orders will be carried out. To the extent that orders are carried out, tasks can be accomplished in such a way that they contribute in an integrated way to the organization's goals. To the extent that orders are not obeyed, there is no way to ensure that the logic of the organization's departmentation and coordination will function effectively. Having discussed sources of power and authority in organizations, we should now therefore turn to a more detailed discussion of obedience to authority: *why people obey.*

Simon and the zone of acceptance.[12]   Prof. Herbert Simon has developed one of the most complete explanations of authority and obedience in organizations. He says there are two basic ways in which behavior of employees can be influenced: One is to establish *in the employees* the attitudes and habits that will lead them to the "right" decision; the second is to *impose* the necessary decisions on them.

The first approach (getting the person to want to do the task) is accomplished by developing loyalty, commitment, and self-control in the employee —for example, through training and indoctrination. The second approach (imposing the decision on the person) relies, according to Simon, on the exercise of authority. Authority to Simon means "the power to make decisions which govern the actions of another," and, in accepting authority, a subordinate suspends his or her own judgment. Technically, as we saw earlier, authority as defined by Simon is exercised only when one person carries out the orders of another without particularly evaluating the merits of the orders; that is, when subordinates suspend their judgment and simply and mechanically "follow orders." When they do this, authority has been exercised; but when they must be persuaded (or must persuade themselves) to carry out the orders, some other mode of influence, like indoctrination, must be used.

A critical question, then, is, "When and under what conditions will a person suspend his own judgment and acquiesce to authority?" According to Simon, a person will suspend his or her own judgment and mechanically follow orders as long as those orders fall within the person's "zone of acceptance." If the superior attempts to carry authority beyond a certain point (beyond the person's "zone of acceptance"), disobedience will follow, and the person will no longer mechanically do what is "right" from the point of view of the organization:

> Once the system of values which is to govern in an organization has been specified, there is one and only one "best" decision. Yet there is an area of acceptance within which the individual will behave "organizationally." When the organizational demands fall outside this area, personal motives reassert themselves and the organization, to that extent, ceases to exist. When a person is behaving impersonally, then, an organizational scale is substituted for his personal value scale as the criterion of "correctness" in his decisions.[13]

Why do people permit themselves to be influenced by the organization? Why, that is, does a person join an organization and then submit to its authority by following those orders that fall within his or her zone of acceptance? According to Simon, the answer lies in the fact that "individuals will do what is required when their behavior contributes indirectly or directly to their own personal goals." Thus, they will join and remain useful members of an organization (they will have a zone of acceptance within which orders will be carried out) as long as, from their point of view, the inducements (like money) provided by the organization equal or exceed the contributions (like the effort) that must be provided in return.

The "width" of the zone of acceptance will vary from person to person and organization to organization. In a voluntary organization, for example, each person's zone of acceptance might be quite narrow, since the organization controls few important rewards or sanctions. But on a military parade ground, the zone of acceptance of each marcher might be quite wide, and each might be willing to unthinkingly carry out orders that cover his behavior down to the smallest detail.

Simon cites several things that affect the width of a person's zone of acceptance. First is the factor of legality: In joining and remaining with an organization, a person agrees to a greater or lesser extent to "follow orders" and to exhibit "an area of acceptance in behavior within which he will follow orders." Beyond this, the width of a person's zone of acceptance is also affected by the quality and quantity of inducements the organization can provide, as well as by the employee's personality. Size of financial rewards, fear of losing a job, and a "follower" mentality are some other factors.

Let us summarize our discussion of Simon's theory of authority. He says the organization can influence employees either by establishing in them the attitudes and desire to do the job, or by imposing on them its decisions. The former involves the use of *influence* modes like persuasion, suggestion, and building of loyalty to the organization—for example, through careful training and selection. The latter involves exercising authority, and in this case, the employee "holds in abeyance his own critical faculties," doing so as long as the order falls within his "zone of acceptance." The former involves tapping the employee's self-control; the latter can be viewed as imposed control.

Simon points out that these forms of influence are interchangeable. For example, as employees become familiar with their jobs through training, they are usually given more discretion and are not as closely supervised. Furthermore:

> Administrators have increasingly recognized in recent years that authority unless buttressed by other forms of influence is relatively impotent to control the decision in any but a negative way. The elements entering into all but the most routine decisions are so numerous and so complex that it is impossible to control positively more than a few. Unless the subordinate is himself able to supply most of the premises of decision, and to synthesize them adequately, the task of supervision becomes hopelessly burdensome.[14]

Thus, says Simon, reliance on the exercise of authority (in which employees mechanically obey those orders that fall within their zone of acceptance) is of limited usefulness unless it is buttressed by the self-control of the employee. In modern organizations, the tasks are often so complex and the contingencies so widespread that it is simply not feasible to rely entirely on an employee's mechanical compliance or a perpetually present supervisor. Instead, the subordinates themselves have to "supply most of the premises of decision" by exhibiting initiative in evaluating different courses of action and choosing the best one. This is why, according to Simon, effectively staffing the organization is so important, since hiring people who can exercise such self-control can greatly reduce the need to rely on their mechanical compliance with imposed authority.

A study of obedience.   Yet it is obvious that an employee's willingness to "follow orders" and to substitute, in Simon's words, an "organizational scale for his personal value scale as the criteria of 'correctness' in his decisions" is still a major factor in compliance.[15] To what extent do subordinates obey authority—"substitute an organizational scale for their own value scale"—because they view that authority as legitimate, and obeying as part of their job? Stanley Milgram carried out a study that shed some startling light on this question.[16]

Milgram's experiments were originally conducted at Yale in 1962–63, and set out to answer the following question: "In a laboratory situation, if an experimenter tells a subject to act with increasing severity against another person, under what conditions will the subject comply, and under what conditions will he disobey?" The design of his study was as follows:

> Two people come to a psychology laboratory to take part in a study of memory and learning. One of them is designated as a "teacher" and the other a "learner." The experimenter explains that the study is concerned with the effects of punishment on learning. The learner is conducted into a room, seated in a chair, his arms strapped to prevent excessive movement, and an electrode attached to his wrist. He is told that he is to learn a list of words; whenever he makes an error, he will receive electric shocks of increasing intensity. (The "learner" is actually one of the researchers, and no electrical shocks are actually given.)
>
> The real focus of the experiment is the teacher. After watching the "learner" being strapped into place, he is taken into the main experimental room and seated before an impressive shock generator. Its main feature is a horizontal line of 30 switches, ranging from 15 volts to 450 volts, in 15-volt increments. There are also verbal designations which range from "slight shock" to "danger—severe shock." The teacher is told that he is to administer the learning test to the man in the other room. When the learner responds correctly, the teacher moves on to the next item; when the other man gives an incorrect answer, the teacher is to give him an electric shock. He is to start at the lowest level (15 volts) and to increase the level each time the man makes an error, going to 30 volts, 45 volts, and so on.
>
> The "teacher" is a genuinely naive subject who has come to the laboratory to participate in the experiment. The learner, or victim, actually re-

ceives no shock at all. The point of the experiment is to see how far a person will proceed in a concrete and measurable situation in which he is ordered to inflict increasing pain on a protesting victim. At what point will the subject refuse to obey the experimenter?

Conflict arises when the man receiving the shock begins to indicate that he is experiencing discomfort. At 75 volts, the "learner" grunts. At 120 volts he complains verbally; at 150 he demands to be released from the experiment. His protests continue as the shocks escalate, growing increasingly vehement and emotional. At 285 volts his response can only be described as an agonized scream.

Observers of the experiment agree that its gripping quality is somewhat obscured in print; for the subject (the "teacher") the situation is not a game, and conflict is intense and obvious. On the one hand, the manifest suffering of the learner presses him to quit. On the other, the experimenter, a legimate authority to whom the subject feels some commitment, enjoins him to continue. Each time the subject hesitates to administer shock, the experimenter orders him to continue. To extricate himself from the situation, the subject must make a clear break with authority. The aim of this investigation was to find when and how people would defy authority in the face of a clear moral imperative.

There are, of course, enormous differences between carrying out the orders of a commanding officer during times of war and carrying out the orders of an experimenter. Yet the essence of certain relationships remains, for one may ask in a general way: How does a man behave when he is told by a legitimate authority to act against a third individual? If anything, we may expect the experimenter's power to be considerably less than that of the general, since he has no power to enforce his imperatives, and participation in a psychological experiment scarcely evokes the sense of urgency and dedication engendered by participation in war.[17]

Findings, interpretations, implications. According to Milgram, the results of his study "are both surprising and dismaying." Although many of his subject "teachers" experienced stress and protested to the experimenter, a substantial portion of them—almost two-thirds—fell into the category of obedient subjects, continuing to the last shock on the generator. These subjects, remember, were not some "sadistic fringe of society," but were "ordinary people drawn from working, managerial, and professional classes." Milgram found that "the ordinary person who shocked the victim did so out of a sense of obligation—a conception of his duties as a subject— and not from any peculiarly aggressive tendencies."

What keeps the subject obeying the experimenter?

First, there is a set of "binding factors" that lock the subject into the situation. They include such factors as politeness on his part, his desire to uphold his initial promise of aid to the experimenter, and the awkwardness of withdrawal. Second, a number of adjustments in the subject's thinking occur that undermine his resolve to break with the authority. The adjustments helped the subject maintain his relationship with the experimenter, while at the same time reducing the strain brought about by the experimental conflict. They are typical of thinking that comes about in obedient persons when they are instructed by authority to act against helpless individuals.[18]

Milgram's findings paint a vivid picture of the adjustments through which obedience to legitimate authority takes place. The subjects, he found, became so absorbed in the "narrow technical aspects" of the task that they lost sight of its broader consequences. (One is reminded of the Watergate affair, which was to follow these studies by ten years.)[19] Furthermore, the obedient subject begins to see himself as not responsible for his own actions, as he "divests himself of responsibility by attributing all initiative to the experimenter, a legitimate authority." Obedient subjects saw themselves not as people acting in a morally accountable way, but as the agents of external authority: When asked after the experiment why they had gone on, the typical reply was, "I wouldn't have done it by myself. I was just doing what I was told." And, Milgram believes, this was not just a "thin alibi concocted for the occasion":

> Rather, it is a fundamental mode of thinking for a great many people once they are locked into a subordinate position in a structure of authority. The disappearance of a sense of responsibility is the far-reaching consequence of submission to authority.[20]

It further appeared that people working under authority did not lose their "moral sense," but instead shifted it to a consideration of how well they were living up to the expectations that *the authority* had for them. Most subjects also saw their behavior in a larger context—the pursuit of scientific truth. Some devalued the victim as a consequence of acting against him, making comments like, "He was so stupid and stubborn he deserved to get shocked."

What Milgram found, therefore, was that people were much more willing than one might have imagined to "just follow orders" and to substitute, in Simon's terms, an organizational scale for their personal value scale. Even in this laboratory setting, where the available rewards and sanctions were few, each subject's zone of acceptance—the zone in which orders were mechanically complied with because they emanated from a legitimate authority—was quite wide. People obeyed simply because they had elected to join the organization (the experiment) and viewed following legitimate orders as part of their jobs. And this phenomenon of obedience, says Milgram, may be largely a result of the process of division of work:

> There was a time, perhaps, when men were able to give a fully human response to any situation because they were fully absorbed in it as human beings. But as soon as there was a division of labor among men, things changed. Beyond a certain point, the breaking up of society into people carrying out narrow and very special jobs takes away from the human quality of work and life. A person does not get to see the whole situation but only a small part of it, and is thus unable to act without some kind of overall direction. He yields to authority but in doing so is alienated from his own actions.[21]

Conclusion. There are many ways an organization can influence its members' behavior. It can build organizational loyalty through various indoctrination techniques and use training, selection, persuasion, and incentives to encourage initiative and self-control. An organization can also impose its authority on its members, by manipulating the dependence of the members on the organization, or by relying on the members' obedience to legitimate authority. In practice, these modes of influence are interchangeable, in that authority, for example, is not relied on to the exclusion of persuasion. Yet it appears that the range of orders with which employees will mechanically comply may be wider than originally thought, and that this wide "zone of acceptance" is the most striking characteristic of the "subordinate" role in organizations.

CONTROL SYSTEMS

Process of Control

Every organization has to ensure that its workers are performing as expected, and *control* is the task of ensuring that activities are providing the desired results. All control systems collect, store, and transmit information on profits, sales, or some other factor. And all control systems are aimed at influencing behavior, which is one reason why "controlling someone" often has negative overtones. Control also requires that targets, standards, or goals be set, and this is why the word *planning* is always used with the word *control*.

Control systems are similar to rules (and close supervision) in that they are imposed on employees for the purpose of ensuring compliance. However, whereas rules can be thought of as simply standards of acceptable behavior, control systems include not only standards but also means (such as budget reports) for *monitoring* compliance with those standards as well as means for taking *corrective action*.

Behavioral consequences of control systems. Researchers have identified a variety of human problems with control systems; these problems have been summarized by Elmer Burack in Figure 9-1.[22] He says that managers often attempt to impose tighter controls in order to improve efficiency of their units, and that symptoms of this include more routine jobs and higher performance standards. However, although these tighter controls may bring about improved performance in the short run, they often result in low morale and high absenteeism. Performance then begins deteriorating. Then, as performance declines, management often reacts with new, tighter controls, which in turn lead to increased alienation on the part of employees, a further deterioration of performance, and attempts by employees to "beat the system." With this in mind, let us discuss some specific human problems of controls.

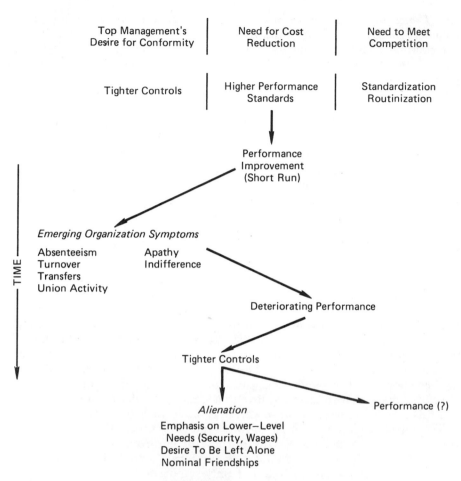

FIGURE 9-1. Behavioral Consequences of Control Systems

Source: Elmer H. Burack, *Organizational Analysis Theory and Applications* (New York: The Dryden Press, Holt, Rinehart and Winston, 1975), p. 159. Copyright © 1975. Reprinted by permission.

Specific Human Problems of Controls

Budgets put supervisors under pressure. In one study, which focused on the reactions of foremen to budgetary controls, Argyris found that budgets were viewed as "pressure devices." He found that budgets were used to evaluate foremen and that having to meet the concrete, written budget standards put the foremen under considerable pressure. They came to view the budgets as "prods" by top management, and they in turn used their budgets to prod their own subordinates. As a result of this pressure, employees formed cohesive antimanagement groups, and the supervisors reacted by making narrow, shortsighted decisions.[23]

Controls result in narrow viewpoints. Managers, in their desire to meet standards, often concentrate on their own assignments and disregard broader organizational goals. For example, one manager refused to make a purchase that would have resulted in a rate of return of 25 percent, because his division was already earning 35 percent. However, the company as a whole was earning only 10 percent, so the purchase would have been good for the company as a whole.[24]

Short run factors are over emphasized. The pressures caused by formal controls also can result in an overemphasis on short-run factors. In one instance, a division manager sold some machinery for scrap in order to lower his investment (and thereby raise his rate of return). Later, the machinery was again needed, and he had to purchase all new equipment.[25] Similarly "long-term" factors like reputation and good will are sometimes disregarded by managers who focus on short-run factors like profits and costs.

Easily measured factors are over emphasized. Some control systems also encourage an over emphasis on easily measured, quantifiable factors. For example, easily measured factors like profits are often over emphasized at the expense of hard to measure factors like reputation and good will. As another example, many schools evaluate their success in terms of how many students are taught, rather than in terms of how well or how much those students are learning.

Some controls result in "politicking." Formal controls like budgets also often result in "politicking" on the part of managers. In developing their budgets, for example, managers may try to withhold or distort important information so that competing managers can't adequately evaluate each others' budget requests. Another tactic involves overstating or "padding" budget needs. Some managers quickly learn, for example, that no matter how honest their budget estimates are, top management typically cuts all budget requests by some arbitrary amount. As a result, even honest managers soon learn that to get their fair share they have to pad their budget estimate.

How Employees Evade Controls

Managers and employees have found many ingenious ways through which to evade controls. In one study departmental efficiency ratings were raised by transferring personnel "on paper" from departments with low efficiencies to those with high ratings. Efficiency ratings then appeared much more consistent from department to department than they actually were. The opposite type of falsification also occurs: managers have knowingly falsified production records in order not to exceed the quota by too great an amount.[26] The list of ways in which employees try to "get around" controls could be expanded. Edward Lawler and John Rhode say, however, that there are three basic ways in which employees resist and evade control systems: they call these "rigid bureaucratic behavior," "strategic behavior," and "invalid data reporting." [27]

"Rigid bureaucratic behavior."   This refers to the tendency of people to try to look good in terms of the control standards. They concentrate their efforts where results are measured, often disregarding the organization's more important goals. The problem stems mostly from incomplete standards. For example, in one state employment agency, employees found that they were measured on the number of job seekers they *interviewed* rather than on the number they placed in jobs. The number of interviews soared but little attention was focused on adequately counseling applicants. When it became apparent what was happening, several new standards (such as the ratio of placements to interviews) were devised. These were aimed at providing a more complete—and acceptable—set of standards for the counselors.[28]

"Strategic behavior."   "Strategic behavior" refers to the tendency of people to provide information in such a way that they look good for a certain time period. As an example, many government agencies assign budgets to departments with the stipulation that any funds not spent by the end of the year be returned. What often happens is that at the end of the year, employees rush to spend all their available funds—often for unnecessary "frills." They look good (they've spent their yearly allocation) but their expenditures are often frivolous. However, you do not have to be in a government agency to incur this problem. It can happen whenever a project you assign must be completed within a certain time period.

Invalid data reporting.   Perhaps the easiest way to evade control systems is to simply report back erroneous, invalid data. In one company, for example, salesmens' activity was "controlled" by requiring them to send in reports listing clients contacted. Management never screened these lists, however, and the salesmen evaded control by listing clients that actually hadn't been seen yet.

The Effectiveness of "Legal Compliance"

Legal compliance is at one extreme of Katz and Kahn's continuum and represents a situation in which organization members obey orders, rules, or control standards because they are perceived as stemming from legitimate sources of authority and because they are enforced by legal sanctions.[29] As you may recall, Katz and Kahn suggest that legal compliance can be used to reduce absenteeism and to bring about acceptable levels of individual performance, particularly where the activity is routine.

Two researchers carried out a study to test this hypothesis.[30] They say that a crucial factor in the success of a strategy to control attendance through legal compliance is recognition and acceptance of the legitimacy of the policy and the policy-making process by the organizational members, and that once the worker knows and accepts the rules of the system, then attendance should be fairly predictable. However, as we have seen, such controls often have unanticipated consequences. The question, therefore, is this: What is the impact of an undeniably legal control system on absenteeism and on performance and satisfaction?

Subjects in this study were 297 undergraduates who had enrolled in an intermediate accounting course at Purdue University. Each student was provided a course syllabus indicating that class attendance was expected, but the specific aspects of the attendance policy were left deliberately vague. In the "compulsory attendance" condition, the instructors announced to one of their two classes that the university regulations stated that attendance was compulsory and that the instructor was required to enforce the policy; consequently, attendance would be taken and included in the computation of the final grade for the course. In the second, "noncompulsory attendance" condition, each instructor acknowledged to his other class the existence of an attendance policy established by the university. These students, however, were informed that the university delegated considerable latitude to instructors to design and enforce an operational attendance policy, that it was the instructor's policy to treat attendance as a voluntary matter, and that it would not be a factor in the determination of the final grade in the course.[31]

The researchers found that absenteeism was substantially reduced by utilizing the compulsory, "legal compliance" control strategy. Furthermore, this strategy not only lowered absenteeism but also increased performance of the accounting students, and it did not result in reduced satisfaction with the instructor or the course. The researchers conclude:

> Since a legalistic control strategy is relatively easy to administer and offers lower initial cost to managers, it may be the most effective control strategy in many organizational settings. It is an empirical question whether similar (or superior) results can be accomplished with the other motivational patterns suggested by Katz and Kahn.[32]

REWARD SYSTEMS

Rewards are another "extrinsic" method for eliciting compliance. Prof. Edward Lawler says that organizations distribute many rewards to their members every day, including pay, promotion, fringe benefits, and status symbols.[33] Such rewards, say Katz and Kahn, can be effective for attracting employees to the organization, for ensuring acceptable quantitative and qualitative performance, and, on rare occasions, for eliciting innovative, creative behavior.

Although there are (as Lawler points out) many types of extrinsic reward systems, pay is perhaps the most important, flexible, and visible,[34] and we therefore stress financial rewards (particularly incentives) in this chapter. However, keep in mind that all or most of the factors that contribute to the effectiveness of *financial* reward systems (factors such as equity and tying pay to performance) are applicable to other types of rewards as well.[35]

Money and Motivation: Background

The use of financial incentives—financial rewards paid to workers whose production exceeds some predetermined standard—was popularized by Frederick Taylor in the late 1800s. As a supervisory employee of the Midvale Steel Company, he had become increasingly concerned with what he called "systematic soldiering," the tendency of employees to work at the slowest pace possible and produce at the bare minimum acceptable levels. What especially intrigued him was the fact that some of these same workers still had the energy to run home and work on their cabins, even after a hard twelve-hour day. Taylor knew that if he could find some way to harness this energy during the workday, huge productivity gains would be possible.

At this time, primitive piecework systems were already in effect. Workers were paid a piece rate (based on informal performance standards) for each piece they produced, although they knew that if their earnings became excessive, the rate would be cut. As a result, most workers produced just enough to earn a decent wage, but little enough so that their piece rate would not be reduced. One of Taylor's great insights was in seeing that what was needed was a standardized, acceptable view of a fair day's wage. And he saw that a fair day's work should depend not on the vague estimates of foremen, but on a careful, formal, scientific process of inspection and observation. It was this need to *scientifically* evaluate each job that led to the scientific-management approach.

Taylor, working in a culture that emphasized Puritan values and the economic rationality of man, proposed that a system of financial incentives be used in order to deal with the question of how to ensure employee compliance, and scientific management was therefore based on the assumption that each worker's main goal was to maximize his economic gains. Later (as we discussed in Chapters 2 and 3), in the 1920s, the human-relations movement emerged. This resulted in a new focus on worker's social needs, and for a time, organization theorists became preoccupied with the notion of ensuring compliance by satisfying employees' "higher-order" needs. Because of this, it is sometimes easy to forget that money, particularly when used as an incentive, has been and is a primary means for motivating employees. As two writers put it:

> Overall, it appears that the charge leveled by human relationists of 50 years ago—that managers overemphasized the importance of money as a motivator—is incorrect today. It appears that managers fail to recognize the full potential of money, properly used, as a way of improving individual employee performance.[36]

Piecework is the oldest type of individual incentive plan, and the most commonly used. Earnings are tied directly to what the worker produces by paying him or her a "piece rate" for each unit produced. Thus, if Smith gets 20¢ apiece for stamping out door jambs, he would make $20 for stamping out 100 a day, and $40 a day for stamping out 200.

Another well-known plan was developed in 1937 by union representative Joseph Scanlon. The Scanlon Plan has two basic features. First, financial incentives aimed at cutting costs (and thereby increasing efficiency) are installed. Second, a network of departmental and plant screening committees are established to evaluate employee and management cost-cutting suggestions. The plan is essentially a suggestion system, and assumes that efficiency requires companywide (or plantwide) cooperation. Usually, all (or virtually all) employees in the plant participate in the plan. Workers, supervisors, and managers make cost-cutting suggestions, which are screened and evaluated by the various screening committees. If a suggestion is implemented and successful, all employees typically share in 75 percent of the savings.

The Scanlon Plan has been fairly successful. Employees make many suggestions, they accept the need for technological changes, and a work climate "hostile to loafing" results. It tends to encourage a sense of partnership and sharing among workers, less overtime, and employee insistence on efficient management.[37] In one recent study, labor costs were cut by about 10 percent and grievances were cut in half after implementation of the Scanlon Plan.[38] However, the plan is generally more successful where there is strong management commitment to it, and where the firm is smaller— say, under 1,000 participants.[39]

Why Incentive Systems Fail

Research findings reveal that although incentive plans can be effective, they are no panacea and in fact often fail.[40] There are a number of reasons why such plans fail, but the main one seems to be that for motivation to take place, the worker must believe that effort on his or her part will lead to rewards, and that the reward must be valuable to the person. In most cases where incentive plans fail, it is because one (or both) of these conditions are not met.

Several specific problems seem to contribute to such failures, but *unfair standards* appear to be the predominant factor. In addition, one of the most persistent problems undermining incentive plans is the belief on the part of employees that standards will be raised if they are met or exceeded.

Peer pressure and *group restrictions* also undermine incentive systems. It appears that if the group views the plan as fair, it can keep "loafers" in line and maintain high production, but that the opposite is also true.[41] If for any reason the group views the plan as not in its best interest, it will— through education, ostracism, or punishment—see that the production levels of group members are held to a minimum.

A number of other problems, some obvious and some not so obvious, can result in the failure of incentive plans. Some plans, for example, fail because employees do not understand them. Perhaps details of the plans are not communicated to the employees, or the communications are simply not understandable. In any case, it is apparent that unless the employees understand how their effort and performance lead to rewards, it is doubtful that the incentive plan will motivate them. Similarly, for the plan to succeed, the employees must see that they have the ability to successfully perform the task; this implies that the necessary structure, tools, training, and so on must be available. Other incentive plans have failed because they created inequitable wage structures within the organization. In one such failure, for example, production workers were placed on an incentive system under which (it turned out) they earned more than higher-skilled workers who were not under the plan. Still other plans have resulted in intergroup conflicts over who has "tight" standards and who has "loose" ones.[42] Some have been unsuccessful because of inadequate or inequitable performance-appraisal systems.

Effects of Extrinsic on Intrinsic Rewards

Some writers have concluded that while incentive plans are generally effective for moderately routine jobs, jobs that are *very* repetitive, boring, and disliked are "apparently much less susceptible to monetary incentives."[43] This seems to suggest that incentive plans cannot by themselves compensate for a very dissatisfying job. Furthermore, these writers have raised the question of whether "highly challenging and intrinsically rewarding" jobs are amenable to incentives: "Are incentives in this situation the cause of mercenary feelings which *detract* from the main source of reinforcement—the job itself—and ultimately lower job effectiveness? Or do they spur the employees on to greater heights?" Since 1966, a good deal of research has gone into studying this question, and, specifically, the question of what effect (if any) extrinsic rewards have on intrinsic rewards. It would be useful to discuss this evidence before turning to our discussion of intrinsic rewards in Chapter 10.

Findings. Until recently, most theorists assumed that the effects of intrinsic and extrinsic reinforcement were additive, and that a worker would be more motivated to complete a task that combined both kinds of rewards than a task where only one kind of reward was available.[44] Such a theory has many practical implications. For one thing, it suggests that putting people like engineers and scientists, who have more challenging (and intrinsically motivating) jobs, on an incentive pay plan should further increase their motivation. Yet a researcher has found that with such tasks, an additional, external reward had no effect on subjects' attitudes.[45] And as a practical matter, individual incentive plans are rarely used for professionals like engineers. A second implication is that installing an incentive plan on a job that is unusually boring or disliked should increase performance, and yet this is not usually the case.[46] Conversely, implementing job-enrichment programs in order to make jobs more challenging has been ineffective where there is extreme dissatisfaction with pay.

In a recent series of studies, Deci and his associates obtained evidence they say shows that a person's intrinsic motivation to perform an activity decreases when he or she receives contingent monetary payment for performing an interesting task.[47] Deci says that financial rewards made contingent on task performance *can reduce the intrinsic motivation to do that task,* and that contingent payment plans are therefore not compatible with "participative management systems" like the ones we discuss in the next chapter that are aimed at developing self-control and organizational commitment.

Basically, Deci's theory assumes that a person is intrinsically motivated when his task is such that he is made to feel competent and self-determining. He says that extrinsic rewards can reduce intrinsic motivation by giving the person the impression that he or she is no longer exerting as much control over rewards (since extrinsic rewards are now being imposed), and by decreasing the person's feeling of competence. Deci's theory has elicited a great deal of interest, and has been both supported and refuted in various studies.[48] On the whole, the findings suggest that extrinsic rewards do seem to detract from intrinsic motivation. Therefore, considerable caution should be used before installing incentive pay plans on jobs that are inherently challenging and intrinsically motivating.

Rewards: Summary and Applications

Incentive rewards can be useful for ensuring employee compliance in terms of meeting or exceeding standards of performance. This appears to be particularly so for "average" jobs that are neither exceptionally boring and disliked or exceptionally challenging and intrinsically motivating. It appears that incentive plans cannot compensate for jobs that are extremely disliked, and that on jobs that are extremely challenging, they may actually diminish rather than increase motivation.

On the whole, the findings are compatible with the predictions made by Katz and Kahn, who proposed that although individual rewards can be effective in motivating people to meet and exceed quantitative or qualitative standards of performance, they are not as useful for eliciting contributions that go beyond the formal requirements of the person's role. It therefore appears that for eliciting innovative and creative behavior some other motivational schemes are required, schemes that revolve around intrinsic rewards and self-control. We turn to these in the next chapter.

SUMMARY

In this chapter, we discussed techniques that are aimed at ensuring compliance through the use of imposed, extrinsic means like authority, formal rules, formal controls, and rewards. We discussed several views of authority and said that the concept of "legal authority" as applied to organizations implies that subordinates who are hired and elect to remain with the organization generally do so with the understanding that they accept this authority as legal; following orders (at least, up to a point) is thus "part of their jobs." Several things determine the width of an employee's "zone of acceptance" (the zone in which orders are followed automatically); these include inducements like wages and, most important, the factor of "legality." In particular, in joining and remaining with an organization, a person agrees (to a greater or lesser extent) to "follow orders" and to exhibit, in Simon's words, "an area of acceptance in behavior within which he will follow orders." Milgram's study suggests that a person's willingness to follow orders and to substitute an "organizational scale for his personal value scale as a criteria of 'correctness' in his decisions" may be greater than originally thought, and in fact a very major element in compliance.

Formal control systems (budgets and the like) are another means for imposing control. Such systems can be dysfunctional, and we discussed some specific human problems with controls. The results of at least one study suggest that legal-compliance techniques like rules can be effective, at least for ensuring attendance and minimally dependable behavior.

Rewards are another extrinsic technique for ensuring compliance. They are useful not only for attracting personnel but for obtaining dependable behavior and (on occasion) innovative behavior as well.

Research findings, we have seen, suggest that incentive rewards can be effective in motivating people to meet and exceed quantitative or qualitative standards, and some incentive plans, for some employees, may even contribute to congruence of the organization's and individuals' goals, and thus to commitment. Yet extrinsic rewards may actually detract from intrinsic motivation, and in general, eliciting creative and innovative behavior requires other motivational schemes, which depend on intrinsic motivation and self-control.

DISCUSSION QUESTIONS

1. Compare and contrast Weber's concept of authority with that of Simon and Barnard.

2. What does Simon mean by "zone of acceptance"? What role does it play in determining whether or not an employee obeys orders?

3. According to Simon, one of the reasons most employees willingly follow orders is simply because, as subordinates, they have agreed to view superior's authority as legitimate—at least up to a point. Does this actually seem to be the case in organizations? What did you base your decision on?

4. "Employees have devised many ingenious ways of evading control systems, and these problems can be especially hard to deal with where jobs require originality and judgment." Discuss whether you agree or disagree with this statement and why.

FOOTNOTES

1 Quotes in Sanford Dornbusch and W. Richard Scott, *Evaluation and the Exercise of Authority* (San Francisco: Jossey Bass, 1975), p. 31.

2 Amitai Etzioni, *Complex Organizations* (New York: Free Press, 1961), pp. 3–22.

3 Dornbusch and Scott, *Evaluation and the Exercise of Authority*, p. 31.

4 Robert Peabody, "Perceptions of Organizational Authority: A Comparative Analysis," *Administrative Science Quarterly*, Vol. 6, No. 4 (1962), 514.

5 Max Weber, *Essays in Sociology* (New York: Oxford University Press, 1946), pp. 294–301.

6 Max Weber, *Essays in Sociology*, p. 299.

7 Herbert Simon, *Administrative Behavior* (New York: Free Press, 1976), p. 133.

8 Herbert Simon, "Authority, Power, and Influence," in *Studies in Managerial Process and Organizational Behavior*, eds. John Turner, Alan Filley, and Robert J. House (Glenview: Scott-Foresman, 1972), pp. 59–64.

9 John R. P. French, Jr., and Bertram Raven, *Studies in Social Power* (Ann Arbor: Institute for Social Research, 1959); reprinted in Henry Tosi and W. Clay Hamner, *Organizational Behavior and Management* (Chicago: St. Clair Press, 1977), pp. 442–56.

10 *Ibid.*, p. 450.

11 David Mechanic, "The Sources of Power of Lower Participants in Complex Organizations," *Administrative Science Quarterly*, Vol. 7, No. 3 (December 1962), 349–64; reprinted in Robert Doktor and Michael Moses, *Managerial Insights* (Englewood Cliffs, N.J.: Prentice-Hall, 1973), pp. 357–67. See also Peabody, "Perceptions of Organizational Authority," p. 512.

12 Herbert A. Simon, *Administrative Behavior* (New York: Free Press, 1976).

13 Simon, *Administrative Behavior*, p. 204.

14 *Ibid.*, p. 227.

15 *Ibid.*, p. 204.

16 Stanley Milgram, *Obedience to Authority: An Experimental View* (New York: Harper & Row, 1974), pp. 1–12. Copyright © 1974 by Stanley Milgram. Reprinted by permission of Harper & Row, Publishers, Inc. Reprinted in Jerome E. Schnee, E. Kirby Warren, and Harold Lazarus, *The Progress of Management* (Englewood Cliffs, N.J.: Prentice-Hall, 1977), pp. 427–36.

17 *Ibid.*, p. 429–30.

18 *Ibid.*, p. 432.

19 From the *Miami Herald*, Wednesday, October 5, 1977:

John Ehrlichman, 52, in a prison camp in Sanford, Ariz., said he got into trouble because "I had an exaggerated sense of my obligation to do as I was bidden without exercising my independent judgment." He told of how he began to rationalize that "things will get better" and eventually saw himself in the White House "as the better of angels." "Looking back, there were all kinds of red flags," he said, "and had I been wiser, I certainly would have checked out when I realized I was in a moral dilemma." But instead, "I abdicated my moral judgments and turned them over to someone else." "I am guilty in law and in fact and in these months in prison I've come to accept this reality."

20 Milgram, *Obedience to Authority*, p. 433.

21 *Ibid.*, pp. 435–36.

22 Elmer H. Burack, *Organization Analysis: Theory and Applications* (Hinsdale, Ill.: The Dryden Press, 1975), pp. 158–60.

23 Chris Argyris, "Human Problems With Budgets," *Harvard Business Review*, Vol. 31, No. 1 (1953), 97–110.

24 Bruce Henderson and John Dearden, "New System for Divisional Control," *Harvard Business Review*, Vol. 44, No. 5 (September–October 1966), 149.

25 *Ibid.*, p. 150.

26 Franch Jasinski, "Use and Misuse of Efficiency Controls," *Harvard Business Review*, Vol. 34, No. 4 (July–August 1956), 105–12; Joseph Berliner, *Factory and Manager in the USSR* (Cambridge: Harvard University Press, 1957).

27 Edward Lawler III and John Grant Rhode, *Information and Control in Organizations* (Pacific Palisades: Goodyear, 1976).

28 P. M. Blau, *The Dynamics of Bureaucracy* (Chicago: University of Chicago Press, 1955), in Lawler and Rhode, *Information and Control in Organizations*, pp. 83–84. V. F. Ridgway, "Dysfunctional Consequences of Performance Measurements," *Administrative Science Quarterly*, Vol. 1, No. 2 (September 1956), 240–47; reprinted in John Turner, Alan Filley, and Robert House, *Studies in Managerial Process and Organizational Behavior* (Glenview: Scott Foresman, 1972), pp. 190–91.

29 See John Baum and Stewart Youngblood, "Impact of an Organizational Control Policy on Absenteeism, Performance, and Satisfaction," *Journal of Applied Psychology*, Vol. 60, No. 6 (1975), 688–94. See also John Baum, "Effectiveness of an Attendance Control Policy in Reducing Chronic Absenteeism," *Personnel Psychology*, Vol. 31, No. 1 (Spring 1978).

30 Baum and Youngblood, "Impact of an Organizational Control Policy on Absenteeism, Performance, and Satisfaction."

31 *Ibid.*, p. 690.

32 *Ibid.*, p. 693.

33 Edward E. Lawler III, "Reward Systems," in J. Richard Hackman and J. Lloyd Suttle, *Improving Life at Work* (Santa Monica, Calif.: Goodyear, 1977), pp. 163–226.

34 *Ibid.*, p. 174.

35 *Ibid.*, p. 226.

36 Orlando Behling and Chester Schreisheim, *Organizational Behavior* (Boston: Allyn & Bacon, 1976), p. 250; see also Gary Yukl, Gary Latham, and Elliot Pursell, "The Effectiveness of Performance Incentives under Continuous and Variable Ratio Schedules of Reinforcement," *Personnel Psychology*, Vol. 29, No. 2 (Summer 1976).

37 David Belcher, *Compensation Management* (Englewood Cliffs, N.J.: Prentice-Hall, 1974), pp. 329–31. Note that one objective of such "profit-sharing" plans is to equate organizational and individual goals; thus, they aim (if not too successfully) at developing self-control.

38 George Sherman, "The Scanlon Concept: Its Capabilities for Productivity Improvement," *Personnel Administrator*, July 1976.

39 J. D. Dunn and Frank Rachel, *Wage and Salary Administration* (New York: McGraw-Hill, 1972), p. 253; Behling and Schreisheim, *Organizational Behavior*, pp. 247–48; and Belcher, *Compensation Management*, pp. 330–32.

40 See, for example, Behling and Schreisheim, *Organizational Behavior*, pp. 247–48.

41 Leonard Sayles, "The Impact of Incentives on Intergroup Work Relations—a Management and Union Problem," *Personnel*, May 1967, pp. 483–90; W. Clay Hamner, "How to Ruin Motivation with Pay," *Compensation Review*, Third Quarter, 1975. See also Lawler, "Reward Systems."

42 Hamner, "How to Ruin Motivation with Pay."

43 Robert Opsahl and Marvin Dunnette, "The Role of Financial Compensation in Industrial Motivation," *Psychological Bulletin*, Vol. 66, No. 2 (1966), 94–118; reprinted in W. E. Scott, Jr., and L. L. Cummings, *Readings in Organizational Behavior and Human Performance* (Homewood, Ill.: Richard D. Irwin, 1973), pp. 350–70.

44 Hamner, "How to Ruin Motivation with Pay."

45 I. W. Andrews, "Wage Inequity and Job Performance: An Experimental Study," *Journal of Applied Psychology*, Vol. 51 (1967), 39–45.

46 See, for example, Opsahl and Dunnette, "The Role of Financial Compensation."

47 Hamner, "How to Ruin Motivation with Pay"; E. L. Deci, "The Effects of Externally Mediated Rewards on Intrinsic Motivation," *Journal of Personality and Social*

Psychology, Vol. 18 (1971), 105–15; E. L. Deci, "The Effects of Contingent and Noncontingent Rewards and Controls on Intrinsic Motivation," *Organizational Behavior and Human Performance,* Vol. 8 (1972), 217–29; E. L. Deci, "Intrinsic Motivation, Extrinsic Reinforcement, and Inequity," *Journal of Personality and Social Psychology,* Vol. 22 (1972), 113–20; E. L. Deci, "Notes on the Theory and Metatheory of Intrinsic Motivation," *Organizational Behavior and Human Performance,* Vol. 15 (1976), 130–45; E. L. Deci, W. Cascio, and J. Krussell, "Cognitive Evaluation Theory and Some Comments on the Calder and Stalk Critique," *Journal of Personality and Social Psychology,* Vol. 31 (1975), 81–85.

[48] See Robert D. Pritchard, Kathleen Campbell, and Donald Campbell, "Effects of Extrinsic Financial Rewards on Intrinsic Motivation," *Journal of Applied Psychology,* Vol. 62, No. 1 (1977), 9–15. See also J. Bobby Calder and Barry Staw, "The Interaction of Intrinsic and Extrinsic Motivation: Some Methodological Notes," *Journal of Personality and Social Psychology,* Vol. 31 (1975), 599–605; W. E. Scott, Jr., "The Effects of Extrinsic Rewards on 'Intrinsic Motivation': a Critique," *Organizational Behavior and Human Performance,* Vol. 15, No. 1 (February 1976); Edward Deci, "Notes on the Theory and Metatheory of Intrinsic Motivation"; Craig Pinder, "Additivity versus Nonadditivity of Intrinsic and Extrinsic Incentives: Implications for Work Motivation, Performance, and Attitudes," *Journal of Applied Psychology,* Vol. 61, No. 6 (December 1976), 693ff.; James Farr, "Task Characteristics, Reward Contingency, and Intrinsic Motivation," *Organizational Behavior and Human Performance,* Vol. 16, No. 2 (August 1976), 296–307; W. Hamner and L. Foster, "Are Intrinsic and Extrinsic Rewards Additive? A Test of Deci's Cognitive Evaluation Theory of Task Motivation," *Organizational Behavior and Human Performance,* Vol. 14, No. 3 (December 1975).

Chapter 10

Self-Control

and Intrinsic Rewards

CHAPTER OVERVIEW

This chapter is a continuation of our discussion of motivation and compliance in organizations. Schemes that depend on imposed controls and extrinsic rewards (discussed in the last chapter) seem sufficient for attracting employees or ensuring minimally acceptable performance levels. However, it appears that innovative, creative behavior requires a different approach—specifically, one aimed at developing intrinsic motivation, commitment, and self-control. So in this chapter, we discuss some techniques for eliciting such self-control—techniques including job enrichment, participation, and management by objectives. According to Katz and Kahn, obtaining compliance through such techniques involves a fundamentally different approach from obtaining it through imposed controls or rewards, since here,

> . . . motivation is so internalized that performance is autonomous. The supervisor does not have to be present to wave a stick or offer candy. The activities carry their own rewards; they are so much a pattern of motive satisfaction that they need no additional incentives.[1]

The outline of this chapter is as follows:

I. Intrinsic Motivation in Organization Theory
   A. Introduction
   B. The Classicists
   C. Herbert Simon

INTRINSIC MOTIVATION
IN ORGANIZATION THEORY

Introduction

The techniques we discuss in this chapter all aim at eliciting intrinsic motivation, motivation that comes from "within" the person and derives from his ability to satisfy higher-order needs for competence, self-determination, and self-actualization.[2]

The superiority of intrinsic motivation—of getting an employee to genuinely *want* to do his or her job—has, of course, been known for ages; John Stuart Mill, for example, in commenting on "close supervision" over 100 years ago, adds, "Nor are the greatest outward precautions comparable in efficacy to the monitor within." [3] However, even though the superiority of intrinsic motivation was understood, its use until the 1930s was rather limited; instead, managers and organization theorists generally emphasized the use of punishment, close supervision, and rewards. Several factors probably accounted for this, including the assumption on the part of managers that workers disliked work and were lazy (McGregor's "Theory X" argument), the fact that jobs tended to be of the routine variety and therefore lent themselves to legal-compliance techniques, and, more recently, the assumption that man as an economic, rational entity sought simply to maximize his income, and so could be motivated through sole reliance on external rewards (Taylor's incentive-pay-plan argument). We can get a useful perspective on the importance of *intrinsic* motivation in organization theory by briefly reviewing what some organization theorists had to say about it.

The Classicists

Classical theorists generally prescribed using legal compliance and rewards for motivating employees. Taylor, for example, sought almost single-mindedly to develop tools and techniques for scientifically analyzing work and developing fair incentive plans. Similarly, Fayol's work is filled with references to using "sanctions" and "constant supervision" for ensuring "discipline."

However, although the classicists emphasized legal compliance and rewards, it would be inaccurate to assume that they didn't understand the usefulness of intrinsic motivation. Fayol, for example, talked in terms of the importance of "subordination of individual interests to general interests," and of "devotion and loyalty"; yet almost every such reference was paired with the fact that such motivation must be developed through legal compliance and rewards. For instance, he wrote of the importance of "respect for authority and discipline" in developing initiative. Furthermore, subordination of individual interests to general interests is important, he said, but the means of effecting it are "firmness and good example on the part of superiors; agreements as far as is possible; constant supervision." [4]

It is probably not so much that these men did not understand the value of intrinsic motivation, but rather that, given the values to which they subscribed, they simply assumed that all behavior in organizations necessarily grows out of economic motives. They assumed, in other words, that workers and entrepreneurs are all rational, economic beings who seek to maximize their benefits, and that these benefits are almost always described in economic terms.

Thus, motivation to the classicists was synonymous with rewards and legal compliance not so much because they did not appreciate the value of intrinsic motivation, but rather because they assumed that man was motivated almost entirely by economic gain.

Herbert Simon

Herbert Simon was one of the first theorists to address the importance of intrinsic motivation. Simon saw that there were two basic ways in which the "behavior of the operative employee" could be influenced:

> These influences fall roughly into two categories: (1) establishing *in the operative employee himself* attitudes, habits, and the state of mind which lead him to reach that decision that is advantageous to the organization and (2) *imposing* on the operative employee decisions reached elsewhere in the organization. The first type of influence operates by inculcating in the em-

ployee organizational loyalties and a concern with efficiency, and more generally by training him. The second type of influence depends primarily upon authority and upon advisory and informational services. It is not insisted that these categories are either exhaustive or mutually exclusive. . . .[5]

Simon feels that three factors contribute to the development of self-control. One is the development of organizational loyalty or identification. Here, the person identifies with the organization, and its goals become his or her own. The second is to inculcate in employees (or hire those who believe in) "the criterion of efficiency." As a result, the employee is motivated "to take the shortest path, the cheapest means, toward the attainment of the desired goals." Training is a third method for developing self-control, according to Simon; it "prepares the organization member to reach satisfactory decisions himself, without the need for the constant exercise of authority or advice."

Behavioral-Systems Writers

Other writers, like McGregor, clearly saw the need for intrinsic motivation, and in fact were often as extreme in their position as were the classicists in theirs. McGregor, you will recall, distinguished between two sets of management assumptions, which he called Theory X and Theory Y. Theory X assumed that man works as little as possible, lacks ambition and responsibility, is inherently self-centered, and requires close supervision to perform adequately. Theory Y, on the other hand, assumes that people are not by nature passive or resistant to organizational needs, that motivation and the capacity for assuming responsibility are present in all people, and that the essential task of management is to arrange "organizational conditions" so that people can achieve their own goals best by directing their own efforts toward organizational objectives. According to McGregor:

> . . . Theory X places exclusive reliance upon external control of human behavior, while Theory Y relies heavily on self control and self direction.[6]

McGregor says that Theory X assumptions manifest themselves in management's attempts to direct and control behavior through a "carrot and stick theory of motivation." Legal compliance through rules, close supervision, and their associated sanctions would in this case be the "sticks," with rewards representing the "carrots." In either case, says McGregor, the carrot-and-stick approach is no longer adequate, because it satisfies only people's lower-level needs, and these needs are already fairly well satisfied in modern societies:

> The philosophy of management by direction and control . . . is inadequate to motivate because the human needs on which this approach relies are today unimportant motivators of behavior. Direction and control are essentially useless to motivating people whose important needs are social and egoistic.[7]

Instead of using "carrots and sticks," says McGregor, managers should concentrate on building self-control to ensure compliance. They can do this, he says, by making employees' jobs more challenging (through job enlargement), and through participation and management by objectives.

Other behavioral-systems writers have come to similar conclusions. Herzberg, for example, prescribes making jobs more challenging and interesting. Katz and Kahn prescribe "craftsmanship" (job enrichment), letting employees participate in decision making, and the selection of employees whose values and goals are the same as or similar to those of the organization.

Contingency Theorists

Contingency theorists like Woodward, Lawrence and Lorsch, and Burns and Stalker also accept the necessity for intrinsic motivation, but they usually tie its use to the nature of the employee's task. Findings here suggest that tapping employees' intrinsic motivation, while perhaps always laudable, is particularly appropriate in more creative, entrepreneurial, organic situations where greater reliance necessarily has to be placed on eliciting self-control and creativity. In more routine, mechanical types of jobs, legal compliance and incentive rewards at least function effectively. As Burns and Stalker put it:

> The distinctive feature of the second, organic system is the pervasiveness of the working organization as an institution. In concrete terms, this makes itself felt in a preparedness to combine with others in serving the general aims of the concern. Proportionately to the rate and extent of change, the less can the omniscience appropriate to command organizations be ascribed to the head of the organization; for executives, and even operatives, in a changing firm it is always theirs to reason why.[8]

And in another place they state:

> The emptying out of significance from the hierarchic command system, by which cooperation is insured and which serves to monitor the working organization under a mechanistic system, is countered by the development of *shared beliefs* about the values and goals of the concern (in the organic system). The growth and accretion of institutionalized values, beliefs, and conduct, in the form of *commitments*, ideology, and manners, around an image of the concern in its industrial and commercial setting make good the loss of formal structure.[9]

In summary, most theorists recognize the advantages of eliciting intrinsic motivation and self-control, and they have prescribed some specific techniques for doing so. We will discuss five of these in this chapter: job enrichment (making jobs more challenging); participatory decision making; developing commitment; management by objectives; and employee selection and orientation.

JOB ENRICHMENT

The Drawbacks of "KITA" (Positive and Negative Incentives)

You will recall from Chapter 8 that Herzberg said you should stress intrinsic "motivators" (like achievement) rather than extrinsic "hygienes" (like money) to motivate employees. He says the use of incentives is popular because "the surest and least circumlocuted way of getting someone to do something is to kick him in the pants—give him what might be called the KITA." [10]

A "kick in the pants" (either carrot or stick) can be useful. Most people work to earn a living, and paying a salary is therefore a requisite for keeping them on the job. And beyond that, incentives (like more pay, fringe benefits, or threats) do "motivate" people—at least, Herzberg says, in the short run. The problem, though, is that once the incentive is removed—or the need for money, security, and so on, is satisfied—the "motivation" often disappears. Thus, KITA results in only short-term movement. As often as not, when you turn your back, you will find that your subordinate is no longer "motivated" (although some schedules of reinforcement can sustain "motivation" better than others). As Herzberg says:

> Why is KITA not motivation? If I kick my dog (from the back or the front) he will move. And when I want him to move again, what must I do? I must kick him again. Similarly I can charge a man's battery, and then re-charge it, and recharge it again. But it is only when he has his own generator that we can talk about motivation He then needs no outside stimulation. He *wants* to do it.[11]

So, in summary, what Herzberg calls KITA is an effective motivation tool—especially for "motivating" short-run bursts of activity. But in the long run, it is more useful (but not always possible) to get subordinates to genuinely *want* to do the job. Operant conditioners would say they *can* use reinforcement to get people to want to do their jobs. Herzberg suggests a different approach, one that more clearly appeals to people's "higher-level" needs.

What Is Job Enrichment?

Herzberg says that the way to motivate someone (to make him or her want to do it) is to build "motivators" like opportunities for growth into the job. One way to do this is through *job enrichment,* in which you reorganize your subordinate's job so as to make it more interesting and challenging. The job is redesigned to be less specialized and more "enriched." Usually, this is accomplished by giving the worker more autonomy and by allowing him to do much of the planning and inspection formerly done by his supervisor.

An example from what Herzberg calls a "highly successful job en-

TABLE 10-1

An Outline of a Successful Job Enrichment Project

Specific Changes Aimed at Enriching Jobs	"Motivators" These Changes Are Aimed at Increasing
A. Removing some controls while retaining accountability	Responsibility and personal achievement
B. Increasing the accountability of individuals for own work	Responsibility and recognition
C. Giving a person a complete natural unit of work (module, division, area, and so on)	Responsibility, achievement, and recognition
D. Granting additional authority to an employee in his activity; job freedom	Responsibility, achievement, and recognition
E. Making periodic reports directly available to the worker himself rather than to the supervisor	Internal recognition
F. Introducing new and more difficult tasks not previously handled	Growth and learning
G. Assigning individuals specific or specialized tasks, enabling them to become expert	Responsibility, growth, and advancement

Source: Frederick Herzberg, "One More Time: How Do You Motivate Employees?" *Harvard Business Review* (January–February 1967). Copyright © 1967 by the President and Fellows of Harvard College; all rights reserved.

richment experiment" is illustrated in Table 10-1. In this case, the jobs were those of people responsible for corresponding with a large corporation's stockholders—answering their questions, and so on. On the left of the figure are listed some of the changes that were aimed at enriching the job, such as "removing some controls while retaining accountability." On the right are listed the "motivators"—such as recognition—these job changes aimed at satisfying.

Why Is Job Enrichment Supposed to Work?

There are two reasons why job enrichment is supposed to result in increased morale and performance. First, by building into the job more challenge and opportunities for achievement, you are supposedly appealing to your employee's higher order needs—such as for achievement. Thus, he should now get so much satisfaction out of doing the job well that he is motivated to do it whether you watch him closely or not. Second, many

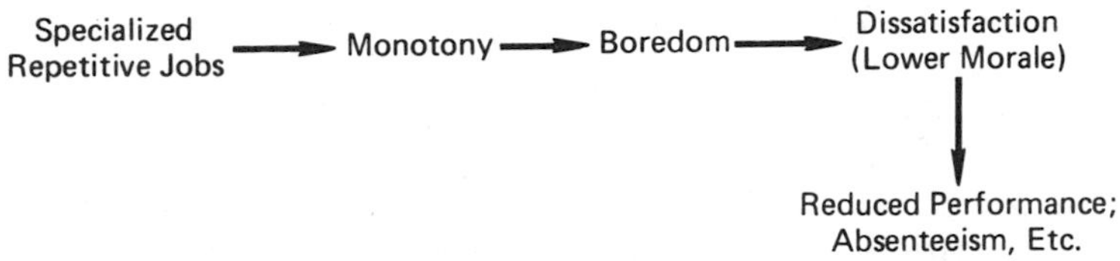

Specialized
Repetitive Jobs ⟶ Monotony ⟶ Boredom ⟶ Dissatisfaction (Lower Morale)

Reduced Performance; Absenteeism, Etc.

FIGURE 10-1. Why Should Unenriched, Repetitive Jobs Be Demoralizing?

Source: Based on Charles Hulin and Milton Blood, "Job Enlargement, Individual Differences, and Worker Responses," *Psychological Bulletin*, Vol. 69 (1968), 41-55.

believe that very specialized jobs are inherently demoralizing. The assumption here is that (as illustrated in Figure 10-1) specialized, repetitive jobs lead to monotony, boredom, and dissatisfaction: This finally leads to absenteeism and reduced performance. Job enrichment is supposed to "short circuit" this by resulting in jobs that are less specialized.

The evidence concerning whether these assumptions are correct is conflicting. Smith, for example, surveyed 72 women performing repetitive work in a knitwear mill.[12] She found that repetitive work was not necessarily related to boredom on the job and that the extent to which a worker was bored with her job was a function of such personal factors as age. In another study of the effects of routine jobs on women workers, researchers interviewed 115 assembly-line operators over a two-year period.[13] They found that fewer than 20 percent felt their work was monotonous or boring; furthermore, monotony and boredom were not necessarily related to dissatisfaction or frustration. The researchers emphasized that repetitive work need not be dissatisfying, particularly when it has *traction*—a smooth process that is not interrupted by outsiders, problems, or excessive pressure for quantity.[14]

A number of studies and literature reviews shed light on the nature of the factors that have been found to influence whether highly specialized tasks are unsatisfying. These surveys often conclude that many of the research findings on the adverse effects of specialization are based upon questionable methodology, and that in any case, personality differences determine how any one worker responds to a routine task.[15]

In summary, we know that the assumptions are more applicable to some situations than to others. We know, for example, that people who are more *"authoritarian,"* or whose major satisfactions come not from work but from nonwork interests such as hobbies, don't find specialized jobs so demoralizing. We also know that many people do not exhibit *strong higher-order* needs, such as for achievement: The design of the job (enriched vs. nonenriched) often has no effect at all on these people.[16] The *job itself* is also important. Jobs that have "traction"—a smooth, uninterrupted machine-like process—are usually not as demoralizing as those where the worker is constantly interrupted by problems and outsiders.[17]

Is Job Enrichment Effective?

Although there is no simple answer to this question, the prevailing evidence seems to say yes—*if* you are careful how and when you implement it. For example, in some companies and in some jobs, particularly those higher in the organization, job enrichment has been successful. Morale rose, quality went up, and production costs went down.[18] Yet in other situations, such as when job enrichment did not involve a commensurate pay raise, workers showed no marked preference for the more enriched jobs. We also know that job enrichment is not recommended where there are severe difficulties—such as low morale due to low pay levels.[19] And usually (as illustrated in Figure 10-2), job enrichment is more successful in improving the *quality* of the work than its quantity.

In summary, how can you help ensure that you use job enrichment most effectively? Based on the research evidence, one should consider using job enrichment as a motivation technique when:

1. Quality of work is a primary consideration.
2. The job requires a good deal of originality and judgment.[20]

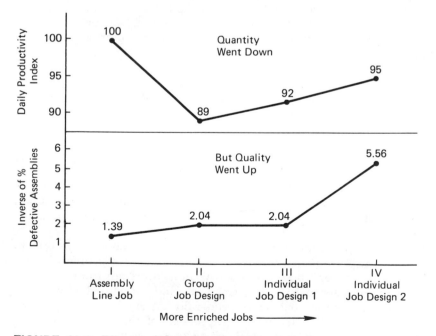

FIGURE 10-2. Effects of One Job Enrichment Program

Source: Adapted from data in Louis Davis, "Job Design and Productivity: A New Approach," *Personnel,* Vol. 31 (March 1957), 425; Filley and House, *Managerial Process and Organizational Behavior* (Glenview, Ill.: Scott Foresman, 1969), pp. 225-26.

Here, the motivation has to come more from *inside* your subordinate.

3. The workers themselves clearly prefer less-structured, less-routine jobs.
4. The organization itself is "organic" and is preoccupied with making creative, entrepreneurial decisions.
5. You know that the employees clearly have strong "higher-order" needs, such as for achievement.
6. The jobs are those of professionals and other higher-level employees.
7. You are not trying to deal with an acute morale problem caused by some "nonjob factor" such as low pay, job security, or poor supervision; in other words, "lower needs" should be fairly well satisfied.

Implementing a Job-Enrichment Program [21]

A group of researchers experimented with a new "technology" for implementing job-enrichment programs. They say that people "get turned on to"—are motivated to perform—their work if the activity is *meaningful* to the person; if the person knows he or she is solely *responsible* for its completion; and if he or she has *knowledge of results* within a few seconds.

According to the researchers, there are five "core job dimensions" that determine whether the person will experience this *meaningfulness, responsibility,* and *knowledge of results:*

1. *Skill variety*—the degree to which a job requires the worker to perform activities that challenge his or her skills and abilities
2. *Task identity*—the degree to which the job requires completion of a "whole" and identifiable piece of work
3. *Task significance*—the degree to which the job has a substantial and perceivable impact on the lives of other people, in the organization or world at large
4. *Autonomy*—the degree to which the job gives the worker freedom and independence
5. *Knowledge of results*—the degree to which the worker gets information about the effectiveness of his job efforts

The first step in developing a job-enrichment program, according to these researchers, is to *diagnose* the problem: Here, you determine if the job is amenable to job enrichment. This process consists of answering four questions. (The researchers have questionnaires to formalize this process.)

1. *Are motivation and satisfaction central to the problem?* Or is there some other problem?—poorly designed production system, etc.

2. *Is the job low in motivating potential?* Is the job the source of the motivation problem identified in question 1?
3. *What specific aspects of the jobs are causing the difficulty?* Here you examine the job on the five "core dimensions" we discussed above.
4. *How "ready" are the employees for change?* As we discussed above, not everyone is motivated by job enrichment. The extent to which job enrichment is effective depends on the worker's *needs* —for achievement, etc.

After diagnosing the problem, the next step is *implementation.* Here, you take specific actions to enrich the jobs; for example:

1. *Form natural work groups.* Here, you change the job in such a way that each person is responsible for—"owns"—an identifiable body of work. For example, instead of having the typists in a typing pool do work for all departments, you might make the work of one or two departments the continuing responsibility of each typist.
2. *Combine tasks.* For example, let one person assemble a product from start to finish, instead of having it go through several separate operations that are performed by different people.
3. *Establish client relationships.* Let the worker have contact, as often as possible, with consumers of the product.
4. *Vertical loading.* Let the worker plan and control his or her own job, instead of having it controlled for him. For example, let him set his own schedules, do his own troubleshooting, decide when to start and stop working, etc.
5. *Open feedback channels.* Finally, find more and better ways for the worker to get quick feedback on his or her performance.

According to the researchers, this system can be very effective. In their study, for example, quantity of work and job attitudes rose markedly while error rates and absenteeism dropped.

BUILDING COMMITMENT

Introduction

Few would argue with the fact that the most powerful way of ensuring compliance is to synchronize the organization's goals with those of its employees; to ensure, in other words, that the two sets of goals are essentially identical, and that by pursuing his or her own goals, the person pursues the organization's goals as well.

Early theorists understood this but generally made the mistake of assuming that goals could be described solely in economic terms. As a result, a series of plans was (and still is) proposed in which the "one best way" to carry out a task is determined, and in which incentive plans are relied upon for employee motivation. As a result of such a plan (the theory goes), the individual worker, by pursuing his or her maximum economic gains, pursues the organization's goal as well, that goal being the maximization of profits. Today, we know that such extrinsic rewards are not usually sufficient for synchronizing the individual's and organization's goals. Instead, other techniques like building commitment, participation, management by objectives, and employee selection are required. In this section we discuss the first of these, building commitment.

Building Loyalty and Commitment

Developing loyalty and commitment among organizational members has occupied theorists from the time of Plato, when writers were concerned with forging the allegiance of citizens to the state.[22] Steers says that organizational commitment may be defined as the relative strength of an individual's identification with and involvement in a particular organization, and that it can be characterized by at least three factors: (1) a strong belief in and acceptance of the organization's goals and values; (2) a willingness to exert considerable effort on behalf of the organization; and (3) a strong desire to maintain membership in the organization.[23] Similarly, Buchanan says that commitment embodies three separate but closely related component attitudes: (1) a sense of identification with the organizational mission; (2) a feeling of involvement or psychological immersion in organizational duties; and (3) a feeling of loyalty and affection for the organization as a place to live and work, quite apart from the merits of its mission or its purely instrumental value to the individual. Furthermore, he says, identification implies the alignment of individual and organizational goals: The employee comes to think of the aims of his organization in personal terms and to incorporate them into his own goal system.[24]

Studies, two of which we discuss in this section, suggest that commitment does result in several valuable outcomes to the organization. Commitment has been found, for example, to be inversely related to employee turnover, and sometimes positively related to employee performance as well.[25] Buchanan asserts that committed people require less supervision and that "the most significant attribute of commitment is its capacity for fusing individual and organizational goals."[26] Two studies shed light on the antecedents and outcomes of organizational commitment.

The Buchanan study. Subjects in this study were 279 managers from eight large organizations in the United States. Buchanan administered questionnaires that measured what he considers the "three component attitudes" of commitment—identification, involvement, and loyalty; they also measured "experiences that fostered commitment among all 279 managers."

He found that the following five "organization experiences" had a significant impact on the employees' commitment:

Personal Importance. The experience of being treated as a productive and valuable member of the organization was far and away the most influential of the five.

Work Group Experiences. . . . In general, the more cohesive (that is, friendly and close-knit) the group, and the more positive the group's overall feeling toward the organization, the more likely was the manager to report strong commitment.

Realization of Expectations. This scale asked managers to evaluate their organizations in terms of such questions as, "Has my organization fulfilled its promises to me and otherwise met my expectations in areas I care about?"

Organization Commitment Norms. Commitment, Buchanan found, is part of a largely implicit network of norms, values, and beliefs that comprise the culture of an organization and that its members are expected to accept as a condition of membership . . . those who sense that their organizations expected them to be committed were more committed than those who did not perceive such an expectation.

First Year Job Challenge. . . . This result suggests that the first job assignment may be of extraordinary importance in setting the tone of a manager's relationship with his organization for years to come. . . .

The Steers study. A recent study by Steers expands on Buchanan's findings.[27] Steers developed a model that we present in Figure 10-3. As you can see, the model consists of two parts: (1) antecedents of commitment, and (2) outcomes of commitment. According to Steers, there are three basic antecedents of commitment: personal characteristics (like need for achieve-

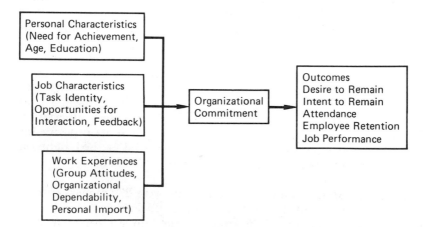

FIGURE 10-3. Hypothesized Antecedents and Outcomes of Organizational Commitment

Source: Richard M. Steers, "Antecedents and Outcomes of Organizational Commitment," *Administrative Science Quarterly,* Vol. 22, No. 1 (March 1977), 47.

ment); job characteristics (how interesting the job is); and work experiences (such as group attitudes). He says these antecedents combine in molding an employee's commitment, which in turn leads to outcomes such as desire to remain with the organization, attendance, and job performance. The purpose of Steers's study was to determine the usefulness of this model.

Subjects came from two organizations. The first was a midwestern hospital; here, subjects were 382 employees, including administrators, nurses, service workers, and clerical employees. The second sample consisted of 119 scientists and engineers employed by a research laboratory. Questionnaires were used to collect the data.

Steers found that six variables were significantly related to commitment in both samples. These included the person's *need for achievement*, his *group's attitude* toward the organization, his *education* (inversely), *organizational dependability* (how dependably the organization was seen to carry out its commitments to employees), the person's *perceived personal importance* to the organization, and *"task identity* (challenging tasks)." [28] At least one of the variables fit into each of Steers's three basic "antecedent" categories, and he says this supports his prediction that all three antecedent categories (personal characteristics, job characteristics, and work experiences) do influence commitment.

Steers also found that several outcomes were related to commitment in both organizations. These included the employees' *desire to remain* with the organization, his or her *intent to remain* with the organization, *attendance* (for the scientists and engineers), and *turnover* (for the hospital employees). *Quantity of work* and the employees' *readiness for promotion* were moderately related to commitment for the hospital employees, but not for the scientists. From this, it appears that commitment is strongly related to the desire and intent of employees to stay with an organization, but that its effects on job performance are inconclusive. One explanation for this, Steers says, may be that performance is a function of not just commitment and motivation, but the employee's skills and expectations that he or she can accomplish the task.[29] In any case, says Steers, developing commitment is still a crucial task for management and involves ensuring that employees' highest level needs are satisfied:

> Individuals come to organizations with certain needs, desires, skills, and so forth and expect to find a work environment where they can utilize their abilities and satisfy many of their basic needs. When the organization provides such a vehicle (for example, where it makes effective use of its employees, is dependable, and so forth), the likelihood of increasing commitment is apparently enhanced. When the organization is not dependable, however, or where it fails to provide employees with challenging and meaningful tasks, commitment levels tend to diminish.[30]

Summary.   Commitment is a person's identification with, involvement in, and loyalty to the organization. It seems to be elicited by feelings of importance the person receives on the job, work-group experiences, realization of expectations, first-year job challenge, the organization's dependability in carrying out its commitment to the individual, and the person's perceived personal importance to the organization. Outcomes of commitment include desire and intent to remain with the organization, reduced turnover, and (sometimes) higher quality work and readiness for promotion.

THE USE OF PARTICIPATION

Participation, "Ownership" of Organizational Goals, and Self-Control

The use of "participation" (encouraging employees to participate actively in developing and implementing decisions directly affecting their jobs) has been popular since the time of the Hawthorne studies. Some writers have pointed out that participation is commonly assumed to be more effective than authoritarian management, and that this assumption is based on the belief that when people become personally involved with their tasks, the execution of those tasks becomes a means for satisfying certain of their needs, such as for achievement.[31] In theory, deriving such satisfaction reinforces successful performance, thus providing a further impetus. On the other hand, authoritarian management supposedly makes work simply the carrying out of the supervisors' will, does not satisfy subordinates' needs, and should thus have a negative affect on performance.

Others feel that participation is effective because employees who participate in decision making become "ego-involved" with the resulting decisons and develop a sense of ownership of the decisions that emerge out of the decision-making process. In other words, participation can increase the degree to which group members "own" their work practices—and therefore the likelihood that the group will develop a norm of support for those practices.[32]

The prevailing evidence does suggest that employees who participate in decision making do develop an ownership of their work practices, and therefore self-control. In one study, for example, participation in the development of an incentive plan for office maintenance workers changed the communication among workers from initial "shared warnings" about management to "helping members (especially new members) come to understand and believe in our plan."[33]

Because of findings like these, participation has been widely used in the implementation of organizational changes: Participants feel they have a sense of ownership of the changes, and are therefore motivated to see these changes put into effect. A classic study of this was carried out by Coch and French.[34] The researchers hypothesized that allowing employees to participate in planning and implementing the necessary procedural change would make a significant difference in their acceptance of the change. The researchers set up four experimental groups. In group I (the control, or "no participation" group), employees went through the usual factory routine. Here, the production department modified the job, a new piece rate was set, and the operators were called in to a meeting and told about the job change. Their questions were answered, and then they went back to work.

Group II was the "participation through representation" group. Here, before any changes took place, a group meeting was held and the need for change was presented dramatically. Management then presented a plan to institute the new work method, and a few representatives of the group were selected to help management work it out.

Groups III and IV were the "total participation" groups. All these employees met with management, and the need for a cost reduction was presented. All the employees in each group discussed the current methods and how they might be improved. When the new methods were agreed on, the operators were trained in them and returned to work.

The results of this study, which appear quite definitive, are presented in Figure 10-4. In group I ("no participation") resistance developed almost immediately, and according to the researchers, 17 percent quit in the first 40 days. Grievances were filed about the piece rate and, as you can see, productivity dropped.

At the other extreme, employees in groups III and IV ("total participation") showed no such signs of resistance. Productivity climbed immediately, and there were no quits during the experiment.[35]

Other studies can also be cited; in summarizing the evidence, Lawler concludes that participation is effective because:

> . . . people become "ego involved" in decisions in which they have had an influence. The decisions become their decisions and they develop expec-

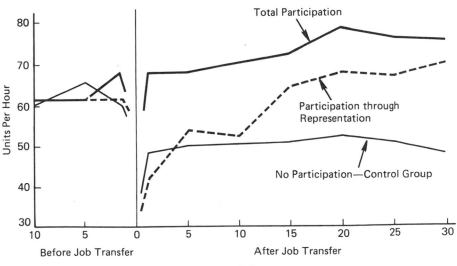

FIGURE 10-4. Effects of Participation

Source: Lester Coch and J. R. French, Jr., "Overcoming Resistance to Change," *Human Relations*, Vol. 1, No. 4 (1948); reprinted in Paul Lawrence and John Seiler, et al., *Organizational Behavior and Administration* (Homewood, Ill.: Irwin/Dorsey, 1965), pp. 931-32.

tancies to the effect that when the decisions are successfully implemented they will experience such intrinsic rewards as feelings of competence and self esteem. Because of this, they work to implement the decision even though no extrinsic rewards are involved.[36]

Participation, Performance, and Attitudes

Although participation may increase commitment and self-control, its effects on performance and attitudes are inconsistent. The subjects in the original and best-known study in this area were 30 ten-year-old boys who met in six groups, which they were told were recreational clubs. These groups were supervised by adults who had been trained to act in either an autocratic, a democratic, or a laissez-faire manner. Each of the experimental groups was exposed to these three styles for six weeks.

Although the quantity of work in autocratic groups seemed to be slightly higher, the quality in democratic groups was usually better. Autocratic groups usually collapsed completely when the leader left the room, whereas the effectiveness of the democratic groups usually decreased only slightly. However, one fact often overlooked by reviewers of this study is that no objective measure of productivity is reported, and it is therefore impossible to assess accurately the effects of the various leadership styles.[37]

Evidence from other studies suggests that a democratic approach may increase job satisfaction but that its relation to productivity remains unclear. In an early study, members of the authoritarian groups were told to obey orders, whereas those in the democratic groups were told to offer suggestions and not blindly follow orders. No differences at all were found in the productivity of the different groups.[38]

On the other hand, the results of one study, which was carried out in two clerical departments of an industrial firm, suggest that while the effects of democratic leadership on productivity may be mixed, its effect on satisfaction is clearly positive. Morse and Reimer exposed work groups to either autocratic or democratic leadership by altering the style of supervision used.[39] In the democratic groups, supervisors were trained to employ more democratic methods, and an attempt was made to delegate more decision making. In the two autocratic groups, a "hierarchically controlled program" was established by moving more of the decision authority to upper management and by increasing the closeness of the supervision. The experiment was continued for about a year and a half.

As seen in Table 10-2, the increase in productivity (measured by cost reduction) for the autocratic groups was considerably higher than for the democratic groups. However, the employees exposed to authoritarian leadership quickly became very dissatisfied. In the democratically supervised group, on the other hand, satisfaction increased and turnover and grievances decreased.

In summary, participation facilitates organizational changes, apparently because it increases the employee's perceived commitment to and "ownership" of the changes. The effects of participation on employee satisfaction are generally positive, and employees who participate more tend to

TABLE 10-2

Comparison of Productivity and Satisfaction for Divisions:
Year Preceding Introduction of Program and Year Following

Experimental Groups	Index of Productivity			Index of Satisfaction with Company		
	Mean for Initial Year	Mean for Experimental Year	Differ- ence	Mean for Initial Year	Mean for Experimental Year	Differ- ence
Democratic Program						
Division A	46.3%	55.2%	+8.9 *	4.16	4.32	+.16 *
Division B	51.0	62.0	+11.0 *	3.83	4.02	+.19
Average	48.6	58.6	+10.0 *	4.01	4.18	+.17 *
Autocratic Program						
Division C	50.2	63.2	+13.0 *	4.04	3.80	−.24 *
Division D	46.8	62.0	+15.2 *	4.26	3.95	−.31 *
Average	48.5	62.6	+14.1 *	4.15	3.88	−.27 *
	High Values Correspond to Higher Productivity			Higher Values Correspond to Higher Satisfaction		

* Statistically significant results.
Source: Adapted from N. C. Morse and E. Reimer, "The Experimental Change of a Major Organizational Variable," *Journal of Abnormal and Social Psychology*, Vol. 52 (1956), 127. Copyright 1956 by the American Psychological Association. Reprinted by permission of the publisher.

be more satisfied. However, the findings concerning the relation between participation and employee performance are inconclusive, and participation has been found to be positively related, negatively related, and unrelated to performance and productivity in a wide range of studies.

Conditions that are conducive to the use of participation. These findings are somewhat curious, in that they suggest that although participation does result in increased employee commitment, self-control, and intrinsic motivation, its results on the employee's ultimate performance may not materialize. Many explanations are plausible, but it seems most reasonable to assume that for many employees and tasks, participation is simply inappropriate.

For example, Victor Vroom found that participative leadership had positive effects only on those employees who had a high need for independence and strong nonauthoritarian values.[40] On the other hand, employees who expressed a high desire for structure and low needs for independence did not react favorably to participative leadership. Similarly, others have found that subordinates' reaction to participative leadership was determined by whether they considered it "legitimate."[41] For example, a researcher found that certain Scandinavian workers do not consider participation a legitimate requirement for workers as Americans do, and that this influences their response to participative leadership.

Vroom and Yetton developed a "situational" model that can help managers decide to what extent they should allow their groups to participate in decision making. They say there are five types of "management decision styles":

A I: You solve the problem or make the decision yourself, using information available to you at that time.

A II: You obtain the necessary information from your subordinates, then decide on the solution to the problem yourself. You may or may not tell your subordinates what the problem is in getting the information from them. The role played by your subordinates in making the decision is clearly one of providing the necessary information to you, rather than generating or evaluating alternative solutions.

C I: You share the problem with relevant subordinates individually, getting their ideas and suggestions without bringing them together as a group. Then you make the decision, which may or may not reflect your subordinates' influence.

C II: You share the problem with your subordinates as a group, collectively obtaining their ideas and suggestions. Then you make the decision, which may or may not reflect your subordinates' influence.

G II: You share a problem with your subordinates as a group. Together you generate and evaluate alternatives and attempt to reach agreement (consensus) on a solution. Your role is much like that of a chairperson. You do not try to influence the group to adopt "your" solution, and you are willing to accept and implement any solution which has the support of the entire group.

They say that the appropriate decision-making style depends on seven attributes of the problem situation—such as how important the quality of the decision is. These seven attributes, along with questions that can be used to diagnose the existence of such attributes, are presented below in Table 10-3. As an example, one could identify the importance of the quality of the decision (the first problem attribute) with the following diagnostic question: "Is there a quality requirement such that one solution is more likely to be more rational than another?"

Finally, Vroom and Yetton present a model for determining the best decision-making style in the form of a "decision tree," and this is presented in Figure 10-5. Notice that it requires the manager to identify the attributes of the problem by asking the seven diagnostic questions, each in its proper sequence. First, for example, you determine whether quality of the decision is important: then you determine if you have sufficient information to make

TABLE 10-3

Problem Attributes Used in Vroom-Yetton Model

Problem Attributes	Diagnostic Questions
A. The importance of the quality of the decision.	Is there a quality requirement such that one solution is likely to be more rational than another?
B. The extent to which the leader possesses sufficient information/ expertise to make a high-quality decision by himself.	Do I have sufficient information to make a high-quality decision?
C. The extent to which the problem is structured.	Is the problem structured?
D. The extent to which acceptance or commitment on the part of subordinates is critical to the effective implementation of the decision.	Is acceptance of decision by subordinates critical to effective implemention?
E. The prior probability that the leader's autocratic decision will receive acceptance by subordinates.	If you were to make the decision by yourself, is it reasonably certain that it would be accepted by your subordinates?
F. The extent to which the subordinates are motivated to attain the organizational goals as represented in the objectives explicit in the statement of the problem.	Do subordinates share the organizational goals to be obtained in solving this problem?
G. The extent to which subordinates are likely to be in conflict over preferred solutions.	Is conflict among subordinates likely in preferred solutions?

Source: Reprinted, by permission of the publisher, from Victor Vroom, "A New Look at Management Decision Making," *Organizational Dynamics,* Spring 1973, © 1973 by AMACOM, a division of American Management Associations. All rights reserved.

a high-quality decision; and so forth. By answering each question "yes" or "no," you can work your way across the decision tree and identify, for the situation you find yourself in, the decision-making style that is best. This model has recently received some empirical support.[42]

In summary, participation can increase commitment, facilitate organizational changes, and increase productivity and morale. Whether it does, however, depends on several things, particularly the employee's personality and the nature of the task. When work outcomes are determined by the worker, rather than by objective factors in the environment, participation should be more effective.[43] Similarly, when employees desire independence, participation should be more effective. Thus, as Lawler points out:

> . . . Participation seems to lead to a greater commitment to decisions that are made. When a commitment exists, people exercise self control because they are intrinsically motivated to carry out the decision. Whether this will

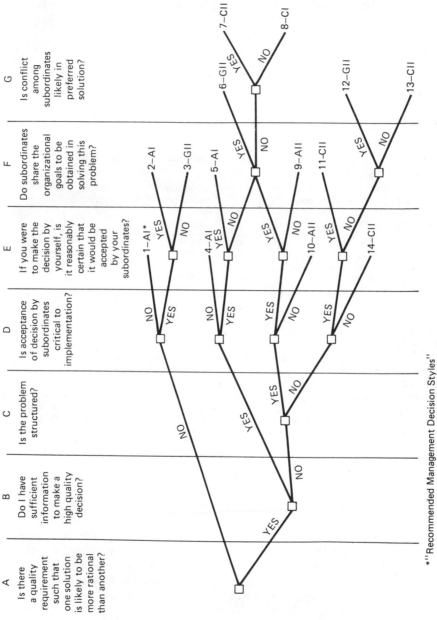

A	B	C	D	E	F	G
Is there a quality requirement such that one solution is likely to be more rational than another?	Do I have sufficient information to make a high quality decision?	Is the problem structured?	Is acceptance of decision by subordinates critical to implementation?	If you were to make the decision by yourself, is it reasonably certain that it would be accepted by your subordinates?	Do subordinates share the organizational goals to be obtained in solving this problem?	Is conflict among subordinates likely in preferred solution?

1–AI*
2–AI
3–GII
4–AI
5–AI
6–GII
7–CII
8–CI
9–AII
10–AII
11–CII
12–GII
13–CII
14–CII

*"Recommended Management Decision Styles"

FIGURE 10-5. Finding the Right Degree of Participation

Source: Reprinted, by permission of the publisher, from Victor Vroom, "A New Look at Managerial Decision Making," *Organizational Dynamics*, Spring 1973, © 1973 by AMACOM, a division of American Management Associations. All rights reserved.

result in higher productivity or greater organizational effectiveness is a function of the nature of the decision that is made.[44]

The Use of Participation: Management by Objectives

The management-by-objectives (MBO) procedure is used to increase employees' commitment by involving them in the development of plans and objectives. MBO originated in managerial practice and was further refined and extended by various researchers and writers. Peter Drucker first publicized the MBO approach in his *Practice of Management,* written in 1954.

Douglas McGregor also advocated the use of the MBO approach.[45] He argued that many performance-appraisal programs fail because both superiors and subordinates resist them. The solution was to have the manager establish short-term goals for himself with the help of his supervisor; the former would then work out the specific plans for implementing these goals. He could then appraise his accomplishments at the end of a short period and discuss this self-appraisal with his superior. McGregor pointed out the following advantages to this approach:

1. It shifts the performance appraisal from an emphasis on weakness to an analysis of strength potentials.
2. It casts the superior in the role of the helper, rather than judge.
3. It facilitates acceptance of organizational goals by emphasizing performance rather than personalities of the persons being appraised.

An effective MBO program usually consists of the following basic steps:

1. *Set organization's goals.* Establishment of organization-wide strategy and goals.
2. *Set departmental goals.* Department heads and their superiors jointly set goals for their departments.
3. *Discuss departmental goals.* Department heads discuss departments' goals with all subordinates in the department and ask them to develop their own individual goals.
4. *Set individual goals.* Each superior and subordinate jointly set goals for the latter and decide on a timetable for accomplishing same.
5. *Feedback.* There are periodic performance review meetings between superior and subordinate to monitor and analyze progress towards latter's goals.[46]

Research foundations of MBO. The MBO approach makes good intuitive sense. Moreover, research evidence also supports its usefulness. This evidence deals with (1) separate components of the MBO approach, such as goal setting, feedback, and participation; and (2) ongoing MBO programs.

Research on goal setting, feedback, and participation suggest that MBO should be effective. For example, researchers have found that *goal setting* resulted in higher levels of performance than merely telling subjects to do their best; even with boring tasks, setting goals increased interest.[47] They found, too, that goal setting increased performance more than did feedback alone. Another researcher found that forcing subjects to set goals increased the level of performance most when the task was difficult.[48] Others have found that goal setting can lead to decreased absenteeism.[49]

Research findings have also supported the usefulness of the *feedback* aspect of MBO. In one study, researchers gave feedback to 13 of 26 groups. Those receiving feedback solved their problems more accurately and were further motivated to solve new problems.[50] In similar studies, others found that life insurance agents who received periodic production bulletins and personal letters commenting on their performance improved their average performance. The average performance of those not receiving feedback remained the same.[51] Similar benefits are claimed for the use of *participation* in the planning process, as we have seen.[52] Participation does seem to lead to greater commitment to and acceptance of decisions, and occasionally to higher productivity and morale as well.[53]

MBO programs. It is not surprising, then, that a number of researchers have found ongoing MBO programs useful. One major research effort was conducted at the General Electric Company, where the program was called "Work Planning and Review." [54] The program grew out of attempts to improve the firm's performance appraisal system and was quite effective. The employees operating under MBO expressed significantly more favorable attitudes on most satisfaction indexes and were much more likely to have taken specific action to improve performance than those operating within a traditional performance-appraisal system.

Similarly, Raia examined the organizational impact of a program called "Goals and Controls," a variant of MBO.[55] He analyzed production records, conducted interviews, and administered questionnaires to 112 managers after the goal-setting program had been instituted. At the end of the first year, productivity had increased, managers were more aware of the firm's goals, and specific goals had been set in more areas than before the new approach. Ivancevich analyzed the performance of the subordinates of 181 MBO-involved superiors and found that the subordinates' performance had improved.[56]

Conditions for success. Carroll and Tosi carried out an extensive questionnaire and interview analysis of an MBO program at the Black & Decker Company.[57] Their findings suggest that a number of factors contribute to the success or failure of the MBO approach. Among these factors are:

1. *Commitment to MBO.* Managers must feel that MBO is important, that the company is serious about it.

2. *Goal clarity.* Organizational goals must become clear, since goal setting at all lower levels is more difficult, perhaps impossible, without clear goals that can be fashioned into departmental or individual goals.

3. *Time and resources.* Managers must have time and resources so that they can utilize MBO.

4. *Need to tailor to individuals.* The results indicate that MBO should be tailored to the individual and his position, rather than be presented as a single, defined approach for all managers.

5. *Feedback.* The manner in which the review process is carried out is of critical importance. The review process is especially important for managers who are lower in ability, lack confidence, and are operating at lower motivational levels.

6. *The review process.* The critical elements in the review process are the amount of effort devoted to it and the interpersonal communication skills of the superior when communicating with subordinates.[58]

Strengths and weaknesses of MBO. One major strength of MBO is that it does seem to increase employees' commitment and their identification with the organization's goals. In addition, Carroll and Tosi list the following advantages.

1. It directs work activities toward organizational goals.
2. It forces and aids in planning.
3. It provides clear standards for control.
4. It provides improved motivation among managers.
5. It makes better use of human resources.
6. It reduces role conflict and ambiguity.
7. It provides more objective appraisal criteria.
8. It better identifies problems.
9. It improves the development of personnel.[59]

There are also a number of problems with the MBO approach. For example, those involved in the program sometimes lack an understanding of how to set clear goals and standards. And, there is sometimes a "tug of war" as the subordinate tries to set the lowest targets possible and the supervisor the highest. Furthermore, Carroll and Tosi found that managers were frequently unaware of all the benefits of the MBO program until significant efforts were made to acquaint them with these. In addition, Raia (as well as Carroll and Tosi) notes that many managers have found MBO to require excessive paperwork.[60] The measurement of performance is still a difficult problem, particularly in those areas (such as personnel development) in which results are not easily quantifiable. All told, however, MBO appears to be a useful technique for eliciting commitment and an identification with organizational goals.[61]

STAFFING AND INTRINSIC MOTIVATION

Introduction

Effectively staffing the organization—recruiting, selecting, placing, and socializing new employees—affects the level of motivation and performance in the organization in several ways. First, performance depends not only on the employee's "motivation" but on his abilities as well, and it is through staffing that employees with the "right" abilities are matched with the right jobs. Furthermore, the staffing process includes orientation and socialization activities, and we will see that these can be useful for inculcating in the employee an appreciation for and identification with the goals of the organization. It is also through staffing that the organization can select people whose values are compatible with those of the organization: through staffing, for example, the civil rights crusader is matched with the Civil Liberties Union; and the arbiters of social injustice are drawn to social work.

The Staffing Process

"Staffing" involves placing the right person in the right job. Specifically, it entails several steps, including (1) job analysis—determining what the job entails and what traits and skills are needed to perform it; (2) personnel planning and recruiting; (3) employee selection—using, for example, application blanks, interviews, and personnel tests; and (4) orientation and training. The combined effect of these activities should be to ensure that employees with the necessary abilities are placed in the appropriate jobs. In addition, these activities ensure (or should ensure) that employees whose values are compatible with those of the organization are selected, and that employees develop an appreciation for and identification with the organization's goals.

Work values and "central life commitment." Selecting employees whose values are compatible with those of the organization can obviously be a crucial element in synchronizing the goals of the organization with those of the individual. A missionary hospital in Africa could hardly expect to keep an income-conscious doctor motivated, and a college devoted to open admissions and maximizing enrollment would find a research-minded professor rapidly becoming demoralized.

Similarly, Simon asserts that hiring employees who believe in the "criterion of efficiency" can help ensure that employees will do their best for the organization. And, in fact, a good deal of research has been carried out to determine if some employees have a stronger "work ethic" than others. In one such study, it was found that job enrichment might not be effective among urban, blue-collar workers, who were found to be "alienated" from Protestant-work-ethic values. In a later study, researchers found that workers from factories located in small towns responded very differently than workers who came from urban factory settings. Specifically, workers from small-town settings tended to be more inclined toward the enriched jobs than were the more "alienated" urban workers.[62] Although there is some debate over what causes some workers to be less alienated from work-ethic values, it does seem apparent that there are significant differences in the values workers bring to their jobs and that these differences affect the way they perform their jobs.

Another line of research has focused on whether work and work experiences constitute a "central life interest" of employed people.[63] This is potentially an important line of research, since one would assume that people for whom work is a "central life interest" might be more committed and motivated employees. In the first study on this subject, 24 percent of the industrial workers in the sample reported *work* as a central life interest. In studies since then, lower percentages of blue-collar workers in a variety of settings have been found to have a central life interest in work—14 percent of lumber workers, and 12 percent of long-distance truck drivers, for example.[64] There was also a wide range among business executives and supervisors, although most tend to have a high central life interest in work. For example, 84 percent of American executives in one study, 82 percent of Japanese middle managers, and 54 percent of industrial supervisors were found to have such a central life interest.[65]

Subjects in a recent study included 409 employees in 37 branches of a bank, and 605 employees from one division of a telephone company. Here, it was found that workers with a central life interest in work had a high level of commitment to their work organization, and also a higher level of attraction to individual features of their organization (such as supervision, immediate work colleagues, and the like) than did workers with other, nonwork central-life-interest orientations. And, workers with a non-job central life interest were found to have a low level of organizational commitment.

Orientation and socialization. Katz and Kahn point out that "the adult socialization process in the organization can build upon the personal values of its members and integrate them around attractive organizational models. People can thus identify with the organizational mission." [66]

Personnel managers have long understood the usefulness of orientation in easing the entry of new employees into the organization. In one study at the Texas Instruments Company, for example, researchers discovered that short orientation programs helped to ease the entry of new employees and thereby to reduce their initial anxiety and significantly reduce their turnover.[67] Orientation programs have also been found to minimize what might be called the "reality shock" some new employees undergo. This reality shock, according to Douglas Hall, is caused by the incompatibility between what employees expect in their new job and the realities they are confronted with.[68] The expectations are concerned with factors like opportunities for advancement, responsibility, and challenge and adventure. Often, however, new employees run into a conflicting set of expectations on the part of the organization, which frequently wants to "monitor" them by closely supervising them in a relatively menial task; the result is "reality shock." Orientation, says Hall, can help overcome this problem by providing for more realistic expectations on the part of new employees. In this way, the organization not only helps ensure that it hires those whose values are compatible with its own, but also ensures that the assimilation and socialization of the employee into the organization is as smooth as possible.

SUMMARY

In this chapter, we discussed techniques for eliciting *intrinsic* motivation and self-control. These techniques included job enrichment, loyalty and commitment, participation, management by objectives, and staffing. Unlike the compliance techniques we discussed in the preceding chapter, these are aimed at getting the employee to identify with his or her job or with the goals of the organization, and thereby be motivated; techniques like legal compliance and rewards, on the other hand, are based on the use of *extrinsic* "carrots" (like rewards), and "sticks" (like punishment).

Classical theorists probably understood the advantages of getting employees to want to do their jobs and to exhibit self-control. But motivation to the classicists was synonymous with rewards and legal compliance, a fact that reflected the prevailing values and tasks of the day. Theorists assumed that workers wanted to simply maximize their rewards, that tasks were routine and easily monitored, and that rewards could easily be tied to efficiency and quantitative measures of output. Today, most theorists agree that eliciting self-control requires appealing to employees' "higher-level" needs, such as those for achievement and self-actualization. Today, too, theorists recognize that workers seek to satisfy a variety of needs, including those for achievement and self-actualization, and that many tasks are no longer easily monitored or quantified. Instead, creativity and innovation are often most important, and to obtain such behavior, self-control (elicited by commitment, and techniques like MBO) is needed. In a sense, therefore, the techniques we discussed in Chapter 9 focused on raising performance directly, whereas those discussed in this chapter focus on building satisfaction, commitment, and the overall "quality" of work life, on the assumption that these will in turn manifest themselves in the accomplishment of the tasks faced by modern workers.

The intrinsic-motivation techniques we discussed in this chapter are often quite effective. *Job enrichment* often results in higher morale and better quality. *Commitment* was found to be inversely related to employee turnover and sometimes positively related to employee performance as well. *Participation* facilitates organizational changes, raises employee morale, and is sometimes related to increased employee performance; the same general conclusions apply to *management by objectives*. Similarly, *staffing* techniques can be used to effectively recruit, hire, and place people whose values and skills are appropriate to your organization.

Yet, although these techniques are often effective, the findings concerning their effects on performance are far from consistent: For example, participation programs often fail, and several reasons probably account for this. First, the technique must be appropriate; for example, job-enrichment programs often fail in situations where lower level needs have not been satisfied yet—as where low pay has resulted in morale problems. Similarly, some people (and tasks) are not amenable to participatory management. Second, it seems that (as illustrated in our model) other factors, like leadership, intergroup conflict, and organization structure, all interact in determining whether organizational effectiveness will emerge. In the last three chapters, we therefore turn to four important "determining" factors: *leadership, groups, intergroup relations and conflict,* and *organizational change and development.*

DISCUSSION QUESTIONS

1. What is meant by job enrichment? Discuss the factors that you would take into consideration before recommending the implementation of a job enrichment program.
2. Herzberg believes that "KITA"—positive and negative incentives—is not as effective at eliciting self-control as are techniques like job enrichment. Based on the research findings we discussed in Chapters 8, 9, and 10, do you agree or disagree with him? Why?
3. Professor Herbert Simon says that techniques like job enrichment that are aimed at eliciting self-control and "imposed control" techniques like close supervision can be substituted for one another, at least up to a point. Do you think this is true? Do you think his statement is more true for some jobs than for others? Why?
4. "There are two things that a manager can do that will ensure his organization's success. First, he must choose the right strategy so that his organization is headed in the right direction and that it has the right niche in its market. Second, he then must effectively staff his organization so that he hires employees who have the commitment and abilities to perform their jobs. With the right strategy and the right staffing, everything else—organization structure, accounting controls, industrial engineering, and so on—are of secondary importance." Do you agree or disagree with this statement? Why?
5. Give several concrete examples of how you would "enrich" the following jobs: tollbooth attendant, assembly line worker in an auto factory, directory assistance operator, bus driver.
6. Discuss the conditions under which job enrichment will more likely result in increased motivation. Based on this, would you, in fact, try to enrich all of the jobs listed in the last question?
7. What (if any) is the relationship between management by objectives and operant conditioning? Are the two similar in any respect? How?
8. Write an essay entitled "How to Motivate Employees in One Easy Lesson."

FOOTNOTES

1 Daniel Katz and Robert L. Kahn, *The Social Psychology of Organizations* (New York: John Wiley, 1966), p. 345.

2 There is something of a debate in the literature as to just what "intrinsic motivation" means. Deci, Cascio, and Krussell say it is a difficult concept to operationalize. Scott implies it may be motivation that emerges in the absence of external rewards. Deci says that "intrinsically motivated behaviors are ones that are involved with the human need for being competent and self determining." E. L. Deci, Wayne Cascio, and J. Krussell, "Cognitive Evaluation Theory and Some Comments on the Calder-Staw Critique," *Journal of Personality and Social Psychology*, Vol. 31 (1975), 81–85; W. E. Scott, Jr., "The Effects of Extrinsic Rewards on Intrinsic Motivation: A Critique," *Organizational Behavior and Human Performance*, Vol. 15 (1975), 117–29; E. L. Deci, *Intrinsic Motivation* (New York: Plenum Publishing Corp., 1975); E. L. Deci, "Notes on the Theory and Metatheory of Intrinsic Motivation," *Organizational Behavior and Human Performance*, Vol. 15 (1976), 130–45.

3 John Stuart Mill, quoted in Alvin Gouldner, "About the Functions of Bureaucratic Rules," in Joseph Litterer, *Organizations* (New York: John Wiley, 1966), p. 379.

4 Henri Fayol, *General and Industrial Management*, trans. Constance Storrs (London: Sir Isaac Pitman, 1949).

5 Herbert Simon, *Administrative Behavior* (New York: Free Press, 1976), p. 11.

6 Douglas McGregor, "The Human Side of Enterprise," *Management Review*, November 1957, pp. 22–28, 88–92; reprinted in Fred Luthans, *Contemporary Readings in Organizational Behavior* (New York: McGraw-Hill, 1972), pp. 38–40.

7 *Ibid.*, p. 24.

8 Tom Burns and G. M. Stalker, *The Management of Innovation* (London: Tavistock, 1961), p. 125.

9 *Ibid.*, p. 122.

10 This section is largely based on Frederick Herzberg, "One More Time: How Do You Motivate Employees?" *Harvard Business Review* (January–February 1968). Also see W. E. Scott and L. L. Cummings, *Readings in Organizational Behavior and Human Performance* (Homewood, Ill.: Richard D. Irwin, 1973), pp. 350–78.

11 Herzberg, "One More Time: How Do You Motivate Employees?" For a discussion of the effects of extrinsic or intrinsic rewards (if any), see Craig Pinder, "Additivity versus Nonadditivity of Intrinsic and Extrinsic Incentives: Implications for Work Motivation, Performance, and Attitudes," *Journal of Applied Psychology*, Vol. 61, No. 6 (December 1976); Robert Pritchard, Kathleen Campbell, and Donald Campbell, "Effects of Extrinsic Financial Rewards on Intrinsic Motivation," *Journal of Applied Psychology*, Vol. 62 (1977), 9–15; James Farr, "Task Characteristics, Reward Contingency, and Intrinsic Motivations," *Organizational Behavior and Human Performance*, Vol. 16, No. 2 (August 1976), 294–307.

12 P.C. Smith, "The Prediction of Individual Differences and Susceptibility to Industrial Monotony," *Journal of Applied Psychology*, Vol. 43 (August 1959), 322–29.

13 A. N. Turner and A. L. Miclette, "Sources of Satisfaction in Repetitive Work," *Occupational Psychology*, Vol. 36 (June 1962), 215–31.

14 See also M. D. Kilbridge, "Turnover, Absence, and Transfer as Indicators of Employee Dissatisfaction with Repetitive Work," *Industrial and Labor Relations Review*, Vol. 15 (1961), 22.

15 A. C. MacKinney, P. F. Wernimont, and W. O. Failtiz, "Has Specialization Reduced Job Satisfaction?" *Personnel*, Vol. 39, No. 1, 8–17.

16 Edward Lawler III and John Grant Rhode, *Information and Control in Organizations* (Pacific Palisades, Calif.: Goodyear, 1976), p. 66; Richard Hackman and Greg Oldham, "Motivation Through the Design of Work: Test of a Theory," *Organizational Behavior and Human Performance*, Vol. 16 (August 1976), pp. 250, 279.

17 For a good review of many of these findings, see Alan Filley, Robert House, and

Steve Kerr, *Managerial Process and Organizational Behavior* (Glenview, Ill.: Scott, Foresman, 1976).

18 See, for example, Frederick Herzberg, "One More Time: How Do You Motivate Employees?"; M. D. Kilbridge, "Reduced Costs Through Job Enlargement: A Case," *Journal of Business*, October 1960, 357–62; Dennis Umstot, Cecil Bell, Jr., and Terrence Mitchell, "Effects of Job Enrichment and Task Goals on Satisfaction and Production: Implications for Job Design," *Journal of Applied Psychology*, Vol. 61 (1976), 379–94.

19 Rollin H. Simmons and John N. Oriff, "Worker Behavior vs. Enrichment Theory," *Administrative Science Quarterly*, Vol. 20 (1975), 606; David Whitsett, "Where Are Your Unenriched Jobs?" *Harvard Business Review*, Vol. 53 (January–February 1976); Greg Oldham, J. R. Hackman, and J. Pearce, "Conditions under Which Employees Respond Positively to Enriched Work," *Journal of Applied Psychology*, Vol. 61 (August 1976), 395–403.

20 See, for example, Saul Gellerman, *Motivation and Productivity* (New York: AMA, 1963), p. 218.

21 J. Richard Hackman, Greg Oldham, Robert Johnson, and Kenneth Purch, "A New Strategy for Job Enrichment," *California Management Review*, Vol. 17, No. 4, 51–71; reprinted in H. Kirk Downey, Don Hellriegel, and John Slocum, Jr., *Organizational Behavior* (St. Paul, Minn.: West, 1977), pp. 304–32.

22 Bruce Buchanan, "To Walk an Extra Mile: The Whats, Whens, and Whys of Organizational Commitment," *Organizational Dynamics*, Spring 1975, pp. 67–80; and Jerome Schnee, Harold Lazarus, and E. Kirby Warren, *The Progress of Management* (Englewood Cliffs, N.J.: Prentice-Hall, 1977).

23 Richard M. Steers, "Antecedents and Outcomes of Organizational Commitment," *Administrative Science Quarterly*, Vol. 22 (March 1977); Lyman Porter, Richard Steers, Richard Mowday, and Paul Boulian, "Organizational Commitment, Job Satisfaction, and Turnover among Psychiatric Technicians," *Journal of Applied Psychology*, Vol. 59 (November 1974), 603–9.

24 Buchanan, "To Walk an Extra Mile."

25 James L. Poch and Richard Steers, "Job Attachment, Satisfaction, and Turnover among Public Employees," Technical Report #6, Office of Naval Research, University of Oregon, 1976; Porter et al., "Organizational Commitment"; and Richard Mowday, Lyman Porter, and Robert Dubin, "Unit Performance, Situational Factors, and Employee Attitudes in Spatially Separated Work Units," *Organizational Behavior and Human Performance*, Vol. 12 (1974), 231–48.

26 Buchanan, "To Walk an Extra Mile"; see also Bruce Buchanan, "Building Organizational Commitment: The Socialization of Managers in Work Organizations," *Administrative Science Quarterly*, Vol. 19 (1974), 533–46.

27 Steers, "Antecedents and Outcomes."

28 See J. Richard Hackman and Edward E. Lawler III, "Employee Reactions to Job Characteristics," *Journal of Applied Psychology*, Vol. 55 (1971) for task identity scale.

29 For additional studies in this area, see Samuel Rabinowitz, Douglas Hall, and James Goodale, "Job Scope and Individual Differences as Predictors of Job Involvement: Independent or Interactive?" *Academy of Management Journal*, Vol. 20, No. 2 (1977), 273–81; Bill McKelvey and Yuma Sekaran, "Toward a Career Based Theory of Job Involvement: A Study of Scientists and Engineers," *Administrative Science Quarterly*, Vol. 22, No. 2 (June 1977), 280–305.

30 Steers, "Antecedents and Outcomes," p. 53.

31 Steven Sales, "Supervisory Style and Productivity: Review and Theory," *Personnel Psychology*, Vol. 19, No. 3 (1966), 275–86.

32 J. Richard Hackman, Edward E. Lawler III, and Lyman Porter, *Behavior in Organizations* (New York: McGraw-Hill, 1975), p. 419.

33 See Kenneth Scheflen, Edward E. Lawler III, and J. Richard Hackman, "Long Term Impact of Employee Participation in the Development of Pay Incentive Plans: A Field Experiment Revisited," *Journal of Applied Psychology*, Vol. 55 (1971), 182–86; and Edward E. Lawler III and J. Richard Hackman, "Impact of Employee Participation in the

Development of Pay Incentive Plans: A Field Experiment," *Journal of Applied Psychology*, Vol. 53 (1969), 467–71.

[34] See "Participation and Decision Making in Work Group Activity," in Paul Lawrence and John Seiler, *Organizational Behavior and Administration* (Homewood, Ill.: Richard D. Irwin, 1965), pp. 931–32.

[35] See also Nancy Morse and Evert Reimer, "The Experimental Change of a Major Organizational Variable," *Journal of Abnormal and Social Psychology*, Vol. 52, No. 1 (January 1956), 120–29.

[36] Edward Lawler III, "Control Systems in Organizations," in Marvin Dunnette, *Handbook of Industrial and Organizational Psychology* (Chicago: Rand McNally, 1976), p. 1281. See also Joseph Alutto and Donald Redenburgh, "Characteristics of Decisional Participation by Nurses," *Academy of Management Journal*, Vol. 20, No. 2 (1977), 341–47.

[37] *Productivity* was measured indirectly—for example, by measuring the number of "work-minded" remarks from each child under various conditions. Also note that drawing inferences from studies such as this, which are not directly concerned with *managerial* behavior, can be dangerous. R. Lippitt, "An Experimental Study of the Effects of Democratic and Autocratic Atmosphere," *University of Iowa Studies in Child Welfare*, No. 16 (1940), 45–195.

[38] H. G. McCurdy and H. W. Eber, "Democratic versus Authoritarian: A Further Investigation of Group Problem Solving," *Journal of Personality*, Vol. 22 (1953), 258–69.

[39] N. C. Morse and E. Reimer, "The Experimental Change of a Major Organizational Variable," *Journal of Abnormal and Social Psychology*, Vol. 52 (1956).

[40] Victor Vroom, "Some Personality Determinants of the Effects of Participation," *Journal of Abnormal and Social Psychology*, Vol. 59 (1959), 322–27; Victor Vroom and F. Mann, "Leader Authoritarianism and Employee Attitudes," *Personnel Psychology*, Vol. 13 (1960), 125–39.

[41] J. R. French, Jr., J. Israel, and D. As, "An Experiment in Participation in a Norwegian Factory: Interpersonal Dimensions of Decision Making," *Human Relations*, Vol. 13, No. 1 (1969), 3–19; U. Foa, "Relation of Workers' Expectation to Satisfaction with Supervisor," *Personnel Psychology*, Vol. 10 (1957), 161–68. See also Ahmed Abdel-Halim and Kendrith Roland, "Some Personality Determinants of the Effects of Participation: A Further Investigation," *Personnel Psychology*, Vol. 29, No. 1 (Spring 1976) for views contradictory to those of Vroom.

[42] Victor Vroom, "A New Look at Managerial Decision Making," *Organizational Dynamics*, Spring 1973; Reprinted, by permission of the publisher, from *Organizational Dynamics*, Spring 1973, © 1973 by AMACOM, a division of American Management Associations. All rights reserved. Henri Tosi, *Readings in Management* (Chicago: St. Clair Press, 1976); Victor Vroom and Arthur Jago, "On the Validity of the Vroom-Yetton Model," *Journal of Applied Psychology*, Vol. 63, No. 2 (1978), 151–62.

[43] Hackman, Lawler, and Porter, *Behavior in Organizations*, p. 420; see also H. G. Kaufman, "Individual Differences, Early Work Challenge and Continuing Education," *Journal of Applied Psychology*, Vol. 60, No. 3 (June 1975); Gary Latham and Gary Yukl, "Assigned versus Participative Goal Setting With Educated and Uneducated Woods Workers," *Journal of Applied Psychology*, Vol. 60, No. 3 (June 1975).

[44] Lawler, "Control Systems in Organizations."

[45] Douglas McGregor, *The Human Side of Enterprise* (New York: McGraw-Hill, 1960).

[46] Stephen J. Carroll, Jr., and Henry L. Tosi, *Management by Objectives* (New York: Macmillan, 1973).

[47] J. F. Bryan and E. A. Locke, "Goal Setting as a Means of Increasing Motivation," *Journal of Applied Psychology*, Vol. 51 (1967), 274–77.

[48] F. W. Fryer, *An Evaluation of Level of Aspiration as a Training Procedure* (Englewood Cliffs, N.J.: Prentice-Hall, 1963).

49 Gary D. Latham and Sydney B. Kinne III, "Improving Job Performance through Training in Goal Setting," *Journal of Applied Psychology,* Vol. 59, No. 2 (1974), 187–91.

50 M. W. Pryer and B. M. Bass, "Some Effects of Feedback on Behavior in Groups," Technical Report #13, Contract N70NR35609 (Baton Rouge: Louisiana State University, 1957).

51 J. A. Weitz, J. Antoinette, and S. R. Wallace, "The Effect of Home Office Contact on Sales Performance," *Personnel Psychology,* Vol. 7 (1954), 381–84.

52 Morse and Reimer, "The Experimental Change of a Major Organizational Variable," pp. 120–29.

53 N. R. F. Maier, *Problem Solving Discussions and Conferences* (New York: McGraw-Hill, 1963).

54 J. R. P. French, Jr., E. Kay, and H. H. Meyer, "Participation and the Appraisal System," *Human Relations,* Vol. 19 (1966), 3–19.

55 A. P. Raia, "A Second Look at Goals and Controls," *California Management Review,* Vol. 8 (1966), 49–58. Stephen J. Carroll, Jr., and Henry L. Tosi, *Management by Objectives* (New York: Macmillan, 1973), p. 11.

56 John M. Ivancevich, "Changes in Performance in a Management by Objectives Program," *Administrative Science Quarterly,* December 1974.

57 Stephen J. Carroll, Jr., and Henry L. Tosi, *Management by Objectives* (New York: Macmillan, 1973).

58 *Ibid.,* p. 45; p. 105.

59 *Ibid.,* pp. 129–38.

60 Raia, "A Second Look at Goals and Controls."

61 MBO's effect may be indirect. For example, Jamieson has suggested that the improved performance may be largely a function of the planning that emerges from detailing and coordinating corporate, unit, and individual objectives. Bruce D. Jamieson, "Behavior Problems with Management by Objectives," *Academy of Management Journal,* Vol. 16, No. 3 (September 1973); Henry Tosi, John Hunter, Rob Chesser, Jim Tartar, and Steven Carroll, "How Real Are Changes Induced by Management by Objectives?" *Administrative Science Quarterly,* Vol. 21, No. 2 (June 1976); Bruce Kirchoff, "A Diagnostic Tool for Management by Objectives," *Personnel Psychology,* Vol. 28 (Autumn, 1975).

62 See John Castellana, "Rural and Urban Differences: One More Time," *Academy of Management Journal,* Vol. 19, No. 3 (1976); A. N. Turner and P. R. Lawrence, *Industrial Jobs and the Worker* (Boston: Harvard University Press, 1965).

63 See, for example, Robert Dubin, "Industrial Workers' Worlds: A Study of the Central Life Interests of Industrial Workers," *Social Problems,* Vol. 3 (1956), 130–142.

64 Kenji Ima, "Central Life Interests of Industrial Workers: A Replication among Lumber Workers," unpublished master's thesis, University of Oregon, cited in Robert Dubin, Joseph Champoux, and Lyman Porter, "Central Life Interests and Organizational Commitment of Blue Collar and Clerical Workers," *Administrative Science Quarterly,* Vol. 20 (September 1975), 411–21.

65 Walter Corrie, Jr., "Work as a 'Central Life Interest': A Comparison of the Amana Coloney Worker with the Nonamana Coloney Worker in a Given Industrial Setting," unpublished doctoral dissertation, University of Iowa, 1957; Calvin Endo, "Career Anchorage Points and Central Life Interests of Japanese Middle Managers," unpublished doctoral dissertation, University of Oregon, 1970; John Mauere, "Work as a Central Life Interest of Industrial Supervisors," *Academy of Management Journal,* Vol. 11 (1968), 329–39.

66 Katz and Kahn, *The Social Psychology of Organizations,* p. 366.

67 Earl Gomersall and M. Scott Myers, "Breakthrough in On-The-Job Training," *Harvard Business Review,* Vol. 44 (July–August 1966), 62–72.

68 Douglas Hall, *Careers in Organizations* (Pacific Palisades, Calif.: Goodyear, 1977).

case for part IV:
the lincoln electric company

The most famous incentive plan of modern times is that of the Lincoln Electric Company of Cleveland, Ohio, a concern with under 2,000 employees.[1] The Lincoln Electric Company has a profit-sharing plan under which approximately 80 percent of the company profits are distributed to the employees. The profit-sharing bonuses are extremely large, amounting to approximately the equivalent of the basic wages and salaries. As a result, the total earnings of the employees are at least double the average earnings in comparable concerns. The interesting question about this plan is why it works so successfully when profit sharing has failed in other companies.

The Lincoln Electric Company is the largest producer of electrodes and arc welding equipment in the United States. The company was founded in 1896. Mr. James F. Lincoln took over as president in 1913 and it was under his management that the incentive system developed. One of his first acts, in 1914, was to establish an Advisory Board, with one elected worker from each department, to advise him on management problems. This committee meets with top management every other Monday. It discusses grievances and suggestions for improving working conditions. New committee members are elected each month, so that memberships continually rotate. There is no union.

The Advisory Board has assisted in introducing changes in the Lincoln Electric Company. For example, the Board helped originate a shorter workweek. The Board assisted in introducing the profit-sharing plan itself in 1934. In fact, Mr. Lincoln was not enthusiastic about the idea at first. It was made clear to the employees that bonuses would have to be earned, that they would arise from increased effort and productivity. Substantial bonuses were earned from the beginning.

The increased productivity under the incentive plan has not only permitted an enormous increase in wages and salaries, but also has enabled the company to cut prices, passing part of the savings in labor time to the consumer. It has also made possible an increase in dividends, though it is interesting that the dividends have increased much less than in most comparable companies. The dividend rate in 1934 was $2.50 per share; in 1943 it was $6 and has not changed much since that time.

The bonus paid to a particular worker depends on several considerations. First, it varies with overall company profits. The individual's portion of the part of profits set aside for bonuses depends, in part, on a merit rating done by his superior. A letter from Mr. Lincoln, dated December 4, 1959, made this announcement:

> The Lincoln Electric Company paid its 1,371 employees in Cleveland and its 38 district offices throughout the country $6,488,167 today in annual incentive pay. Each employee received a check representing payment for his or her extra contribution to the success of the company for the year. The amount of each check was determined by an individual merit rating of performance on the job for the year.

Lincoln has paid this incentive every year since 1934, during which time the company has paid a total of $93,985,308 in addition to regular earnings and other benefits all of which are standard for the industry. This year the company also purchased $1,000,000 in retirement annuities covering each employee. The company also guarantees continuous employment to all employees with over two years' service, thus securing them against layoffs.

Mr. Lincoln's letter indicates that the average bonus per employee was about $4,730. This [was in 1959] more than the total wages of most nonsupervisory employees in the United States.

Mr. Lincoln personally determines the bonuses of his immediate subordinates. All profit-sharing bonuses are paid at the end of the year. In addition, payments are made for cost-saving suggestions at the rate of one-half of expected savings during the first year. A Suggestion System Board reviews suggestions once a week. The Board is careful to explain to workers the impracticality of suggestions not adopted.

Great care is taken in the selection of new employees, with emphasis on intelligence quotients and extracurricular activities (such as athletics). The average age of foremen is kept down by promoting older supervisors to staff positions. The foremen are encouraged to discuss companywide problems in weekly meetings. This gives the foremen a broader managerial viewpoint, prepares them for higher positions, and provides them with information to answer questions within their departments.

Mr. Lincoln has written at length about his ideas on incentives. He argues that too much emphasis is placed upon profits as the sole purpose of industry. This emphasis, he feels, distracts management from its main objective and tends to alienate the employees. The goal should instead be one of making a better product to be sold at a lower price, with profits a by-product of performing service. The aim in dealing with company personnel should be to develop latent abilities by stimulating the desire to develop. This can be done by providing challenging jobs, by building up a sense of teamwork and of individual responsibility to the team, by continually applying pressure for more and better work, and by promoting only on the basis of ability and performance. Mr. Lincoln argues that supervisors should be leaders rather than bosses; they should accept their subordinates as members of a team. He also emphasizes selection of employees with ability and initiative.

Mr. Lincoln stresses the importance of recognition. He states that the "worker must feel that he is recognized in accordance with his contribution to success. If he does not have that feeling of self-respect and the respect of others because of his skill, he will think he is being 'played for a sucker' if he increases his output so the owners can have more profit."

"It is not necessary that this reward be solely in money. As a matter of fact, the amateur athlete gets no money, yet he tries harder than the professional who is paid. This athlete, however, does get the respect and position resulting from his achievement. That is his reward." [2]

Mr. Lincoln also stresses competition as a driving force. While it is desirable to have a sense of team membership, he feels that it is also important to stress the drive to be outstanding in the group.

Mr. Lincoln's views on profit sharing are of special interest. "Profit sharing, in its many forms as generally applied, fails and for the same fundamental reasons. Profit sharing does not distinguish the worker. He is likely to consider the share of the profit given him in the usual profit-sharing split somewhat in the nature of a tip to a Pullman porter. . . . The worker knows that manufacturing is necessary to the consumer. He is not so sure about profit. He thinks that the salary that the boss gets should satisfy him without any profit. Profit should be a by-product of service to the consumer, not an end in itself."

Mr. Lincoln stresses that it is not enough to impose an incentive system from above. The problem is to get the employees to want the plan. For example, if the plan is tried out by a small group at first, the rest of the personnel may insist on being included. The workers must feel that the added effort they will put in under the plan will produce large rewards, both monetary and nonmonetary. Mr. Lincoln favors stock-ownership plans, such as the one available to the employees of the Lincoln Electric Company, but he does not think that the company should put pressure on the employees to buy stock. Stock ownership creates a sense of responsibility for company success and acts as a powerful incentive in itself.

QUESTIONS

(Please answer these questions before reading the conclusion below.)

1. Does the success of the Lincoln plan indicate that financial rewards themselves, if they are large enough, can result in innovative behavior and self-control?

2. What specific actions have apparently been taken at Lincoln to elicit self-control and provide intrinsic rewards?

3. "The workers at Lincoln are actually more like owners than workers." Is this true? If so, how would it explain the success of the Lincoln incentive plan?

CONCLUSION

The Lincoln Electric plan is one technique that has been used to elicit self-control. As such, it illustrates several important features of an effective, practical motivation system.

First, as we discussed in the last few chapters, one effective way (perhaps the most effective way) of eliciting self-control is to somehow coordinate each employee's goals with those of the organization, and it is such a coordination that the Lincoln plan aims at achieving. Under this plan, workers appear to be driven to increased productivity, since it increases both the organization's and their own rewards. To a large extent, their goals and those of the firm become one and the same, and the result is a group of highly committed, loyal, and motivated employees.

Yet other incentive plans have been tried and have failed; in fact, even implementing the Lincoln plan is no guarantee of success. And we discussed the fact that extrinsic rewards by themselves are not usually sufficient for eliciting the kind of innovative, creative behavior that employees at the Lincoln firm seem capable of exhibiting. What, then, accounts for the Lincoln plan's success?

The answer, probably, is that the Lincoln plan is far more than simply a financial incentive plan. In addition to the substantial financial rewards that accrue to employees, the plan relies on other important elements, including companywide participation, careful staffing, job enrichment, and an emphasis on building employee commitment. There is, for example, a suggestion system aimed at encouraging suggestions for new methods and products. There is an employees' association, the objective of which is to provide a cooperative group apart from the management to promote social and athletic activities among the workers. An advisory board elected by employees meets periodically with management in order to discuss grievances and complaints and to make suggestions regarding the improvement of working conditions.

In summary, there are many ways to interpret the success of the Lincoln Electric firm's incentive plan. It is possible, for example, that the financial rewards accruing to the workers are so enormous that it is in fact the rewards and not the other elements like participation that account for the plan's success. And it is difficult to determine whether the Lincoln Electric Company would not generate more profits for its owners by eliminating the incentive plan and its associated bonuses, even though productivity might decrease. In any case, there is little doubt that the Lincoln experiment contains an important lesson, in that it represents one company's approach to harmonizing its goals with those of its employees.

FOOTNOTES

1 This case was taken from W. Warren Haynes and Joseph Massie, *Management* (Englewood Cliffs, N.J.: Prentice-Hall, 1969), pp. 233–36.

2 James F. Lincoln, *Incentive Management* (Cleveland, O.: Lincoln Electric Company, 1951), p. 81.

PART V

SOCIAL INFLUENCES ON ORGANIZATION EFFECTIVENESS

In this part of the book, we discuss leadership processes, group processes, intergroup relations and conflict, and organizational change and development. Although an effective *structure* and the establishment of *compliance* are important determinants of organization effectiveness, other factors—like the ones discussed in this part—also influence effectiveness (often through their effects on structure and compliance). Therefore, one important question raised in most of these chapters is, "How does this particular factor (leadership, group processes, and so on) influence organization structure and compliance?"

Chapter 11

Leadership Processes

and Organization Theory

CHAPTER OVERVIEW

In this chapter we present a survey of leadership-effectiveness theories. We discuss trait theories (which focus on what the leader *is*), behavioral theories (which focus on what the leader *does*), and contingency theories (which tie the leader's effectiveness to the nature of the "situation").

We also relate leadership to organization theory and discuss its relationship to organization structure and compliance. With respect to structure, for example, no organization chart or job description can ever be totally complete and so the leader therefore carries out a "structuring" function, filling in the "gaps" on a day-to-day basis.

Leaders are also instrumental in ensuring compliance. How do they do this? We discuss the classicists' solution (close supervision), the human-relations solution (raise morale), and Katz and Kahn's solution (participative leadership). As you read this chapter, ask:

1. How does "context" influence leadership?
2. How does leadership influence organization structure?
3. How does leadership influence organizational compliance?

The outline of this chapter is as follows:

I. A Survey of Leadership-Effectiveness Theories
   A. Trait Theories of Leadership Effectiveness
   B. Behavioral Theories: Styles of Leadership
   C. Fiedler's Contingency Theory of Leadership

A SURVEY
OF LEADERSHIP-EFFECTIVENESS THEORIES

Leadership effectiveness theories fall into three categories: the trait, behavioral (style), and contingency theories of leadership.

Trait Theories of Leadership Effectiveness

Background. Trait theories of leadership assume that effective leaders have a finite number of identifiable traits or characteristics that distinguish them from ineffective leaders. These theories emerged out of work done by the American Psychological Association at the beginning of World War I.[1] A committee of psychologists had been appointed to assist the U.S. Army in screening and selecting military personnel, and a number of useful tools, including the Army Alpha Test of Intelligence, were developed at this time. After the war, it seemed logical to try to apply the same techniques or methods in industrial situations, and the early, "traitist" leadership research grew out of this personnel-testing movement.

Most of the early research on leadership traits was inconclusive: Specific traits were found to be related to leader effectiveness, but none were found to be so related in a variety of different studies and situations. For example, traits classified as physical, social background, intelligence and ability, and personality were found to differentiate leaders from followers and effective leaders from ineffective leaders in specific studies. However, most reviewers were in agreement that the use of various traits had not proved very useful for the selection of leaders.[2] More recently, Palmer concluded that his own investigation "showed no support for the hypothesis that management effectiveness, as evaluated by subordinate managers, is a function of the personality characteristics of the individual. . . ."[3]

The Ghiselli research. More recently, a number of researchers, most notably Edwin Ghiselli,[4] have carried out multicompany studies that suggest it may be possible to identify traits that distinguish effective from ineffective leaders in a variety of settings.

Ghiselli's subjects included 306 middle managers, ranging in age from 26 to 42. They were employed by 90 different businesses and industrial organizations throughout the United States; an average of three to four men were drawn from each firm. The firms were in the transportation, finance, insurance, manufacturing, utilities, and communications industries. About 90 percent of the subjects were college graduates; all had had at least some

TABLE 11-1

Portion of Ghiselli's Self-Description Inventory

The purpose of this inventory is to obtain a picture of the traits you believe you possess and to see how you describe yourself. There are no right or wrong answers, so try to describe yourself as accurately and honestly as you can.

In each of the pairs of words below, check the one you think *most* describes you.

1.___capable	11.___unaffected
___discreet	___alert
2.___understanding	12.___sharp-witted
___thorough	___deliberate
3.___cooperative	13.___kind
___inventive	___jolly
4.___friendly	14.___efficient
___cheerful	___clear-thinking
5.___energetic	15.___realistic
___ambitious	___tactful
6.___persevering	16.___enterprising
___independent	___intelligent
7.___loyal	17.___affectionate
___dependable	___frank
8.___determined	18.___progressive
___courageous	___thrifty
9.___industrious	19.___sincere
___practical	___calm
10.___planful	20.___thoughtful
___resourceful	___fair-minded

Source: Edwin E. Ghiselli, *Explorations in Managerial Talent* (Pacific Palisades, Calif.: Good-year, 1971), p. 139.

college education. Because of this and the fact that they were all middle managers, Ghiselli says that "these 306 managers do not constitute a representative sample of American executives and administrators [although] there is sufficient variation both in managers and in firms that the results we obtained from our study should have a good deal of generalizability."

The test used in these studies is called the Self-Description Inventory, a portion of which is presented in Table 11-1. Subjects are asked to describe themselves by checking those of a series of adjectives that apply to them. In the table, for example, a person might describe himself as discreet, thorough, cooperative, and cheerful.

Based upon his work with this inventory, Ghiselli has identified important leadership traits, classified as follows:

I. *Abilities*
   Supervisory ability

  Intelligence
  Initiative

  II. *Personality traits*
  Self-assurance
  Decisiveness
  Masculinity/femininity
  Maturity
  Working-class affinity

  III. *Motivations*
  Need for occupational achievement
  Need for self-actualization
  Need for power over others
  Need for high financial reward
  Need for job security

Supervisory ability measures the capacity of a person to direct the work of others, and to organize and integrate their activities so that the goal of the work group can be obtained. Characteristics reflecting high supervisory ability include, for example, cheerful, energetic, clear-thinking, tactful, and farsighted. *Intelligence,* "the cognitive capacity of the mind, . . . gives an overall picture, even though a crude one, of the individual's general level of competence." *Initiative* reflects the "independence and inventiveness of the person." [5]

Self-assurance "refers to the extent to which the individual perceives himself to be effective in dealing with the problems that confront him." *Decisiveness* measures the degree to which the subject is a "ready, quick, and self confident decision maker." *Masculinity/femininity* reflects the fact that "there are a number of qualities that tend to be associated with one sex, and that complement the other sex." Commonly, for example, "robustness and forcefulness are taken to be a part of masculinity, and gentleness and understanding to be a part of femininity," according to Ghiselli.[6] *Maturity* "is usually taken to refer to the extent to which an individual is more like those that are older than he is, rather than those who are younger than he is." *Working-class affinity* reflects the degree to which a person, whatever his occupation, "would prefer to be with, to work with, and to share the common problems of those of the working class." [7]

Need for occupational achievement reflects the degree to which people "are impelled to achieve appointments to high level positions in business and industry." Need for *self-actualization* reflects the degree to which people need and seek the opportunity to utilize their talents to the fullest extent.[8] Ghiselli's other needs—for power over others, high financial reward, and job security—are self-explanatory.

Findings. Ghiselli's findings are summarized in Figure 11-1, which presents the relative importance of the 13 traits to managerial talent. First, you can see that supervisory ability—the capacity to direct the work of others, and to organize and integrate their activities so that the goal of the

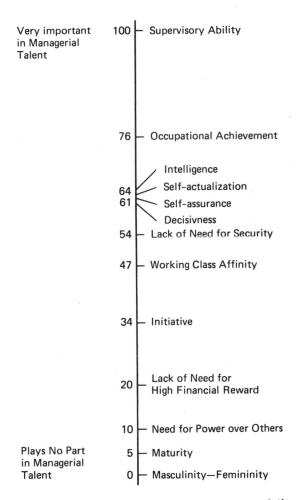

Very important in Managerial Talent	100	— Supervisory Ability
	76	— Occupational Achievement
	64	— Intelligence, Self-actualization
	61	— Self-assurance, Decisivness
	54	— Lack of Need for Security
	47	— Working Class Affinity
	34	— Initiative
	20	— Lack of Need for High Financial Reward
	10	— Need for Power over Others
Plays No Part in Managerial Talent	5	— Maturity
	0	— Masculinity—Femininity

FIGURE 11-1. The Relative Importance of the Thirteen Traits to Managerial Talent

Source: Edwin E. Ghiselli, *Explorations in Managerial Talent* (Pacific Palisades, Calif.: Goodyear, 1971), p. 165.

work group can be attained—seems to be the most powerful trait for predicting leader effectiveness. According to Ghiselli, "it is the trait which plays the most important role, and stands out clearly and is apart from all of the other traits."

Next in importance is a cluster of five traits: the need for occupational achievement, intelligence, the need for self-actualization, self-assurance, and decisiveness. According to Ghiselli, "the traits in this cluster are just about equally important, and can be said to play a major role in managerial talent."

Below these, and fairly well spread out, are a number of traits that can be characterized as playing a minor role in managerial talent. These include the need for security, working-class affinity, initiative, need for high financial reward, need for power, maturity, and masculinity/femininity.[9]

Trait theory: Discussion. Ghiselli found that six traits (supervisory ability, occupational achievement, intelligence, self-actualization need, self-assurance need, and decisiveness) characterized effective managers, and it is probably reasonable to assume that these traits characterize, more narrowly, effective leaders as well. These findings suggest that trait theory is probably of some use in predicting leader effectiveness, but several caveats are in order. First, Stogdill points out that many studies of leader effectiveness have been carried out in formal organizations where "severe screening processes" have already acted to ensure that leaders are similar to each other.[10] Furthermore, even though Ghiselli's research tapped a wide range of firms and subjects, more work is needed before we can generalize his findings in regard to other, specific organizations. In summary, the trait approach is useful, but at this point it is necessary to identify traits that predict leader effectiveness within specific organizations (perhaps using Ghiselli's findings as a starting point). These traits can then be used to screen leader candidates.

Behavioral Theories: Styles of Leadership

Behavioral leadership theories focus on what the leader does and how he behaves in carrying out his leadership functions, rather than on traits like intelligence or initiative. Trait theory attempts to explain leadership on the basis of what the leader *is,* behavioral theory on the basis of what the leader *does.*

Robert Bales carried out a famous study some years ago in which he established a series of five-man discussion groups that had to arrive at a single solution to a human-relations problem within a specified time. Group members were relative strangers, and the groups met four times. After each session, they had to answer a number of simple questions, such as, Whom did you like? Whom did you dislike? Who did most to guide the discussion? Who contributed the most ideas?

Bales found that after the first session, the best-liked member was usually the one who had contributed the most ideas or guidance. However, by the end of the last session, he was no longer the person best liked; in fact, the one who contributed most was usually the most disliked man.[11]

Bales's findings draw attention to a major assumption underlying the behavioral leadership theories. Specifically, there are two major functions that leaders can perform—accomplishing the task and satisfying the needs of group members—and the same person will not necessarily fill both roles. Bales found that as the task leader continued to force people to focus on their jobs, certain of their needs (for affiliation, say) were frustrated. What emerged was a social leader, one whose role was to reduce tensions and make the job more pleasant. The behavior of this leader helped to boost morale and crystalize and defend the values, attitudes, and beliefs of the group. It is generally recognized that the task and people dimensions of leader behavior are not mutually exclusive. They are usually thought of as independent, with most leaders exhibiting elements of both people and task orientation simultaneously.[12]

There are a number of different leadership styles typically associated with these basic task and people dimensions of leadership. Writers distinguish between structuring and considerate leaders, and close and general leaders, for example. The research evidence, which we discuss next, suggests that considerate styles of leadership are frequently associated with higher employee satisfaction, but that structuring styles are often associated with high employee performance and, on occasion, with high employee satisfaction as well.

Structuring and considerate styles. *Initiating structure* and *consideration* are two of the most frequently used descriptions of leader behavior. These two factors were developed out of research begun in 1945 at Ohio State University that was aimed at constructing an instrument for describing various leadership styles.[13] On the basis of conversations with various specialists, researchers developed a list of nine dimensions or categories of leadership behavior. Descriptive items were then written for each, and a final instrument, known as the Leader Behavior Description Questionnaire (LBDQ) was produced, which included a total of 150 of these descriptive items.

The LBDQ was further refined by Halpin and Wiener, who collected data from a number of air-force personnel.[14] They used 130 items of the original questionnaire and concluded that four independent factors could be used to summarize the 130 items:

1. *Consideration.* Behavior indicative of mutual trust, friendship, support, respect, and warmth.
2. *Initiating structure.* Leader behavior by which he organizes the work to be done; also, he must define relationships or roles and the channels of communication, and the ways of getting jobs done.
3. *Production emphasis.* Behavior which reflects attempts by the leader to motivate greater activity by emphasizing the job to be done.
4. *Sensitivity (social awareness).* Leader's sensitivity to, and his awareness of, social interrelationships and pressures inside or outside the group.

The Halpin and Wiener version of the LBDQ (or some adaptation of it) is probably the most widely used today. The researchers eventually dropped the third and fourth factors because they provided too little additional information, and *consideration* and *initiating structure* have therefore become almost synonymous with the "Ohio State" dimensions of leadership. An adaptation of the consideration and initiating-structure scales is presented in Table 11-2.[15]

TABLE 11-2

Selection of Items Representing Consideration and Initiating Structure

	Ratings by Judges *	
	Consideration	Initiating Structure
Consideration		
1. He expresses appreciation when one of us does a good job.	1.48	3.15
2. He stresses the importance of high morale among those under him.	1.39	4.55
3. He treats all his foremen as his equals.	1.97	5.21
4. He is friendly and can be easily approached.	1.52	4.61
Initiating Structure		
1. He rules with an iron hand.	5.85	1.48
2. He insists that his foreman follow standard ways of doing things in every detail.	5.39	1.48
3. He insists that he be informed on decisions made by foremen under him.	4.30	2.30
4. He "needles" foremen under him for greater effort.	6.30	1.94
5. He decides in detail what shall be done and how it shall be done.	4.85	1.12

* On a scale from 1.0 (always characteristic) to 7.0 (never characteristic)

Source: A. E. Lowin, W. J. Hrapchak, and M. J. Kavanagh, "Consideration and Initiating Structure: An Experimental Investigation of Leadership Traits," *Administrative Science Quarterly,* Vol. 14 (1969), 239-40.

Findings: Leader consideration. Leader consideration is generally found to be positively related to employee satisfaction, but its effects on employee performance are still unclear. In one major study, Stogdill surveyed over 1,000 managers in 27 organizations, including those in the metals, chemicals, textiles, aircraft, and retail-store industries, and in government agencies. While few relationships (between leadership and morale or performance) were found that characterized *all* the organizations of a given type, leader consideration was generally related to the employee's satisfaction, and especially, to how satisfied he or she was with freedom on the job.[16] No consistent relation was found between consideration and employee performance.

The finding that considerate leaders have the most satisfied employees has been supported by many other researchers.[17] In one classic study, Fleishman and Harris surveyed 57 foremen in a truck manufacturing plant. As you can see in Figure 11-2, they found that leader consideration and grievances (or turnover) were curvilinearly related. Consideration seemed to reduce grievances up to a point, but beyond that it had little or no effect on employee turnover or grievances. In summary, as Gary Yukl recently

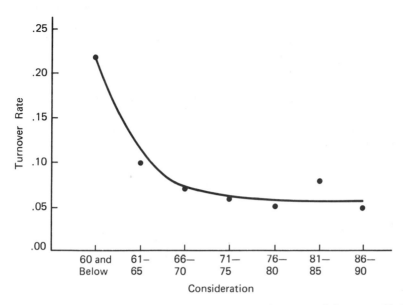

FIGURE 11-2. Relation between Consideration and Grievance Rates

Source: E. A. Fleishman and E. F. Harris, "Patterns of Leadership Behavior Related to Employee Grievances and Turnover," *Personnel Psychology,* Vol. 15 (1962), 42-56.

put it, "the research literature indicates that in most situations, considerate leaders will have more satisfied subordinates."

Findings: Initiating structure. The effects of *initiating structure* on subordinate satisfaction or performance, however, are inconsistent. In their study, Fleishman and Harris found structure and grievance rates to be directly related, but *where consideration was high,* leader structure and grievances were unrelated. Most researchers have failed to find any consistent relationship between initiating structure and satisfaction or performance.[18]

In summary, we will conclude that (1) leader consideration is positively related to employee satisfaction, although its effects on employee performance are unclear; and (2) one cannot generalize about the effects of initiating structure, except to say that its relation to employee satisfaction and performance may be positive, negative, or nonexistent, depending on the situation.[19]

Production-centered and employee-centered leadership styles. At about the same time that researchers at Ohio State were undertaking the construction of their LBDQ, a similar program was being instituted at the University of Michigan's Survey Research Center.[20] This line of research led to the identification of two dimensions of leader behavior, which were called *employee orientation* and *production (job) orientation.* The former was described as behavior by a leader indicating that he views his employees as human beings of intrinsic importance and accepts their individuality and personal needs. Production orientation is behavior that stresses production and the technical aspects of the job and reflects an assumption that employees are simply means to an end.

This line of research was developed by Rensis Likert of the University of Michigan. Likert and his associates have carried out many studies to determine which leadership style appears most effective. He concludes:

> Supervisors with the best record of performance focus their primary attention on the human aspects of their subordinates' problems and on endeavoring to build effective work groups with high performance goals.[21]

Although Likert and his associates have claimed that the employee-centered leader is the most effective one, even their own data suggest that at times a production-centered one is best. For example, he has found a number of instances in which employee-centered leadership was associated with low productivity; [22] and in at least one instance, the production-centered supervisor had a high-producing unit.[23]

Close and general styles of leadership. These styles of leadership were originally defined and studied by researchers at the University of Michigan.[24] They developed their leadership styles on the work previously carried out at the Survey Research Center. *Close supervision* was conceptualized as "one end of a continuum that describes the degree to which a supervisor specifies the roles of the subordinates and checks up to see that they comply with the specifications." [25] The *laissez-faire* leader, who takes a completely hands-off policy with his subordinates, would be at the other extreme, with the *general* leader somewhere in the middle of the continuum.

Most of the early research findings suggested that close leadership was associated with lower subordinate satisfaction. For example, Morse obtained data from female workers in a large metropolitan insurance firm and found that workers subjected to close supervision were usually less satisfied with the reasonableness of the supervisor's expectations and with the rules she enforced.[26] Similarly, Katz and Kahn reported finding a relation between closeness of supervision and aggressive feelings of workers in a tractor plant.[27] However, the results are far from definitive. Katz and his associates found no relationship at all between close or general supervision and worker aggression.[28] In another study, researchers attempted to ascertain the effects of close versus general styles of leadership.[29] They found that close supervision was related to employee aggressiveness, but that the specific effects of close supervision depended largely on the self-esteem of the subordinate, with increases in aggressive feelings occurring only in those with low self-esteem.

Common elements of leadership styles. We have discussed these various pairs of leadership styles individually here, but in practice they overlap. For example, many writers place the employee-centered, general, and considerate styles into one category, and the production-centered, close, and structuring styles into a second.[30]

Such categories seem valid. For example, in one study, researchers concluded that employee-centered supervisors tended to be democratic, to supervise in a general way, and to be nonpunitive.[31] One writer points out that these same styles seem to be components of the "consideration" styles described by the Ohio State LBDQ.[32] Likert equates close and general styles of leadership with job- and employee-centered styles.[33]

On the whole, therefore, these several pairs of styles do have much in common, and there seems to be validity in reducing them to two broad— "people" and "task"—leadership styles. We have to be careful, however, not to carry such categorizations too far. For example, "production-centered" leadership need not be devoid of consideration, and a "close" leadership style need not be a "punitive" one.

Leadership styles: A situational approach. Although a prevailing view is that a more considerate leader style is "best," the research findings are mixed. Usually, the more employee-centered styles are associated with higher levels of subordinate satisfaction, but the findings are not consistent. Furthermore, the structuring leader sometimes has the more productive work group.

Part of the reason for these inconsistent findings may well be that the styles are not mutually exclusive: Subordinates may see their authoritarian leader as considerate and supportive (a "benevolent autocrat"). Furthermore, many of the writers in this area have perhaps made the same mistake for which they blame the classical theorists: They often assume that some particular style, such as employee orientation, is universally applicable regardless of the nature of the situation. They usually disregard such leadership traits as intelligence and initiative and take the personality of the subordinate into account only insofar as they assume that all subordinates prefer greater freedom and independence.[34] Finally, these theorists usually ignore the nature of the work group's task; thus, an implicit assumption is that a particular style is as appropriate on an assembly line as in a research facility.

This need to take the "situation" into account when studying the relation between leadership style and subordinate satisfaction and behavior is apparently quite important.[35] Based upon an exhaustive review of the literature, for example, four writers concluded that a variety of situational factors influence which style of leadership is appropriate. A sampling of the situational factors and their expected effects follows:

Job pressure. The higher the job pressure—due to time pressure, conflict, physical danger, etc.—the more tolerant will subordinates be of attempts by the leader to structure the situation.

Intrinsic job satisfaction. The more satisfying the job itself, the less impact leader consideration has on subordinate satisfaction.

Subordinate's need for information. The higher the subordinate's need for information—due to his personality, the ambiguity of the job, etc. —the more tolerant he will be of the leader's attempts to structure the job.

Leader's consideration. The more considerate the leader is, the more he will be able to structure the task without causing his subordinates to become dissatisfied.[36]

Fiedler's Contingency Theory of Leadership

Behavioral scientists have long recognized the importance of situational factors in explaining leader effectiveness. Stogdill, after reviewing a large number of leadership studies, concluded that the traits or skills required in a leader are largely determined by the situation in which he is to exercise leadership.[37] Similarly, as we have seen, no one style of leadership has been found to be universally effective—a fact that led Tannenbaum and Schmidt to conclude that "effective leadership depends on the leader, his followers, the situation, and the interrelationships between them." [38]

Despite this general acceptance of the importance of situational factors in leader effectiveness, there have been few attempts to establish controls for such factors. Consequently, we have seen a series of studies in which the observed relationships between leader and subordinate behavior are applicable only to the unique research setting. Lowin and his associates pointed out, for example, that initiating structure and consideration have been correlated both positively and negatively with effectiveness and morale indexes.[39] Korman carried out an extensive review of the relevant literature and came to a similar conclusion.[40]

The contingency model of leadership effectiveness grew out of a comprehensive program of research begun at the University of Illinois by Fred E. Fiedler in 1951. Although Fiedler's work has recently been subjected to some rather sharp criticism, he and his colleagues have answered many of their critics' questions, and the debate appears to be a continuing one.

The theory. Fiedler originally sought to determine whether a leader who was very lenient in evaluating his associates was more or less likely to have a high-producing group than the leader who was highly demanding and discriminating. At the core of this research program is the "esteem for the least preferred coworker," or LPC scale, a measure of leader orientation. The person who fills it out is asked to think of all the people with whom he has ever worked and to focus on the one person with whom he "had the most difficult time in getting a job done"—that is, his least-preferred coworker. The rater is then asked to describe this person on a series of bipolar, 8-point, descriptive adjective scales whose extremes are labeled in the following fashion:

Pleasant . . . . Unpleasant

Intelligent . . . . Stupid

Although Fiedler originally felt that the LPC was measuring a personality trait, some of his recent papers suggest that the LPC is actually measuring a style of leadership, ranging from considerate leadership (high LPC) to structuring leadership (low LPC).

At the base of Fiedler's theory are three situational dimensions that he feels influence and determine whether considerate or structuring leader styles are called for:

266

1. *Position power.* "The degree to which the position itself enables the leader to get his group members to comply with and accept his direction and leadership."
2. *Task structure.* How routine and predictable the work group's task is.
3. *Leader–member relations.* The extent to which the leader "gets along" with his men, and the extent to which they have confidence in him and are loyal to him.

Findings. Fiedler claims to have found that "the appropriateness of the leadership style for maximizing group performance is contingent upon the favorableness of the group-task situation." [41] As shown in Figure 11-3, Fiedler feels that where the situation is either favorable or unfavorable to the leader (where leader–member relations, task structure, and leader position power are either very high or very low), a more task-oriented, structuring leader is appropriate. On the other hand, in the mid-range, where these factors are more mixed and the task is not as clear-cut, a more considerate, relationship-oriented leader is appropriate. To explain these findings, Fiedler says:

> In the very favorable conditions in which the leader has power, informal backing, and a relatively well-structured task, the group is ready to be directed, and the group members expect to be told what to do. . . . In the relatively unfavorable situation, we would again expect that the task oriented leader will be more effective than will the considerate leader who is concerned with interpersonal relations (the group will fall apart without the leader's active intervention and control). . . . In situations which are only moderately favorable (or moderately unfavorable) for the leader, a considerate, relationship-oriented attitude seems to be most effective. . . . Here the leader must provide a nonthreatening, permissive environment if members are to feel free to make suggestions and to contribute to discussions. . . .[42]

Criticisms. The results of recent studies cast some doubt on the validity of Fiedler's findings and theory. Graen and his associates carried out laboratory experiments in which they obtained results strongly contradicting the Fiedler model.[43] Others have found that task structure seems to be the only important situational factor.[44] A number of writers, including Fiedler, have pointed out fundamental deficiencies in the contingency model.[45] For example, a situation of high position power in one study might be considered one of low position power in another.

Other criticisms attack the measure of leadership style, the LPC. Fiedler suggested that high LPC reflected a considerate, relationship-oriented leader and low LPC a task-oriented leader.[46] However, a number of studies in which a leader's style and behavior on the LPC were compared with the consideration and initiating-structure scales of the Ohio State LBDQ do not support this assertion.[47] Furthermore, it has been found that the LPC is not a very reliable scale; indeed, the same person may obtain significantly

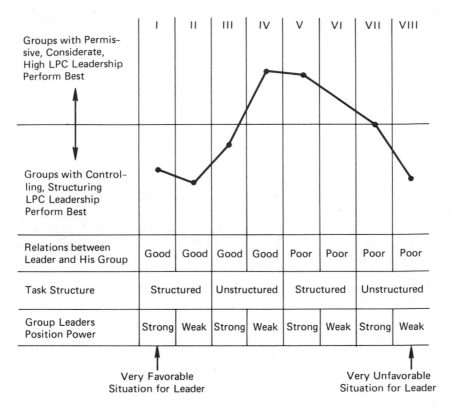

	I	II	III	IV	V	VI	VII	VIII
Relations between Leader and His Group	Good	Good	Good	Good	Poor	Poor	Poor	Poor
Task Structure	Structured		Unstructured		Structured		Unstructured	
Group Leaders Position Power	Strong	Weak	Strong	Weak	Strong	Weak	Strong	Weak

Groups with Permis-sive, Considerate, High LPC Leadership Perform Best

Groups with Control-ling, Structuring LPC Leadership Perform Best

Very Favorable Situation for Leader

Very Unfavorable Situation for Leader

FIGURE 11-3. Fiedler's Findings on How Leadership Effectiveness Varies with the Situation

Source: Adapted from Frederick E. Fiedler, *A Theory of Leadership Effectiveness* (New York: McGraw-Hill, 1967), p. 146. Used by permission of McGraw-Hill Book Company.

different LPC scores on different days.[48] This may result from some funda-mental flaw in the scale, or it may occur because the characteristics them-selves, measured by the LPC, vary with the task. Thus, Fiedler found that the high-LPC leader, as the situation becomes more threatening, tends to become both more considerate *and* more critical, task-oriented, and struc-turing.[49]

In summary, the Fiedler theory has generated a great deal of interest and research and has contributed to our knowledge of leader effectiveness. However, it has several flaws, and it is doubtful that the theory, by itself, can consistently predict leader effectiveness.[50] There is little doubt that other factors like the leader's supervisory ability and intelligence also in-fluence his effectiveness; furthermore, the effects of *combinations* of con-siderate and structuring leadership must be considered.

LEADERSHIP FINDINGS AND
ORGANIZATION THEORY

The Functions of Leadership
in Organization Theory

There is a common theme underlying most of the theories of leadership we've discussed so far, and it is that there are two major functions that leaders can perform. Robert Bales calls these *accomplishing the task* and *satisfying the needs of group members.*[51] The Ohio State researchers call them *initiating structure* and *consideration.* Katz and Kahn say that "the two basic dimensions of the leader–follower relationship are *task direction* and *socioemotional supportiveness.*"[52] In keeping with the terminology we've used in this book, leaders thus have two interrelated functions, and these are ensuring the motivation and compliance of their people, while also ensuring that the task is adequately structured and "do-able."

The Leader's "Structuring" Function

Katz and Kahn have pointed out that no organization chart or set of rules and procedures can ever be totally complete, and where there are gaps, it is the leader's job to provide the necessary "incremental" structure, instructions, tools, and procedures.

This seems to suggest that a leader's structuring behavior might be more successful when there are such "gaps," and when he is thus *required* to clarify duties, provide instructions, and so forth. Perhaps, then, this is why styles like "initiating structure" have been found to be positively, negatively, and not related to employee satisfaction and performance.

The House path-goal theory of leadership. Robert J. House has proposed a theory of leadership that helps explain the "situational" nature of the leader's structuring function. His theory states that the functions of a leader consist largely of increasing personal rewards for subordinates for goal attainment and of making the path to these rewards easier to follow—by clarifying it, reducing roadblocks and pitfalls, and increasing the opportunities for personal satisfaction en route. This theory is based on the expectancy theory of motivation as proposed by Vroom. Recall that the central concept of expectancy theory states that motivation is a function of both the person's ability to accomplish the task, and his or her desire to do so.[53] House says that a leader can increase an employee's motivation by ensuring that the person has the ability to accomplish the task, and that the leader can do this by providing "structure" (in terms of instructions, and so forth) when needed.

House's basic thesis is as follows. He says that ambiguous, uncertain situations have the potential for being frustrating and that, in such situa-

269

tions, the structure provided by the leader will be viewed as legitimate and satisfactory by subordinates. On the other hand, in routine situations, such as might be encountered on assembly-line tasks, the additional structure provided by a production-oriented leader might be viewed as illegitimate and redundant by the subordinates, who might therefore become dissatisfied. House's view of leader structure is therefore quite similar to Katz and Kahn's "incremental structure" view of the leader's functions.

House and his associates have carried out a number of studies to determine the usefulness of his model. One study found some modest support for his hypothesis,[54] but two others found that the effect of leader structure on employee satisfaction was influenced by a variety of factors, including how considerate the leader was and to what extent the subordinate disliked unstructured, ambiguous tasks.[55]

Others have found that "Expectancy Theory has the capacity to predict and explain leader behavior," a finding that provides some indirect support for the path-goal theory.[56] Evans found that a path-goal theory was more useful in predicting the behavior of subordinates who were more "rational." [57] Two researchers collected data from a total of 1,161 hospital employees, and their findings supported the path-goal theory as it applied to the relationship between leader behavior and subordinate satisfaction, but not as it applied to subordinate performance.[58]

In total, the findings suggest that this theory of leader effectiveness is useful. The ideas that the appropriate level of leader structure depends on how ambiguous the task is, and that the necessary level of leader consideration varies with the intrinsic satisfaction of the task, have both received support.

The Leader's Compliance Function

What can a leader do to ensure that his subordinates carry out their tasks? House's path-goal theory aims at providing at least part of the answer: By structuring the task as needed, the leader increases his subordinate's ability to do the task and thus his motivation to do so.

Many other suggestions have been made concerning how a leader should behave in order to best ensure employee compliance. The classical theorists, for example, prescribed close supervision, the human relations theorists supportive leadership, and Katz and Kahn participative leadership. Let us briefly review the "compliance" prescriptions of these theorists.

The classicists' prescription: Close supervision. In Chapter 2, we saw that when classicists like Fayol addressed the problem of motivation and compliance, they usually prescribed the use of sanctions, constant supervision, and a subordination of individual interests to those of the firm, rather than trying to make the two compatible. For example, about the only explicit statement Fayol makes in regard to using something other than sanctions or close supervision in motivating workers is his mention of managers "setting a good example," and also letting subordinates make more decisions in order to tap their initiative.

How effective is close supervision as a compliance tool? Most of the research on close supervision as a leadership style has focused on its effect on employee satisfaction, rather than on performance. These findings (as we discussed above) suggest that closely supervised subordinates are less satisfied and more aggressive toward their leaders than are employees who are not closely supervised. In terms of *performance*, findings like those of Bell suggest that close supervision can increase compliance on routine tasks, but that on non-routine tasks a more general type of supervision is best.[59]

The human-relations prescription: supportive leadership.

The essence of the human-relations movement that grew out of the Hawthorne studies was that leaders could increase productivity by increasing the morale of their employees.[60] The human-relations solution for ensuring compliance therefore calls for leaders to be more considerate and supportive, on the assumption that this will increase satisfaction and thereby increase performance.

We have seen that leader consideration *is* generally related to employee morale, so these theorists' *consideration* ⟶ *satisfaction* link seems accurate. However, the findings concerning the link between employee morale and performance are inconclusive. The findings from the Hawthorne studies and a number of other studies suggest that high satisfaction leads to high performance.[61] Other researchers take the opposite position. For example, Porter and Lawler say that satisfaction *results from* high performance, and, in fact, most people have probably experienced the enormous feeling of satisfaction that comes from having accomplished some task like making the dean's list, building a radio, or making a sale. Finally, there are those who claim that there is no consistent relation between morale and performance; Vroom reviewed 22 pertinent studies and found significant relationships between morale and performance in only five of them.[62] These inconsistent findings may reflect the fact that the effects of consideration (like those of close supervision) vary with the type of task. For example, it seems reasonable to expect that consideration and morale may have more effect on the performance of employees whose tasks call for creativity and autonomy than they will on those employees who work on machine-paced assembly lines.

On the other hand, the relation between morale and *attendance* on the job is very clear and consistent. Employees with higher morale clearly have better attendance records and stay on their jobs longer than do employees with low morale, and this can directly affect the organization's profitability.[63] Therefore, to this extent at least, the prescriptions of human-relations theorists seem to be generally applicable.

Katz and Kahn's prescription: Participative leadership.

Katz and Kahn say that "the most consistent and thoroughly demonstrated difference between successful and unsuccessful leadership . . . has to do with the distribution or sharing of the leadership function." [64] They say that participative leadership results in more-motivated employees because employees "have greater feelings of commitment to decisions in which they have a part, or in which they act autonomously." [65]

Although such conclusions are intuitively attractive, the research findings that we discussed in Chapter 10 suggest that the effects of participative leadership are not clear-cut. There is a tendency for democratic leadership to be associated with high satisfaction, but the cause–effect relation here is frequently unknown. Furthermore, the effect of participative leadership on productivity is not at all clear, and the evidence suggests that *authoritarian* leadership often results in higher productivity, at least in the short run. Why should this be the case? Sales has pointed out that to prescribe democratic leadership assumes that the task is such that the subordinate will see task accomplishment as a way of satisfying certain of his needs.[66] But if the situation is such that allowing the subordinate to set his own goals and make his own decisions does not materially increase the extent to which this occurs (as it might not on a machine-paced assembly line), then democratic leadership might be ineffective.

SUMMARY

All the leadership theories outlined in this chapter are of value. From the trait theorists, it seems that the more effective leader exhibits initiative, self-assurance, and decisiveness. In addition, he or she is intelligent and is able to analyze problems, come to grips with their central issues, and consistently come up with the correct solutions. He tends to be somewhat withdrawn, but competitive.

Second, from the behavioral theorists, this effective leader is considerate and supportive of his or her subordinates. This does not necessarily mean that he does not give orders and provide structure where needed. Rather, this leader recognizes that each of his people is an individual who wants to be made to feel important and useful, and he acts in such a way as to support those needs.

Third, according to the situational theorists, in addition to these universally applicable characteristics, the effective leader has *supervisory ability*, which we might define as the ability to provide the right amount of structure and centralization for the task.[67]

How does the "context" influence leadership? The findings we discussed in this and other chapters suggest that different situations call for different types of leaders. For example, in moderately unpredictable environments, a more participative leader seems to be appropriate. In very ambiguous situations, a more structuring leader who can clarify relationships and provide the needed direction seems more appropriate. In very routine situations, one might imagine (for example, from House's path-goal theory) that less leader structure is required, but some findings (like Bell's) reveal that routine situations are usually associated with close supervision.

Leader *consideration* seems to be appropriate regardless of the situation but might be more necessary where jobs are inherently dissatisfying.

How does leadership influence organization structure? No organization chart and set of job descriptions can ever be so complete as to specify every action that employees might have to take. This is why "innovative" behavior is necessary, behavior that is aimed at doing more than simply what is called for in the job description.

Leadership can serve a similar purpose: An effective leader can provide an increment of structure—"fill in the gaps" in a structure—by defining tasks, relationships, and direction when situations arise that aren't covered by the formal organization structure. At the extreme, ambiguous, uncertain tasks can lead to frustration and ineffectiveness, and in these situations, leader structure seems especially appropriate. In summary, leadership can supplement organization structure by clarifying direction and relationships for the employees involved.

How does leadership influence organizational compliance? Much (if not most) of what leaders do is aimed at ensuring that subordinates not only can but *will* carry out their tasks. Many leadership behaviors including close supervision, supportive leadership, and participative leadership have been proposed for accomplishing this. Close supervision is a form of imposed compliance and appears to be more useful where work tasks are routine. Supportive leadership aims to increase employee morale, and in so doing, employee performance. Findings here suggest that high morale may be more important when the job requires creativity and innovation than when it is routine. Participative leadership can lead to job identification and an internalization of the organization's goals. However, whether it does, and whether it leads to higher performance depends at least partly on whether the job is such that the person exercises some degree of control over it.

DISCUSSION QUESTIONS

1. How would you define the phrase "failed to exert leadership"?
2. You have just been asked to give a short lecture to a group of new supervisors on "How to Be an Effective Leader." What would you tell them?
3. Do you think it is more important for a leader to be respected or popular? Why?
4. What leadership style would you exhibit under the following conditions:

   You have just been given a job as director of marketing services for an organization and have been told by the president to "get those division managers to use some up-to-date marketing tools." He has also told you that you have no position power or authority over those division managers. How would you act as a leader?

   You have just been named the new manager of a large division. They have had four managers in three years; profits are declining; morale is at an all-time low; and a recent consultant's report states that "nobody knows what he is doing or what he is supposed to be doing." How would you act as a leader?

The president of Central Steel Company wants to get his company into some new businesses and has asked you to take charge of a recently organized new-ventures department. The steel company has always been highly centralized, with top management making virtually all important decisions; everyone has always "played it by the rules"; and requests for deviations from standard practices traditionally have to be funnelled through the formal chain of command, a process that can take up to one year. How would you act as a leader?

5. Who is the most effective leader you ever met? Describe his or her characteristics and style and any conditions that you feel contribute to that person being so effective.

6. What sort of a leader are you? Do you think you are people or task oriented? How do your traits measure up to those of successful leaders? In what situation would you be most effective as a leader?

FOOTNOTES

1 Ralph Stogdill, "Historical Trends in Leadership Theory and Research," *Journal of Contemporary Business*, Vol 3. No. 4 (Autumn 1974), 1–17; reprinted in Harold Koontz and Cyril O'Donnell, *Management* (New York: McGraw-Hill, 1976).

2 Ruth Nutting, "Characteristics of Leadership," *School and Society*, Vol. 18 (1923), 387–90; C. Bird, *Social Psychology* (New York: Appleton-Century, 1940); W. O. Jenkins, "A Review of Leadership Studies with Particular References to Military Problems," *Psychological Bulletin*, 44 (1947), 54–79; R. M. Stogdill, "Personal Factors Associated with Leadership: A Survey of Literature," *Journal of Psychology*, 25 (1948), 35–71; R. D. Mann, "A Review of the Relationships between Personality and Performance in Small Groups," *Psychological Bulletin*, 56 (1959), 241–70; T. O. Jacobs, *Leadership and Exchange in Formal Organizations* (Alexandria, Va.: Human Resources Research Organizations, 1970); R. M. Stogdill, *Handbook of Leadership* (New York: Free Press, 1974).

3 Walter J. Palmer, "Management Effectiveness as a Function of Personality Traits of the Manager," *Personnel Psychology*, Vol. 27 (1974), 283–95.

4 Information here is based on Edwin E. Ghiselli, *Explorations in Managerial Talent* (Pacific Palisades, Calif.: Goodyear, 1971).

5 Ghiselli, *Explorations*, pp. 39, 45, 49.

6 *Ibid.*, pp. 57, 61, 65.

7 *Ibid.*, p. 71.

8 *Ibid.*, p. 82.

9 Strictly speaking, Ghiselli's was a study of managerial rather than leadership effectiveness, and to some extent, "supervisory ability" itself measures leadership ability, which is only one of the manager's many duties. In addition to having to lead, for example, managers have to organize their work properly, exercise control, plan the work of each of their subordinates, etc. Therefore, traits like supervisory ability, occupational achievement, and intelligence can be said to be predictors of managerial effectiveness, not leadership effectiveness, and while (according to Ghiselli) an effective manager must be an effective leader, an effective leader need not necessarily be an effective manager. In any

case, Ghiselli found that the traits we discussed do predict managerial effectiveness in a variety of situations, and most writers would probably agree that they predict leadership effectiveness as well.

10 Stogdill, "Historical Trends."

11 Robert Bales, "The Equilibrium Problem in Small Groups," in *Working Papers in the Theory of Action,* eds. T. Parsons et al. (New York: Free Press, 1953).

12 However, the matter of whether the dimensions are independent of each other is still under debate. See, for example, Peter Weissenbert and Michael J. Kavanagh, "The Independence of Initiating Structure and Consideration: A Review of Evidence," *Personnel Psychology,* Vol. 25 (1972), 119–30; Leopold Gruenfeld and Saleem Kassum, "Supervisory Style and Organizational Effectiveness in a Pediatric Hospital," *Personnel Psychology,* Vol. 26 (1973), 531–44; and Michael J. Kavanagh, "Leadership Behavior as a Function of Subordinate Competence and Task Complexity," *Administrative Science Quarterly,* December 1972, pp. 591–600.

13 R. M. Stogdill and A. E. Coons, eds., *Leader Behavior: Its Description and Measurement* (Columbus: Bureau of Business Research, Ohio State University, 1957).

14 E. W. Halpin and B. J. Wiener, "A Factorial Study of Leader Behavior Description," in Stogdill and Coons, *Leader Behavior.*

15 Schriesheim and Kerr note that the various versions of the Ohio State scales differ from one another and suffer from a number of shortcomings (such as a tendency for responses to some items to be skewed). They suggest that at least one version (LBDQ XII) seems to be more useful than the others. Chester Schriesheim and Steven Kerr, "Psychometric Properties of the Ohio State Leadership Scales," *Psychological Bulletin,* Vol. 81, No. 1 (November 1974), 756–65.

16 Ralph Stogdill, *Managers, Employees, Organizations* (Columbus: Bureau of Business Research, Ohio State University, 1965).

17 Gary Yukl, "Toward a Behavioral Theory of Leadership," *Organizational Behavior and Human Performance,* Vol. 6, No. 4 (July 1971), 414–40, reprinted in W. E. Scott and L. L. Cummings, *Readings in Organizational Behavior and Human Performance* (Homewood, Ill.: Richard D. Irwin, 1973); L. R. Anderson, "Leader Behavior, Member Attitudes, and Task Performance of Intercultural Discussion Groups," *Journal of Social Psychology,* 69 (1966), 305–19; E. A. Fleishman and E. F. Harris, "Patterns of Leadership Behavior Related to Employee Grievances and Turnover," *Personnel Psychology,* 15 (1962), 43–56; A. W. Halpin, "The Leader Behavior and Effectiveness of Aircraft Commanders," in Stogdill and Coons, *Leader Behavior*; and Halpin and Wiener, "A Factorial Study of the Leader Behavior Descriptions."

18 Scott and Cummings, *Readings in Organizational Behavior,* p. 462.

19 See Chester Schriesheim, Robert J. House, and Steven Kerr, "Leader Initiating Structure: A Reconciliation of Discrepant Research Results and Some Empirical Tests," *Organizational Behavior and Human Performance,* Vol. 15, No. 2 (April 1976); and M. N. Petty and Gorden J. Lee, Jr., "Moderating Effects of Sex of Supervisor and Subordinate on Relationships between Supervisory Behavior and Subordinate Satisfaction," *Journal of Applied Psychology,* Vol. 60, No. 5 (October 1975).

20 Rensis Likert, *New Patterns of Management* (New York: McGraw-Hill, 1961).

21 *Ibid.,* p. 7.

22 *Ibid.,* Chap. 2.

23 This suggests that other situational factors may influence the appropriateness of various leadership styles.

24 D. Katz and R. L. Kahn, "Leadership Practices in Relation to Productivity and Morale," in *Group Dynamics,* eds. D. Cartwright and A. Zander (Evanston, Ill.: Row, Peterson, 1960), pp. 554–70.

25 Robert C. Day and Robert L. Hamblin, "Some Effects of Close and Punitive Styles of Leadership," *American Journal of Sociology,* Vol. 69 (1964), 499–510.

26 Nancy Morse, *Satisfactions in the White Collar Job* (Ann Arbor: Survey Research Center, University of Michigan, 1953).

27 Katz and Kahn, "Leadership Practices."

28 Daniel Katz and Robert Kahn, "Some Recent Findings in Human Relations Research in Industry," in *Readings in Social Psychology*, ed. G. E. Swanson et al. (New York: Holt and Company, 1950), pp. 650–52.

29 Day and Hamblin, "Some Effects of Close and Punitive Styles of Leadership."

30 See, for example, Alan Filley, Robert House, and Steven Kerr, *Managerial Process and Organizational Behavior* (Glenview, Ill.: Scott, Foresman, 1976), pp. 399–405.

31 M. Argyle, G. Gardner, and F. Cioffi, "The Measurement of Supervisory Methods," *Human Relations*, Vol. 10 (1957), 295–314.

32 J. G. Hunt, "Organizational Leadership: Some Theoretical and Empirical Considerations," *Business Perspectives*, Vol. 4, No. 4 (Summer 1968), 16–24; reprinted in James Gibson, John Ivancevich, and James Donnelly, *Readings in Organization*, rev. ed. (Dallas: Business Publications Inc., 1976).

33 See also Gary Yukl and J. G. Hunt, "An Empirical Comparison of the Michigan Four-Factor and Ohio State LBDQ Leadership Scales," *Organizational Behavior and Human Performance*, Vol. 17, No. 1 (October 1976), 45–65.

34 Some recent findings suggest that there may in fact be some logic in combining the trait and behavioral theories. Pinder and Pinto studied 200 American managers and found that the leader's style ("autocratic," "organized," "consultative") was related to such leader characteristics as his age, departmental affiliation, primary values orientation, and educational level. See Craig C. Pinder and Patric R. Pinto, "Demographic Correlates of Managerial Style," *Personnel Psychology*, Vol. 27 (1974), 257–70.

35 Steven Kerr, Chester A. Schriesheim, Charles J. Murphy, and Ralph M. Stogdill, "Toward a Contingency Theory of Leadership Based upon the Consideration and Initiating Structure Literature," *Organizational Behavior and Human Performance*, Vol. 12 (1974), 62–82.

36 See also Eugene M. Foder, "Group Stress, Authoritarian Style of Control, and Use of Power," *Journal of Applied Psychology*, Vol. 61, No. 3 (June 1976); Robert Miles and M. M. Petty, "Leader Effectiveness in Small Bureaucracies," *Academy of Management Journal*, Vol. 20, No. 2 (1971), 238–50; Enzo Valenzi and Gary Dessler, "Relationships of Leader Behavior, Subordinate Role Ambiguity, and Subordinate Job Satisfaction," *Academy of Management Journal*, in press; and Chester Schriesheim and Charles Murphy, "Relationships between Leader Behavior and Subordinate Satisfaction and Performance: A Test of Some Situational Moderators," *Journal of Applied Psychology*, Vol. 61, No. 5 (October 1976), 634.

37 Ralph Stogdill, "Personal Factors Associated with Leadership."

38 Robert Tannenbaum and Warren Schmidt, "How to Choose a Leadership Pattern," *Harvard Business Review*, Vol. 36 (March–April 1958), 95–101.

39 A. Lowen, W. Hrapchak, M. Kavanagh, "Consideration and Initiating Structure: An Experimental Investigation of Leadership Traits," *Administrative Science Quarterly*, Vol. 14 (1969), 239–44.

40 Abraham Korman, "Consideration, Initiating Structure and Organizational Criteria—A Review," *Personnel Psychology*, Vol. 19 (1966), 349–61.

41 Frederick E. Fiedler, *A Theory of Leadership Effectiveness* (New York: McGraw-Hill, 1967), p. 147.

42 Fiedler, *A Theory of Leadership Effectiveness*, p. 147.

43 G. Graen, K. Alvares, J. B. Orris, and J. A. Martella, "Contingency Model of Leadership Effectiveness: Antecedent and Evidential Results," *Psychological Bulletin*, Vol. 74 (1970), 285–96. See also Graen, Orris, and Alvares, "Contingency Model of Leadership Effectiveness: Some Experimental Results," *Journal of Applied Psychology*, Vol. 55 (1971), 196–201.

44 J. P. Campbell, M. D. Dunnette, E. E. Lawler, and K. E. Weick, *Managerial Behavior, Performance and Effectiveness* (New York: McGraw-Hill, 1970).

45 Terence Mitchell, Anthony Biglan, Gerald Oncken, and Frederick Fiedler, "The Contingency Model: Criticisms and Suggestions," *Academy of Management Journal*, Vol. 13, No. 3 (September 1970), 253–67.

46 Fiedler, *A Theory of Leadership Effectiveness*, p. 45.

47 For example, see Martin M. Chemers and Robert W. Rice, "A Theoretical and Empirical Examination of Fiedler's Contingency Model of Leadership Effectiveness," in *Contingency Approaches to Leadership*, eds. J. G. Hunt and L. Larson (Carbondale: Southern Illinois University Press, 1974), pp. 91–123.

48 Mitchell et al., "The Contingency Model: Criticisms and Suggestions."

49 The literature on the LPC is voluminous. In addition to the studies mentioned, see, for example, Martin G. Evans, "A Leader's Ability to Differentiate the Subordinate's Performance," *Personnel Psychology*, Vol. 26 (1973), 385–95; Joe E. Stinson and Lane Tracy, "Some Disturbing Characteristics of the LPC Score," *Personnel Psychology*, Vol. 27 (1974), 477–85; Martin G. Evans and Jerry Dermer, "What Does the Least Preferred Co-worker Scale Really Measure?" *Journal of Applied Psychology*, Vol. 59, No. 2 (1974), 202–6; Lars Larson and Kendrith M. Rowland, "Leadership Style and Cognitive Complexity," *Academy of Management Journal*, Vol. 17, No. 1 (March 1974), 37–45; Marshall Sashkin, F. Carter Taylor, and Rama C. Tripathi, "An Analysis of Situational Moderating Effects on the Relationship between Least Effective Co-worker and Other Psychological Measures," *Journal of Applied Psychology*, Vol. 59, No. 6 (1974), 731–40; Robert Rice and Martin Chemers, "Personality and Situational Determinants of Leader Behavior," *Journal of Applied Psychology*, Vol. 60, No. 1 (February 1975); and William Fox, "Reliabilities, Means, and Standard Deviations, for LPC Scales: Instrument Refinement," *Academy of Management Journal*, Vol. 19, No. 3 (September 1976), 450–61.

50 This is my conclusion based on the research findings obtained up to this point. For a good summary of the opposing view, see Chemers and Rice, "A Theoretical and Empirical Examination of Fiedler's Contingency Model"; also, Steven Green, Delbert Nebeker, and M. Allen Boni, "Personality and Situational Effects on Leader Behavior," *Academy of Management Journal*, Vol. 19, No. 2 (June 1976), 184; Paul Bons and Fred Fiedler, "Changes in Organizational Leadership and the Behavior of Relationship and Task Oriented Leaders," *Administrative Science Quarterly*, Vol. 21, No. 3 (September 1976), 453; and Robert P. Vecchio, "An Empirical Examination of the Validity of Fiedler's Model of Leadership Effectiveness," *Organizational Behavior and Human Performance*, Vol. 19, No. 1 (June 1977), 180–206.

51 Bales, "The Equilibrium Problem in Small Groups."

52 Daniel Katz and Robert L. Kahn, *The Social Psychology of Organizations* (New York: John Wiley, 1966), p. 311.

53 J. W. Atkinson, ed., *Motives in Fantasy, Action, and Society* (New York: Van Nostrand Reinhold, 1958).

54 Robert J. House, "A Path-Goal Theory of Leader Effectiveness," *Administrative Science Quarterly*, Vol. 16 (1971), 321–38.

55 Robert J. House and Gary Dessler, "A Path-Goal Theory of Leadership: Some Post-Hoc and A-Priori Tests," in Hunt and Larson, eds., *Contingency Approaches to Leadership*; and Gary Dessler, "Investigation of a Path-Goal Theory of Leadership," unpublished doctoral dissertation, 1973, City University of New York.

56 Robert M. Nebeker and Terence B. Mitchell, "Leader Behavior: An Expectancy Theory Approach," *Organizational Behavior and Human Performance*, Vol. 11 (1974), 355–67.

57 Martin G. Evans, "Extensions of a Path-Goal Theory of Motivation," *Journal of Applied Psychology*, Vol. 59, No. 2 (1974), 172–78.

58 Andrew D. Szilagyi and Henry P. Sims, Jr., "An Exploration of the Path-Goal Theory of Leadership in a Health-Care Facility," *Academy of Management Journal*, Vol. 17, No. 4 (December 1974), 622–34. See also Gary Dessler and Enzo Valenzi, "Initiation of

Structure and Subordinate Satisfaction: A Path Analysis of Path-Goal Theory," *Academy of Management Journal*, June 1977.

[59] Gerald D. Bell, "The Influence of Technological Components of Work upon Management Control," *Journal of the Academy of Management*, Vol. 8, No. 2 (1965), 127–32. See also Gerald D. Bell, "Predictability of Work Demands and Professionalization as Determinants of Worker's Discretion," *Journal of the Academy of Management*, Vol. 9, No. 1 (March 1966), 20–28.

[60] Victor Vroom, *Work and Motivation* (New York: John Wiley, 1964); L. L. Cummings and W. E. Scott, *Readings in Organizational Behavior and Human Performance* (Homewood, Ill.: Richard D. Irwin, 1969), Chap. 3.

[61] F. Herzberg, B. Mausner, and D. B. Schneiderman, *The Motivation to Work* (New York: John Wiley, 1959).

[62] Vroom, *Work and Motivation*.

[63] H. Mann and H. Baumgartel, "Absence and Employee Attitudes in an Electric Power Company," Survey Research Center, University of Michigan, December 1965; Ernest J. McCormick and Joseph Tiffin, *Industrial Psychology* (Englewood Cliffs, N.J.: Prentice-Hall, 1974), pp. 325–30; Philip Mirvis and Edward Lawler, "Measuring the Financial Impact of Employee Attitudes," *Journal of Applied Psychology*, Vol. 62, No. 1 (1977), 1–8.

[64] Katz and Kahn, *The Social Psychology of Organizations*, p. 332.

[65] *Ibid.*

[66] Steven Sales, "Supervisory Style and Productivity: Review and Theory," *Personnel Psychology*, Vol. 19, No. 3 (1966), 275–86.

[67] Keep in mind that most studies of leadership correlate various leadership styles with "dependent" variables such as subordinate satisfaction and performance, and while it is usually assumed that leadership style "causes" the satisfaction or findings, there is considerable evidence that to a large extent it is employee satisfaction or performance that in fact "causes" leadership style. Lowen and Craig found that subordinate performance affects the manager's closeness of supervision, initiating structure, and consideration, for example, Aaron Lowen and James Craig, "The Influence of Level of Performance on Managerial Style: An Experimental Object-Lesson in the Ambiguity of Correlational Data," *Organizational Behavior and Human Performance*, Vol. 3 (1968), 440–458; Barrow found that increasing performance levels of workers caused a leader to be more supportive-considerate, while decreasing performance levels resulted in heavier use of punitive-performance emphasis and autocratic behaviors. (Jeffrey Barrow, "Worker Performance and Task Complexity as Causal Determinants of Leader Style and Flexibility," *Journal of Applied Psychology*, Vol. 61, No. 4 (August 1976), 433–40; Jeffrey Pfeffer, "The Ambiguity of Leadership," *Academy of Management Review*, Vol. 2, No. 1 (January 1977), 104–12).

Chapter 12

Group Processes and Organization Theory

CHAPTER OVERVIEW

In terms of our model, group processes play a critical role in organization theory for two reasons. First, groups affect how their members define their self-interest, and therefore affect their compliance; as Elton Mayo says:

> If a number of individuals work together to achieve a common purpose, a harmony of interests will develop among them to which individual self interest will be subordinated. This is a very different doctrine from the claim that individual self interest is the solitary human motive.[1]

Second, groups influence (and are influenced by) organization structure. Groups, we will see, can add to or detract from the formal organization structure, by filling in the "gaps" in an inadequate structure, or short-circuiting an adequate one. Therefore, because groups do exert a powerful influence on both structure and worker compliance, we discuss group processes and their effects on these factors in this chapter.

We first discuss the Hawthorne studies, which were briefly introduced in Chapter 3. It was as a result of these studies that organization theorists first became fully cognizant of how employees' work groups, attitudes, and needs affect their motivation and behavior. And the studies provide a fascinating example of the scientific method applied to organizational questions.

Next we discuss the "Homans Model," a theory of group influence that George Homans developed, based in part on the Hawthorne findings. And, since a work group's *cohesiveness* determines the extent to which the group can influence its members, we then discuss some factors (like the size of the group) that influence group cohesiveness.

We next treat the subject of groups and organization theory, and specifically the relationship between groups and organization structure, and compliance. We say you can view the organization as a "structure of groups," and we also discuss the effect organization structure has on groups and groups in turn can have on organization structure. A person's work group also influences his or her compliance, and so we discuss norms—a group's rules of behavior—and some specific effects that groups have on individual behavior and compliance. As you read this chapter, ask:

1. What is the process through which groups influence their members?
2. How do groups influence compliance?
3. How are groups and organization structure related?

The outline of this chapter is as follows:

THE EFFECTS OF GROUPS ON INDIVIDUALS: THE HAWTHORNE STUDIES

The experiments at the Hawthorne works of Western Electric are of tremendous importance in organization theory, for several reasons. First, it was during these studies that organization theorists first became fully cognizant of how employees' work groups, attitudes, and needs affected their motivation and behavior. In addition, the Hawthorne studies remain to this day a classic, one that Blum and Naylor call "the most significant research program undertaken to show the enormous complexity of the problem of production in relation to efficiency." As a work of research, these studies are far from perfect. Still, they provide a fascinating example of the scientific method applied to organizational questions, of the need for hypothesis testing and controlled experimentation, and of the need to maintain an open, inquisitive mind while in the pursuit of truth through science. For these reasons, we will discuss these studies at some length.[2]

Introduction

During the spring of 1927, a series of experimental studies was begun at the Hawthorne works of the Western Electric Company in Chicago. The results of these studies literally changed the course of organization theory, in that they introduced the notion that a person's work group (and his attitudes) are important determinants of his motivation and compliance. The four Hawthorne studies we will focus on are:

The illumination studies
The relay assembly test room studies
The interviewing program
The bank wiring observation room studies

The Illumination Studies

While the illumination studies are often viewed as part of the Hawthorne studies, they actually preceded the main studies, and lasted from November 1924 through April 1927. Their importance lies in the fact that their findings provided the stimulus for the later Hawthorne studies.

The illumination experiments began as a straightforward industrial engineering study to determine the relation between level of illumination and worker productivity. The organization theory that prevailed at that time assumed economic rationality on the part of workers and generally assumed that they were "motivated" solely by external factors like pay and the physical conditions of their surroundings. In line with these assumptions, the illumination researchers expected that productivity would increase with increasing levels of illumination, and they set out to determine what the optimum level of illumination was.

There were actually three separate illumination experiments, each aimed at clarifying the somewhat startling findings of the preceding one. In the first experiment, workers in three Western Electric departments were exposed to various levels of illumination. The researchers found that while productivity increased with greater illumination, it did not do so in direct proportion to the increase in illumination. Of more importance, however, production efficiency "did not always fall off with the decrease in illumination." [3]

In the second illumination experiment, the researchers attempted to carry out more of a "controlled" study. Only one of the original three departments was chosen for this study, and its workers were divided into two groups, "each group composed of an equal number of operators of about the same experience":

> One group, called the "test group," was to work under variable illumination intensities; the other group, called the "control group," was to work under an intensity of illumination as nearly constant as possible. The groups were located in different buildings in order to reduce the influence of any spirit of competition. . . . It was thought that by this method the differences in production efficiency could be related directly to differences in illumination intensity.[4]

In this experiment, as in the first, productivity did not vary in direct proportion to level of illumination. Instead:

> This test resulted in very appreciable production increases in both groups and of almost identical magnitude. The difference in efficiency of the two groups was so small as to be less than the probable error of the values. Consequently, we were again unable to determine what definite part of the improvement in performance should be ascribed to improved illumination.[5]

The researchers thought these findings might have resulted from the fact that both groups were exposed to both artificial and natural light and that the latter varied during the day. A third illumination experiment was therefore carried out. Now the control group was provided with a constant level of illumination, and the test group with a carefully controlled series of changes in illumination level. The productivity of the test and control groups both *increased* as illumination *decreased* until the productivity of the control group finally leveled off when the level of illumination in their enclosure became constant. However, the productivity of the test group continued to *increase* with *decreases* in illumination, until the illumination finally got so low that workers protested, "saying that they were hardly able to see what they were doing." [6]

These experiments failed in their basic purpose—determining the relation between effort and illumination—but probably had a more profound effect on the evolution of organization theory than any other experiments before or since, because they raised important questions that were seized upon by a group of perceptive and open-minded scientists. The illumination experiments suggested, for example, that light was only one factor, and apparently a minor one, among many that affect employee output. And they also suggested that more carefully controlled experiments had to be used in further experimentation with workers. Based upon these implications, the researchers began what have become known as the Hawthorne studies, a series of experiments aimed at determining—under carefully controlled conditions—what factors influence productivity and behavior.

The Relay Assembly Test Room Studies

From the findings of the illumination studies, "it was decided to isolate a small group of workers in a separate room somewhat removed from the regular working force, where their behavior could be studied carefully and systematically." [7] Researchers felt that this procedure would enable them to study the factors influencing worker productivity while controlling the number of variables "which inevitably creep into a large group situation." For example, "such influences as the amount of work ahead of the operators, changes in type of work, the introduction of inexperienced operators, and the shifting of personnel because of fluctuation in work schedules could be largely eliminated." [8] Experimental conditions could be imposed with less chance of having them disrupted by departmental routines, and finally, "in a small group there was the possibility of establishing a feeling of mutual confidence between investigators and operators, so that the reactions of the operators would not be distorted by general mistrust." [9]

The job. The job finally chosen involved the assembly of telephone relays, an operation performed by women, which consisted of putting together about 35 small parts in an assembly fixture and securing them by four machine screws. The various parts were put in front of the operators in small bins. The selection of the parts was done by the operator, using both hands, and considerable skill was required in picking them up and placing them in the pile-up in front of her. The complete operation required about one minute, and the task was therefore highly repetitive; each operator assembled about 500 relays each day. A photo of the relay assembly test room operators, taken during the Hawthorne experiment, is presented in Figure 12-1.

The subjects. The subjects for the relay assembly test room were chosen as follows: Two experienced operators who were known to be friendly with each other were asked to participate in the test, and to choose the remaining members of the group. The group selected consisted of six women—five to do the actual assembly operation and a sixth to act as layout operator. The latter's duties "were of a minor supervisory character and consisted of assigning work and procuring parts for each assembler." This arrangement of having a layout operator serve the assemblers was identical with that in the regular relay assembly department, "with the exception

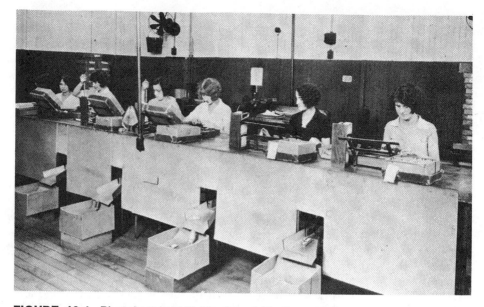

FIGURE 12-1. Photograph of Relay Assembly Test Room

Source: F. J. Roethlisberger, et al., *Management and the Worker* (Cambridge, Mass.: Harvard University Press, 1939), p. 24.

that quite frequently in the regular department one layout operator served six or seven girls instead of five as in the test room."

In addition, there was a "test room observer" whose function was to keep accurate records of all that happened, and to create and maintain a friendly atmosphere in the room. The test room occupied about 560 square feet of floor space in a corner of one of the regular shop rooms and was enclosed by a board partition that extended partway to the ceiling.

The purpose. The relay assembly test room studies have also been called the rest-pause experiments, since they aimed at determining, under carefully controlled conditions, the effects of rest pauses and fatigue on employee productivity. (The topic of fatigue was a controversial one in industrial circles at the time, and the illumination studies had cast some doubt on the accuracy of preceding findings on the effects of rest pauses.) The original relay assembly test room studies therefore set out to answer six questions:

Do employees actually get tired out?

Are rest pauses desirable?

Is a shorter working day desirable?

What are the attitudes of employees toward their work and toward the company?

What is the effect of changing the type of working equipment?
Why does production fall off in the afternoon?

The study. As summarized in Table 12-1 the relay assembly test was organized into 13 periods, each period representing one in which a specific condition of work was enforced. Periods 1–3 constituted an introductory phase, the purpose of which was preparation for experimentation. During period 1, the operators were still in the regular department; period 2 permitted them time to become familiar with their new test room surroundings; and in period 3, a change in wage payment was introduced, "a necessary step before the experiment proper could begin." The researchers' description of their findings during the remaining periods paints a fascinating picture of the problems and potential of organizational research, and of the application of observation, generalization, and experimentation to studying organizational phenomena.

Periods 4-7. In periods 4–7, experiments concerned entirely with rest periods were carried out. In period 4, the investigators began with short rest periods of five minutes each, one during the morning and the other in the afternoon. Because the researchers wanted to place these rest periods where they would be most advantageous, a meeting was called at the superintendent's office. The women were shown their output curves, and the low and high points in the day were pointed out. "When asked at what times they would like to have their rests, they unanimously voted in favor of 10 o'clock in the morning and 2 o'clock in the afternoon." Accordingly, the investigators agreed to institute the rest pauses at these times. (As we will see, the Hawthorne experiments were filled with such attempts by the researchers to maintain the friendly, cooperative attitudes of their subjects.)

Based on the generally favorable attitude of the operators to these rest pauses, ten-minute rests were instituted in period 5. Here again (as had been the case in period 4), the operators' output rate increased so that even with the "nonproductive" rest pauses, they were producing—and earning—more than they had previously.

In period 6, the operators were again asked for their opinions concerning the length of the rest periods to be introduced. However, although they expressed a preference for two fifteen-minute breaks, a series of six five-minute pauses was instituted. The operators clearly disliked this new situation and expressed their dislike by returning late from work breaks, laughing and talking on the job, and generally acting "troublesome and rebellious."

In period 7, there was a fifteen-minute rest in the morning and a ten-minute rest in the afternoon. This period was chiefly notable for the emergence of a "personnel problem," in which two of the operators became increasingly hostile toward the researchers. For their part, the researchers sought to keep employee attitudes a "constant" so as to better assess effects of factors like rest pauses on worker activity. Given the researchers' attempts to maintain high employee morale, the attitudes of the two hostile women

TABLE 12-1

Schedule of Test Periods: Relay Assembly Test Room

Period Number	Special Feature	Dates Included	Duration in Weeks	Times of Rest Pauses		
				A.M.		P.M.
1	In regular department	4-25-27 to 5-10-27	Approx. 2		None	
2	Introduction to test room	5-10-27 to 6-11-27	5		None	
3	Special group rate	6-13-27 to 8-6-27	8		None	
4	Two 5-min. rests	8-8-27 to 9-10-27	5	10:00		2:00
5	Two 10-min. rests	9-12-27 to 10-8-27	4	10:00		2:00
6	Six 5-min. rests	10-10-27 to 11-5-27	4	8:45, 10:00, 11:20		2:00, 3:15, 4:30
7	15-min. A.M. lunch and 10-min. P.M. rest	11-7-27 to 1-21-28	11	9:30		2:30
8	Same as 7 but 4:30 stop	1-23-28 to 3-10-28	7	9:30		2:30
9	Same as 7 but 4:00 stop	3-12-28 to 4-7-28	4	9:30		2:30
10	Same as 7	4-9-28 to 6-30-28	12	9:30		2:30
11	Same as 7 but Sat. A.M. off	7-2-28 to 9-1-28	9	9:30		2:30
12	Same as 3 (no lunch or rests)	9-3-28 to 11-24-28	12		None	
13	Same as 7 but operators furnish own lunch, company furnishes beverage	11-26-28 to 6-29-29	31	9:30		2:30

Source: F. J. Roethlisberger and William Dickson, *Management and the Worker* (Cambridge, Mass.: Harvard University Press, 1939), p. 30.

was viewed as a failure for which the women themselves were held responsible.[10]

The results and conclusions of this portion of the relay assembly test room studies may be summarized as follows: Productivity (average hourly output per week) generally increased for periods 1 through 7, and the researchers concluded that this was due to the introduction of rest pauses. A second, more tentative conclusion was that the operators' attitudes toward one another and toward the group influenced their productivity. (For example, there was a tendency for the output of the two uncooperative operators to vary similarly.) Very soon, this latter conclusion, concerning the effects of employee attitudes and relations on productivity, was to become the pivotal finding of the Hawthorne studies, as the researchers—through a process of observation, generalization, and experimentation—attempted to develop and test new hypotheses for explaining their findings. As the researchers point out:

> In looking back it is clear that two essentially different sorts of changes occurred in the first seven periods of the experiment. There were those changes introduced by the investigators in the form of experimental conditions; these were well noted and recorded. There was another type of change, however, of which the investigators were not so consciously aware. This was manifested in two ways: first, in a gradual change in social interrelations among the operators themselves, which displayed itself in the form of new group loyalties and solidarities; secondly, in a change in the relation between the operators and their supervisors. The test room authorities had taken steps to obtain the girls' cooperation and loyalty and to relieve them of anxieties and apprehensions. From this attempt to set the proper conditions for the experiment, there rose indirectly a change in human relations which came to be of great significance in the next stage of the experiment, when it became necessary to seek a new hypothesis to explain certain unexpected results of the inquiry.[11]

Periods 8–13. Periods 8 through 13 focused on the effects on productivity of shorter working days and weeks. During period 8, the two uncooperative operators were replaced with two new workers who were chosen by the foreman. Also in this period, the working day was shortened by stopping work at 4:30 instead of 5:00, and the rest periods (a fifteen-minute break in the morning, and a ten-minute afternoon break) were continued.

Although the workday had now been shortened considerably, output had still not diminished, and the investigators therefore used period 9 "to find out what would happen to output if the working day was shortened still further, and at what point in this process the total weekly output would begin to fall off." [12] After the approval of the operators was obtained, the daily working hours were therefore reduced by an additional half hour. Although the workers were in favor of this shorter working day, it apparently proved too drastic a cut, and total weekly output and earnings dropped.

In period 10, investigators began a process aimed at lengthening the work week and reducing rest pauses to what they were when the experiments began. At the end of period 10, the situation was identical with period 7—a full forty-eight-hour workweek, with a morning rest of fifteen minutes and an afternoon rest of ten minutes. The operators now complained of fatigue and tiredness, a complaint they had not expressed in period 7.

In period 11, the operators worked only five days, with Saturday mornings off (they normally worked five and a half days). Rest pauses as in period 7 were continued, and weekly working hours were reduced to about 42 hours. The return to the original hours of work (forty-eight hours per week with no rest pauses) commenced on September 3, 1928, during period 12. In preparation for the elimination of rest pauses, the operators were told that it was "just another experimental feature" and that as usual they should work at a "natural pace." It was apparent from the operators' comments, however, that they strongly disliked the return to the full 48-hour week.

In period 13, rest pauses were reinstated and again were fifteen minutes in the morning and ten minutes in the afternoon. This period lasted for seven months, the longest interval for any of the experimental periods, and its length reflected a number of important changes that were noted during it. For example, there was a significant increase in group morale, and this manifested itself in a high degree of group cooperation. Apparently partly as a result of the return of the rest pauses, the operators exhibited new pride in their work, and worked hard to beat their former output records. More important, they worked hard to help each other:

> If one girl wished to slack off, another girl, generally her neighbor alongside, would agree to speed up. Instead of antagonistic competition, there was concerted effort toward a common goal.[13]

Researchers' hypotheses to explain major findings. Generally speaking, output had risen regardless of breaks or work hours, and the researchers developed five hypotheses to explain this puzzling upward trend. First, they hypothesized that *improved conditions and work methods* in the test room might account for their findings, but they concluded that the improvements were not significant and that in some respects working conditions were not as good as in the plant at large. They next hypothesized that the rise in output may have resulted from the *reduction in fatigue* that the rest pauses provided, but concluded (based on later experiments) that fatigue was never a significant problem in the test room. They hypothesized that the rest pauses had been effective not so much in reducing fatigue as in *reducing the monotony* of work; they were never able to discount this hypothesis, pointing out that "monotony in work is primarily a state of mind and cannot be assessed on the basis of output data alone."

Fourth, they hypothesized that the new *incentive wage plan* might account for the improvement in output. However, based on later studies, they concluded that "there was absolutely no evidence in favor of the hypothesis that the continuous increase in output in the relay assembly test room during the first two years could be attributed to the wage incentive factor alone." [14]

Their fifth and final hypothesis was that the increased output and improved attitude in the test room could best be related to the change *in the method of supervision* that had gradually taken place. Proponents of this view felt that the experimental periods "had been essentially carriers of social value." [15] They had been effective as a means of gaining the operators' confidence and of establishing effective working relations between operators and supervisors. In countless ways, for example, the test room observer "had shown his personal interest in the girls and their problems. He had always been sympathetically aware of their hopes and fears. He had granted them more and more privileges." [16] Furthermore:

> No longer were the girls isolated individuals, working together only in the sense of an actual physical proximity. They had become participating members of a working group with all the psychological and social implications peculiar to such a group. . . . In period 13 the girls began to help one another out for the common good of the group. They had become bound together by common sentiments and feelings of loyalty.[17]

As they looked back on their experiment, it became obvious to the researchers that a number of significant differences existed between social conditions in the test room and those in the plant at large. It was obvious to the girls, for example, that they had become the focus of considerable attention from top management. Furthermore, they were exposed to a completely new system of control. Supervision outside the test room "meant upholding all the rules and practices intended to maintain efficiency in the department." For the experimenters, however, control meant a "controlled experiment," and for this they needed willing and cooperative subjects. Toward this end, operators were advised of and consulted about changes to be made and were questioned sympathetically about their reactions to the different conditions of work. Ironically, therefore, the researchers' attempts to maintain a "controlled experiment" had drastically altered the social conditions of work, as well as the attitudes and output of the operators!

Relay room: Conclusion. Thus, "the chief result of the first two years of experimentation in the relay assembly test room, then, had been to demonstrate the importance of employee attitudes and preoccupations." The rest pauses were obviously desirable (and were to be continued throughout the plant), but management—and later, organization theorists—would no longer draw any simple cause-and-effect equations between working conditions and output:

> [Management] began to see that such factors as hours of work and wage incentives were not things in themselves having an independent effect on employee efficiency; rather, these factors were no more than parts of a total situation and their effects could not be predicted apart from that total situation.[18]

The relay assembly test room (and the earlier illumination experiments) thus became the basis of a new organization theory, one in which the social and technical aspects of work were viewed as interrelated and in which the social conditions of work and employee attitudes took on a new importance. To this day, the relay assembly test room studies, although far from a perfect model of scientific investigation, stand out as perhaps the most important example of scientific inquiry and theory building in the social sciences.

The Interviewing Program

Based on the relay assembly test room results, it was apparent that supervisor behavior was an important ingredient in employee morale and productivity. However, little was known at the time about employee complaints or what sorts of supervisor behaviors contributed to high or low employee morale. In order to obtain this information, the researchers decided to interview a group of employees in order to learn more about their opinions with respect to their work, working conditions, and supervision. The interviews began on a small scale in the inspection department, and gradually grew to the point where the likes, dislikes, complaints, and attitudes of more than 21,000 employees were obtained through interviews.

At first, researchers tried to relate employees' comments regarding satisfaction and dissatisfaction to their physical environment. But it was quickly determined that even people working in similar surroundings did not react in the same way to those surroundings; for example, "some expressed satisfaction, some dissatisfaction with similar plant conditions, wages, and working conditions."

Eventually, the researchers began to focus on the *personal situations* of the interviewees as a source of their complaints, and several important conclusions were drawn. For example, in one of the earliest descriptions of the need to build achievement and self-actualization into work, the researchers concluded from the interview data that "the meaning a person assigns to his position depends on whether or not that position is allowing him to fulfill the social demands he is making of his work." They further concluded that psychological factors (and particularly a person's background and "previous social conditioning") help determine whether he or she will be satisfied or dissatisfied in any particular work situation.[19] Finally, the researchers concluded that it was not simply working conditions or a person's personality that determines his attitudes, but also his work group and his relationship to it:

> It became clear that many employee comments which had formerly been interpreted in terms of the interviewees' personal situation could be better understood if they were interpreted in light of the employee's existing social relations within the plant: the social organization of the group with which he worked and his position in that group.[20]

In summary, the interviewing program emphasized the importance of group processes to employee attitudes and productivity, and one symptom of this relation was restriction of output: Specifically, the researchers found that the plant's incentive systems were not working as planned and that work-group pressure for restriction of output appeared to be the main reason.

The Bank Wiring Room Studies

As a result of these observations, it was decided to study more intensively the mechanics of small-group processes—"to obtain more exact information about social groups within the company." [21] This time, however, the researchers took steps to avoid the problems that had confounded the earlier, relay assembly test room studies. For example, although the fourteen men chosen as subjects were taken out of their regular department and placed in a special room, no other change was made in their conditions of work except that an investigator was present to observe their behavior.

One of his first observations was that the employees in the test room had a clear notion of a "proper day's work." [22] As soon as these employees felt they could finish what they considered enough for the day, they slacked off, and as a result, the output graph from week to week tended to be a straight line. To facilitate this, the employees also reported more or less output than they actually produced so as to ensure what appeared to be a constant rate of production.

The researchers discovered that the workers were able to do this because they had developed an informal social organization—a cohesive work group. Although friendships sprang up and two cliques formed, the fourteen workers shared a common body of sentiments: that a person should not turn out too much work, and that if he did, he was a "rate buster." Ironically, the industrial engineers who had designed the plant's incentive plan had assumed that the work group would pressure slower workers to maintain a high pace of work and therefore ensure high pay for all group members. Instead, it was found that the employees brought pressure to bear *not on the slower workers but on the faster ones,* often through a process called "binging," slapping the errant worker on the arm. The workers never made clear why they wished to hold production even from week to week, although they alleged that "someone" would "get them" by reducing their wage rates if output rose too high.

The researchers also found that the informal organization of the group served both *external* and *internal* purposes. Internally, the informal organization functioned to control and regulate the behavior of its members. Externally, however, it functioned as a protective mechanism. "It served to protect the group from outside interference by manifesting a strong resistance to change, or threat of change, in conditions of work and personal relations."

The workers' behavior was usually not based on their actual experience with Western Electric, since the company's policy was that piece rates would not be changed unless there was a change in manufacturing process. Instead, the researchers found that the group's resistance seemed to derive in some complicated fashion from the position of that group in the total company structure and its consequent relations with other groups within the company. This position usually dictated that this group be on the receiving end of a constant series of technical changes emanating from higher in the organization; they felt they were always getting "dumped on" by "higher-ups."

As a result of the group's perceptions (or misperceptions), the researchers found that otherwise "logical" plans often did not work as intended. Partly because the workers saw themselves as having to accommodate themselves frequently to changes they did not initiate—changes that often seemed to further subordinate them in the company's social structure—and partly because the technical innovations caused changes in the workers' jobs and perceived status, otherwise "logical" changes were often resisted. As the researchers put it:

> The study of the bank wiremen showed that their behavior at work could not be understood without considering the informal organization of the group and the relation of this informal organization to the total social organization of the company. The work activities of this group, together with their satisfactions and dissatisfactions, had to be viewed as manifestations of a complex pattern of interrelations. In short, the work situation of the bank wiring group had to be treated as a social system; moreover, the industrial organization in which this group was a part also had to be treated as a social system.[23]

The Researchers' Theory and Conclusions

The Hawthorne researchers made several important contributions to organization theory, but probably the most basic was their notion of an industrial organization as a *sociotechnical system*:

> The two aspects into which an industrial plant can be roughly divided —the technical organization and the human organization—are interrelated and interdependent. The human organization is constantly molding and recreating the technical organization either to achieve more effectively the common economic purpose or to secure more satisfaction for its members. Likewise, changes in the technical organization require an adaptation on the part of the human organization.[24]

Relatedly, the researchers concluded that *employee attitudes and morale* appeared to be a major determinant of productivity and that a variety of factors, including the worker's personality and his supervisor's behavior, influenced his attitudes and morale. They concluded that a person's *work group* had a prevailing effect on his or her attitudes and productivity and that the group's attitudes were in turn a complex function of its perceived relationship to the rest of the organization. Later research findings would cast doubt on the notion that morale had determining effects on productivity, but the researchers' basic conclusions concerning the organization as a sociotechnical system and the effects of groups on their members are accepted today.

Criticisms of the Hawthorne Studies

The Hawthorne studies and the human-relations school they spawned have been severely criticized, and our discussion would be incomplete without a brief discussion of these criticisms.

Philosophy. The most vehement criticisms relate not so much to the Hawthorne studies themselves, but to the human-relations school and philosophy that Elton Mayo and others built on their interpretations of the Hawthorne findings. The empirical studies themselves, objectively reported in major works like *Management and the Worker*, have generally escaped this criticism. However, later works like Mayo's *Human Problems of Industrial Civilization* are laden with the human-relations writers' one-sided interpretations of the Hawthorne findings, and it is this one-sided interpretation—and the underlying philosophy implicit in it—that has been criticized.[25] Several economists, for example, write that by encouraging workers to develop loyalties to anything but their own self-interests, and by preaching collaboration instead of competition, human relations would eventually lead to reduced efficiency. Others point out that it is difficult to understand Mayo's work "unless one realizes how much he abhors conflict, competition, or disagreement: conflict to him is a social disease and cooperation is a social help." [26] Finally, critics charge that the human-relations movement, built as it is on a philosophy of worker–management harmony, is not only antithetical to a viable capitalistic system but impractical as well.

Methodology. Others have attacked the methodology of the Hawthorne studies.[27] With respect to the relay assembly test room studies, for example, Alex Carey points out that there was no attempt to establish sample groups "representative of any larger population than the groups themselves," and that no generalization is therefore legitimate. Furthermore:

> There was no attempt to employ control data from the output records of the girls who were not put under special experimental conditions [and] even if these points had been met, the experiments would still have been of only minor scientific value since a group of five subjects is too small to yield statistically reliable results.[28]

In his analysis, Carey asserts that the objective evidence obtained from these studies does not support any of the conclusions derived by the Hawthorne investigators and that it is only by "massive and relentless reinterpretation" that the researchers were able to draw the conclusions they did.

Findings. Related to this criticism are some concerning the *findings* of the Hawthorne studies. Carey, for example, says that the Hawthorne researchers grossly overstated their case for the importance of employee attitudes and that their findings may well simply reflect "a rather old world view about the value of monetary incentives, driving leadership, and discipline." Others accuse Carey of himself overstating the case; they point out that, far from underrating the importance of financial incentives, the Hawthorne researchers take pains to state that wage incentives *alone* could not account for their findings.[29]

The Hawthorne researchers' conclusions concerning the cause-and-effect relation between employee morale and productivity has also been widely criticized. Here, the prevailing evidence does suggest that there is no simple cause-and-effect relation and that, as often as not, (1) high productivity *leads* to high morale, or (2) the two are unrelated.[30]

Contributions of the Hawthorne Studies: Summary

Criticisms like these are not without merit and it is probably true that the Hawthorne researchers and their proponents overstated their case.[31] Yet it would be a mistake to disregard the Hawthorne findings, as Carey suggests, as "worthless scientifically." Even though those findings may have been oversimplified and overstated, they were responsible for adding new and essential dimensions to organization theory. They introduced the idea of the organization as an *open system* in which the technical and human segments are closely intertwined. They emphasized the importance of employee attitudes in an era when wage incentives and physical work conditions were often viewed as the only requirements for high productivity. Finally, they showed how cohesive *work groups* act to protect their self-interest by restricting output, resisting change, and undermining otherwise "rational" wage incentive plans. Later research strongly supported the conclusion that groups have an influence on their members, and we will discuss such group processes in the remainder of this chapter.

THEORY OF GROUP INFLUENCE

It was clear from the Hawthorne findings that groups have a profound influence on their members; researchers turned next to determining how—the process and mechanics through which—these group effects emerged.

The Homans Model

George Homans developed one of the earliest theories of group influence, and the so-called Homans Model has become something of a classic. It was developed from the Hawthorne findings and emphasizes the relation between the activities that are *required* of the group, and those that *emerge* from within the group itself.[32]

Three basic elements.   According to Homans, all group behavior consists of one or more "basic elements," which he calls "activities," "interactions," and "sentiments."

> *Activities.* Activities are things that people do, such as planting, cutting, smoking, walking. To be precise, says Homans, all activities "refer in the end to movements of the muscles of men. . . ."
>
> *Interactions.* Interactions are communications of any sort between individuals. These communications need not be verbal and in fact may be nonverbal: "Perhaps the simplest example of interaction, though we should find it complex enough if we studied it carefully, is two men at opposite ends of a saw, sawing a log. When we say that the two are interacting, we are not referring to the fact that both are sawing—in our language, sawing is an activity—but to the fact that the push of one man on the saw is followed by the push of the other. In this example, the interaction does not involve words."
>
> *Sentiments.* Sentiments are "internal states of the human body" and include motives, drives, emotions, feelings, effective states, sentiments, and attitudes. Sentiments thus range from fear and hunger to affection. Unlike activities and interactions, sentiments cannot be seen or observed.

External and internal systems.   Homans says group behavior can be observed in terms of an external system and an internal system. Each system contains its own activities, interactions, and sentiments.

The *external* system is composed of those required activities, interactions, and sentiments that the group must carry out to survive. For example, in the bank wiring room at Hawthorne, the required *activities* included wiring equipment and soldering connections. Similarly, "there were the necessary *interactions* between a solderman and the three wiremen he worked for, between an inspector and the wiremen and soldermen whose work he passed judgment on, [and] between the group chief and all the men in the room." [33] Finally, the bank wiremen's external system contained given and required *sentiments*. The given sentiments were those attitudes, values, and motives that the wiremen brought with them to their jobs and that were "generated by the circumstances of their lives outside the plant"; [34] the required sentiments were those that were required for adequate job performance—for example, wanting to do a good job.

On the other hand, the Hawthorne researchers discovered that the activities, interactions, and sentiments that *emerged* from the work groups were different (and often at odds with) those of the external system, a phenomenon that Homans comments on as follows:

> When a number of persons have come together to form a group, their behavior never holds to its first pattern. Social life is never wholly utilitarian: it elaborates itself, complicates itself, beyond the demands of the original situation.[35]

What emerges, says Homans, is an *internal* system, "the elaboration of group behavior that simultaneously arises out of the external system and reacts upon it." This system is also composed of activities, interactions, and sentiments, but in this case, these elements *emerge* out of the group's situation rather than being required by it:

> Instead of the motives for getting a job done, we shall have to deal with sentiments developed on the job, such as liking or disliking for others, approval or disapproval of the things other persons do. Instead of activities demanded by the job, we shall have to deal with activities spontaneously evolved that serve to express the attitudes of persons toward one another. And instead of interactions required for the coordination of practical activities, we shall have to deal with interactions elaborated socially—for fun, so to speak.[36]

The Homans model is illustrated in Figure 12-2. According to this model, background factors like technology, job design, and rules combine to determine the required and given behavior (the external system) in terms of required activities, interactions, and sentiments. In turn, an internal system (also composed of activities, interactions, and sentiments) emerges as the group members interact with one another. For example, special sentiments called norms develop; these are "laws" governing things like desirable output level. Also, new communications channels and new activities (like restricting output) emerge. As a result, the output of the group, in terms of productivity, satisfaction, and individual development, is often quite different from that expected by management.

Factors That Influence Group Cohesiveness

What determines the extent to which a group can influence the behavior and compliance of its members? To a large extent, it depends on the attraction the group has for its members—on its *cohesiveness*. Therefore, in this section we will discuss some of the factors that influence group cohesiveness.

Group size. The size of the group is one important factor. In one study, Seashore collected data on almost 6,000 people in industry and found that group cohesiveness declined as group size increased, up to about 20 members; beyond this size, cohesiveness leveled off.[37] In fact, group size seemed to have more of an influence on group cohesiveness than did such things as similarity in education or age. Part of the reason for this is that communication and interaction are prerequisites for the existence of a cohesive group; and as group size becomes too large, the number of possible interactions becomes so large that both interaction and communication begin to break down.

Intragroup and intergroup competition. Intragroup competition undermines group cohesiveness. In one study, management put production supervisors under considerable pressure to minimize departmental costs. Then a situation occurred in which certain goods were damaged at some unknown point in the production process. Normally, the cost of the damage would have been absorbed by the negligent department. In this case, the plant manager called a meeting of his subordinates to determine who was to be charged with the expense. Every department head emphatically denied that his department was responsible, and the meeting ended with the department managers blaming one another for the damaged merchandise. Thus, the competition created by the cost-minimization program resulted in hostilities and ill feeling that drastically reduced the cohesiveness and unity of the foremen group. In the end, the plant manager had to charge the loss against general plant overhead.

Whereas intragroup competition can undermine group cohesiveness, intergroup competition can frequently increase it. In one study, groups were assigned problems and then had to compete with each other in a situation in which only one group could win.[38] The researchers found that the newly created competitive environment increased group cohesiveness. Of equal importance, however, is that whether a group wins or loses has important implications for its cohesiveness. In losing groups, researchers have found that tension emerges that can upset internal relationships and undermine group cohesion.

Status.   Group cohesiveness is directly related to *group status.*[39] Such status may reflect many things, including differences in organizational level, overall performance, the work that the group is doing, or the amount of discretion extended to the group. However, there are a number of exceptions to this rule. For example, in those low-status groups whose members could not easily leave, the group did exhibit relatively high cohesion. On the other hand, a high-status group that was unsuccessful in carrying out its goals had relatively low cohesiveness.

Goals.   One reason a person joins a group is his feeling that the group can help him accomplish his goals. Agreement over goals, therefore, increases cohesiveness; differences undermine it.[40] Similarly, major disagreements over how the goal is to be accomplished (assuming that all group members agree on the goal) have disruptive effects on cohesiveness.

Environment and proximity.   Walker and Guest have found that the noise that often attends an assembly line inhibits verbal interaction and group cohesiveness.[41] However, a more basic factor inhibiting cohesiveness in such a situation may be the nature of the work itself, which usually requires little or no exchange of tools, or reciprocal or team action.

Stable relationships.   The existence of stable relationships is another requisite for a cohesive group. For example, studies of California aircraft factories concluded that groups that were frequently disturbed or rearranged did not become cohesive, but exhibited high rates of absenteeism and turnover.[42]

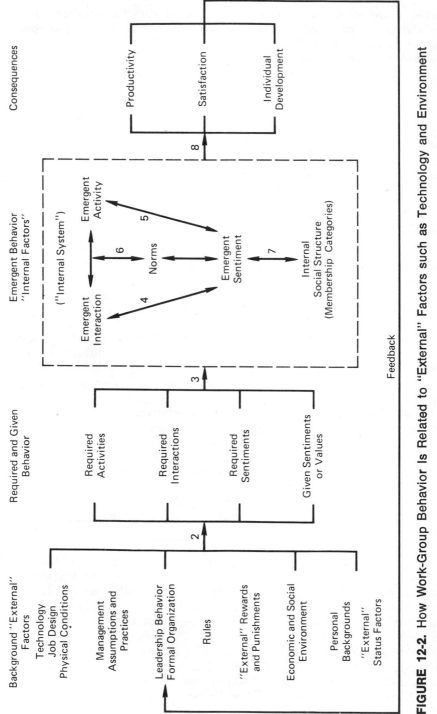

FIGURE 12-2. How Work-Group Behavior Is Related to "External" Factors such as Technology and Environment

Source: Arthur Turner, "A Conceptual Scheme for Describing Work-Group Behavior." Copyright © 1961 by the President and Fellows of Harvard College. Reproduced by permission.

GROUP NORMS AND MEMBER COMPLIANCE

What Are Norms?

Groups control their members through the use of norms, which Hare calls "rules of behavior, proper ways of acting, which have been accepted as legitimate by members of a group [and which] specify the kinds of behavior that are expected of group members." [43] Hackman says that norms have five characteristics, as follows:

1. Norms are structural characteristics of groups that summarize and simplify group influence processes. In other words, a norm summarizes and highlights those processes within the group that are intended to regulate and regularize group member behavior.
2. Norms apply only to behavior—not to private thoughts and feelings. According to Hackman, "behavioral compliance does not necessarily reflect the true private attitudes and beliefs of group members." He says that through the use of norms, a group member can be coerced into agreeing (or saying he agrees) with the group as a whole, but that his or her attitudes and beliefs may continue to conflict with those of the group.
3. Norms are generally developed only for behaviors that are viewed as important by most group members, and only for behaviors that otherwise would have to be controlled by direct and continuous social influence.
4. Norms usually develop gradually, but the process can be short-cut if members want. Hackman says that norms about behavior typically develop gradually and informally as members learn what behaviors are, in fact, important for the group to control, but that "if for some reason group members decide that a particular norm would be desirable or helpful, they simply agree to such a norm suddenly by declaring that 'from now on' the norm exists."
5. Not all norms apply to everyone. For example, high-status members often have more "freedom" to deviate from the letter of the norm than do other people.[44]

A Model of Group Norms

Jackson has developed what he calls a Return Potential Model (RPM) that quantitatively illustrates the approval or disapproval a norm-governed behavior evokes. As an example, Figure 12-3 shows a hypothetical RPM for the activity "talking during a group meeting." Both too little and too much talking (according to this model) would be disapproved of, but the *intensity* of the disapproval is somewhat stronger for someone who talks too much.

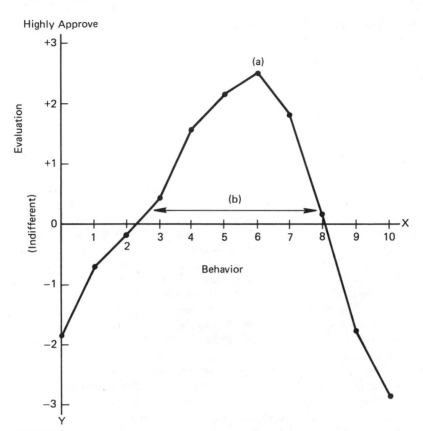

FIGURE 12-3. Schematic Representation of the Return Potential Model (RPM) of Normative Structure

Note: Ordinate is an axis of evaluation; abscissa is an axis of behavior.

Source: J. Richard Hackman, "Group Influences on Individuals," p. 1497. (Adapted from Jackson, "Structural Characteristics of Norms," in I. D. Steiner and M. Fishbein, eds., *Current Studies in Social Psychology* (New York: Holt, Rinehart and Winston, 1965).

To develop such a model, one would obtain from group members (or from observations of these group members) the amount of approval or disapproval associated with various levels of an activity and from these data plot a Return Potential Curve. The curve itself then provides information on the level of behavior that generates the highest approval or disapproval, the range of tolerable behavior, the approval and disapproval associated with various levels of the behavior, and "crystalization"—the degree of consensus among group members regarding the amount of approval or disapproval associated with each point on the behavior dimension.

Jackson and his associates have used the RPM idea successfully. It allows quantification of norms, thereby permitting comparison of different norms within a group and of the same norm between different groups. An RPM can also be used for "raising implicit norms to the level of explicit awareness and discussion," thereby getting a group to recognize the need for making some change.

How Groups Influence Perception and Behavior

Social control: Imposed versus self-control. Hare calls the process through which group members put pressure on the individual "social control." Through social control, "behavior is confined to acceptable limits, limits which maximize the possibilities of survival for the individual and the group."

Social control is sometimes *imposed* on deviant group members. For example, by educating, ostracizing, or on occasion physically punishing the deviant, group members put pressure on him or her. But Hare says that in most cases, social control is *self-control*:

> This is the self control which takes place during the initial phase of the social act when the individual modifies his behavior as a result of his anticipation of the response of the other person. . . . This process of modification of behavior may range from an individual's conscious attempts to conform to norms to the unconscious acceptance of group or individual directives.[45]

Effects of groups on perception and judgment. Groups can influence their members' behavior *indirectly* by influencing their perception and judgment. The classic study of this phenomenon was carried out by Asch. The subjects were asked to compare and to match lines of various lengths, and Asch arranged for all but one of the subjects to give erroneous answers so that Asch could study the responses of the naive subject.

Of the 50 naive subjects, about one-fourth reported the true length of the lines, although this contradicted the length reported by the rest of the group. Asch reports that the rest of the subjects "yielded" for one (or more) of three reasons:

> *Distortion of perception.* A small minority of the naive subjects reported that they were unaware that their estimates had been distorted by the majority and that they actually came to perceive the majority estimates as correct.
>
> *Distortion of judgment.* Most of the subjects who yielded belonged to this category. These subjects lacked confidence in their own perceptions and came to believe that their perceptions were inaccurate while those of the majority were accurate.
>
> *Distortion of action.* These subjects did not come to view their perceptions as inaccurate nor did the group distort their true perceptions. Instead, these subjects yielded because of what they felt was an overwhelming need to go along with the group. They were afraid to ap-

pear different or as outsiders and therefore willingly parroted the majority position although they knew it was incorrect.[46]

Conditions determining compliance with the majority. What are the factors that determine whether the individual will in fact comply with the opinion of the group majority? Research suggests at least interrelated factors:

> *Characteristics of the environment.* First, where the items on which decisions must be made are *ambiguous or unclear*, there tends to be much greater reliance on the group and a greater tendency to go along with the group majority's decision.
>
> *Characteristics of the perceiver.* Second, individuals who are *insecure*, or who feel poorly qualified to assess the situation, are more apt to go along with the group majority's decision.
>
> *Characteristics of the group.* Finally, a group that is seen as being highly *credible* will for obvious reasons evoke more compliance than a group that is not. Similarly, where there is a greater *unanimity of views* among group members, individual group members can be expected to comply more with the group majority than where there is not such unanimity.[47]

Effects of Groups on behavior and compliance. Writers since the time of the Hawthorne studies have recognized the fact that groups influence the behavior and compliance of their members. Exactly what effects do groups have on the productivity of their members? Two representative studies, one by Schachter and one by Seashore, help answer this question.

In a laboratory study, Schachter was able to manipulate two independent variables. First, he was able to categorize the group as either high-cohesive or low-cohesive. He was also able to categorize the group according to whether it had positive or negative norms (that is, whether the group agreed with the performance standards it had to meet).[48]

Schachter's findings are summarized in Table 12-2. They indicate that a highly cohesive group with positive norms can cause a significant increase in group production, whereas a highly cohesive group with negative norms can bring about a significant decrease. On the other hand, there is some indication that a low-cohesive group with positive norms can still result in increased production, but that a low-cohesive group with negative norms has very little effect on production.

Seashore's study was conducted in a heavy-machinery company and focused on the relationship between work-group cohesiveness and various measures of anxiety and productivity.[49] The employees were well educated, mostly married, of various ages, and about 93 percent male. Questionnaires were administered to a total of 5,871 employees, who were the constituents of 228 work groups.

To measure group cohesiveness, the researchers constructed an "index of cohesiveness" based upon responses to questions such as, "Do you feel that you are really a part of your work group?" and, "If you had a chance

TABLE 12-2

Relationship between Group Cohesiveness, Production Norms, and Change in Production

	Change in Production for Positive Norm	Change in Production for Negative Norm
High-Cohesive Groups	+5.92	−2.16
Low-Cohesive Groups	+5.09	−.42

Source: S. Schachter, et al., "An Experimental Study of Cohesiveness and Productivity," *Human Relations* (Fall 1951), p. 233.

to do the same kind of work for the same pay in another work group, how would you feel about moving?" This index was then correlated with measures of anxiety, perceived company "supportiveness," and productivity.

The researchers found that members of high-cohesive groups were much less anxious and tense than members of low-cohesive groups. Specifically, they were less likely to report feeling "jumpy" or "nervous" or perceiving a lack of "supportiveness" by the company. Furthermore, members of high-cohesive groups where the production was at least average were less likely to report feeling under pressure for high production.

Cohesiveness also had two effects on group productivity. First, there was less *variability* in actual productivity within high-cohesive groups. Second, the actual *level* of production might be either high or low, depending upon whether the high-cohesive group members had a favorable attitude toward the company.

In summary, high group cohesiveness is associated with low anxiety and tension as well as with a greater ability to withstand complaints, abuse, or pressure emanating from the group's environment. High cohesiveness is also associated with less variability in production; however, whether such a stable, uniform production rate is high or low seems to depend largely upon whether the group views management's goals as acceptable.

Therefore, groups influence their members' perception, judgment, behavior, and compliance. We turn next to an analysis of how groups affect —and are affected by—the organization's structure.

GROUPS AND ORGANIZATION STRUCTURE

The Organization as a Structure of Groups

According to Rensis Likert, an organization will function best when its personnel function not as individuals but as members of highly effective work groups with high performance goals. Therefore, he says, management

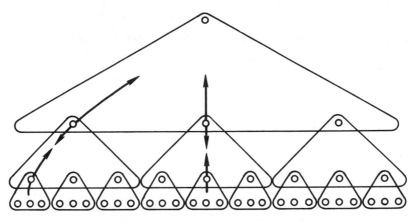

(The Arrows Indicate the Linking Pin Function)

FIGURE 12-4. The Linking Pin and Overlapping Groups

Source: Rensis Likert, *New Patterns of Management* (New York: McGraw-Hill, 1961), p. 113.

should deliberately endeavor to build these effective work groups, linking them into an organization structure by means of people who hold over- lapping group membership (as in Figure 12-4). His theory of the organiza- tion as a structure of groups is built on his "principle of supportive rela- tionships":

> The leadership and other processes of the organization must be such as to insure a maximum probability that in all interactions and all relationships with the organization each member will, in the light of his background, values, and expectations, view the experience as supportive and one which builds and maintains his sense of personal worth and importance.[50]

The desire to achieve and maintain a sense of personal worth is clearly a central concept of this principle. According to Likert, "the most important source of satisfaction for this desire is the response we get from the people we are close to . . . the face to face groups with whom we spend the bulk of our time are, consequently, the most important to us." As a result:

> Management will make full use of the potential capacities of its human resources only when each person in an organization is a member of one or more effectively functioning work groups that have a high degree of group loyalty, effective skills of interaction, and high performance goals.[51]

As in Figure 12-4 the supervisors in the most effective organizations function as "linking pins" between their own supervisors and their sub- ordinates. Likert says that to function effectively in this role, the supervisor must have enough influence with his own superior to be able to affect the superior's decisions. To the extent that a supervisor cannot perform this linking-pin function, the effectiveness of the organization as a structure of effective work groups is reduced, since the contributions that the supervisors' group might otherwise have made to problem solving and decision making in the organization are lost or reduced.

How Organization Structure Affects
Group Functioning

Structure both affects and is affected by group processes; we first discuss the influence of structure on groups.

Task structure. There are several ways in which the design of the task or organization influences group behavior. First as we have seen, proximity and the ability to interact are prerequisites to group formation, and in situations where proximity or opportunities for interaction are reduced, group cohesiveness tends to be reduced as well.[52]

Similarly, the workflow implicit in the organization structure determines required interactions and status, which in turn affect group functioning. In a classic study of restaurants, for example, Whyte found that the work flow placed higher-status employees (like cooks) in a position of taking orders from lower-status employees (like waitresses), and as a result, workgroup functioning suffered.[53] (Eventually, the problem was partially solved by having the waitresses clip their orders to a revolving clipboard, thus eliminating the interaction between the cook and waitress.)

In another famous study, Trist and his associates investigated the effects of converting from a "short-wall" to a "long-wall" method of coal mining in British coal mines.[54] In the former, each miner was proficient at all the necessary mining tasks, and the miners, working as a highly cohesive group, took turns carrying out these tasks. This system was replaced by a "long-wall" system, in which miners worked across a long mine face and each worker had a single task. With the long-wall method, the first shift of miners carried out their single task, the second shift carried out a second task, and the third shift carried out the third basic mining task.

The long-wall method was not successful. Ability to face the dangers of deep mining is perhaps the most important characteristic miners must have, and this ability tends to be higher within cohesive work groups. In the case of the long-wall method, these cohesive work groups were broken down by changes in the required activities and interactions of group members. Miners now had specialized jobs to do and no longer shared common tasks (or a common pay rate); and they were now more independent of one another and often worked widely separated from one another. These structural changes undermined group cohesiveness and functioning.

Walker and Guest, in their studies of work groups on assembly lines, made a number of useful observations of the structural and technological factors that undermine group functioning.[55] According to them, "the first and most obvious barrier is noise. In many of the sections along the line, verbal interaction, at least, is difficult or impossible." More important, the technical nature of assembly-line work "neither suggests nor compels inter-action," so that groups have less of a formal need to emerge. Furthermore, assembly lines put a good deal of distance between workers (particularly those on opposite ends of the line), and this too reduces interactions and group formation. However, Walker and Guest found that although group formation had usually been hampered by these structural and technological factors, in some cases cohesive groups had emerged. This was generally be-cause more effective foremen took specific action (such as holding periodic meetings with their men) to cultivate cohesive groups. Task structure also affects group functioning in many other ways. For one thing, as we have seen, departmentation results in *differentiation* whereby departments each develop their own goals and point of view. Therefore, where a unit is placed on the organization chart has implications for its functioning. For example, the quality control group that reports to the production manager might develop a very different—and less independent—point of view than one re-porting to the president. The placement of groups or work units lower or higher on the organization chart also has implications for each unit's status, and thus the resulting group and intergroup behavior.

Group size. Organization structure can also influence group func-tioning more indirectly through its effect on group size. The span of con-trol implicit in an organization structure determines the number of subor-dinates reporting to a supervisor and, therefore, the size of each work group. To the extent that group size and cohesiveness are inversely related, smaller groups should foster more satisfaction than large ones and this seems to be the case. The findings relating group size and performance, however, are mixed. Most have found that small groups produce more, perhaps because coordination is easier. It is likely though that the impact of group size depends on how structured the group's task is. Researchers have found that group size was positively related to performance for highly structured tasks, possibly because the leader could watch each man closely. On the other hand, the size-performance relationship was negative where the task was unstructured.[56]

"Ambient stimuli." Hackman says that ambient stimuli—"stimuli which potentially are available to all group members"—affect group func-tioning. Among these stimuli are the other people in the group, the materials and task the group is working on, and aspects of the groups' workplace.[57] He says that "the ambient stimuli which characterize a given group can strongly affect a group member's behavior-outcome expectancies" (that is, his perceptions of "what leads to what" for that group). For exam-ple, the layout that characterizes a traditional elementary school class—chairs lined up in rows and bolted to the floor, communications routinely passing from teacher to student in one direction, and the like—provide a new group member (student) with a good deal of information about be-havior-outcome contingencies, such as that sitting quietly at a desk will result in no unpleasant interactions with the teacher. In summary, says Hackman, "the ambient stimuli present in a group setting often prompt

fairly strong inferences by group members regarding what behaviors are likely to be appropriate and inappropriate in that group."

Engineering the task. Hackman says that managers can and should attempt to "engineer" a group's ambient stimuli so as to affect group behavior in specified ways. He says there are three primary "sources" of ambient stimuli that are potentially manipulable: "(A) the particular *people* who compose the group, (B) the *situation or environment* in which the group functions, and (C) the *task* of the group." For example, it is often possible to manipulate the characteristics of the task or situation so as to highlight the availability of certain rewards (or punishments). Similarly, managers can influence group cohesivensss by changing the particular people who compose the group, and by influencing the proximity and work flow of those people.[58]

How Groups Affect Organization Structure: The Informal Organization

Groups that emerge in an organization can also modify the organization structure. Stieglitz says that "to some people, that mystical entity known as the 'informal' organization is the real organization. It is how things really get done." This informal organization, he says, encompasses all relationships and channels of communication that mature, reasonable people are expected to develop and use in order to meet organizational objectives. This informal organization is informal "only in the sense that nobody has found it necessary to inundate the organization with memorabilia that fully spell out its workings." [59] Katz and Kahn point out that this informal organization (which itself is composed of groups or "role-sets" that emerge spontaneously) is necessary because it is impossible to specify in advance every required task or to plan for every contingency: instead, informal relationships emerge through which the formal organization is expanded and elaborated.

Woodward presents some useful anecdotal findings in this regard. In her study:

> It was found, for example, that organizational objectives were frequently achieved through the informal rather than the formal organization. A dysfunctional formal organization could be compensated by contributive informal relationships. This was particularly noticeable in relation to technical change.[60]

In three of the firms the Woodward team studied, changes in organization structure were planned and put into effect at the same time as the technical change. In the remaining firms, however, technical changes were made without changing the formal organization, "it having been taken for granted that the existing organizational structure would prove adequate for the new technology." However, in every case this proved not to be so:

The first thing that happened was that informal organization began to respond to the new situational demands imposed upon it. The result was a serious discrepancy between formal and informal organizations, and the achievement of organizational goals almost entirely through an informal network of relationships. In general, senior management were sophisticated enough to be aware that this was happening, and after a varying period of time had elapsed changes were made in formal organization. Either the existing informal relationships were defined and formalized or mechanisms were introduced to minimize the discrepancy. For example, in one firm a production committee was set up to allow people to establish contact with those to whom they were not related in the formal hierarchy.[61]

SUMMARY

Groups play a crucial role in organization theory because they influence and are influenced by organization structure, and because they affect their members' behavior and compliance. In this chapter, therefore, we discussed group processes and their relation to organization theory.

It was during the Hawthorne studies that organization theorists first became fully cognizant of how employees' work groups, attitudes, and needs affect their motivation and behavior. Furthermore, even though as a work of research these studies are far from perfect, they still provide a fascinating example of the scientific method applied to organizational questions, of the need for hypothesis testing and controlled experimentation, and of the need to maintain an open, inquisitive mind while in the pursuit of truth through science. These studies introduced the idea of the organization as an open system, emphasized the importance of employee attitudes in an era when wage incentives were viewed as paramount, and showed how cohesive work groups act to protect their self-interest by restricting output and resisting change.

What is the process through which groups influence their members? We discussed one explanation, that of George Homans, which he based partly on the Hawthorne findings. He distinguishes between activities, interactions, and sentiments, and explains how required activities, interactions, and sentiments are often very different from those that emerge from the work group. The extent to which the group can influence the behavior and compliance of a member depends largely on the attraction the group has for that person, and so we next discussed some factors, such as group size, that influence group cohesiveness.

How do groups influence employee compliance? We found that groups can influence their members' perception, judgment, and behavior. We concluded that high group cohesiveness is associated with low anxiety and tension; with greater ability to withstand complaints, abuse, or pressure emanating from the group's environment; and with less variability of production. Whether the production rate is high or low, however, seems to depend largely on whether the group accepts management's goals.

How are groups and organization structure related? Groups influence and are influenced by organization structure. Likert, in fact, describes organization structure as a system of overlapping groups in which supervisors perform "linking-pin" functions. We saw that organization structure (in terms of task design, work layout, group size, and ambient stimuli) can affect group functioning, and that to improve group functioning, "engineering the task" is sometimes advisable. We also saw that groups can influence organization structure by filling in what is not on the organization chart; it was found, for example, that "a dysfunctional formal organization could be compensated by contributive informal relationships."

In summary, groups exert a powerful influence on both the structure of the organization and their members' compliance, and the topic of groups is, therefore, an important one in the subject of organization theory.

DISCUSSION QUESTIONS

1. "Supervisors should always strive to have cohesive groups." Discuss whether you agree or disagree with this statement and why.
2. Discuss the factors that influence group cohesiveness.
3. Describe how the Homans model of work group behavior underscores the contingency or situational aspects of group behavior.
4. What role did the Hawthorne studies play in changing the direction of organization theory?
5. Do you agree that as a research study the Hawthorne experiments were "worthless scientifically"? Why or why not?
6. Describe what Homans means by activities, interactions, and sentiments. How useful do you think his theory is for explaining work group behavior?
7. Explain specifically how you would go about increasing the cohesiveness of some work group.
8. "One cannot predict the effectiveness of an organization structure or of a leader without understanding the group processes that exist in the situation." Explain whether you agree or disagree with this statement and why.
9. Under what conditions are group members more likely to comply with the opinion of the group majority?

FOOTNOTES

1 Elton Mayo, *The Political Problems of an Industrial Civilization* (Boston: Graduate School of Business, Harvard University, 1947), p. 21.

2 This section is based on F. L. Roethlisberger and William Dickson, *Management and the Worker* (Cambridge, Mass.: Harvard University Press, 1939); and Henry Landsberger, *Hawthorne Revisited* (Ithaca, N.Y.: Cornell University Press, 1958).

3 Roethlisberger and Dickson, *Management and the Worker*, p. 15.

4 *Ibid.*, p. 16.

5 *Ibid.*

6 *Ibid.,* p. 17.

7 *Ibid.,* p. 19.

8 *Ibid.*

9 *Ibid.,* p. 20.

10 *Ibid.,* p. 54.

11 *Ibid.,* pp. 58–59.

12 *Ibid.,* p. 62.

13 *Ibid.,* p. 73.

14 *Ibid.,* p. 160.

15 *Ibid.,* p. 88.

16 *Ibid.,* p. 72.

17 *Ibid.,* p. 72.

18 *Ibid.,* p. 185.

19 *Ibid.,* pp. 373–75.

20 *Ibid.,* p. 374.

21 *Ibid.,* p. 385.

22 See George Homans, *Fatigue of Workers: Its Relation to Industrial Production* (New York: Rinehart, 1941), pp. 77–86; reprinted in Paul Lawrence and John Seiler, *Organizational Behavior and Administration* (Homewood, Ill.: Richard D. Irwin, 1965).

23 Roethlisberger and Dickson, *Management and the Worker,* p. 551.

24 *Ibid.,* p. 553.

25 See Landsberger, *Hawthorne Revisited,* Chap. 3.

26 *Ibid.,* p. 31.

27 For a discussion of this, see Alex Carey, "The Hawthorne Studies: A Radical Criticism," *American Sociological Review,* June 1967, pp. 403–16.

28 *Ibid.*

29 See Jon Shepard, "On Alex Carey's Radical Criticism of the Hawthorne Studies," *Academy of Management Journal,* March 1971, 23–31.

30 See, for example: Dennis Organ, "A Reappraisal and Reinterpretation of the Satisfaction Causes Performance Hypothesis," *Academy of Management Review,* Vol. 2, No. 1 (1977), 46–53; J. E. Sheridan and J. W. Slocum, Jr., "The Direction of the Causal Relationship between Job Satisfaction and Work Performance," *Organizational Behavior and Human Performance,* Vol. 14, No. 2 (October 1975), 159–72.

31 See, for example, Edwin Locke, "Nature and Causes of Job Satisfaction," in Marvin Dunnette, *Handbook of Industrial and Organizational Psychology* (Chicago: Rand McNally, 1976), p. 1299.

32 This information is based on George Homans, *The Human Group* (New York: Harcourt Brace Jovanovich, 1950), pp. 25–40, 90–107, 108–13, and 118–19; and Joseph Litterer, *Organizations* (New York: John Wiley, 1969), Vol. I, pp. 167–88.

33 Litterer, *Organizations,* p. 180.

34 *Ibid.,* p. 178.

35 *Ibid.,* p. 185.

36 *Ibid.,* p. 186.

37 Stanley F. Seashore, *Group Cohesiveness in the Industrial Work Group* (Ann Arbor: Survey Research Center, University of Michigan, 1954), pp. 90–95. For an excellent discussion of group cohesiveness see Joseph A. Litterer, *The Analysis of Organizations* (New York: Wiley, 1965), pp. 91–101.

38 Robert R. Blake and Jane S. Mouton, "Reactions to Intergroup Competition under Win-Lose Conditions," *Management Science,* Vol. 7 (1961), 432.

39 John W. Thibaut, "An Experimental Study of Cohesiveness of Underprivileged Groups," *Human Relations*, Vol. 3 (1950), 251–78.

40 John R. P. French, Jr., "The Disruption and Cohesion of Groups," The *Journal of Abnormal and Social Psychology*, Vol. 36 (1941), 361–77.

41 C. R. Walker and R. H. Guest, *The Man on the Assembly Line* (Cambridge, Mass.: Harvard University Press, 1952), pp. 135–40.

42 Elton Mayo and George H. Lombard, "Teamwork and Labor Turnover in the Aircraft Industry of Southern California," Business Research Report #32 (Boston: Graduate School of Business Administration, Harvard University, 1944), p. 8.

43 A. P. Hare, *Handbook of Small Group Research* (New York: Free Press, 1962), p. 24.

44 J. Richard Hackman, "Group Influences on Individuals," in Marvin Dunnette, ed., *Handbook of Industrial and Organizational Psychology*, p. 1494, p. 1497. Copyright © Rand McNally College Publishing Company, 1976.

45 Hare, *Handbook of Small Group Research*, p. 25.

46 S. E. Asch, "Effects of Group Pressure upon the Modification and Distortion of Judgments," in Guy Swanson, Theodore Newcomb, and Eugene Hartley, *Readings in Social Psychology* (New York: Henry Holt and Company, 1952), pp. 6–7; and Michael Olmstead, *The Small Group* (New York: Random House, 1959), pp. 67–81.

47 For a good review of these findings, see Hare, *Handbook of Small Group Research*, and Hackman, "Group Influences on Individuals."

48 S. Schachter, N. Ellerston, D. McBridge, and D. Gregory, "An Experimental Study of Cohesiveness and Productivity," *Human Relations*, Fall 1951, 229–38.

49 Seashore, *Group Cohesiveness in the Industrial Work Group*.

50 Rensis Likert, *New Patterns of Management* (New York: McGraw-Hill, 1961), p. 103.

51 *Ibid.,* p. 104.

52 See, for example, A. K. Rice, "Productivity and Social Organization in an Indian Weaving Shed," *Human Relations*, Vol. 6 (1953), 311; E. L. Trist and K. W. Bamforth, "Some Social and Psychological Consequences of the Long Wall Method of Coal-Getting," *Human Relations*, Vol. 4 (1951), 1–38.

53 William F. Whyte, *Human Relations in the Restaurant Industry* (New York: McGraw-Hill, 1948).

54 Trist and Bamforth, "Some Social and Psychological Consequences."

55 Charles Walker, Robert Guest, and Arthur Turner, *The Foremen on the Assembly Line* (Boston: Harvard University Press, 1956).

56 Edwin Thomas and Clinton Fink, "Effects of Group Size," *Psychological Bulletin*, Vol. 60, No. 4 (1963), 371–84; A. P. Hare, "A Study of Interaction and Consensus in Different Sized Groups," *American Sociological Review*, Vol. 17 (1952), 261–67; Stanley F. Seashore, *Group Cohesiveness in the Industrial Work Group* (Ann Arbor: Survey Research Center, University of Michigan, 1954), pp. 90–95; and Robert C. Cummins and Donald C. King, "The Interaction of Group Size and Task Structure in an Industrial Organization," *Personnel Psychology* (1973), pp. 87–94.

57 J. Richard Hackman, "Group Influences on Individuals," in Dunnette, *Handbook of Industrial and Organizational Psychology*, pp. 1455–1526.

58 *Ibid.,* p. 1471.

59 Harold Stieglitz, "What's Not on the Organization Chart," *The Conference Board Record*, November 1964, pp. 7–10.

60 Joan Woodward, *Industrial Organization: Theory and Practice* (London: Oxford University Press, 1965), p. 239.

61 *Ibid.*

Chapter 13

Intergroup Relations and Conflict

CHAPTER OVERVIEW

Intergroup conflict is a familiar aspect of organizations, and one that has important implications for organization structure and therefore theory. The effectiveness of a structure depends on the departments working together effectively. Intergroup conflict—between line and staff units, or production and sales units, for example—can be useful, but can also reduce communication and collaboration between departments, so that the structure no longer functions effectively. In this chapter, we therefore turn to a discussion of intergroup relations, and in particular, conflict—its sources, processes, and management. A question we ask is, "How are organization structure and intergroup conflict related?"

The outline of this chapter is as follows:

I. Types of Conflict
   A. Functional and Dysfunctional Conflict
   B. Individual, Organizational, and Interorganizational Conflict
   C. Line–Staff Conflict

II. Sources of Intergroup Conflict
   A. Interdependencies and Shared Resources
   B. Intergroup Differences in Goals, Values, or Perceptions
   C. Authority Imbalances
   D. Ambiguity

III. Models of Intergroup Conflict
   A. Pondy: Organizational Conflict—Concepts and Models

TYPES OF CONFLICT

Functional and Dysfunctional Conflict

Today, we view intergroup conflict as a very real and often useful aspect of organizations, but such a view did not always prevail. Classical theorists, for example, regarded organizational conflict as an aberration. To these classicists, with their mechanical, closed-system view of organizations, conflict simply could not—or should not—arise, since a network of financial incentives and close supervision supposedly assured unanimity of goals throughout the organization, and a rigid chain of command provided an ever-present vehicle for resolving disagreements.

The human-relations theorists were more realistic in their views of conflict, and they acknowledged its existence. But while they recognized its existence they too viewed it as an aberration: for example (as we saw in Chapter 12), one cannot perhaps fully appreciate human-relations theory without understanding how much Mayo ". . . abhors conflict, competition, and agreement: conflict to him is a social disease and cooperation is a social help." [1]

Today, according to Stephen Robbins, theorists hold a more positive view of organizational conflict. This positive view:

1. Recognizes the absolute necessity of conflict,
2. Explicitly encourages opposition,
3. Defines conflict management to include stimulation as well as resolution methods, and
4. Considers the management of conflict as a major responsibility of all administrators.

Robbins says the classicists' belief that conflicts were inherently destructive has been replaced with what he calls the "interactionists' " view. This view recognizes the necessity of conflict and explicitly encourages a certain amount of controlled conflict in organizations. The basic case for this view is that some conflict is necessary if an organization is to avoid stagnation and myopic decision making, and an example often cited is a paper by Janis called "Group-Think." In this paper, Janis describes how potential critics of the abortive Bay of Pigs invasion were put under tremendous pressure not to express their opposition. For example, then Attorney General Robert Kennedy at one point took Arthur Schlesinger aside and asked him why he was opposed to the invasion. According to Janis, Kennedy listened coldly and then said, "You may be right or you may be wrong, but the President has made his mind up. Don't push it any further. Now is the time for everyone to help him all they can." [2]

Janis feels that if Kennedy and his staff had encouraged the expression of more criticism, many of their questionable assumptions would have been challenged and much better decisions would have resulted. As Robbins puts it:

> Constructive conflict is both valuable and necessary. Without conflict, there would be few new challenges; there would be no stimulation to think through ideas; organizations would be only apathetic and stagnant.[3]

This generally positive picture of conflict appears to be supported by surveys of current management practice. In one recent survey of top and middle managers, for example, managers rated "conflict management" as of equal (or slightly higher) importance to topics like planning, communication, motivation, and decision making. They reportedly spent about 20 percent of their time on conflicts; yet they did not consider the conflict level in their organizations to be excessive. Instead, they rated it as about right—that is, at the midpoint of a scale running from "too low" to "too high." [4]

Individual, Organizational, and Interorganizational Conflict

According to March and Simon, we can identify three main classes of conflict: *individual, organizational,* and *interorganizational.* "Role conflict" is a familiar example of conflict within the *individual.* Role conflict occurs when a person is faced with conflicting orders, such that compliance with one would make it difficult or impossible to comply with the other.

Organizational conflict includes conflict between individuals, between individuals and groups, and between groups. Intergroup conflict, which we stress in this chapter, often involves two or more organizational units that, while interdependent (like production and sales), find themselves with conflicting goals.

Concerning *interorganizational* conflict, the third class of conflict proposed by March and Simon, they point out:

> Many of the phenomena of intergroup conflict within organizations are

almost indistinguishable from the phenomena that we might consider under the [heading of interorganizational conflict].[5]

In other words, March and Simon recognize the fact that interorganizational conflict—conflict between two or more organizations—can arise. However, they believe that the sources and processes of such conflict are usually quite similar to those involving competing units within single organizations.

Line–Staff Conflict

Line and staff units are highly interdependent by design, and line–staff conflict may be viewed as a special case of conflict between interdependent units. Many authors have argued that controversy and conflict are inherent in the concept of line and staff.[6] Although there may be some question as to whether the controversy and conflict are inherent, there is little doubt that they exist. Theorists have suggested a number of sources of line–staff conflict, including the fact that the creation of a staff unit tends to diminish the line manager's authority.[7] In addition, the staff unit is frequently in the position of gatekeeper relative to the line manager and can often control the resources and rewards flowing to him. One example of this is a plant personnel manager who has a staff position but has easy access to the plant manager and thereby exercises considerable indirect influence over plant foremen.

Such problems are frequently compounded by differences in personnel characteristics between line and staff managers. Dalton found that staff men were usually younger and came from different social backgrounds from line managers.[8] He also found that the staff managers were better educated and more embroiled in the politics of the organization. In addition, since staff men had fewer organizational levels to advance to, each frequently tried to enlarge his own "empire." The interdependence of line and staff units tends to further aggravate the situation: While the success and existence of the staff men frequently depends on their obtaining acceptance for their ideas from the line managers, the latter often fear the staff people as a group that undermines line authority.

An underlying assumption of many of these sources of conflict is that line and staff managers differ in their views of what activities are legitimate for the staff manager. Two researchers carried out a study that sheds some light on the nature of this problem.[9] They collected two types of data from 71 organizations in western New York about perceptions of the role of the top-level staff personnel manager in each organization. The first set of data concerned the extent to which the personnel administrator and other staff and line managers agreed on the *current* responsibilities of the personnel administrator. These included supervising subordinates, representing the company, union activities, and so forth. The second set of data concerned the agreement between these groups of managers as to what the personnel administrator's responsibilities *should be*.

The researchers found that there was a consensus among the managers about the personnel administrator's current responsibilities, but that there were significant differences in what the three groups of managers thought the legitimate responsibilities of the personnel administrator should be:

> Both personnel administrators and other managers agreed that the former should participate more fully in organizational decisions. However, the personnel manager expressed the much stronger desire, and this seemed to lead to the conflict.[10]

The researchers interpret their finding to mean that conflict is not inherent in the line–staff structure. The conflict in this case arose out of the desire of the personnel administrators to be more involved in legitimate "personnel" areas such as hiring and collective bargaining.

However, regardless of whether line–staff conflict is inherent in the structure, it is still a very real problem, and one of its symptoms may be the lower levels of satisfaction generally found among staff managers. Three studies by the Opinion Research Corporation reported that engineers and scientists in staff positions were less satisfied with their jobs than were engineers and scientists in line positions.[11] Another study surveyed line and staff managers. Line managers reported a greater incidence of desirable conditions of work, and seemed to believe that their important needs were better satisfied than did the staff managers.[12] Similarly, Dalton found that staff managers in three plants had a turnover rate between two and four times that of line managers.[13]

SOURCES OF INTERGROUP CONFLICT

Many factors contribute to intergroup conflict. In one recent study, for example, the researchers listed the following sources of conflict:

Misunderstanding (communication failure)
Personality clashes
Value and goal differences
Substandard performance
Differences over method
Responsibility issues
Lack of cooperation
Authority issues
Frustration and irritability
Competition for limited resources
Noncompliance with rules and policies [14]

But although there are obviously many sources of intergroup conflict, research findings suggest that four factors create most of the problems: interdependencies and shared resources; intergroup differences in goals, values, or perceptions; authority imbalances; and ambiguities.

Interdependencies and Shared Resources

The existence of what March and Simon call a "felt need for joint decision making" is one important antecedent to intergroup conflict. Walton and Dutton define interdependence as "the extent to which two units depend on each other for assistance, information, compliance, or other coordinative acts in the performance of their respective tasks." [15] For obvious reasons, intergroup conflict is unlikely between units that are *not* required to interact with each other. Dutton and Walton have found that although interdependence can provide an incentive for collaboration, it also presents an occasion for conflict, and that interdependence thus tends to heighten the intensity of either antagonisms or friendliness between units. It also increases the *consequences* of interunit conflict for organizational performance.

Similarly, conflict potential increases when two units depend upon a common pool of scarce resources, such as capital funds or a typing pool. As Walton and Dutton state:

> If the two units have interdependent tasks, the competition for scarce resources will tend to decrease interunit problem solving and coordination. Also, if competition for scarce resources is not mediated by some third unit and they must agree on their allocation, they will come into direct conflict.[16]

Intergroup Differences in Goals, Values, or Perceptions

Differences in goals. Differences in goals are a familiar source of intergroup conflict. Dutton and Walton, for example, found that the preference of production units for long, economical runs conflicted with the preference of sales units for quick delivery for good customers, and that these differing goals often led to intergroup conflict.[17] Similarly, Dalton found that line–staff conflicts often arose because staff units valued change, whereas line units valued stability.[18] Other fundamental differences in goals that have been found to lead to conflicts include an emphasis on flexibility versus stability; emphasis on short-run versus long-run performance; emphasis on measurable versus intangible results; and emphasis on organizational goals versus societal needs.[19]

Differences in values and perceptions. Dalton's study of line–staff conflict provides some clear examples of how differences in values and perceptions can lead to conflicts. He found that conflicts between line and staff managers arose because:

1. Staff personnel tend to be younger, more educated, of a higher

social-status class, and more ambitious and restless than line managers.

2. The older, often more experienced line managers tend to dislike having to take advice from younger staff managers. They fear being "shown up."

3. Line managers tend to view staff as agents on trial, as people who must constantly prove themselves. The staff person, on the other hand, views himself as an expert.

4. Line managers frequently feel that staff is encroaching on their duties and prerogatives.

5. Line managers also complain that staff does not give sound advice, steals credit, and fails to see the "whole picture."

6. Staff managers, on the other hand, feel that line managers are "bullheaded," do not give staff enough authority, and resist new ideas.

Organizational differentiation. In their study of plastics, container, and food firms, Lawrence and Lorsch found that "differentiation" can lead to intergroup conflict.[20] *Differentiation* was defined as the "segmentation of the organizational system into subsystems, each of which tends to develop particular attributes in relation to the requirements posed by its relevant external environment." As you may recall (see Figure 6-15), they found that departments in firms in the three industries faced different amounts of uncertainty and diversity. For example, the "techno-economic" (production) department in the plastics firms tended to have fairly predictable tasks, whereas the scientific (research and development) departments tended to have extremely unpredictable environments. As we discussed in Chapter 6, Lawrence and Lorsch found that as a result of these differences in tasks, departments were differentiated from each other in terms of (1) degree of structure (tightness of rules, and so on), (2) posture toward the environment (scientific knowledge versus customer problems, and the like), (3) time orientation (long versus short time perspective), and (4) orientation toward other people (openness versus autocratic). These researchers found that greater differentiation appeared to result in more *potential* for conflict. However, they say that whether conflict actually resulted depended on several things, particularly how the organization achieved "integration" (coordination between departments), and the mode of conflict resolution used.

Authority Imbalances

We also know that when a department's actual authority is inconsistent with its prestige, intergroup conflicts are more likely to develop. Seiler diagnosed interdepartmental conflict in several firms; his findings are summarized in Table 13-1. As you can see, Seiler concluded that intergroup conflicts arise either because points of view are in conflict (the "differences in goals,

TABLE 13-1

Summary of Seiler's Findings on Organizational Conflict

	Where Points of View Are Closely Allied	Where Points of View Are In Conflict
Where Authority * Is Consistent with Prestige Differences	We Will Tend to Find . . . . . . Collaboration and productive conflict	We Will Tend to Find . . . . . . Energies absorbed by efforts to force points of view on other groups. Relations will be formal and often arbitrated by outsiders.
Where Authority Is Inconsistent with Prestige Differences	We Will Tend to Find . . . . . . Energies devoted to regaining a "proper" authority relationship. Relations will usually be distant and between low hierarchical levels of the two groups (e.g. messengers).	We Will Tend to Find . . . . . . Energies initially expended on forcing points of view and righting authority relations. But the task will be so patently fruitless that the groups will break off contact rather than expose themselves to further threat.

* As indicated by work flow.

Source: John A. Seiler, "Diagnosing Interdepartmental Conflict," *Harvard Business Review*, September-October, 1963, pp. 121-32.

values, and perceptions" problem we discussed above), or because a department's authority is inconsistent with its prestige. As an example of the latter, Seiler found that in one company, the production department was in the position of having to accept instructions from a production engineering department composed of men with skills no greater than (and in fact quite similar to) those possessed by production employees. As a result, "production managers spent an inordinate amount of time checking for consistency among the various items produced by production engineering." [21]

Ambiguity

Dutton and Walton found that where responsibility for a problem could not clearly be assigned to a department, there was an increase in conflict between units. Similarly, Dalton, in his study of line–staff conflict, found that conflicts often arose when it was difficult to determine whether a contribution had been made by the line or the staff unit. Conflict is also a familiar phenomenon in organizations where departmental responsibilities are not clearly delineated and where "power vacuums" arise and intergroup conflicts ensue as each department fights to fill those vacuums.

MODELS OF INTERGROUP CONFLICT

Theorists have developed a number of models to explain and describe the emergence and process of intergroup conflict—conflict, for example, between production and sales departments. We will discuss four well-known models in this section, then summarize these models and derive some implications for the management of interunit conflict.

Pondy: Organizational Conflict— Concepts and Models

Louis Pondy has developed a model that views intergroup conflict as a consequence of interlocking "conflict episodes." [22]

Types of conflicts. Pondy distinguishes between three major classes of intergroup conflict in organizations. He calls these the "bargaining model," the "bureaucratic model," and the "systems model":

1. *Bargaining model.* This is designed to deal with conflict among interest groups in competition for scarce resources. This model is particularly appropriate for the analysis of labor–management relations, budgeting processes, and staff–line conflicts.
2. *Bureaucratic model.* This is applicable to the analysis of superior-subordinate conflicts, or, in general, conflicts along the vertical dimension of a hierarchy.
3. *Systems model.* This is directed at lateral conflict, or conflict among the parties to a functional relationship. Analysis of the problems of coordination is the special province of this model.

Pondy says that although these represent three different types of conflict, they have an underlying similarity, in that they are each made up of a "sequence of interlocking conflict episodes."

His model identifies five stages in such a conflict episode: (1) latent conflict (conditions); (2) perceived conflict (cognition); (3) felt conflict (effect); (4) manifest conflict (behavior); and (5) conflict aftermath (conditions). The model is presented in Figure 13-1.

The latent-conflict stage. According to Pondy, a conflict episode begins with "latent conflict." This stage represents the basic conditions or sources of intergroup conflict, which Pondy believes can be classified as (1) competition for scarce resources, (2) drives for autonomy, and (3) differences of subunit goals. Pondy calls this the "latent conflict" stage because, even though the *sources* of conflict exist, the conflict itself is still only latent and may or may not emerge.

The perceived-conflict stage. Sometimes, says Pondy, conflicts fail to arise even though the conditions for them exist, because of two important

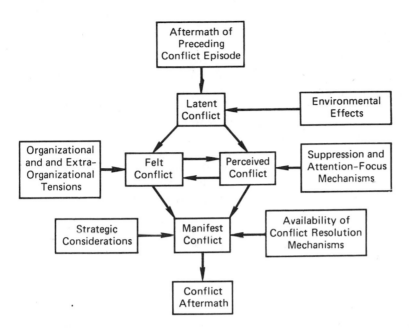

FIGURE 13-1. Pondy's Model: The Dynamics of a Conflict Episode

Source: Louis Pondy, "Organizational Conflict: Concepts and Models," *Administrative Science Quarterly,* Vol. 12, No. 2 (September 1967).

mechanisms that reduce the *perception* of conflict. First, "individuals tend to block or suppress conflicts that are only mildly threatening out of awareness." Second, "organizations are characteristically faced with more conflicts than can be dealt with given available time and capacities." As a result, employees focus attention on just a few of the conflicts, particularly those for which short-run, routine solutions are available.

Conversely, conflict may sometimes be perceived even though no conditions of conflict (latent conflict) exist. The most familiar example of this occurs when there is a "communications breakdown" or misunderstanding between groups with respect to each other's true position. Here, basic sources of conflict—like competition for scarce resources, drives for autonomy, and differences in goals—do not actually exist, but owing to misunderstandings, group members misperceive the true positions of the members of the other group.

The felt-conflict stage. Pondy says there is an important distinction between perceiving conflict and feeling conflict:

> A may be aware that B and A are in serious disagreement over some policy, but it may not make A tense or anxious, and it may have no effect whatsoever on A's affection towards B. The personalization of conflict is the mechanism which causes most students of organization to be concerned with

the dysfunctions of conflict. There are two common explanations for the personalization of conflict.[23]

First, says Pondy, conflict can become personalized or internalized (and therefore "felt") because people in the organization *feel under pressure or tension* and seek to displace these tensions by venting their frustrations on suitable targets. By this line of reasoning, conflicts are often symptoms of underlying problems, like low morale.

On the other hand, conflicts sometimes become personalized (and thereby felt) when the person becomes "ego-involved" in a conflict relationship. He may, for example, identify so completely with the goals and values of his group that he views the actions of competing groups personally.

The manifest-conflict stage.   This stage is characterized by open conflict behavior. Open, violent aggression is the most extreme example of such behavior, but this would be unusual in most work organizations. Yet the motivation driving such aggression may remain, and may manifest itself in sabotage, defensive coalitions, apathy, or rigid adherence to rules.[24]

Conflict aftermath.   Pondy says that each conflict episode "is but one of a sequence of episodes that constitute the relationships among organization participants, and the manner in which the conflict episode is managed and resolved has important implications for whether the episode results in a more cooperative relationship, or in continued aggravation and conflict." He says that if the conflict is confronted and resolved to the satisfaction of all participants, the basis for a more cooperative relationship may be laid. On the other hand, "if the conflict is merely suppressed but not resolved, the latent conditions of conflict may be aggravated and explode in more serious form until they are rectified or until the relationship dissolves." This legacy of a conflict episode is what Pondy calls "conflict aftermath."

Walton and Dutton: A General Model of Intergroup Conflict

Walton and Dutton have developed a "general model" of interunit conflict that they suggest is:

> . . . applicable to all lateral relations between any two organizational units (departments, divisions, sections, and so on) that engage in any type of transaction, including joint decision making, exchanging information, providing expertise or advice, and auditing or inspecting.[25]

Their model includes the following sets of related variables: antecedents to conflict, attributes of the lateral relationship, management of the interface, and consequences of the relationship. The model is presented in Figure 13-2.

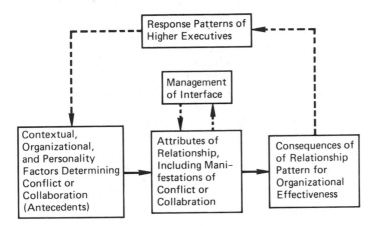

FIGURE 13-2. Walton and Dutton's General Model of Interunit Conflict

Source: Richard E. Walton and John M. Dutton, "The Management of Interdepartmental Conflict: A Model and Review," *Administrative Science Quarterly*, Vol. 14, No. 1 (March 1969), 552.

Antecedents to interunit conflict and collaboration. These writers say that manifest conflict results largely from factors that originate outside the particular lateral relationship or that antedate the relationship. Many of these factors or conditions for conflict are thus "built into" the relationship by those who design the structure and technology of the organization. For example, conflict sources like interdependence, authority–prestige imbalances, rewards, ambiguities, and sharing of common resources are often part of the environment of the groups, and are factors over which the groups have little or no control. Other factors, like communication breakdowns, dissatisfaction, and interunit differences in values and perceptions, are usually at least partly under the control of the group members themselves.

The interdepartmental relationship. The nature of the interdepartmental relationship is the next important factor in these writers' model of the conflict process. They distinguish between "integrative" and "distributive" lateral relationships. These differ as follows: Decision making in the integrative relationship emphasizes problem solving and free exchange of information, whereas that in the distributive relationship emphasizes bargaining and information distortion. Interactions in the integrative relationship are flexible and open; those in the distributive relationship are rigid and formal. The attitudes toward the other unit when an integrative relationship prevails are positive and friendly; those for the distributive relationship are negative and suspicious. These writers say that developing an integrative relationship is advisable, and that a distributive relationship always results in conflict.

Management of the interface. Walton and Dutton say that even though the conflict potential of a situation is largely determined by the antecedents and nature of the interunit relationship, some organizations are more successful at controlling conflict because of the *conflict-management strategies* they use; these strategies are what they mean by "management of the interface." For example, is there an *open confrontation* of conflict, a *problem-solving* orientation, or a "smoothing over" of problems?

Consequences of interunit conflicts. Intergroup conflicts, say Walton and Dutton, can result in competition, concealment, rigidity, appeals to superiors, and low trust and suspicion. However, they say, whether the conflict results in positive or negative consequences will depend on things such as the personalities of the participants and the conflict-management strategies used. Illustrative consequences (both positive and negative) of interunit conflict are presented in Table 13-2.

Schmidt and Kochan: A Model of the Conflict Process

Conflict defined. Schmidt and Kochan conceptualize conflict as the overt behavioral *outcome* of the conflict process. Specifically conflict is:

> The overt behavior arising out of a process in which one unit seeks the advancement of its own interests in its relationship with the others. . . . Units

TABLE 13-2
Consequences of Interunit Conflict

Attributes of Conflictful Lateral Relationships	Illustrative Consequences
Competition in general	Motivates or debilitates Provides checks and balances
Concealment and distortion	Lowers quality of decisions
Channeled interunit contacts	Enhances stability in the system
Rigidity, formality in decision procedures	Lowers adaptability to change
Appeals to superiors for decisions	Provides more contact for superiors
	May increase or decrease quality of decisions
Decreased rate of interunit interaction	Hinders coordination and implementation of tasks
Low trust, suspicion, hostility	Psychological strain and turnover of personnel or decrease in individual performance.

Source: Richard Walton and John Dutton, "The Management of Interdepartmental Conflict: A Model and Review," *Administrative Science Quarterly,* Vol. 14, No. 1 (March 1969), 78.

are not in conflict when deliberate interference is absent, or if they have agreed on their final position but events beyond their control prevent or hamper them from realizing it.[26]

A model of the conflict process. Their model of the conflict process, presented in Figure 13-3, assumes that three basic factors are necessary preconditions for conflict. The first is "perception of goal incompatibility" and "implies that goal attainment by one unit is seen to prevent others from achieving their goals under the same circumstances or with equivalent outcomes." In other words, each unit must feel that it can accomplish its goals only at the expense of the competing unit.

A second precondition is that the units must "share resources," and the more each unit perceives itself as dependent on the common resource, the more it will tend to view its success as contingent on the other group's behavior. Finally, according to these writers, "interdependence of activities" is the third precondition to conflict.

Types of conflict. These writers distinguish between three types of conflict, according to *where the actual blocking behavior that characterizes the conflict occurs.* They say that one unit can attempt to block the other (1) at the point where resources must be shared, (2) at the point where activities are interdependent, or (3) at both stages. These are illustrated in Figure 13-3. In all three types of conflict, the goals of the groups are incompatible.

In type I conflict, the blocking activities take place at the point where resources must be shared. Here, for example, two departments that share

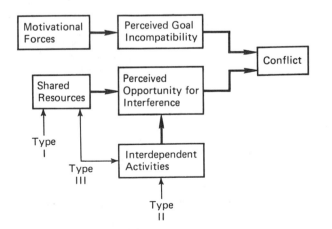

FIGURE 13-3. The Process of Conflict: Schmidt and Kochan

Source: Stuart Schmidt and Thomas Kochan, "Conflict: Toward Conceptual Clarity," *Administrative Science Quarterly,* Vol. 17, No. 3 (September 1972), p. 363.

a typing pool might engage in various blocking activities aimed at inhibiting each other's use of the pool—say, by inundating the pool with work.

In type II conflict, the blocking behavior occurs at the point where the interdependent activity must be carried out. One example is the situation in which a production department tries to undermine the engineering department by rejecting its production schedules.

In type III conflict, the blocking activities occur both at the point of resource sharing *and* at the interdependent activity stage. A study by Dutton and Walton illustrates this situation. Here, the departments studied were production and sales. Although these two departments were highly interdependent, they had opposing and narrowly defined goals. As a result, each group tried to block the other, and conflict ensued. The sales department refused to transmit sales data to the production unit (blocking at the shared-resources stage), which made cost estimates and production forecasts difficult. And, the production department would claim it did not have the materials to produce an order, thereby inhibiting the sales department's efforts to service its customers (blocking at the interdependent-activity stage).[27]

Potential for conflict. The extent to which any of these three types of conflict emerge depends, say Schmidt and Kochan, on the three preconditions—on the extent to which resources are shared, on the degree of interdependence, and on the perceived incompatibility of goals. This is illustrated in Figure 13-4: note that a situation's conflict potential can be reduced by reducing one or more of the three preconditions.

Research findings. Three researchers, in carrying out a test of the Schmidt and Kochan conflict model, pointed out that the model is based on two underlying assumptions: (1) that *goal incompatibility* among interdependent parties provides the motivation to engage in conflict, and (2) that for overt conflict to occur among parties with incompatible goals, the parties must have the ability to *interfere* with one another's goal attainment.[28] (This ability to interfere in turn depends on the extent to which resources are shared and activities are interdependent.)

The researchers tested the model by examining conflict among city management officials who were engaged in collective bargaining with unions. Managements in 228 cities were surveyed, with questionnaires mailed to each city's management negotiator, city manager or mayor, fire chief, a sample of three council members, and members of the civil service commission.

The questionnaire was aimed at obtaining two types of information. First, it sought to determine the extent to which these officials agreed or disagreed on the importance of each of eleven possible collective-bargaining goals. This provided a measure of the *goal incompatibility* among the officials in each city. Second, the questionnaire aimed at determining the extent to which the managers in each city had the ability to *interfere* with one another's goal attainment.[29]

The findings of this study generally support the Schmidt and Kochan

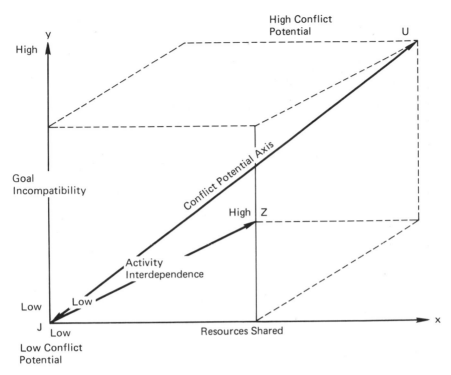

FIGURE 13-4. Potential for Conflict Behavior: Schmidt and Kochan

Source: Stuart Schmidt and Thomas Kochan, "Conflict: Toward Conceptual Clarity," *Administrative Science Quarterly*, Vol. 17, No. 3 (September 1972), p. 366.

model. Specifically, they substantiate the basic argument of the model "that both motivational factors (goal incompatibility) and ability factors (interference capability) are antecedents of perceived open conflict." [30]

Ruble and Thomas: A Two-Dimensional Model of Conflict Behavior

Ruble and Thomas have refined and tested a model of conflict behavior developed by Blake and Mouton.[31] The model, presented in Figure 13-5, is different from the other models we have discussed in that it assumes that conflict is not simply one end of a cooperation–conflict dimension; rather, it recognizes that people involved in conflictful situations often describe their behaviors in terms of *both* evaluative (good versus bad) and dynamic (strong and active versus weak and passive) dimensions.[32] Therefore, these writers see conflict as having *both an assertiveness dimension and a cooperativeness dimension*, and the type of conflict behavior reflects both these components. For example, highly uncooperative behavior may result in

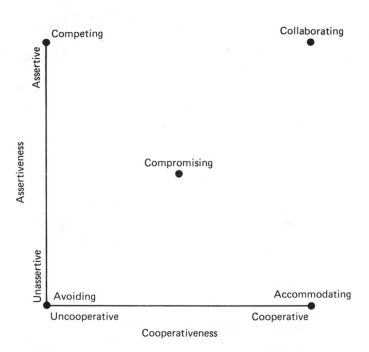

FIGURE 13-5. Two-dimensional Model of Conflict Behavior

Source: Thomas Ruble and Kenneth Thomas, "Support for a Two-Dimensional Model of Conflict Behavior," *Organizational Behavior and Human Performance*, Vol. 16 (June 1976), 145.

either *avoidance* or *competing*, depending upon the assertiveness of the groups involved, and cooperative behavior may result in either *accommodation* or *collaboration*, again depending on the assertiveness of the parties.

Models of Conflict: Summary and Implications

These models are summarized in Table 13-3, in which some commonalities and differences are apparent. The models differ insofar as they are aimed at accomplishing different things. Both Pondy and Walton and Dutton sought to explain the *process* of conflict and the sequence of steps leading to a "conflict episode." Schmidt and Kochan, on the other hand, focused more on different *types* of conflict: They distinguish between conflict that occurs where resources are shared, where activities are interdependent, and where both occur. Unlike these other theorists, Ruble and Thomas assume that conflict depends on the degree of both cooperativeness *and assertiveness* of the parties involved; "assertiveness" is thus an important contributor to conflict in their model.

Yet these models have much in common, and their commonalities and differences allow us to combine them into a general model of the conflict

TABLE 13-3

Summary: Models of Intergroup Conflict

Theorist	Sources of Intergroup Conflict	Major Components of Model
Pondy	Competition over scarce resources (bargaining); control and reactions to control (bureaucratic); interdependence (systems)	A "conflict episode" model: latent conflict → perceived conflict → felt conflict → manifest conflict → conflict aftermath.
Walton and Dutton	"Antecedents" include interdependence, authority–prestige imbalances; rewards; ambiguities; common resources; communications breakdowns; dissatisfaction; interunit differences in values, goals, or perceptions	Existence of "antecedent" factors combined with quality of interdepartmental relationship (distributive versus integrative) plus how interface is managed (confrontation, problem solving, smoothing over) largely determines whether conflicts are managed effectively.
Schmidt and Kochan	Three necessary "preconditions": perception of goal incompatibility; shared resources; interdependence	Type I conflict occurs when blocking is at point where resources shared; Type II occurs at point where activity is interdependent; Type III occurs where blocking is at both points. Both goal incompatibility *and interference capability* are required for conflict to arise.
Ruble and Thomas	Conflict has both assertiveness and cooperativeness dimensions	Five different conflict behaviors (competing, avoiding, accommodating, compromising, collaborating) are identified and viewed as combinations of the *cooperativeness* and *assertiveness* of the parties.

process. It is presented in Figure 13-6 and consists of three components: antecedents of conflict, conflict moderators, and actual, manifest conflict.

Pondy, Walton and Dutton, and Schmidt and Kochan all conclude that the conflict process begins with certain *antecedents*. For Pondy, these antecedents include, for example, competition for scarce resources, drives for autonomy, and differences of subunit goals. For Walton and Dutton, they include interdependence, authority–prestige imbalances, sharing of common resources, and rewards and ambiguities. For Schmidt and Kochan, the antecedents include goal incompatibility, shared resources, and interdependent activities (the last two have been summarized as "interference capability").

Second, most of these theorists agree that several factors *moderate* or influence whether conflict in fact occurs. Pondy, for example, says that whether conflict becomes perceived and felt depends on several things, like

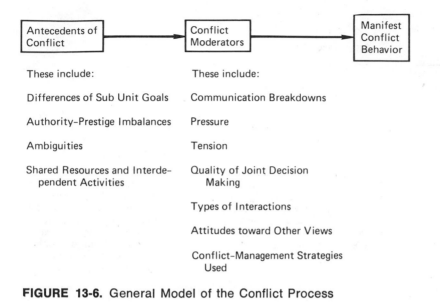

Antecedents of Conflict		Conflict Moderators		Manifest Conflict Behavior

These include:

Differences of Sub Unit Goals

Authority-Prestige Imbalances

Ambiguities

Shared Resources and Interdependent Activities

These include:

Communication Breakdowns

Pressure

Tension

Quality of Joint Decision
Making

Types of Interactions

Attitudes toward Other Views

Conflict-Management Strategies
Used

FIGURE 13-6. General Model of the Conflict Process

communications breakdowns, and pressure and tension. Walton and Dutton talk in terms of the quality of joint decision making, the type of interaction, and the attitudes toward the other units, as well as the conflict-management strategies that are used. Ruble and Thomas say each group's assertiveness helps determine if conflicts arise.

Finally, there is an actual or *manifest* conflict stage, which, say Schmidt and Kochan, can occur either where resources are shared, where activities are interdependent, or at both points.

Some implications of this discussion (and of our previous discussion on the sources of conflict) are these: There are various sources or *antecedents* of conflict, including interdependencies and shared resources; differences in goals, values, or perceptions; authority imbalances; and ambiguities. Furthermore, whether conflict arises depends on such things as the quality of joint decision making and the strategies used to *manage* any conflicts. Therefore, techniques for reducing specific antecedents of conflict and for more effectively *managing* conflicts should be useful, and we turn to such techniques in the next section.

MANAGING INTERGROUP CONFLICT

There are many strategies for managing or resolving conflicts, but they generally fall into one of three categories. The first involves establishing "superordinate" goals and thus creating an area of commonality between the previously competing groups. The second includes various structural approaches—for example, reducing the interdependencies between the competing groups, or referring the disagreement to a common superior. Finally, various conflict-resolution behaviors can be used; these include *avoiding* the problem, *confronting* the problem, and *negotiating* a solution. We will discuss each of these three major conflict-management strategies in this section.

Common Goals and Conflict Management

Most of the conflict models we discussed assume that incompatible goals are a necessary antecedent for the development of conflict.[33] Conversely, it is generally acknowledged that the existence of "superordinate" goals—goals "which have a compelling appeal for both [groups] but which neither could achieve without the other"—reduces dysfunctional conflict.[34] Edgar Schein, for example, points out:

> The fundamental problem of intergroup competition is the conflict of goals and the breakdown of interaction and communication between the groups; this breakdown in turn permits and stimulates perceptual distortion and mutual negative stereotyping. The basic strategy of reducing conflict, therefore, is to find goals upon which groups can agree and to reestablish valid communication between the groups. The tactics to employ in implementing this strategy can [include] . . . locating a common enemy [and] locating a superordinate goal.[35]

The Sherif experiments in group conflict. Sherif carried out a series of experiments in intergroup conflict and common goals using groups of boys in a summer camp.[36] His working hypothesis was that "when two groups have conflicting aims—i.e., when one can achieve its end only at the expense of the other—their members will become hostile to each other even though the groups are composed of normal, well-adjusted individuals." To test this hypothesis, his research team produced friction between the groups of boys by arranging a tournament of games, including baseball, touch football, a tug-of-war, and a treasure hunt. They found that although the tournament started in a spirit of good sportsmanship, as it progressed, this good feeling soon evaporated.

Between the groups, there sprang up enmity, as members began calling their rivals "sneaks" and "cheaters." They refused to have anything to do with those in the opposing group, and boys often turned against buddies they had chosen as "best friends" when they first arrived at the camp. The rival groups made threatening posters and planned raids against each other. In one case, a group burned a banner left behind by the opposing team, only to have its own banner seized the next morning. Name-calling, scuffles, and raids were the rule of the day.

Within each group, solidarity increased, and there were other important changes as well. One group deposed its leader because he could not "take it" in the contest with the adversary. Another group made a hero of a boy who had previously been regarded as a bully. Generally speaking, morale and cooperativeness within each group became stronger.

Sherif and his associates then hypothesized that "just as competition generates friction, working in a common endeavor should promote harmony." They therefore set about creating a series of "urgent and natural" situations that would face their competing groups with the need to work together to accomplish superordinate goals. On one occasion, the researchers rigged a breakdown in the pipeline supplying water to the camp. They called the boys together to tell them of the crisis, and both these initially hostile groups promptly volunteered to search the water line for the trouble. The two groups worked together harmoniously, and before the end of that afternoon, they had located and corrected the difficulty.

Another time, the two groups were taken on an outing some distance from the camp. A truck was to go to town for food, but when everyone was hungry and ready to eat, it was found that the truck would not start, a situation that had been arranged by the researchers. The boys got a rope, and both groups pulled together to start the truck.

Yet the researchers found that joint efforts like these did not immediately dispel hostility:

> At first the groups returned to the old bickering and name calling as soon as the job at hand was finished. But gradually the series of cooperative acts reduced friction and conflict. The members of the two groups began to feel more friendly to each other. . . . The boys stopped shoving in the meal line. They no longer called each other names, and sat together at the table. New friendships developed between individuals in the two groups. In the end the groups were actively seeking opportunities to mingle, to entertain, and "treat each other." [37]

On the basis of such findings, Sherif concluded:

> What our limited experiments have shown is that the possibilities for achieving harmony are greatly enhanced when groups are brought together to work toward common ends. Then favorable information about a disliked group is seen in a new light, and leaders are in a position to take bolder steps toward cooperation. In short, hostility gives way when groups pull together to achieve overriding goals which are real and compelling to all concerned.[38]

Incentive systems. Wieland and Ullrich point out that "goal differentiation can also be reduced through the use of incentive systems designed to reward activities that benefit the larger system, as opposed to those that are primarily in the interest of subunits." [39] Many (perhaps most) organizational reward systems, by rewarding the performance of individuals (or individual departments), often result in a "win-lose" mentality in the organization. The quality-control department, for example, may be rewarded for the number of defects it finds, but its rewards are obviously received at the expense of another department, usually production.

The Sears, Roebuck Company recently revised the method used in rewarding store managers, and the change is a good example of the use of reward systems to reduce intergroup conflict. For years, Sears store managers were rewarded for increasing the sales of their own stores. In recent years, however, it became apparent that this system was breeding conflictual behavior by store managers. For example, managers in the same geographical area were generally not inclined to advertise areawide sales, and they resisted transferring merchandise from one store to another. Under the new reward system, a store manager's reward is based not only on the sales of his own store but on the sales of all Sears stores in his area, and this has resulted in a marked increase in collaborative behavior by store managers.

Structural Approaches to Conflict Management

Various structural approaches have been used to manage or resolve intergroup conflicts. Several of them are described below.

Appeal to power and the superior. Classical theorists prescribed using the chain of command for solving interunit disagreements, and a study by Stagner suggests this is still a widely used method. His subjects were top executives in major corporations.[40]

Stagner found, first, that conflicts were usually resolved not on the basis of logical arguments concerning profitability and such, although the arguments were often couched in economic terms. Instead, most conflicts were resolved by resorting to power, power that was based on things like ability to provide rewards. Second, even in more "decentralized" firms, Stagner found the power of the chief executive to be the most widely used arbiter of disagreements. In some cases, the chief executive simply resolved the conflict through decree, and in other cases, he acted as mediator or arbitrator. As an alternative, some corporations let the executive vice-president arbitrate the conflict; this left open the possibility of appealing the decision to the president if necessary.

Reduce interdependencies. Conflicts rarely arise between groups not required to work interdependently, and so one way to reduce conflict is to reduce the required interunit interdependencies. James Thompson distinguished three types of interdependence—pooled, sequential, and reciprocal —and his proposal has recently received some empirical support.[41]

Pooled interdependence is exemplified by a fully divisionalized, decentralized organization in which the separate divisions are relatively self-contained and independent. On the other hand, as you can see in Figure 13-7, *sequential* interdependence results in a greater degree of interdependence between units, since the output of one unit now becomes the input to a second unit in the sequence, with the receiving unit quite dependent for its success on the sending unit. (An example here would be the dependence of a production department on a purchasing department.) Finally, Thompson suggests that units are most interdependent when that interdependence is *reciprocal*. In this situation, the output of various units become input for the others:

> This is illustrated by the airline which contains both operations and maintenance units. The production of the maintenance units is an input for

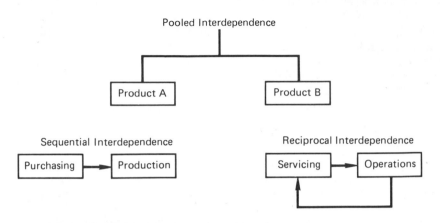

FIGURE 13-7. Types of Interdependence

Source: Based on James Thompson, *Organizations in Action* (New York: McGraw-Hill, 1967), Ch. 2

operations, in the form of serviceable aircraft; and the product (or by-product) of operations is an input for maintenance, in the form of an aircraft needing maintenance. Under conditions of reciprocal interdependence, each unit involved is penetrated by the other. . . .[42]

According to the models of conflict we have discussed, the potential for conflict should increase as the interdependencies between two groups increase. One alternative for preventing or managing conflicts is therefore to reduce interdependencies by moving from reciprocal to sequential and finally to pooled interdependence. At the extreme, this might involve what Galbraith calls the creation of "self-contained tasks," an arrangement that is thus useful for managing conflicts as well as for reducing the amount of information to be processed by the chief executive.

Rather than separating the units organizationally, a similar alternative involves separating them physically. Neilsen says that "physically separating the conflicting groups has the distinct advantage of preventing more damage from being done and of preventing the creation of further rationales for fighting." On the other hand, this tactic "may require continuous surveillance to keep the parties separate, especially if tempers are hot and energy levels high." [43] Also, physical separation does not encourage confronting basic problems or working through solutions; it is therefore more of a stop-gap measure than a cure.

Reduce shared resources. When two units are required to share scarce resources, the potential for intergroup conflict increases, and so another structural conflict-management approach involves reducing such sharing. March and Simon say that one technique for accomplishing this is increasing the available resources to the point where they are no longer considered "scarce."

Exchange of personnel.   Conflict theorists have long prescribed having conflicting groups trade personnel for a specified time period as a way to reduce and manage conflicts.[44] An exchange of people is very similar to a tactic psychologists call "role reversal," which is aimed at creating greater understanding between people by forcing each to present and defend the other's position.[45]

In one relevant study, 62 three-person groups composed of students each acted as either a "manufacturer" or a "wholesaler" of medical instruments; their goal was to get agreement on the selling price and quantity of these instruments. The researchers created a conflict situation in several ways. For example, they told the members of each group that their dollar earnings would depend on their group's performance relative to all other groups that had assumed corresponding positions in previous trials. To test the usefulness of role reversal, 30 minutes into the bargaining session a random selection of groups were handed a memo that said the chief executive officers of each firm had decided to undertake a temporary exchange of personnel; to this end, the "manufacturer's salesman" and "wholesaler's purchasing agent" were to trade positions for 20 minutes. The subjects were physically exchanged, and when 20 minutes had elapsed, the "salesman" and the "purchasing agent" were returned to their "home" companies. The bargaining then continued until the trial ended.

The researchers concluded (from their analysis of various measures of intergroup conflict and collaboration) that the exchange-of-personnel program was effective at reducing conflict and speeding agreement. In fact, they point out, it was successful even though it was mandatory, involved the least influential members of the organizations, and was of relatively short duration.

Create special "integrators."   Lawrence and Lorsch found that in certain situations (particularly where there was much differentiation between departments in terms of time span, goals, and values), the use of special "integrator" departments or individuals facilitated the management and resolution of interdepartmental conflicts.[46] As you can see in Table 13-4, several factors determined how successful these integrators were at resolving interdepartmental conflicts. For example, the integrators were particularly effective where they were viewed as about *intermediate* in position between the conflicting departments, where they were viewed as *high in influence,* and where they perceived that their *rewards* were tied to the total performance of the two groups they were integrating.

Frequent interaction.   Schein says that frequent interaction and communication between groups can increase intergroup coordination and reduce the potential for conflict.[47] On the other hand, interaction can also have the reverse effect, and so its usefulness depends in part on the existence of a relatively healthy, problem-solving environment.

TABLE 13-4

Summary of Effective Conflict Resolution Relative to Differentiation, Integration, and Performance

Organization	I Intermediate Position of Integrative Organization [a]	II Influence of Integrators Derived from Technical Competence [a]	III Integrators Perceive Rewards Related to Total Performance [a]	IV High Influence throughout the Organization [a]	V Delegation: Influence Centered at Requisite Level [a]	VI Right Approach to Conflict Resolution [a]	Degree of Differentiation	Degree of Integration	Organization System Performance
High A	High	High	Medium	High	High	High	High (9.4)	High (5.7)	High
High B	Medium	High	High	High	Medium	High	High (8.7)	High (5.6)	High
Medium A	Medium	Low	High	High	Medium	Medium	Low (7.5)	High (5.3)	Medium
Medium B	Medium	Low	Medium	High	Medium	Medium	High (9.0)	Low (5.1)	Medium
Low A	Low	Low	Low	Low	Low	Low	High (9.0)	Low (4.9)	Low
Low B	Medium	Low	Low	Low	Low	Low	Low (6.3)	Low (4.7)	Low

[a] High, medium, or low indicates relative extent to which each organization met each determinant.

Source: Paul R. Lawrence and Jay W. Lorsch, *Organization and Environment* (Boston: Harvard University Press, 1967), p. 80. Reprinted by permission of Harvard University Press, from *Organization and Environment* by Paul R. Lawrence and Jay W. Lorsch, Boston, Mass.: Division of Research, Graduate School of Business Administration, Harvard University, copyright © 1967 by the President and Fellows of Harvard College.

Conflict-Resolution Behaviors

The actual *behaviors* through which conflicting groups try to resolve differences and hammer out agreements represent a third important class of conflict-management strategies.

Possible behaviors. A variety of conflict-resolution behaviors have been proposed. March and Simon say an organization can react to conflict by (1) problem solving, (2) persuasion, (3) bargaining, and (4) "politics." [48] Ruble and Thomas distinguish between five types of conflict-management behavior:

> Competing ("The other person took a stand and stuck to it")
> Avoiding ("The other person tried to avoid the task of negotiating")
> Accommodating ("The other person gave in to my position")
> Compromising ("The other person suggested a middle ground or compromise")
> Collaborating ("The other person communicated all of his/her information and encouraged me to do the same") [49]

Lawrence and Lorsch, in their study of differentiation and integration, distinguish between three types of conflict management behavior that they call *confrontation, smoothing,* and *forcing.* They present the following as actual examples of each:

> *Confrontation.* "In recent meetings we have had a thrashing around about manpower needs. At first we did not have much agreement, but we kept thrashing around and finally agreed on what was the best we could do."
> *Smoothing.* "I thought I went to real lengths in our group to cause conflict. I said what I thought in the meeting, but it did not bother anybody. I guess I should have been harsher. I could have said I won't do it unless you do it my way. If I had done this, they couldn't have backed away, but I guess I didn't have the guts to do it. I guess my reaction was—well, I made a fool of myself in the meeting and nothing happened so I'll sit back and feel real comfortable. I guess I didn't pound the bushes hard enough. . . ."
> *Forcing.* "If I want something very badly and I am confronted by a roadblock, I go to top management to get the decision made. If the research managers are willing to go ahead (my way), there is no problem. If there is a conflict, then I take the decision to somebody higher up." [50]

Research findings. Lawrence and Lorsch analyzed the effectiveness of confrontation, smoothing, and forcing behavior for resolving interdepartmental conflicts. They found that:

TABLE 13-5

Modes of Conflict Resolution

Organization	Confrontation	Smoothing	Forcing
High performer A	13.0 [a]	8.9	9.5
High performer B	13.1 [a]	9.3	9.5
Medium performer A	12.4 [a]	9.0	9.0 [b]
Medium performer B	12.0 [a]	9.8 [b]	9.7
Low performer A	11.7 [a]	9.0	9.8
Low performer B	11.8 [a]	9.8 [b]	8.5 [b]

Higher score indicates *more* typical behavior.

[a] Pairs of organizations (high performers, medium performers and low performers) significantly different from other organizations at .01 (Orthogonal comparison).

[b] Significantly different from other organizations at .01 (Orthogonal comparison).

Source: Paul R. Lawrence and Jay W. Lorsch, *Organization and Environment.* (Boston: Harvard University Press, 1967), p. 77. Reprinted by permission of Harvard University Press from *Organization and Environment* by Paul R. Lawrence and Jay W. Lorsch, Boston: Division of Research, Graduate School of Business Administration, Harvard University, copyright © 1967 by the President and Fellows of Harvard College.

Reliance on confrontation (or a problem-solving approach) seems to lead to effective conflict resolution and to the desired states of differentiation and integration. The high-performing organizations met this determinant most clearly, the medium-performing ones to a moderate extent, and the low performers the least.[51]

Thus they found that managers in the high-performing organizations used confrontation more than did those in the other organizations. Furthermore, managers in medium- and low-performance organizations were more prone to smooth over conflicts than were managers in the high-performing organizations (see Table 13-5). In this study (which focused on the highly uncertain plastics-industry firms), Lawrence and Lorsch concluded that although reliance on confrontation seemed essential, it was also important for organizations to have a "backup mode" of conflict resolution that relied on some forcing (appeals to a superior) and a relative absence of "smoothing over" behavior.

In another study, Patricia Renwick found that the *topic* and *source* of the disagreement influenced how the conflict was managed.[52] Subjects in her study were 72 employees from two large manufacturing firms in the San Francisco Bay area. They were drawn from diverse departments, including sales, marketing, accounting, production, research and development, and computer operations, and occupied a variety of positions.

The employees completed a questionnaire that asked them first to indicate how likely they were to use various conflict-management behaviors to deal with differences and disagreements. The conflict-management behaviors were measured as follows:

Behavior	Questionnaire Items
Withdrawal	Refrain from argument, try not to get involved (very unlikely 1 2 3 4 5 very likely)
Smoothing	Play down the differences and emphasize common interests (very unlikely 1 2 3 4 5 very likely)
Compromise	Search for an intermediate position, try to find a compromise (very unlikely 1 2 3 4 5 very likely)
Forcing	Use the power of my position or knowledge to win acceptance of my point of view (very unlikely 1 2 3 4 5 very likely)
Confrontation	Bring the problem clearly into the open and carry it out to resolution, even if feelings are likely to get hurt (very unlikely 1 2 3 4 5 very likely)

Specifically, employees were asked to indicate the extent to which they would use each of these conflict-management behaviors for conflicts involving each of three different *topics*: (1) salaries, promotions, and performance appraisals; (2) personal habits and mannerisms; and (3) physical working conditions and organizational policies and procedures. Then they were asked to indicate the extent to which they would use each of these behaviors if they thought the *source* of the conflict was based on (1) differences in knowledge or factual material, (2) personality differences, or (3) differences in attitudes or opinions.

The results are presented in Table 13-6. Renwick found that employees "were inclined to *confront* topics involving salaries, promotions, or performance appraisal and were likely to rely on *compromise* to deal with conflicts concerning personal habits and mannerisms." [53] When the topic of the conflict concerned physical working conditions and organizational procedures however, no striking preferences in conflict-management behaviors were observed.

The *source* of the conflict also seemed to influence the type of conflict-management behavior that was preferred. For example, disagreements originating from substantive factors (like differences in knowledge or factual material) were more likely to elicit confrontation than was any other behavior.

Renwick, like Lawrence and Lorsch, also found a tendency for subjects to use "backup" behaviors should the primary conflict-management behavior fail. For example, she found that compromise and smoothing were likely to be used together, and that confrontation and compromise were often paired. Finally, her findings also suggest that individuals seem to have preferences for particular conflict-management behaviors, and that "they will be predisposed to adopt a specific method of conflict resolution to deal with a variety of topics and sources of disagreement." [54]

TABLE 13-6

Likelihood of Using Methods of Conflict Resolution
Across Sources

Method	Source *		
	Differences in Knowledge or Factual Material	*Personality Differences*	*Differences in Attitudes or Opinions*
Withdrawal	1.46	2.90	2.36
Smoothing	2.35	3.47	3.28
Compromise	2.82	3.69	3.75
Forcing	2.94	2.10	2.24
Confrontation	3.93	2.57	2.97

Likelihood of Using Methods of Conflict Resolution
Across Topics

Method	Topics *		
	Salaries, Promotions, and Performance Appraisal	*Personal Habits and Mannerisms*	*Physical Working Conditions and Organizational Policies and Procedures*
Withdrawal	1.82	2.69	1.81
Smoothing	2.86	3.06	2.79
Compromise	3.17	3.54	3.40
Forcing	2.47	2.38	2.81
Confrontation	3.49	2.90	3.38

* Higher number indicates more likely use of the behavior.

Source: Patricia Renwick, "Impact of Topic and Source of Disagreement on Conflict Management," *Organizational Behavior and Human Performance,* Vol. 14 (December 1975), 420-21.

Managing Intergroup Conflict: Summary

Various techniques can be used to successfully head off or manage intergroup conflicts, so such conflict need not undermine the effectiveness of an organization or its structure. Common, "superordinate" goals can be established between the groups or departments, for example through the use of incentive systems. Various structural approaches to conflict management can be used, including appealing to the superior, reducing interdependencies and shared resources, exchanging personnel, creating special integrators, and providing for frequent interaction. Finally, the evidence suggests that certain conflict-resolution behaviors, such as confrontation, are often more effective than are ones like the "smoothing over" of problems.

SUMMARY

Intergroup conflict has important implications for organization structure and theory. The effectiveness of a structure depends on the resulting departments working together effectively, and where intergroup conflicts occur organizational effectiveness can suffer. In this chapter we therefore discussed the sources, processes, and management of intergroup conflict. Sources include interdependencies and shared resources; differences in goals, values, and perceptions; authority imbalances; and ambiguities. The process, we said, can be viewed in terms of antecedents ——→ moderators ——→ and actual conflicts. Conflict-management strategies aimed at developing common goals, changing the organization structure, and choosing the best conflict-management behavior were shown to be effective.

How are organization structure and intergroup conflict related? In several ways. First, the effectiveness of a structure depends on the resulting departments' working together effectively. Intergroup conflict—between line and staff units, or production and sales units, for example—can be useful, but can also reduce communication and collaboration between departments so that the structure no longer functions effectively.

Second, there are several structural antecedents of conflict—for example, interdependencies, differences in goals and values (which may derive from the structural position of one department vis-à-vis another), authority imbalances, and ambiguity—that are based in the structure of the organization.

Finally, the structure of the organization provides a useful vehicle for reducing or managing conflict. This might involve, for example, referring conflicts to a common superior, reducing interdependencies, reducing shared resources, exchanging personnel, or creating special integrator departments or positions.

DISCUSSION QUESTIONS

1. Compare and contrast the Pondy, Walton and Dutton, Schmidt and Kochan, and Ruble and Thomas models of intergroup conflict.
2. Does intergroup conflict always have to be dysfunctional? Explain the conditions under which it might and might not be dysfunctional.
3. Explain some of the techniques you could use to manage interdepartmental conflicts.
4. Explain the sources of intergroup conflict.
5. What is the relationship between intergroup conflict and organization design?

FOOTNOTES

1 Henry Landsberger, *Hawthorne Revisited* (Ithaca: Cornell University Press, 1968), p. 31.

2 I. L. Janis, *Victims of Groupthink* (Boston: Houghton Mifflin, 1972).

3 Stephen P. Robbins, "Managing Organizational Conflict," in Jerome Schnee, E. Kirby Warren, and Harold Lazarus, *The Progress of Management* (Englewood Cliffs, N.J.: Prentice-Hall, 1977), pp. 163–76.

4 Kenneth Thomas and Warren Schmidt, "A Survey of Managerial Interests with Respect to Conflict," *Academy of Management Journal,* June 1976, pp. 315–18.

5 James March and Herbert Simon, *Organizations* (New York: John Wiley, 1966), p. 131.

6 Robert C. Sampson, *The Staff Role and Management: Its Creative Uses* (New York: Harper & Row, 1955).

7 Joseph A. Litterer, "Conflict in Organizations: A Re-Examination," *Academy of Management Journal,* Vol. 9, September 1966; Robert Golembiewski, *Organizing Men and Power* (Chicago: Rand McNally, 1967), pp. 61–89.

8 M. Dalton, "Conflicts between Staff and Line Managerial Officers," *American Sociological Review,* Vol. 15, No. 3 (1950), 342–51. Also, "Changing Line–Staff Relations," *Personnel Administration,* March–April 1966, pp. 3–5.

9 James A. Belasco and Joseph A. Alutto, "Line Staff Conflicts: Some Empirical Insights," *Academy of Management Journal,* Vol. 12, No. 4 (December 1969), 469–77.

10 *Ibid.*

11 Opinion Research Corporation, *The Conflict between the Scientific and the Management Mind* (Princeton, N.J.: ORC, 1959). See also Lyman Porter and Edward Lawler III, "Properties of Organization in Relation to Job Attitudes," *Psychological Bulletin,* Vol. 64, No. 1 (1965), pp. 23–51.

12 Lyman W. Porter, "Job Attitudes in Management: III. Perceived Deficiencies in Need Fulfillment as a Function of Line Versus Staff Type of Jobs," *Journal of Applied Psychology,* Vol. 47 (1963), 267–75.

13 Dalton, "Conflicts between Staff and Line Managerial Officers."

14 Thomas and Schmidt, "A Survey of Managerial Interests."

15 Richard Walton and John Dutton, "The Management of Interdepartmental Conflict: A Model and Review," *Administrative Science Quarterly,* Vol. 14, No. 1 (March 1969), 73–84.

16 *Ibid.,* p. 82.

17 J. M. Dutton and R. E. Walton, "Interdepartmental Conflict and Cooperation: Two Contrasting Studies," *Human Organization,* Vol. 25 (1966), 207–20.

18 M. Dalton, *Men Who Manage* (New York: John Wiley, 1959).

19 H. A. Landsberger, "The Horizontal Dimension in a Bureaucracy," *Administrative Science Quarterly,* Vol. 6 (1961), 298–333.

20 Paul R. Lawrence and Jay W. Lorsch, *Organization and Environment* (Boston: Division of Research, Graduate School of Business Administration, Harvard University, 1967).

21 John Seiler, "Diagnosing Interdepartmental Conflict," *Harvard Business Review,* September–October 1963, pp. 121–32.

22 Louis R. Pondy, "Organizational Conflict: Concepts and Models," *Administrative Science Quarterly,* Vol. 12, No. 2 (September 1967), 296–320.

23 Pondy, "Organizational Conflict."

24 Dalton, "Conflicts between Line and Staff Managerial Officers"; David Mechanic, "Sources of Power of Lower Participants in Complex Organizations," *Administrative Science Quarterly,* Vol. 7, No. 3 (December 1962), 349–64.

[25] Walton and Dutton, "The Management of Interdepartmental Conflict."

[26] Stewart Schmidt and Thomas Kochan, "Conflict: Toward Conceptual Clarity," *Administrative Science Quarterly,* Vol. 17 (1972), 359–70.

[27] *Ibid.*

[28] Thomas Kochan, George Huber, and L. L. Cummings, "Determinants of Intraorganizational Conflict in Collective Bargaining in the Public Sector," *Administrative Science Quarterly,* Vol. 20 (March 1975), 10–23.

[29] The researchers measured perceived opportunity for interference by measuring such things as how widely power and control were dispersed among city officials, rather than using the factors "shared resources" and "interdependent activities" of the original Schmidt and Kochan model.

[30] Kochan, Huber, and Cummings, "Determinants of Intraorganizational Conflict," p. 21.

[31] R. R. Blake and J. S. Mouton, *The Managerial Grid* (Houston: Gulf Publishing, 1964); Thomas Ruble and Kenneth Thomas, "Support for a Two-Dimensional Model of Conflict Behavior," *Organizational Behavior and Human Performance,* Vol. 16 (June 1976), 143–55.

[32] C. E. Osgood, J. G. Suci, and P. H. Tannenbaum, *The Measurement of Meaning* (Urbana: University of Illinois Press, 1957); H. H. Kelley, G. H. Schure, M. Deutch, C. Faucheux, J. T. Lanzetta, S. Moscovici, J. M. Nuttin, J. M. Rabbie, and J. W. Thibaut, "A Comparative Experimental Study of Negotiation Behavior," *Journal of Personality and Social Psychology,* Vol. 16 (1970), 411–38.

[33] See, for example, Schmidt and Kochan, "Conflict."

[34] Muzafer Sherif, "Experiments in Group Conflict," *Frontiers of Psychological Research,* ed. Stanley Coopersmith, *Scientific American,* November 1956, pp. 112–16; R. R. Blake and J. S. Mouton, "The Intergroup Dynamics of Win-Lose Conflict and Problem Solving Collaboration in Union Management Relations," in M. Sherif, ed., *Intergroup Relations and Leadership* (New York: John Wiley, 1962); D. W. Johnson and R. J. Lewicki, "The Initiation of Superordinate Goals," *Journal of Applied Behavioral Science,* Vol. 5 (1969), 9–24.

[35] Edgar Schein, *Organizational Psychology* (Englewood Cliffs, N.J.: Prentice-Hall, 1970).

[36] Sherif, "Experiments in Group Conflict."

[37] *Ibid.,* p. 116.

[38] *Ibid.,* p. 117. For an example of a study in which superordinate goals did *not* seem to reduce intergroup conflict, see Louis Stern, Brian Sternthal, and C. Samuel Craig, "Strategies for Managing Interorganizational Conflict: A Laboratory Paradigm," *Journal of Applied Psychology,* Vol. 60, No. 4 (August 1975), 472–82.

[39] George Wieland and Robert Ullrich, *Organizations: Behavior, Design, and Change* (Homewood, Ill.: Richard D. Irwin, 1976), p. 286.

[40] Ross Stagner, "Corporate Decision Making: An Empirical Study," *Journal of Applied Psychology,* Vol. 53 (1969), 1–13; Ross Stagner, "Conflict in the Executive Suite," in Warren Bennis, ed., *American Bureaucracy* (Chicago: Aldine, 1970), pp. 85–95; Wieland and Ullrich, *Organizations: Behavior, Design, and Change,* pp. 271–73.

[41] James Thompson, *Organizations in Action* (New York: McGraw-Hill, 1967); Thomas A. Mahoney and Peter Frost, "The Role of Technology in Models of Organizational Effectiveness," *Organizational Behavior and Human Performance,* Vol 11 (1974), 122–38.

[42] Thompson, *Organizations in Action,* p. 55.

[43] Eric Neilsen, "Understanding and Managing Intergroup Conflict," in Paul Lawrence, Louis Barnes, and Jay Lorsch, *Organizational Behavior and Administration* (Homewood, Ill.: Richard D. Irwin, 1976), p. 297.

[44] Stern, Sternthal, and Craig, "Strategies for Managing Interorganizational Conflict."

45 J. Cohen, "The Technique of Role Reversal: A Preliminary Note," *Occupational Psychology*, Vol. 25 (1951), 64–66; M. Deutsch, "Psychological Alternatives to War," *Journal of Social Issues*, Vol. 18 (1962), 97–119.

46 Lawrence and Lorsch, *Organization and Environment*.

47 Schein, *Organizational Psychology*.

48 March and Simon, *Organizations*, p. 129.

49 Ruble and Thomas, "Support for a Two-Dimensional Model," pp. 146–47.

50 Lawrence and Lorsch, *Organization and Environment*, pp. 74–75.

51 *Ibid.*, p. 78.

52 Patricia Renwick, "Impact of Topic and Source of Disagreement on Conflict Management," *Organizational Behavior and Human Performance*, Vol. 14 (December 1975), 416–25.

53 *Ibid.*, p. 423.

54 *Ibid.*, p. 424.

Chapter 14

Organizational Change and Development

CHAPTER OVERVIEW

Organizations and their contexts are dynamic, and are constantly undergoing change: Competitors introduce new products, new production technologies are developed, employees retire or resign, intergroup conflicts arise, or productivity inexplicably drops. These changes and others are the kinds that managers face daily. And very often, an effective response involves the implementation of one or more of the organizational change and development techniques we discuss in this chapter. These include changing the structure of the organization (perhaps to make it more adaptable); changing the technology of the organization (to increase productivity); or changing the people (their attitudes and behavior, for example). Organizational change and development is thus important to a study of organization theory because it literally involves the modification of the structure, technology, and/or people in the organization for the purpose of increasing the organization's effectiveness. Therefore, as you study this chapter, keep the following questions in mind:

1. How does the context of an organization influence the organization's need for organizational change and development?

2. How does organizational change and development affect organizational structure and design?

3. How does organizational change and development affect compliance in organizations?

The outline of this chapter is as follows:

STAGES IN THE CHANGE PROCESS

Experts agree that most organizational changes do not take place overnight; instead, they proceed in stages.[1] One way to think of these stages was proposed by psychologist Kurt Lewin years ago. He identified three stages of change and called them unfreezing, changing, and refreezing. The first, *unfreezing stage*, is necessary for prodding people into seeing the need for change. Here, some provocative problem or event is usually necessary to get people to recognize the need for a change and to search for new solutions.

In the second, *change stage*, the change is introduced and implemented. In the last, *refreezing stage*, the necessary reinforcement is provided to ensure that the new behavior patterns are adopted on a more permanent basis.

Others propose a similar step-by-step change process. They say that implementing a change involves four stages: (1) *diagnosing* organization problems, (2) *planning* for the change, (3) *making* the change, and (4) *evaluating* the change.

These two views of organizational change stages complement each other. Lewin's three-stage process is important because it underscores the need to "unfreeze" the parties and then "refreeze" them once the changes are made. The other, four-stage view provides a different perspective on the change process and especially underscores the need to start by diagnosing the problem.

DIAGNOSING THE PROBLEM

The first step in organizational change and development is to diagnose the problem, and this is a step that is often missed. Some managers note a deficiency and immediately assume it is a "training" problem of some sort. Yet the fact is that the problem may actually be the result of poor selection, inadequate incentives, low salary, or any of a number of other factors. It is therefore important to accurately diagnose the problem, a process we will assume has three steps, as follows.

Step 1. Analysis of the Organization

Organizational change programs should be aimed at preparing employees to better achieve the *goals of the organization*. Therefore, the first step in developing such a program is to analyze the organization's goals and current performance.[2] This is one reason why "organizational analysis"—reviewing the organization's goals, plans, environment, practices, and performance—is important: It will help identify problems, and develop solutions that are in keeping with the organization's goals.

Organizational analysis is also important because many of the change programs that fail do so because they lack the backing and full commitment of top management.[3] One way to ensure this commitment is to have top management participate in developing change programs that it sees as vehicles for achieving the goals it has set for the organization.

Step 2. Identification of Important Performance Discrepancies

The next step is to determine if there is a discrepancy between the employees' actual and desired performance, and there are many ways to do this. One might, for example, observe *problems*, like poor-quality production, or interdivisional arguments. Questionnaires might be used to identify morale problems. Or the problems could be identified as a by-product of the performance appraisal or from management suggestions.

Robert Mager and Peter Pipe say that you then have to decide whether the performance discrepancy is *important* or not.[4] They suggest completing the sentence, "The discrepancy is important because . . ." Ask, "What will happen if I leave the discrepancy alone?" This will "force into the open the reasons why someone says the discrepancy is important."

Step 3. Problem Identification

The next step is to identify the "real problem." For example, suppose you discover important conflicts between members of two departments: They are always arguing with one another, they don't return each other's calls, and so on. How would you define the problem?

Many managers would probably fall into the trap of identifying "interdepartment conflict" as the problem. They would assume that it could be alleviated by training employees to be more sensitive and understanding toward one another. But if they dug deeply enough, they might find that the real problem does not lend itself to a "training" solution at all.

For example, in one company, the kind of conflict we just described resulted because the company had inadequate job descriptions, and it was therefore hard to pinpoint who was responsible for what. A tug-of-war ensued, in which each department tried to obtain more responsibility and authority for itself. As soon as the consultants assigned clear, unambiguous job descriptions to each employee, the tug-of-war ceased and conflict all but disappeared.

If it is not a "training" problem, what is it? In Table 14-1, William Tracey has summarized some suggested procedures for identifying training and development requirements. Notice that very often "training" is not the solution. Instead, reorganization, clearer policies, improved job design, or better work methods are called for. Mager and Pipe suggest trying to isolate a "motivation" problem by asking four questions:

1. *Is the desired performance punishing?* For example, ask, What is the consequence of performing as desired? Is it punishing to perform as expected?
2. *Is nonperformance rewarding?* For example, ask, What is the result of doing it his way instead of my way? What does he get out of his present performance in the way of rewards? Does he get more attention for misbehaving than for behaving?
3. *Does performing really matter?* For example, ask, Does performing as desired matter to the performer? Is there a favorable outcome for performing? Is there an undesirable outcome for not performing? (Is the reward important to the person?)

TABLE 14-1

A Checklist for Identifying Training and Development Requirements

1: Determine immediate needs.
   a. Evaluate current training and development programs to determine whether the training produces the desired behavioral changes.
      (1) Evaluate ongoing training programs.
         a) Review training documents for adequacy.
         b) Observe trainers, trainees in learning environment of classroom, shop, laboratory.
         c) Analyze in-course and end-of-course test results.
         d) Interview trainers and trainees.
      (2) Evaluate the *products* of the training system.
         a) Interview line supervisors.
         b) Interview and observe trainees at the workplace.
         c) Review personnel records and performance ratings.
         d) Administer questionnaires to supervisors and trainees; analyze questionnaires.
   b. List and analyze shortfalls in process or products. Determine whether they are due to:
      1) Poor organization.
      2) Inadequate supervision.
      3) Unclear policies.
      4) Poor communications.
      5) Improper personnel selection policies or procedures.
      6) Poor job design.
      7) Equipment or material problems.
      8) Work methods.
      9) Inappropriate work standards.
     10) Inadequate operator or supervisor training.
   c. Survey all aspects of enterprise operations to determine areas where additional training is required.
      1) Compare job descriptions and applicant specifications with personnel records.
      2) Analyze performance ratings.
      3) Analyze all enterprise records for areas of possible deficiency.
      4) Identify and analyze operating problems.
      5) Use interviews, questionnaires, group conferences, tests, and work samples to determine training problems.
      6) Subject each problem to careful analysis to determine whether the problem is due to:

a) Poor organization.	f) Poor job design.
b) Inadequate supervision.	g) Equipment or material
c) Unclear or ambiguous policies.	deficiencies.
d) Poor communications.	h) Improper work methods.
e) Improper personnel	i) Inappropriate work standards.
selection policies.	j) Training deficits.

2: Determine long-range training needs.
   a. Analyze enterprise plans, policies, and forecasts to determine their potential impact on staffing needs.
   b. Identify and analyze future systems, equipment, techniques, and procedures to determine their impact on personnel requirements.
   c. Determine whether current training systems will support future personnel requirements in terms of
      1) Operative personnel (workers)
      2) Supervisory personnel.
      3) Managerial personnel.
   d. Identify training system shortfalls.
3: For each training requirement, determine whether the training should be provided

TABLE 14-1

A Checklist for Identifying Training and Development Requirements (*cont.*)

---

on or off the premises, and whether it should be formal or on-the-job. Consider:
a. Comparative costs
b. Availability of in-house personnel, equipment, and facilities resources.
4: Summarize training needs.
5: For off-the-premises programs, develop objectives, prepare contract specifications, solicit and evaluate proposals and select a contractor.
6: For in-house programs, develop objectives and guidelines following the procedures described in the remainder of this chapter.

---

4. *Are there obstacles to performing?* For example, ask, What prevents him from performing? Does he know what is expected of him? Does he know when to do what is expected of him? Are there conflicting demands on his time? Does he lack the authority, time, or tools? Is he restricted by policies, or by a "right way of doing it" that ought to be changed? (Has the person the ability to do the job—could he do it if he *wanted* to?)

PLANNING THE CHANGE

Diagnosing the problem will help you determine what sort of change is called for; then, a main "planning" question is, "What change and development technique should I use?" Harold Leavitt says that there are three types of techniques you can use to bring about a change: You can change the structure, technology, or people in the organization.[5]

Structural Approaches

Leavitt says that several types of structural approaches can be identified. The first is structural change in terms of reorganizing departments, changing span of control, and the like, the major mechanism of the "classical" organization theorists. Recall that these theorists evolved a set of "principles" of organization that they felt could be applied in increasing the effectiveness of an organization and its structure. Structural changes of this sort (often called "reorganizations") are still widely used.

A second approach to change, says Leavitt, involves the idea of decentralization. Here, "profit centers" are often established, and managers are delegated the authority to make a wider range of decisions than they had previously. This supposedly increases their motivation, while at the same time increasing the flexibility of the organization.

Technological Approaches

The classical examples of technological change are those of the type proposed by Frederick Taylor and his disciples. These theorists developed a new skill—industrial engineering—the purpose of which was to scientifically measure work methods and recommend improvements. Leavitt says that more recent technical innovations, like operations research and computerization, are contemporary examples of the sort of technological approaches to organizational change first espoused by Taylor.

People Approaches

Leavitt says that the people approaches to organizational change aim at changing the organization by changing the behavior of the people in it. These "people" approaches, in other words, aim at bringing about some fundamental change in the attitudes or values of people, on the assumption that behavioral changes will follow.

Dealing with Resistance to Change

Whether you elect to change the structure, technology, or people in the organization, you will have to be able to deal with employee resistance to change. This is because such resistance can quickly undermine and destroy the change efforts, and can manifest itself in many ways including decreased output, absenteeism, strikes, and hostility.

Why do people resist change? Most now agree that resistance is not a necessary concomitant of change and that a change—if handled correctly—may evoke little or no resistance. This is because it is generally not the "technical" aspects of the change that employees resist but rather the social change. For example, they may see in the change diminished responsibilities for themselves and therefore lower status in the organization and less job security.

This has implications for how you implement the change. Larry Greiner says there are three basic ways to implement any change.[6] You can use a top-down unilateral "decree approach" and simply force the change through. You can use a "shared power" participative approach and let the employees help recommend changes. Or, you can use a "delegated power" approach in which you delegate the problem to your employees who then develop and implement the changes themselves.

Each of these approaches to organizational change can be useful. For example, in some chaotic situations a unilateral approach to change (in which you simply issue your decree and ram through the change) may be appropriate. (As you might imagine, this approach can backfire if not used prudently.) [7] In other situations, a "delegated power" approach is called for; here you use techniques like "organizational development" or "sensitivity training" to get your people themselves to work out the necessary changes.

But as often as not it's going to be Greiner's middle-of-the-road "shared

351

power" approach that you will find useful. It involves gaining the *active participation* of your employees in selecting from several alternative solutions. We discussed the use of participation in Chapter 10.

CHANGING ORGANIZATIONS BY CHANGING STRUCTURE

Reorganization

Reorganization involves a redesign of the organization structure; a change, in other words, in the departmentation, coordination, span of control, or centralization of decision making in an organization. Reorganization is a relatively direct and quick method for changing an organization, and the technique is widely used and often effective. In his studies, Chandler found that after World War II, the rapid rate of new-product development and differentiation of markets rendered ineffective the centralized organization structure at Westinghouse and General Electric. In response to these problems, both firms began to decentralize their organizations. Recall that at Westinghouse, merchandise divisions were established for electric appliances; these allowed a group of executives to make most of the sales, engineering, and manufacturing decisions for products in their divisions. Similarly, General Electric established a decentralized organization with vice-presidents for such divisional groups as consumer products, aerospace, and construction materials.

Another successful reorganization recently took place at General Motors.[8] By the end of 1973, gas mileage had become an overriding concern for the automobile industry, and it was clear to GM that its entire product line would have to be redesigned and "downsized." Normally, such product redesigning, which involved development of new soundproofing materials, shock absorbers, and so on, would have been done by each GM division, with some centralized policy making done at headquarters. In this case, however, GM felt that its normal design organization was too ponderous, so in 1974, a project center was adopted to coordinate the efforts of the five automobile divisions. The "Ad Hoc" project center is made up of engineers lent by the divisions, and it works on parts of engineering problems common to all divisions (such as frames, electrical systems, steering gear, and brakes).

According to *Fortune* magazine, the project center was probably GM's most important managerial tool in carrying out its downsize decision: "It has eliminated a great deal of redundant effort, and has speeded numerous new technologies into production."

Other Structural Approaches to Change

We have already discussed other structural approaches to change in this book, and we need only mention some of them at this point. Job enrichment, through which individual jobs are made more challenging, is one of these. In the preceding chapter, we saw that various structural techniques can be used to reduce or manage intergroup conflict; these techniques include reducing interdependencies, and reducing ambiguities by more clearly specifying job requirements. Similarly, the introduction of special "integrator" individuals or departments can facilitate coordination and reduce intergroup conflict in appropriate situations.

CHANGING ORGANIZATIONS BY CHANGING TECHNOLOGY: THE IMPACT OF COMPUTERIZATION

Technological changes are changes in the work methods used by the organization to accomplish its tasks. These could be the introduction of new production technologies, industrial engineering "time and motion" studies, introduction of new performance-appraisal procedures (including management by objectives), and so forth. Perhaps the most major and far-reaching technological change facing most organizations today is computerization—the substitution of computer systems on jobs formerly carried out by people—so we focus on the impact of computerization in this section.[9]

The Effect of Computers on Organization Structure

Thomas Whisler had studied the question of how computers affect organization structure. From his analysis of the research evidence, he concluded that the introduction of a computer system in an organization generally tends to cause the following changes in the structure of the organization:

1. Departments are consolidated.
2. The number of levels in the hierarchy is reduced.
3. The span of control is reduced.
4. Parallel departments are replaced by functional departments.
5. Control becomes more centralized.
6. Control is shifted laterally between major executives and departments.
7. The technology becomes part of the control structure.[10]

Notice that most of the changes result in relatively more "mechanistic" organizations. For instance, spans of control are reduced (#3), divisionalized "profit center" structures are replaced by the more traditional functional departmentation (#4), and control becomes more centralized. This is probably because such computer systems make their major contribution (according to Whisler) "by improving coordination and control." In other words, computer systems greatly increase management's capacity for monitoring and for processing information. Therefore, with the computer system, there is less need for organizational devices like profit centers and decentralization for reducing the information processing load on top management.

Effect on Tasks and People

The individual's discretion. Does modern technology such as computerization make man simply an appendage to a machine? That it does is a favorite argument of opponents of computerization, and some research lends support to their view.

In one study of computerization in an insurance company, it was found that more jobs were routinized than enlarged at the clerical level, while the reverse was true at the supervisory level. The enlargement in supervisory jobs appears to have been a consequence of having to understand computer systems and participate in their effective use. Even where supervisors have had their jobs enlarged, however, they still tend to have reduced control over the timing and patterning of their activities as a result of the deadline pressure imposed by computers. The results here seem to indicate that "where technology is important, complex, and directly involves others, the human being becomes an 'appendage' who must submit to the discipline of a routinized performance." [11]

Communication and interaction with others. Computerization also affects the communication patterns in the organization. It does this in two ways: First, in a "systems" sense, one person's actions directly affect more people, more quickly than before. Ironically, though, computerization is also associated with reduced interpersonal communication, at least at the clerical level. In one study, it was found that computerization increased the percentage of time that clerks worked alone, so it also changed their pattern of communication; they spoke with other clerks less frequently, for example. On the other hand, interpersonal communication between managers increased.

Level of required skill. Although computerization results in increased job routinization, the level of skills demanded of employees tends to increase. The explanation for this paradox is apparently that the demands on the employee increase: Each must perform precisely as the system demands, and greater *reliability* in performance is required. These new demands are translated into higher "skill" requirements.

Summary. Technological changes like computerization often drastically change the organization and its people. Computerization, for example, is generally associated with increased centralization, a less "divisionalized" structure, and less discretion on the part of most employees.

CHANGING ORGANIZATIONS
BY CHANGING PEOPLE:
ORGANIZATIONAL DEVELOPMENT

Introduction

There are a variety of techniques that can be used to change the people in the organization but as House points out:

> If development is to be successful, it must be geared not only to the participants' needs and learning abilities, but also to the particular requirements and practices of the organization in which he manages.[12]

Similarly, Roger Harrison emphasizes that development methods require various degrees of emotional involvement, depending upon how private, individual, and hidden are the issues and processes concerned. He suggests that "surface" interventions, such as those stressing change in skills, are more appropriate where mechanistic conditions prevail. These surface development techniques include lectures, conferences, and reorganizations, for example.

On the other hand, says Harrison, "in-depth" interventions, such as the sensitivity training we will discuss in this chapter, are more appropriate for developing organic organizations to meet rapidly changing conditions.[13] These organizational-development techniques are aimed at changing the attitudes, values, and behavior of participants with the specific objective of getting the people themselves to develop more open, supportive, organic types of organizations.

What Is Organizational Development?

The environments in which many organizations operate are becoming increasingly unpredictable. As a result, new forms of organizations are emerging—ones that are more organic and adaptable to change. These organic organizations are characterized by flexible organization structures; open, supportive organizational climates; values and attitudes that espouse trust and openness; and open, democratic leadership styles. Perhaps a formerly mechanistic organization is faced with some exigency that forces it to become adaptable and organic. Or an organic organization may be faced with emerging internal conflict or a gradual deterioration of its flexibility. In such instances, some type of developmental activity may be necessary to bring factors like structure or group cohesiveness into line with the needs for openness and adaptability.

According to Bennis, organizational development (OD) is:

> A response to change, a complex educational strategy intended to change the beliefs, attitudes, values and structure of organization so that they can

better adapt to new technologies, markets, and challenges, and the dizzying rate of change itself.[14]

Objectives of OD. Although the specific objectives of organizational-development programs vary, a number of broad objectives emerge with some consistency. These programs are aimed at increasing:

1. The level of support and trust among participants and development of open, authentic communications
2. Open confrontation of organizational problems, as well as situations in which position authority is augmented by authority based on expertise and knowledge
3. The openness and authenticity of organizational communications
4. Personnel enthusiasm and self-control [15]

OD reverses the normal change process: It attempts to change skills, structures, and relationships *by changing the values and attitudes of participants.* As Blake and Mouton point out:

> Organization development deliberately shifts the emphasis away from the organization's structure, from technical skill, from wherewithal and results per se, as it diagnoses the organization's ills. Focusing on organization purpose, the human interaction process, and organization culture, it accepts these as the areas in which problems are preventing the fullest possible integration within the organization.[16]

The overall objective of OD is to change the values, attitudes, and beliefs of people. Hampton and his associates put it this way:

> It is the change in personal values in the system, coupled with the change in ways in which people treat one another, which come first. . . . Operating procedures, costs, job descriptions, production schedules—the whole rational side of the firm—become dependent upon how a group of people feel about themselves as people and about others as people. . . .[17]

Characteristics of OD. Bennis lists seven distinguishing characteristics of organizational development.[18] First, OD is an *educational strategy* adopted to bring about some planned organizational change. Second, changes sought are usually directly related to the *exigency* or demand with which the organization is trying to cope. This demand, which typically arises in new and rapidly expanding organizations, frequently results in problems of communication, intergroup conflict, organizational identity and destination, and so forth, which are uniquely amenable to solution through organization development. Third, the OD effort almost always relies on a strategy that emphasizes *direct experience.* This may take the form of data feedback, sensitivity training, or confrontation meetings. Fourth, the OD effort utilizes a *change agent* who is almost always an external consultant. Fifth, the change agent enters into a *collaborative relationship* with organization members and works actively with them. Sixth, the change agent usually has a social philosophy or set of values concerning people and organizations that parallels those of *McGregor's "Theory Y"* (see Chapter 3). Seventh, the change agent often has a set of *normative goals* based on his social philosophy. Although the goals will differ from one agent to another, he most commonly seeks such goals as improvement in interpersonal competence, better methods of conflict resolution, more effective team management, increased understanding, and the establishment of a value system in which human feelings are considered legitimate. Furthermore, change agents usually aim at developing organic rather than mechanistic systems. These characteristics make OD a more appropriate strategy where organic systems are themselves appropriate.

An Actual OD Change Program: An Example

Here is a brief summary of an actual OD program that was carried out recently:

1. *Initial diagnosis:* The diagnosis consisted of three stages. First, a series of *interviews* was held with a sample of 15 supervisory and managerial personnel (including the plant manager and his immediate staff). Second, *group meetings* were held with those interviewed to examine the results and to identify problem areas and priorities. Finally, the plant manager, his immediate staff, and the external consultants met to finalize the *"change design"* (the OD training program).

2. *Team skills training:* Foremen, general foremen, assistant superintendents, and superintendents participated with their peers (in groups of approximately 25) in a series of experience-based exercises during a 2½-day workshop.

3. *Data collection:* Immediately following the team skills training, all foremen completed two questionnaires. The first concentrated on organizational "health" and effectiveness. The second asked them to describe the behavior of their immediate supervisor—general foremen or assistant superintendents.

4. *Data confrontation:* In this phase, various work groups were asked to review the data described above and determine problem areas, establish priorities in these areas, and develop some preliminary recommendations for change.

5. *Action planning:* Based on the data, and conversations during the data confrontation, each group developed some recommendations for change and plans for the changes to be implemented. The plans included what should be changed, who should be responsible, and when the action should be completed.[19]

6. *Team building:* Each natural work group in the entire system, including the plant manager and his immediate staff of superin-

tendents, then met for two days. The agenda consisted of identifying blocks to effectiveness for the specific group and the
development of change goals and plans to accomplish the desired
changes.

7. *Intergroup building:* This phase consisted of two-day meetings
between groups that were interdependent in the plant. The groups
met for the purpose of establishing mutual understanding and
cooperation and to enhance collaboration on shared goals or
problems.

The sequence in which the interventions occurred is outlined in
Table 14-2.

Strategy in Organizational Development

There are as many methods of organizational development as there are consultants, but its basic strategy consists of three steps:

1. Gathering of data about organizational operations, attitudes, and
behavior
2. Feedback of data to the parties involved
3. Team planning of the solutions

Some OD practitioners refer to this three-step strategy as *action research,*
implying, as Bennis puts it, that it is similar to all types of applied research
except that "the relationship of researchers and subject may reverse—the
subjects becoming the researchers." [20]

The data-gathering and feedback steps comprise a diagnosis stage.
Some applied-behavioral scientists also use the term *unfreezing* to denote
this stage. The term implies that people in organizations have a tendency

TABLE 14-2

Actual Timetable for O. D. Program Described in Text

Intervention	Initiated	Completed
Initial diagnosis	12-1-69	12-31-69
Team skills training	1-9-70	2-28-70
Data collection	1-10-70	3-1-70
Data confrontation	5-9-70	8-19-70
Action planning	9-1-70	12-31-70
Team building	1-1-71	2-1-71
Intergroup building	2-2-71	2-28-71
Data Collection	3-15-71	3-15-71

Source: John Kimberly and Warren Neilson, "Organization Development and Change in Organizational Performance," *Administrative Science Quarterly,* Vol. 20, No. 2 (June 1975), 193.

to become "frozen" into attitudes of conflict or competition, as well as into out-of-date operating policies and customs.

A preliminary step in the diagnosis is usually for the consultant and key client (the plant manager, a company president, or the division vice-president, for example) to meet and develop an initial assessment of the organization's strategic problems. Subordinates of the key client might also be interviewed at this point, to obtain additional data. On the basis of this initial assessment, it may turn out that the problem is technological or that the key client is unwilling to delve more deeply into his organization's problems. But the diagnosis might also suggest a number of other alternatives, including postponing the development effort or hiring additional specialists (such as in finance or information systems), or it might lead to the second step of the process.

Assuming that the consultant and client agree that the development should continue, additional data are usually gathered. This is frequently done through interviews, at least in part, because this personal contact builds a cooperative relationship between the consultant and the client group. In addition, questionnaires in the context of what has been called *survey feedback* have also been used with success.

These data then form the basis for the feedback provided by the consultant to the client, often during two- or three-day off-site meetings. The consultant provides his feedback in terms of some of the fundamental problems that have been identified during the data-gathering phase. The client group is then encouraged to set some priorities on the problems and to discuss them under the guidance of the consultant. Throughout these meetings, the consultant (who is also sometimes referred to as the change agent or the trainer) acts as an educator, training the participants in how to confront and analyze the problems under discussion.

Having eliminated some or all of the problems, the OD effort moves into its third, action-planning or refreezing stage. At this point, the client group sets about developing new ways of operating. The participants, having new attitudes and values, might at this point develop new job descriptions, policies and procedures, organization structures, and solutions to residual problems.

The specific OD method used will vary with the organization and the consultant. A great number are currently in use; in the following sections, we will discuss four widely used, representative OD methods:

1. Survey feedback
2. Confrontation meetings
3. Sensitivity training
4. The managerial grid

Some of the other methods are coaching and counseling activities, planning and goal-setting activities, third-party peacemaking activities, and techno-structural activities.

Survey Feedback

Many managers use attitude surveys, though usually not as effectively as they might. In most cases the forms are administered to employees by outside consultants, and the results are tallied and sent to top management. And as often as not, that is the last the employees hear about the attitude survey (at least until next year's routine survey).

Attitude surveys (as in Figure 14–1) can actually be quite useful as an organizational change technique. They can be used to dramatically underscore the existence of some problem (like low morale), thereby "unfreezing" the system. And they can be used as a basis for discussion among employees and for developing alternative solutions. Finally, they can also be used to "follow-up" on the change to see if it has been successful ("refreezing"). While it is an OD technique, survey feedback generally does not involve a high degree of emotional soul searching on the part of participants.

The "involvement" approach. Scott Meyers has proposed what he calls an involvement approach to using attitude surveys.[21] At the Texas Instruments Company, where this approach was developed, a questionnaire (like that in Figure 14–1) is administered to a 10–20 percent sample of employees throughout the company. Profiles (as in Figure 14–2) are prepared from the results and delivered to each of the approximately 160 department managers. The heavy solid line shows the *company* average for this year, and is the same on every department's profile. The thin solid line is this year's *department* results, while the dotted line is last year's results. As you can see, each department manager can therefore compare his or her department's results for each item to both the total company results and to his or her last year's profile.

In order to avoid making department managers defensive, survey results are fed directly back to them (rather than to top management). The department head presents and discusses these results in general terms in a group meeting of his or her department, and then hands them to a committee of employees. These five or six people meet as often as necessary to analyze the results and make recommendations to the department manager. The latter, in turn, analyzes these recommendations with his boss and the final recommendations are transmitted back to departmental employees. Some examples of "problems" and "recommendations" are presented in Table 14-3.

The Confrontation Meeting

The *confrontation meeting* is a type of focused exercise in which the total management group meets with the change agent to discuss and come to grips with operating problems that have arisen. The typical confrontation meeting lasts from four to eight hours; it usually begins with the consultant's discussing in general terms such topics as organizational communi-

This questionnaire is designed to help you give us your opinions quickly and easily. There are no "right" or "wrong" answers—it is your own, honest opinion that we want. Please do not sign your name.

DIRECTIONS:
Check ( ) one box for each statement to indicate whether you agree or disagree with it. If you cannot decide, mark the middle box.

EXAMPLE:

I would rather work in a large city than in a small town .... Agree 2☐ ? 1☐ Disagree 0☐

	Agree 2	? 1	Disagree 0
1. The hours of work here are O.K.	☐	☐	☐
2. I understand how my job relates to other jobs in my group	☐	☐	☐
3. Working conditions in TI are better than in other companies	☐	☐	☐
4. In my opinion, the pay here is lower than in other companies	☐	☐	☐
5. I think TI is spending too much money in providing recreational programs	☐	☐	☐
6. I understand what benefits are provided for TIers	☐	☐	☐
7. The people I work with help each other when someone falls behind, or gets in a tight spot	☐	☐	☐
8. My supervisor is too interested in his own success to care about the needs of other TIers	☐	☐	☐
9. My supervisor is always breathing down our necks; he watches us too closely	☐	☐	☐
10. My supervisor gives us credit and praise for work well done	☐	☐	☐
11 I think badges should reflect rank as well as length of service	☐	☐	☐
12. If I have a complaint to make, I feel free to talk to someone up-the-line	☐	☐	☐
13. My supervisor sees that we are properly trained for our jobs	☐	☐	☐
14. My supervisor sees that we have the things we need to do our jobs	☐	☐	☐
15. Management is really trying to build the organization and make it successful	☐	☐	☐
16. There is cooperation between my department and other departments we work with	☐	☐	☐
17. I usually read most of Texins News	☐	☐	☐
18. They encourage us to make suggestions for improvements here	☐	☐	☐
19. I am often bothered by sudden speed-ups or unexpected slack periods in my work	☐	☐	☐
20. Qualified TIers are usually overlooked when filling job openings	☐	☐	☐
21. Compared with other TIers, we get very little attention from management	☐	☐	☐
22. Sometimes I feel that my job counts for very little in TI	☐	☐	☐
23. The longer you work for TI the more you feel you belong	☐	☐	☐
24. I have a great deal of interest in TI and its future	☐	☐	☐
25. I have little opportunity to use my abilities in TI	☐	☐	☐

	Agree 2	? 1	Disagree 0
26. There are plenty of good jobs in TI for those who want to get ahead	☐	☐	☐
27. I often feel worn out and tired on my job	☐	☐	☐
28. They expect too much work from us around here	☐	☐	☐
29. The company should provide more opportunities for employees to know each other	☐	☐	☐
30. For my kind of job, working conditions are O.K.	☐	☐	☐
31. I'm paid fairly compared with other TIers	☐	☐	☐
32. Compared with other companies, TI benefits are good	☐	☐	☐
33. A few people I work with think they run the place	☐	☐	☐
34. The people I work with get along well together	☐	☐	☐
35. My supervisor has always been fair in his dealings with me	☐	☐	☐
36. My supervisor gets employees to work together as a team	☐	☐	☐
37. I have confidence in the fairness and honesty of management	☐	☐	☐
38. Management here is really interested in the welfare of TIers	☐	☐	☐
39. Most of the higher-ups are friendly toward us	☐	☐	☐
40. I work in a friendly environment	☐	☐	☐
41. My supervisor lets us know what is expected of us	☐	☐	☐
42. We don't receive enough information from top management	☐	☐	☐
43. I know how my job fits in with other work in this organization	☐	☐	☐
44. TI does a poor job of keeping us posted on the things we want to know about TI	☐	☐	☐
45. I think TI informality is carried too far	☐	☐	☐
46. You can get fired around here without much cause	☐	☐	☐
47. I can be sure of my job as long as I do good work	☐	☐	☐
48. I have plenty of freedom on the job to use my own judgment	☐	☐	☐
49. My supervisor allows me reasonable leeway in making mistakes	☐	☐	☐
50. I really feel part of this organization	☐	☐	☐
51. The people who get promotions in TI usually deserve them	☐	☐	☐
52. I can learn a great deal on my present job	☐	☐	☐

(PLEASE CONTINUE ON REVERSE SIDE)

FIGURE 14-1. Texas Instruments Incorporated—Attitude Questionnaire

	Agree ? Disagree		Agree ? Disagree
53. My job is often dull and monotonous	2☐ 1☐ 0☐	75. I'm really doing something worthwhile in my job	2☐ 1☐ 0☐
54. There is too much pressure on my job	2☐ 1☐ 0☐	76. I'm proud to work for TI	2☐ 1☐ 0☐
55. I am required to spend too much time on the job	2☐ 1☐ 0☐	77. Many TIers I know would like to see the union get in	2☐ 1☐ 0☐
56. I have the right equipment to do my work	2☐ 1☐ 0☐	78. I received fair treatment in my last performance review	2☐ 1☐ 0☐
57. My pay is enough to live on comfortably	2☐ 1☐ 0☐	79. During the past six months I have seriously considered getting a job elsewhere	2☐ 1☐ 0☐
58. I'm satisfied with the way employee benefits are handled here	2☐ 1☐ 0☐	80. TI's problem-solving procedure is adequate for handling our problems and complaints ...	2☐ 1☐ 0☐
59. I wish I had more opportunity to socialize with my associates	2☐ 1☐ 0☐	81. I would recommend employment at TI to my friends	2☐ 1☐ 0☐
60. The people I work with are very friendly	2☐ 1☐ 0☐	82. My supervisor did a good job in discussing my last performance review with me	2☐ 1☐ 0☐
61. My supervisor welcomes our ideas even when they differ from his own	2☐ 1☐ 0☐	83. My pay is the most important source of satisfaction from my job	2☐ 1☐ 0☐
62. My supervisor ought to be friendlier toward us	2☐ 1☐ 0☐	84. Favoritism is a problem in my area	2☐ 1☐ 0☐
63. My supervisor lives up to his promises	2☐ 1☐ 0☐	85. I have very few complaints about our lunch facilities	2☐ 1☐ 0☐
64. We are kept well informed about TI's business prospects and standing with competitors	2☐ 1☐ 0☐	86. Most people I know in this community have a good opinion of TI	2☐ 1☐ 0☐
65. Management ignores our suggestions and complaints	2☐ 1☐ 0☐	87. I usually read most of my division newspaper	2☐ 1☐ 0☐
66. My supervisor is not qualified for his job	2☐ 1☐ 0☐	88. I can usually get hold of my supervisor when I need him	2☐ 1☐ 0☐
67. My supervisor has the work well organized	2☐ 1☐ 0☐	89. Most TIers are placed in jobs that make good use of their abilities	2☐ 1☐ 0☐
68. I have ample opportunity to see the end results of my work	2☐ 1☐ 0☐	90. I receive adequate training for my needs	2☐ 1☐ 0☐
69. My supervisor has enough authority and backing to perform his job well	2☐ 1☐ 0☐	91. I've gone as far as I can in TI	
70. I do not get enough instruction about how to do a job	2☐ 1☐ 0☐	92. My job seems to be leading to the kind of future I want	2☐ 1☐ 0☐
71. You can say what you think around here	2☐ 1☐ 0☐	93. There is too much personal friction among people at my level in the company	2☐ 1☐ 0☐
72. I know where I stand with my supervisor	2☐ 1☐ 0☐	94. The amount of effort a person puts into his job is appreciated at TI	2☐ 1☐ 0☐
73. When terminations are necessary, they are handled fairly	2☐ 1☐ 0☐	95. Filling in this questionnaire is a good way to let management know what employees think	2☐ 1☐ 0☐
74. I am very much underpaid for the work I do	2☐ 1☐ 0☐	96. I think some good will come out of filling in a questionnaire like this one	2☐ 1☐ 0☐

97   Please check on term which most nearly describes the kind of work you do: 1 ☐ Clerical or office   2 ☐ Production

3 ☐ Technical   4 ☐ Maintenance   5 ☐ Manufacturing   6 ☐ R & D   7 ☐ Engineering   8 ☐ Other

98   1 ☐ Hourly   2 ☐ Salaried   99   1 ☐ Male   2 ☐ Female   100   Do you supervise 3 or more TIers?   1 ☐ Yes   2 ☐ No

Name of your department:

Please write any comments or suggestions you care to make in the space below.

FIGURE 14-1 (continued)

Source: Courtesy of Texas Instruments Incorporated; reprinted in Sanford, *Human Relations,* pp. 348-49.

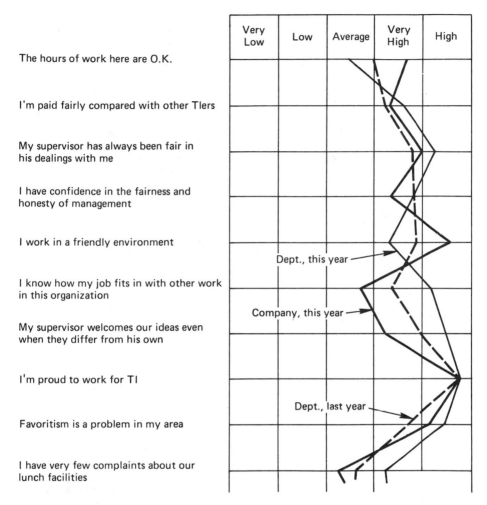

	Very Low	Low	Average	Very High	High
The hours of work here are O.K.					
I'm paid fairly compared with other TIers					
My supervisor has always been fair in his dealings with me					
I have confidence in the fairness and honesty of management					
I work in a friendly environment					
I know how my job fits in with other work in this organization					
My supervisor welcomes our ideas even when they differ from his own					
I'm proud to work for TI					
Favoritism is a problem in my area					
I have very few complaints about our lunch facilities					

Dept., this year

Company, this year

Dept., last year

FIGURE 14-2. Employee Attitude Profile

Source: M. Scott Meyers, "How Attitude Surveys Help You Manage," *Training and Development Journal,* Vol. 21 (October 1967), 34-41; reprinted in Beach, *Personnel,* pp. 311-16.

cation, the need for mutual understanding, and the need for members of the management team to share responsibility for accomplishing the organization's goals. In such a meeting, the discussion might turn to an analysis of the organization's operating problems, including how advertising budgets are arrived at, how sales commissions are computed, and how financial controls are imposed. On the other hand, some types of confrontation meetings focus exclusively on such human-organization problems as conflict between line and staff personnel.

Bennis describes a confrontation meeting that was supposed to deal

TABLE 14-3

Problems and Committee Suggestions

Committee Report for XYZ Department	
Problems	*Recommendations*
1. New employees are sometimes hired for good jobs that old employees are qualified to fill.	1. Post job openings on bulletin boards and explain procedure for bidding on these jobs.
2. Sometimes employees are not told till Friday night that they are expected to work on Saturday.	2. Give at least two days' notice of the requirement to work on weekends.
3. Some believe that salary comparisons with other companies do not take into consideration overtime pay practices in effect in other companies.	3. Define the normal work week for salaried personnel which serves as the basis for salary comparisons with other companies.
4. We sometimes read about company events in local newspapers before we hear about them in the company.	4. Let employees hear first about company events through department meetings, newspaper, bulletins and supervisors
5. We are often pulled off a job before it's finished and put on another rush job.	5. Better planning and more consideration on the part of supervision could correct most of this.
6. Some items on attitude survey are confusing.	6. Give Corporate Personnel a list of confusing items with suggested changes.
7. Because the attitude survey is done on a sample basis, a lot of people feel "left out."	7. Increase the size of the samples or explain why you can't.

Source: M. Scott Meyers, "How Attitude Surveys Help You Manage," *Training and Development Journal,* Vol. 21 (October 1967), 34-41; reprinted in Beach, *Personnel,* pp. 311-16.

with this sort of intergroup conflict. The meeting took place during a State Department conference held at the Massachusetts Institute of Technology and dealt with conflict between Foreign Service officers and the administrative staff of the State Department. The problem was that:

> The stereotyping and mutual distrust, if not downright hostility, blocked communication and reduced effectiveness enormously, for each "side" perceived the other as more threatening than any realistic overseas enemy.

The two groups of officers were assigned to separate rooms and were asked to discuss three questions:

1. What qualities best describe our group?
2. What qualities best describe the other group?
3. What qualities do we predict the other group would assign to us?

Each group was asked to develop a list of words or phrases that it felt best described its answers to each question. The results were as follows:

The Foreign Service officers saw themselves as being:

1. Reflective
2. Qualitative
3. Humanistic, subjective
4. Cultural, with broad interests
5. Generalizers
6. Interculturally sensitive
7. Detached from personal conflicts

The Foreign Service officers saw administrative officers as being or having:

1. Doers and implementers
2. Quantitive
3. Decisive and forceful
4. Noncultural
5. Limited goals
6. Jealous of us
7. Interested in form more than substance
8. Wave of the future! [exclamation mark theirs]
9. Drones but necessary evils

The Foreign Service officers predicted that the administrative officers would see them as being:

1. Arrogant, snobbish
2. Intellectuals
3. Cliquish
4. Resistant to change
5. Inefficient, dysfunctional
6. Vacillating and compromising
7. Effete

The administrative officers saw themselves as being or having:

1. Decisive, guts
2. Resourceful, adaptive
3. Pragmatic
4. Service-oriented
5. Able to get along
6. Receptive to change
7. Dedicated to job
8. Misunderstood

9. Useful

10. Modest! [added by the person doing the presenting]

The administrative officers saw the Foreign Service officers as being:

1. Masked, isolated
2. Resourceful, serious
3. Respected
4. Inclined to stability
5. Dedicated to job
6. Necessary
7. Externally oriented
8. Cautious
9. Rational
10. Surrounded by mystique
11. Manipulative
12. Defensive

The administrative officers predicted that the Foreign Service officers would see them as being or having:

1. Necessary evils
2. Defensive, inflexible
3. Preoccupied with minutiae
4. Negative and bureaucratic
5. Limited perspective
6. Less culture (educated clerks)
7. Misunderstood
8. Practical
9. Protected
10. Resourceful

The two groups of officers then assembled together and proceeded to discuss their own lists and those made by the other group. They questioned each other about the lists, and after several hours, "it appeared as if each side moved to a position where they at least understood the other side's point of view." [22]

Sensitivity Training

Sensitivity or *T-group training* is a highly controversial development method that impinges upon the attitudes and personalities of the participants to a degree far exceeding that of other methods we discuss. The T-group, according to Argyris, is:

. . . a group experience designed to provide maximum possible opportunity for the individuals to expose their behavior, give and receive feedback, experiment with new behavior, and develop . . . awareness and acceptance of self and others. . . .[23]

According to the National Training Laboratory (NTL), which specializes in conducting such training, the primary purposes of T-groups are:

1. To provide managers with the sensitivity for themselves and others and with skills necessary to more effectively guide and direct changes in social arrangements and relationships
2. To develop in managers the sensitivity, understanding, and skill to participate effectively both as group leaders and members
3. To discover and develop tested principles and improved methods of human-relations training

The T-group process. Although the T-group procedure varies from trainer to trainer, the usual framework has been described as follows: A group of 10 to 15 meets, usually away from the job, and no activities or discussion topics are planned. The focus is on the "here and now" (including the feelings and emotions of the group members), and the participants are encouraged to portray themselves *in the group* rather than in terms of past experiences or future problems. Breaks in the discussions are often filled by feelings of frustration, expressions of hostility, and eventual attempts by some to organize and impose a hierarchical structure on the rest. Such attempts are usually blocked spontaneously by the group or through the trainer's intervention. Since the group's behavior is the principal topic of conversation, the success of the training group depends largely on the process of feedback. Specifically, participants must be able to inform each other of how their behavior is being seen, and be able to describe and interpret the kinds of feelings it produces. This feedback must be articulate and meaningful, since it is the primary channel through which the trainers learn. In turn, the success of the feedback process depends upon the member's being able to discover how deficient his earlier behavior was, and upon a climate of *psychological safety*. In other words, the person should feel safe to reveal himself in the group, to expose his feelings, drop his defenses, and try out new ways of interacting.[24]

Criticisms. T-group training is very personal in nature, so it is not surprising that it is an extremely controversial subject. Odiorne describes a training session in which, during one "horrible weekend," an inadequately trained trainer "broke down the barriers of formal courtesy that had substituted quite successfully for human relations in this successful lab for many years." [25] Everyone spoke frankly of his hostilities, and by the time the participants returned to their job, organized politicking and conflict reigned. Many senior scientists quit, and candid observations helped to sever ties between former colleagues. Odiorne points out several specific shortcomings of T-group training:

1. Not only are the participants unaware of what the outcome will be, but in many instances, since there are no controls, neither are the trainers.
2. Sensitivity training is based on creating stress situations for their own sake.
3. At present, anybody with a registration fee can attend.
4. Finally, the real flaw is that it isn't consistent with the business and economic world we live in.[26]

A number of writers have also attacked T-group training on the grounds that it may constitute an invasion of privacy. House points out that when participation in a T-group program is "suggested" by one's superior, attendance cannot be considered strictly voluntary.[27]

Argyris has tried to answer some of these objections. He has said that laboratory training of this type does have objectives, and even though the training session led by an inadequately prepared trainer could have poor effects, the policy at NTL, at least, is to utilize only highly trained people. In over 10,000 cases, there have been only "about four individuals" who had psychotic episodes and who became seriously ill, and "all of these people had previous psychiatric histories." [28]

Delbecq suggests considering several caveats before employing laboratory training. Programs should be voluntary, and careful screening should take place. A great deal of attention should be spent on building in mechanisms for transferring the learning to the organizational setting, and better methods for evaluating the effectiveness of laboratories should be employed.[29]

Research findings and discussion.   There is little doubt that sensitivity training, done properly, can result in more supportive behavior, more considerate managers, and more sensitive people.[30] Campbell and Dunnette note that changes in the direction of greater openness and self-understanding and improved communications and leadership skills were reported, although these changes would have been influenced by factors other than simply the T-group training. Trainees usually do become more sensitive to others and more open after going through T-group training. Furthermore, researchers have found that sensitivity training can also increase company performance and profits.[31]

Yet, the nagging question is still whether sensitivity training can change organizations, or change them in the right way.[32] Thus, the emphasis on flexibility, openness, and participation may not be compatible with the needs of the organization, particularly a mechanistic one. In addition, a typical problem of off-the-job training is an inability or unwillingness to apply the learning to the workplace. Since T-group training is concerned

TABLE 14-4

Four Basic Leadership Styles Represented on the Managerial Grid

Type of Leader as Ranked on Grid	Type of Concern for People	Type of Concern for Production
(1-1)	Low	Low
(1-9)	High	Low
(9-1)	Low	High
(9-9)	High	High

Source: Based on material in Robert R. Blake and Jane S. Mouton, *The Managerial Grid* (Houston: Gulf Publishing, 1964).

with the here and now *of the group*, it may have little relevance to actual organizational problems.

The Managerial Grid

The *managerial grid* is another technique sometimes used to bring about a change in employee attitudes or values. The grid itself, as summarized in Table 14-4, represents several possible leadership "styles." The two basic orientations—concern for people and concern for production—are conceptually similar to the consideration and initiating-structure leader-behavior dimensions of the Ohio State LBDQ. The different leader styles reflect different combinations of these two factors. For example, the 1–9 leader ranks high in his concern for people but low in his concern for production. At the opposite extreme, the 9–1 leader emphasizes production but deemphasizes the needs of his people.

Blake and Mouton's managerial-grid program assumes that it is possible for managers to work toward and develop a 9–9 grid score.[33] The program is composed of a six-phase program that usually lasts three to five years:

Phase I consists of laboratory-seminar training and is typically a one-week conference aimed at studying the theory of managerial effectiveness that underlies the grid program.

In *phase II*, the superior and his group utilize the climate of openness —which phase I anticipates—to develop and analyze their managerial styles and group practices.

In *phase III*, the experiences of phase II are extended to include the interrelationships of related organizational units. The objective here is joint problem solving.

In *phase IV*, top management works with other groups to develop an ideal corporate model for the future management of the organization.

Phase V uses a number of the procedures of phase I to develop operational tactics for moving the company to the ideal organizational model developed in phase IV.

Finally, in *phase VI*, the achievements of phases I through V are evaluated, with the objective of identifying weaknesses and taking corrective actions as necessary.[34]

Research findings. Although this is a widely used OD technique, the research evidence of its effectiveness is sketchy. Few studies have evaluated the effects of an overall managerial-grid program, and most of those have been by Blake and Mouton or their associates. One study was carried out in the "Sigma plant" of the Piedmont Corporation.[35] Among the problems identified here were intergroup conflict between the operating and engineering departments, and strained relations between the plant and parent organizations. The grid program began in November 1962 with 40 managers, and phase I continued until the summer of 1963, by which time 800 managers and technicians had completed it. The results of the study, which suggest a rise in plant efficiency, are presented in Table 14-5.

Productivity and profits increased during the period in which the grid program was in effect. However, Sigma's business involved widely fluctuating market prices, and higher revenues or lower materials costs might explain the doubling of profits. An overall manpower reduction of 600 employees during this period may also have contributed to increased profits.[36] The researchers attempted to measure behavioral changes but could not or did not develop adequate measurement scales. However, they did find an increase of 31 percent in formal meetings and of about 12½ percent in "team problem-solving" meetings. In addition, managers felt that group and interdepartmental relations had improved.

In another study, researchers tested hypotheses based on Blake and

TABLE 14-5

Changes in Relevant Operating Figures During and After
Grid Program (in Percentages)

	1960 *	*1961*	*1962*	*1963*
Gross revenue	100	101.6	98.2	106.6
Raw-material costs	100	98.8	97.2	103.2
Noncontrollable operating costs	100	97.5	101.8	104.6
Controllable operating costs	100	95.0	94.1	86.2
Net profit before taxes	100	229.0	118.0	226.0
Number of employees	100	95.5	94.1	79.5
Total production units	100	98.5	98.2	102.2

* 1960 is used as a base year, since it was the first year that Sigma's records could be compared with postmerger years.
Source: Robert R. Blake, Jane S. Mouton, Louis B. Barnes, and Larry E. Greiner, "Breakthrough in Organization Development," *Harvard Business Review*, Vol. 42 (November–December 1964), 142.

Mouton's Grid in a large midwestern manufacturing firm.[37] Their results suggested that where a person placed on the Grid was a poor predictor of either managerial effectiveness or conflict resolution methods used, a finding that has been disputed by Blake and Mouton.[38]

EVALUATING THE DEVELOPMENT EFFORT

The final step in organizational change and development should be to evaluate the change and development effort. Although organizations may assume that their development efforts are achieving their intended objectives, such faith is sometimes unwarranted. To determine the effectiveness of a development program, the organization must go through a systematic evaluation process. This is a complex subject, and we will touch on only some important points.

Basic Concepts in Evaluation

Basic procedure. In comparing various approaches to evaluation, one writer notes that the only procedure that provides a solid basis for evaluation is controlled experimentation, in which both a training group and a control group are used.[39] Relevant data should be obtained both before and after work in the training group, and before and after a corresponding work period in the control group. This procedure can be used both to evaluate the effectiveness of a particular development program and to compare the effectiveness of two or more different OD methods. However, such practical considerations as time and expense sometimes make it difficult to use this approach.

Bases of evaluation. Exactly what effects should be measured? The number of measurable effects is obviously large, and virtually all the topics we discussed in previous chapters (for instance, coordination, leadership style, satisfaction) might be relevant criteria. However, two writers have suggested a useful four-category outline of criteria:

Reaction. How well do the trainees like the program?

Learning. To what extent did the trainees learn the facts, principles, and approaches included in the training?

Behavior. To what extent did their job behavior change because of the program?

Results. What final results were achieved (reduction in cost, reduction in turnover, improvement in production, etc.)? [40]

Although these items can represent four types of criteria, the implication is that the *results* are clearly the most appropriate criteria in most instances. Where objective measures of results are available, such criteria might include measures of quantity and quality, for example.

Current Evaluation Practices

A survey. How many organizations actually evaluate their development efforts? Two researchers questioned 110 organizations that were known to be involved in various development programs.[41] Approximately 78 percent of these reported that they attempted to measure trainee reactions, and about half reported attempts to evaluate learning, behavior, and/or results. More detailed questionnaires were then sent to this half, and 47 companies responded. Although many of the organizations attempted to measure learning both before and after the training programs, fewer than half attempted to measure behavior, and only about a third tried to measure results. Where results were measured, it was usually on the bases of observation, interviews, analysis of production reports, and other indexes. It is apparent that the number using control groups was negligible.

In summary, two conclusions seem warranted concerning the evaluation of development programs. First, although huge sums of money are spent every year on various training and development programs, there seem to be few instances in which organizations carefully evaluate the effectiveness of their programs. Second, more managers can and should build an evaluation phase into their development efforts. Such evaluation would ideally include both control groups and pretests so that before and after results can be compared and the contribution of the training measured. Such evaluation programs have proved both feasible and useful.[42]

SUMMARY

Organizational change and development involves changing the structure, technology, or people in an organization in order to increase the organization's effectiveness. The change process consists of diagnosing the problem, planning for the change, implementing the change, and evaluating the change. Structural approaches to the change involve major reorganizations as well as more limited structural changes, such as job enrichment and development of more complete job descriptions. Technological changes are changes in work methods, and we discussed the impact of computerization at some length. Changing or developing the people in the organization is based on the assumption that by changing their values and attitudes, behavioral (as well as structural and technological) changes will follow.

How is the change and development process influenced by the organization's context—by its environment, for example? Here, it is apparent that change and development both influences and is influenced by the organization's context. First, context influences the change. Thus, we know that the organization structure in more effective organizations is appropriate to the "situation"—that, for example, organic organizations are more appropriate for unpredictable, entrepreneurial tasks. Therefore, structural changes should be made with the aim of adapting the structure to contextual demands. Similarly, development methods like OD are primarily a response to change, a "complex educational strategy intended to change the beliefs, attitudes, values, and structure of organizations so that they can better adapt to new technologies, markets, and challenges, and the dizzying rate of change itself." Organizational change and development can also influence the organization's context, as is the case where, for example, major technological changes such as computerization take place. In turn, changes to the organization's technology result in changes in organization structure and in the tasks and people in the organization.

How does organizational change and development affect organizational structure? Here, we saw that reorganization is perhaps the most direct and quickest way to change an organization. Organizational-development techniques (like sensitivity training) reverse the "normal" change process in that they try to change skills, structures, and relationships by changing the values and attitudes of participants.

How does organizational change and development affect employee compliance? Organizational change and development has an important influence on whether compliance derives from imposed control or self-control. OD techniques like sensitivity training, for example, are generally aimed at developing (among other things) a higher level of self-control among participants. On the other hand, technological changes like computerization very often reduce individual discretion, substituting instead a centralized network of computerized control.

DISCUSSION QUESTIONS

1. Why do people resist change?
2. What are three approaches to organizational change? Give some examples of conditions under which each would probably be more appropriate.
3. How does the "involvement" approach to attitude surveys differ from simply administering surveys and returning the results to top management?
4. Your company's consultants have just suggested to you that you put all your subordinates through sensitivity training. What are some of the questions you would ask of your consultants at this point?
5. Your boss has just suggested that you attend a sensitivity training laboratory. What are some of the questions you would ask of him or her?
6. Compare and contrast several organizational development techniques.

FOOTNOTES

[1] See Larry Greiner and Lewis Barnes, "Organizational Change and Development," in Paul Lawrence, Lewis Barnes, and Jay W. Lorsch, *Organizational Behavior and Administration* (Homewood, Ill.: Richard D. Irwin, 1976), pp. 621–33.

[2] Irwin Goldstein, *Training: Program Development and Evaluation* (Monterey, Calif.: Brooks/Cole, 1974), p. 19.

[3] Robert J. House, *Management Development: Design, Evaluation, and Implementation* (Ann Arbor: Bureau of Industrial Relations, Graduate School of Business Administration, University of Michigan, 1967), pp. 45–64.

[4] Robert Mager and Peter Pipe, *Analyzing Performance Problems* (Belmont, Calif.: Fearon, 1970), pp. 7–15.

[5] Harold Leavitt, *New Perspectives in Organization Research* (New York: John Wiley, 1964). Reprinted in Paul Lawrence, Lewis Barnes, and Jay Lorsch, *Organizational Behavior and Administration* (Homewood, Ill.: Richard D. Irwin, 1976), pp. 652–67.

[6] Larry Greiner and Lewis Barnes, "Organizational Change and Development," in Paul Lawrence, Lewis Barnes, and Jay Lorsch, *Organizational Behavior and Administration* (Homewood, Ill.: Irwin, 1976), pp. 621–33.

[7] Douglas T. Hall, James Goodale, Samuel Rabinowitz, and Marilyn Morgan, "Effects of Top-Down Departmental and Job Change Upon Perceived Employee Behavior and Attitudes: A Natural Field Experiment," *Journal of Applied Psychology*, Vol. 63, No. 1 (1978), 62–72.

[8] "How G.M. Turned Itself Around," *Fortune*, January 16, 1978.

[9] This section is based on Thomas Whisler, *Information Technology and Organizational Change* (Belmont, Calif.: Wadsworth, 1970).

[10] *Ibid.*, p. 68.

[11] *Ibid.*, p. 74. For a different point of view, see Herbert Simon, *The New Science of Management Decision* (Englewood Cliffs, N.J.: Prentice-Hall, 1977), Chap. 3.

[12] House, *Management Development*, p. 11.

[13] Roger Harrison, "Choosing the Depth of Organizational Intervention," *Journal of Applied Behavioral Science*, Vol. 2 (April/May/June 1970), 181–202.

[14] Warren G. Bennis, *Organizational Development: Its Nature, Origins, and Prospects* (Reading, Mass.: Addison-Wesley, 1969), p. 2.

[15] "What is O.D.?" *News and Reports from N.T.L. Institute for Applied Behavioral Science*, Vol. 2 (June 1968), 1–2.

[16] R. R. Blake and J. S. Mouton, "Grid Organization Development," *Personnel Administration*, January–February 1967, 11.

[17] David R. Hampton, Charles E. Summer, and Ross A. Webber, *Organizational Behavior and the Practice of Management* (Glenview, Ill.: Scott, Foresman, 1973), p. 850.

[18] Bennis, *Organization Development*, p. 10.

[19] John R. Kimberly and Warren R. Nielson, "Organization Development and Change in Organizational Performance," *Administrative Science Quarterly*, Vol. 20, No. 2 (June 1975).

[20] Warren Bennis and H. Shepard, "A Theory of Group Development," *Human Relations*, Vol. 9, No. 4 (1965).

[21] M. Scott Meyers, "How Attitude Surveys Help You Manage," *Training and Development Journal*, Vol. 21 (October 1967), 34–41; reprinted in Beach, *Personnel*, pp. 311–16; see also Robert Solomon, "An Examination of the Relationship between a Survey Feedback O.D. Technique and the Work Environment," *Personnel Psychology*, Vol. 29, No. 4 (Winter 1976).

[22] Bennis, *Organization Development*, p. 4-6. Reprinted with permission.

[23] Chris Argyris, "A Brief Description of Laboratory Education," *Training Director's Journal*, October 1963.

24 Based on J. P. Campbell and M. D. Dunnette, "Effectiveness of T-Group Experiences in Managerial Training and Development," *Psychological Bulletin*, Vol. 70 (1968), 73–104. Reprinted in W. E. Scott and L. L. Cummings, *Readings in Organizational Behavior and Human Performance* (Homewood, Ill.: Irwin, 1973), p. 571.

25 George S. Odiorne, "The Trouble with Sensitivity Training," *Training Director's Journal*, October 1963.

26 *Ibid.*

27 House, *Management Development,* p. 71.

28 Chris Argyris, "In Defense of Laboratory Education," *Training Director's Journal*, October, 1963.

29 Andre L. Delbecq, "Sensitivity Training," *Training and Development Journal*, January 1970, pp. 32–35.

30 Robert J. House, "T-Group Training: Good or Bad," *Business Horizons* (December 1969), pp. 69–77. Campbell and Dunnette, "Effectiveness of T-Group Experiences."

31 Kimberley and Nielsen, "Organizational Development," p. 203; see also Peter B. Smith, "Controlled Studies of the Outcome of Sensitivity Training," *Psychological Bulletin*, Vol. 82 (1976), 597–622.

32 House, "T-Group Training: Good or Bad." See also R. M. Powell and J. E. Stinson, "The Worth of Laboratory Training," *Business Horizons*, Vol. 14, No. 4 (1971), 87–95.

33 Robert R. Blake and Jane S. Mouton, *The Managerial Grid* (Houston: Gulf Publishing, 1964).

34 See R. R. Blake and J. S. Mouton, *Building a Dynamic Corporation through Grid Organizational Development* (Reading, Mass.: Addison-Wesley, 1969), p. 16.

35 Robert Blake, Jane Mouton, Lewis Barnes, and Larry Greiner, "Breakthrough in Organization Development," *Harvard Business Review*, Vol. 42 (November–December 1964). See also Robert Blake, Jane Mouton, Richard L. Sloma, and Barbara P. Lofton, "A Second Breakthrough in Organization Development," *California Management Review*, Vol, 11 (Winter 1968), 73–78.

36 The researchers themselves caution against drawing simple cause-and-effect conclusions about the effectiveness of this grid program.

37 H. John Bernardin and Kenneth M. Alvarez, "The Managerial Grid as a Predictor of Conflict Resolution Method and Managerial Effectiveness," *Administrative Science Quarterly*, Vol. 21, No. 1 (March 1976).

38 Robert Blake and Jane S. Mouton, "When Scholarship Fails, Research Falters: A Reply to Bernardin and Alvarez," *Administrative Science Quarterly*, Vol. 21, No. 1 (March 1976).

39 A. C. MacKinney, "Progressive Levels in the Evaluation of Training Programs," *Personnel*, Vol. 34, No. 3 (November–December 1957), 72–78. Ernest McCormick and Joseph Tiffin, *Industrial Psychology* (Englewood Cliffs, N.J.: Prentice-Hall, 1974), pp. 268–71.

40 R. E. Catalanello and D. L. Kirkpatrick, "Evaluating Training Programs—The State of the Art," *Training and Development Journal*, Vol. 22, No. 5 (May 1968), 2–9.

41 *Ibid.*

42 Kerry Bunker and Stephen Cohen, "The Rigors of Training Evaluation: A Discussion and Full Demonstration," *Personnel Psychology*, Vol. 30, No. 4 (Winter 1977).

case for part V:
texana petroleum corporation [1]

During the summer of 1966, George Prentice, the newly designated executive vice-president for domestic operations of the Texana Petroleum Corporation, was devoting much of his time to thinking about improving the combined performance of the five product divisions reporting to him (see Figure 1). His principal concern was that corporate profits were not reflecting the full potential contribution which could result from the close technological interdependence of the raw materials utilized and produced by these divisions. The principal difficulty, as Prentice saw it, was that the division general managers reporting to him were not working well together:

> As far as I see it, the issue is, where do we make the money for the corporation? Not how do we beat the other guy. Nobody is communicating with anybody else at the general manager level. In fact they are telling a bunch of secrets around here.

RECENT CORPORATE HISTORY

The Texana Petroleum Corporation was one of the early major producers and marketers of petroleum products in the southwest United States. Up until the early 1950s, Texana had been almost exclusively in the business of processing and refining crude oil and in selling petroleum products through a chain of company-operated service stations in the southwestern United States and in Central and South America. By 1950 company sales had risen to approximately $500 million with accompanying growth in profits. About 1950, however, Texana faced increasingly stiff competition at the retail service station level from several larger national petroleum companies. As a result, sales volume declined sharply during the early 1950s, and by 1955, sales had fallen to only $300 million and the company was operating at just above the breakeven point.

At this time, because of his age, Roger Holmes, who had been a dominant force in the company since its founding, retired as President and chief executive officer. He was replaced by Donald Irwin, forty-nine, who had been a senior executive with a major chemical company. William Dutton, fifty-five, was appointed chairman of the board to replace the retiring board chairman. Dutton had spent his entire career with Texana. Prior to his appointment as chairman he had been senior vice-president for Petroleum Products, reporting to Holmes.

Irwin and Dutton, along with other senior executives, moved quickly to solve the problems facing Texana. They gradually divested the company's retail outlets and abandoned the domestic consumer petroleum markets. Through both internal development and acquisition, they expanded and rapidly increased the company's involvement in the business

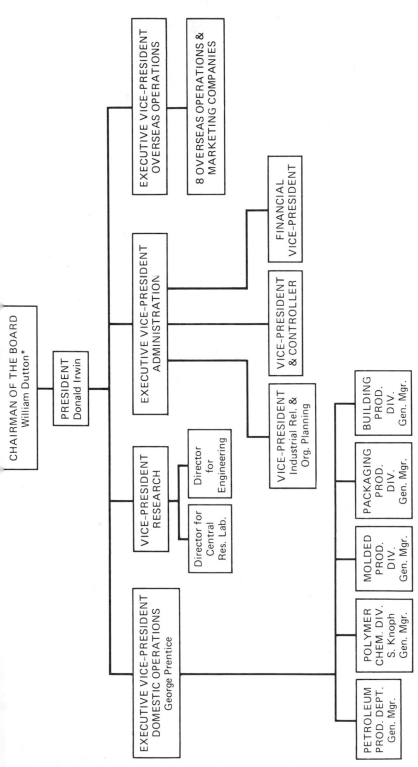

FIGURE 1. Texana Petroleum Company—Partial Organization Chart, 1966

CHAIRMAN OF THE BOARD
William Dutton*

PRESIDENT
Donald Irwin

EXECUTIVE VICE-PRESIDENT
OVERSEAS OPERATIONS

8 OVERSEAS OPERATIONS &
MARKETING COMPANIES

EXECUTIVE VICE-PRESIDENT
ADMINISTRATION

FINANCIAL
VICE-PRESIDENT

VICE-PRESIDENT
& CONTROLLER

VICE-PRESIDENT
Industrial Rel. &
Org. Planning

VICE-PRESIDENT
RESEARCH

Director
for
Engineering

Director for
Central
Res. Lab.

EXECUTIVE VICE-PRESIDENT
DOMESTIC OPERATIONS
George Prentice

PETROLEUM
PROD. DEPT.
Gen. Mgr.

POLYMER
CHEM. DIV.
S. Knoph
Gen. Mgr.

MOLDED
PROD.
DIV.
Gen. Mgr.

PACKAGING
PROD.
DIV.
Gen. Mgr.

BUILDING
PROD.
DIV.
Gen. Mgr.

*Names included for persons mentioned in the case.

of processing petroleum for chemical and plastic products. In moving in this direction, they were rapidly expanding on initial moves made by Texana in 1949, when the company built its first chemical processing plant and began marketing these products. To speed the company's growth in these areas, Irwin and Dutton selected aggressive general managers for each division and gave them a wide degree of freedom in decision making. Top management's major requirement was that each division general manager create a growing division with a satisfactory return on investment capital. By 1966, top management had reshaped the company so that in both the domestic and foreign market it was an integrated producer of chemicals and plastics materials. In foreign operations, the company continued to operate service stations in Latin America and in Europe. This change in direction was successful, and by 1966, company sales had risen to $750 million, with a healthy rise in profit.

In spite of this success, management believed that there was a need for an increase in return on invested capital. The financial and trade press, which had been generous in its praise of the company's recovery, was still critical of the present return on investment, and top management shared this concern. Dutton, Irwin, and Prentice were in agreement that one important method of increasing profits was to take further advantage of the potential cost savings which could come from increased coordination between the domestic operating divisions, as they developed new products, processes, and markets.

DOMESTIC ORGANIZATION 1966

The product divisions reporting to Mr. Prentice represented a continuum of producing and marketing activities from production and refining of crude oil to the marketing of several types of plastics products to industrial consumers. Each division was headed by a general manager. While there was some variation in the internal organizational structure of the several divisions, they were generally set up along functional lines (manufacturing, sales, research and development). Each division also had its own controller and engineering activities, although these were supported and augmented by the corporate staff. While divisions had their own research effort, there was also a central research laboratory at the corporate level, which carried on a longer range research of a more fundamental nature, and outside the scope of the activities of any of the product divisions.

The *petroleum products division* was the remaining nucleus of the company's original producing and refining activities. It supplied raw materials to the polymer and chemicals division and also sold refining products under long-term contracts to other petroleum companies. In the early and mid-1950s, this division's management had generated much of the company's revenue and profits through its skill of negotiating these agreements. In 1966, top corporate management felt that this division's management had accepted its role as a supplier to the rest of the corporation, and felt that there were harmonious relations between it and its sister divisions.

The *polymer and chemicals division* was developed internally during the late 1940s and early 1950s as management saw its share of the consumer petroleum market declining. Under the leadership of Seymour Knoph (who had been general manager for several years) and his predecessor (who was in 1966 executive vice-president of administration), the division had rapidly developed a line of chemical and polymer compounds derived from petroleum raw materials. Most of the products of this division were manufactured under licensing agreement or were materials the formulation of which was well understood. Nevertheless, technical personnel in the division had developed an industrywide reputation for their ability to develop new and improved processes. Top management of the division took particular pride in this ability. From the beginning, the decision of what products to manufacture was based to a large extent upon the requirements of the molded and packaging products divisions. However, polymer and chemicals division executives had always attempted to market these same products to external customers, and had been highly successful. These external sales were extremely important to Texana, since they assured a large enough volume of operation to process a broad product line of polymer chemicals profitably. As the other divisions had grown, they had required a larger proportion of the division's capacity, which meant that polymer and chemical division managers had to reduce their commitment to external customers.

The *molded products division* was also an internally developed division, which had been formed in 1951. Its products were a variety of molded plastic products ranging from toys and household items to automotive and electronic parts. This division's major strengths were its knowledge of molding technology and particularly its marketing ability. While it depended upon the polymer and chemicals division for its raw materials, its operations were largely independent of those of the packaging products and building products divisions.

The *packaging products division* was acquired in 1952. Its products were plastic packaging materials, including films, cartons, bottles, etc. All of these products were marketed to industrial customers. Like the molded products division, the packaging division depended on the polymer and chemical division as a source of raw materials, but was largely independent of other end-product divisions.

The *building products division* was acquired in 1963 to give Texana a position in the construction materials market. The division produced and marketed a variety of insulation roofing materials and similar products to the building trade. It was a particularly attractive acquisition for Texana, because prior to the acquisition it had achieved some success with plastic products for insulation and roofing materials. Although the plastic products accounted for less than 20 percent of the total division sales in 1965, plans called for these products to account for over 50 percent of division sales in the next five years. Its affiliation with Texana gave this division a stronger position in plastic raw materials through the polymer and chemicals division.

Selection and Recruitment of Management Personnel

The rapid expansion of the corporation into these new areas had created the need for much additional management talent, and top management had not hesitated to bring new men in from outside the corporation, as well as advancing promising younger men inside Texana. In both the internally developed and acquired divisions, most managers had spent their careers inside the division, although some top division managers were moved between divisions or into corporate positions.

In speaking about the type of men he had sought for management positions, Donald Irwin described his criterion in a financial publication:

> We don't want people around who are afraid to move. The attraction of Texana is that it gives the individual responsibilities which aren't diluted. It attracts the fellow who wants a challenge.

Another corporate executive described Texana managers:

> It's a group of very tough-minded, but considerate gentlemen with an enormous drive to get things done.

Another manager, who had been with Texana for his entire career, and who considered himself to be different from most Texana managers, described the typical Texana manager as follows:

> Texana attracts a particular type of person. Most of these characteristics are personal characteristics rather than professional ones. I would use terms such as cold, unfeeling, aggressive, and extremely competitive, but not particularly loyal to the organization. He is loyal to dollars, his own personal dollars. I think this is part of the communication problem. I think this is done on purpose. The selection procedures lead in this direction. I think this is so because of contrast with the way the company operated ten years ago. Of course, I was at the plant level at that time. But today the attitude I have described is also in the plants. Ten years ago the organization was composed of people who worked together for the good of the organization, because they wanted to. I don't think this is so today.

Location of Division Facilities

The petroleum products, chemical and polymer, and packaging products divisions had their executive offices on separate floors of the Texana headquarters building in the Chicago Loop. The plants and research and development facilities of these divisions were spread out across Oklahoma, Texas, and Louisiana. The molded products division had its headquarters, research and development facilities, and a major plant in an industrial suburb of Chicago. This division's other plants were at several locations in the Middle West and on the East Coast. The building products division's headquarters and major production and technical facilities were located in Fort Worth, Texas. All four divisions shared sales offices in major cities from coast to coast.

Evaluation and Control of Division Performance

The principal method of controlling and evaluating the operations of these divisions was the semiannual review of division plans and the approval of major capital expenditures by the executive committee.[2] In reviewing performance against plans, members of the executive committee placed almost sole emphasis on the division's actual return on investment against budget. Corporate executives felt that this practice, together with the technological interdependence of the divisions, created many disputes about transfer pricing.

In addition to these regular reviews, corporate executives had frequent discussions with division executives about their strategies, plans, and operations. It had been difficult for corporate management to strike the proper balance in guiding the operations for the divisions. This problem was particularly acute with regard to the polymer and chemicals division, because of its central place in the corporation's product line. One corporate staff member explained his view of the problem:

> This whole matter of communications between the corporate staff and the polymer and chemical division has been a fairly difficult problem. Corporate management used to contribute immensely to this by trying to get into the nuts and bolts area within the chemical and polymer organization, and this created serious criticisms; however, I think they have backed off in this matter.

A second corporate executive, in discussing this matter for a trade publication report, put the problem this way:

> We're trying to find the middle ground. We don't want to be a holding company, and with our diversity we can't be a highly centralized corporation.

Executive Vice-President—Domestic Operations

In an effort to find this middle ground, the position of executive vice-president of domestic operations was created in early 1966, and George Prentice was its first occupant. Prior to this change, there had been two senior domestic vice-presidents—one in charge of the petroleum and polymer and chemicals divisions and the other in charge of the end use divisions. Mr. Prentice had been senior vice-president in charge of the end-use divisions before the new position was created. He had held that position for only two years, having come to it from a highly successful marketing career with a competitor.

At the time of his appointment, one press account described Mr.

Prentice as "hard-driving, aggressive, and ambitious—an archetype of the self-actuated dynamo—Irwin has sought out."

Shortly after taking his new position, Prentice described the task before him:

> I think the corporation wants to integrate its parts better and I am here because I reflect this feeling. We can't be a bunch of entrepreneurs around here. We have got to balance discipline with entrepreneurial motivation. This is what we were in the past, just a bunch of entrepreneurs, and if they came in with ideas we would get the money, but now our dollars are limited, and especially the polymer and chemical boys haven't been able to discipline themselves to select from within ten good projects. They just don't seem to be able to do this, and so they come running in here with all ten good projects which they say we have to buy, and they get upset when we can't buy them all.

> This was the tone of my predecessors (senior vice-presidents). All of them were very strong on being entrepreneurs. I am going to run it differently. I am going to take a marketing and capital orientation. As far as I can see, there is a time to compete and a time to collaborate, and I think right now there has been a lack of recognition in the polymer and chemicals executive suite that this thing has changed.

Other Views of Domestic Interdivisional Relations

Executives within the polymer and chemicals divisions, in the end-use divisions, and at the corporate level shared Prentice's view that the major breakdown in interdivisional relations was between the polymer and chemicals division and the end-use divisions. Executives in the end-use divisions made these typical comments about the problem:

> I think the thing we have got to realize is that we are wedded to the polymer and chemicals division whether we like it or not. We are really tied up with them. And just as we would with any outside supplier or with any of our customers, we will do things to maintain their business. But because they feel they have our business wrapped up, they do not reciprocate in turn. Now let me emphasize that they have not arbitrarily refused to do the things that we are requiring, but there is a pressure on them for investment projects and we are low man on the pole. And I think this could heavily jeopardize our chances for growth.

> $\cdot \qquad \cdot \qquad \cdot \qquad \cdot \qquad \cdot$

> I would say our relationships are sticky, and I think this is primarily because we think our reason for being is to make money, so we try to keep Polymer and Chemicals as an arm's-length supplier. For example, I cannot see, just because it is a polymer and chemicals product, accepting millions of pounds of very questionable material. It takes dollars out of our pocket, and we are very profit-centered.

> $\cdot \qquad \cdot \qquad \cdot \qquad \cdot \qquad \cdot$

> The big frustration, I guess, and one of our major problems, is that you can't get help from them [Polymer and Chemicals]. You feel they are not

interested in what you are doing, particularly if it doesn't have a large return for them. But as far as I am concerned, this has to become a joint venture relationship, and this is getting to be real sweat with us. We are the guys down below yelling for help. And they have got to give us some relief.

.   .   .   .   .

My experience with the polymer and chemicals division is that you cannot trust what they say at all, and even when they put it in writing, you can't be absolutely sure that they are going to live up to it.

Managers within the polymer and chemicals division expressed similar sentiments:

Personally, right now I have the feeling that the divisions' interests are growing further apart. It seems that the divisions are going their own way. For example, we are a polymer producer but the molding division wants to be in a special area, so that means they are going to be less of a customer to us, and there is a whole family of plastics being left out that nobody's touching, and this is bearing on our program. . . . We don't mess with the building products division at all, either. They deal in small volumes. Those that we are already making we sell to them, those that we don't make we can't justify making because of the kinds of things we are working with. What I am saying is that I don't think the corporation is integrating, but I think we ought to be, and this is one of the problems of delegated divisions. What happens is that an executive heads this up and goes for the place that makes the most money for the division, *but* this is not necessarily the best place from a corporate standpoint.

.   .   .   .   .

We don't have as much contact with sister divisions as I think we should. I have been trying to get a liaison with guys in my function but it has been a complete flop. One of the problems is that I don't know who to call on in these other divisions. There is no table of organization, nor is there any encouragement to try and get anything going. My experience has been that all of these operating divisions are very closed organizations. I know guys up the line will say that I am nuts about this. They say to just call over and I will get an answer. But this always has to be a big deal, and it doesn't happen automatically, and hurts us.

The comments of corporate staff members describe these relationships and the factors they saw contributing to the problem:

Right now I would say there is an iron curtain between the polymer and chemicals division and the rest of the corporation. You know, we tell our divisions they are responsible, autonomous groups, and the polymer and chemicals division took it very seriously. However, when you are a three-quarter-billion-dollar company, you've got to be coordinated, or the whole thing is going to fall apart—it can be no other way. The domestic executive vice-president thing has been a big step forward to improve this, but I would say it hasn't worked out yet.

.   .   .   .   .

The big thing that is really bothering [the polymer and chemicals division] is that they think they have to go develop all new markets on their own. They are going to do it alone independently, and this is the problem they are faced with. They have got this big thing, that they want to prove that they are a company all by themselves and not rely upon packaging or anybody else.

Polymer and chemicals division executives talked about the effect of this drive for independence of the divisional operating heads on their own planning efforts:

> The polymer and chemicals division doesn't like to communicate with the corporate staff. This seems hard for us, and I think the [a recent major proposal] was a classic example of this. That plan, as it was whipped up by the polymer and chemicals division, had massive implications for the corporation both in expertise and in capital. In fact, I think we did this to be a competitive one-up on the rest of our sister divisions. We wanted to be the best-looking division in the system, but we carried it to an extreme. In this effort, we wanted to show that we had developed this concept completely on our own. . . . Now I think a lot of our problems with it stemmed from this intense desire we have to be the best in this organization.

> .   .   .   .   .

> Boy, a big doldrum around here was shortly after Christmas (1965) when they dropped out a new plant, right out of our central plan, without any appreciation of the importance of this plant to the whole polymer and chemicals division's growth. . . . Now we have a windfall and we are back in business on this new plant. But for a while, things were very black and everything we had planned and everything we had built our patterns on were out. In fact, when we put this plan together, it never really occurred to us that we were going to get it turned down, and I'll bet we didn't even put the plans together in such a way as to really reflect the importance of this plant to the rest of the corporation.

A number of executives in the end-use divisions attributed the interdivisional problems to different management practices and assumptions within the polymer and chemicals division. An executive in the packaging division made this point:

> We make decisions quickly and at the lowest possible level, and this is tremendously different from the rest of Texana. I don't know another division like this in the rest of the corporation.

> Look at what Sy Knoph has superfluous to his operation compared to ours. These are the reasons for our success. You've got to turn your guys loose and not breathe down their necks all the time. We don't slow our people down with staff. Sure, you may work with a staff, the wheels may grind, but they sure grind slow.

> Also, we don't work on detail like the other divisions do. Our management doesn't feel they need the detail stuff. Therefore, they're [Polymer and Chemical] always asking us for detail which we can't supply, our process doesn't generate it and their process requires it, and this always creates problems with the polymer and chemicals division. But I'll be damned if I am going to have a group of people running between me and the plant, and I'll

be goddamned if I am going to clutter up my organization with all the people that Knoph has got working for him. I don't want this staff, but they are sure pushing it on me.

This comment from a molding division manager is typical of many about the technical concerns of the polymer and chemicals division management:

> Historically, even up to the not too distant past, the polymer and chemicals division was considered a snake pit as far as the corporate people were concerned. This was because the corporate people were market-oriented and polymer and chemicals division was technically run and very much a manufacturing effort. These two factors created a communication barrier and to really understand the polymer and chemicals division problems, they felt that you have to have a basic appreciation of the technology and all the interrelationships.
>
> Building on this strong belief, the polymer and chemicals divisions executives in the past have tried to communicate in technical terms, and this just further hurt the relationship, and it just did not work. Now they are coming up with a little bit more business or commercial orientation, and they are beginning to appreciate that they have got to justify the things they want to do in a business or commercial orientation, and they are beginning to appreciate that they have got to justify the things they want to do in a business sense rather than just a technical sense. This also helps the problem of maintaining their relationships with the corporation, as most of the staff is nontechnical; however, this has changed a little bit in that more and more technical people have been coming on, and this has helped from the other side.
>
> They work on the assumption in the polymer and chemicals division that you have to know the territory before you can be an effective manager. You have got to be an operating guy to contribute meaningfully to their problems. However, their biggest problem is this concentration on technical solutions to their problems. This is a thing that has boxed them in the most trouble with corporation and the other sister divisions.

These and other executives also pointed to another source of conflict between the polymer and chemicals division and other divisions. This was the question of whether the polymer and chemicals division should develop into a more independent marketer, or whether it should rely more heavily on the end-use divisions to "push" its products to the market.

Typical views of this conflict are the following comments by end-use division executives:

> The big question I have about Polymer and Chemicals is, what is their strategy going to be? I can understand them completely from a technical standpoint, this is no problem. I wonder, what is the role of this company? How is it going to fit into what we and others are doing? Right now, judging from the behavior I've seen, Polymer and Chemicals could care less about what we are doing in terms of integration of our markets or a joint approach to them.

· · · · · ·

I think it is debatable whether the polymer and chemicals division should be a new product company or not. Right now we have an almost inexhaustible appetite for what they do and do well. As I see it, the present charter is fine. However, that group is very impatient, aggressive, and they want to grow, but you have got to grow within guidelines. Possibly the polymer and chemicals division is just going to have to learn to hang on the coattails of the other divisions, and do just what they are doing now, only better.

.   .   .   .   .

I think the future roles of the polymer and chemicals division is going to be, at any one point in time for the corporation, that if it looks like a product is needed, they will make it. . . . They are going to be suppliers, because I will guarantee you that if the moment comes and we can't buy it elsewhere, for example, then I darn well know they are going to make it for us regardless of what their other commitments are. They are just going to have to supply us. If you were to put the polymer and chemicals division off from the corporation, I don't think they would last a year. Without their huge captive requirements, they would not be able to compete economically in the commercial areas they are in.

A number of other executives indicated that the primary emphasis within the corporation on return on investment by divisions tended to induce, among other things, a narrow, competitive concern on the part of the various divisional managements. The comment of this division executive was typical:

As far as I can see it, we [his division and Polymer and Chemicals] are 180 degrees off on our respective charters. Therefore, when Sy Knoph talks about this big project, we listen nicely and then we say, "God bless you, lots of luck," but I am sure we are not going to get involved in it. I don't see any money in it for us. It may be a gold mine for Sy but it is not for our company; and as long as we are held to the high profit standards we are, we just cannot afford to get involved. I can certainly see it might make good corporate sense for us to get it, but it doesn't make any sense in terms of our particular company. We have got to be able to show the returns in order to get continuing capital, and I just can't on that kind of project. I guess what I am saying is that under the right conditions we could certainly go in, but not under the present framework; we would just be dead in terms of dealing with the corporate financial structure. We just cannot get the kinds of returns on our capital that the corporation has set to get new capital. In terms of the long run, I'd like very much to see what the corporation has envisioned in terms of a hook-up between us, but right now I don't see any sense in going on. You know, my career is at stake here too.

Another divisional executive made this point more succinctly:

Personally, I think that a lot more could be done from a corporate point of view, and this is frustrating. Right now all these various divisions seem to be viewed strictly as an investment by the corporate people. They only look at us as a banker might look at us. This hurts us in terms of evolving some of these programs because we have relationships which are beyond financial relationships.

The remarks of a corporate executive seemed to support this concern:

> One of the things I worry about is where is the end of the rope on this interdivisional thing. I'm wondering if action really has to come from just the division. You know, in this organization when they decide to do something new, it always has been a divisional proposal—they were coming to us for review and approval. The executive committee ends up a review board; not us, working downward. With this kind of pattern, the talent of the corporate people is pretty well reduced into asking questions and determining whether a thing needs guidelines. But I think we ought to be the idea people as well, thinking about where we are going in the future, and if we think we ought to be getting into some new area, then we tell the divisions to do it. The stream has got to work both ways. Now it is not.

QUESTIONS

(Please answer these questions before proceeding to the conclusion below.)

1. What are the *antecedents* of conflict in this situation? The *moderating factors*? How is conflict *manifesting* itself?
2. How would you go about managing the conflict inherent in this situation? Texana has tried to handle it by appointing an executive vice-president for internal operations, but it is doubtful that this move by itself will be sufficient. Develop your own prescriptions for managing conflict at Texana. You might suggest, for example, such conflict-management techniques as developing superordinate goals, installing an improved incentive system, and structural approaches (special integrators, reduced interdependency, and the like); and conflict-resolution behaviors such as confrontation, smoothing, and forcing.
3. What organizational change and development techniques seem necessary here? Why?
4. Does there seem to be a high degree of "differentiation" between the end-use divisions and polymer and chemical divisions? What implications does this have for how "integration" (coordination) should be achieved?
5. Is the organization structure adequate? How would you change it?
6. Is there a need to build more commitment on the part of employees? What do you base this on? How would you do so?

CONCLUSION

This case helps illustrate, amongst other things, a number of the characteristics of intergroup relations and conflict we discussed in Chapter 13.

There are several sources or *antecedents* of conflict inherent in the way this company is now organized and managed. For one thing, the divisions are interdependent. The petroleum division is a supplier to other divisions, and the molded products, packaging products, and building products divisions are all dependent on the polymer and chemicals division for their raw materials. However, even though the divisions are highly interdependent, there are significant intergroup differences in terms of goals, values, and management styles. The performance of each division is measured by its own return on investment, a situation that seems to discourage interdivisional collaboration. And as an example of the differences in management styles between divisions, an employee says that in his division, they prefer making quick decisions at the lowest possible level, whereas in Polymer and Chemicals, employees always seem to want more "details," a process that slows down the decision process. By way of conflict antecedents, there is also some ambiguity. For example, there is no table of organization, so employees in each division don't know who their counterparts are in other divisions and can't communicate with them as they would like to.

Viewed in terms of the models of conflict we discussed, it is apparent why conflict has emerged at Texana. Not only are there numerous conflict antecedents, as we just discussed, but a number of moderating factors are acting to attenuate the effects of these antecedents. There is an absence of effective communication between divisions, and managers describe themselves as "180 degrees apart." Managers in the end-use divisions have come to assume that those in the polymer and chemicals division view them as "low man on the pole" and that "they have us wrapped up and do not reciprocate when we try to be helpful." There is no effective liaison between divisions. To make matters worse, the top executives in each division are assertive, aggressive, and competitive, a fact that probably increases further the likelihood that the conflict antecedents will lead to manifest conflict.

FOOTNOTES

1 This case was prepared by Jay W. Lorsch from data collected by Paul R. Lawrence, James A. Garrison, and himself. Copyright © 1967 by the President and Fellows of Harvard College. Reprinted by permission. Case material of the Harvard Graduate School of Business Administration is intended as a basis for class discussion rather than to illustrate either effective or ineffective handling of an administrative situation. The case was reprinted in Robert Coffey, Anthony Athos, and Peter Reynolds, *Behavior in Organizations* (Englewood Cliffs, N.J.: Prentice-Hall, 1975), pp. 557–68.

2 The executive committee consisted of Messrs. Dutton, Irwin, and Prentice, as well as the vice-president of research, executive vice-president of administration, and executive vice-president of foreign operations.

PART VI

ORGANIZATIONAL EFFECTIVENESS

Chapter 15

Organizational Effectiveness

CHAPTER OVERVIEW

The purpose of this last chapter is to discuss the meaning of organizational effectiveness and the usefulness of our framework for understanding, explaining, and predicting it. Although our framework is useful, it is not the only way to conceptualize the determinants of effectiveness, and we discuss another. This latter emphasizes that organizations should actively try to alter their environments, rather than just react to them by reorganizing. Finally, we end with a brief discussion of some questions we first raised in Chapter 1.

The outline of this chapter is as follows:

I. What Is Organizational Effectiveness?
   A. Introduction
   B. Single-Criterion Measures of Effectiveness
   C. Multiple-Criteria Measures of Effectiveness
   D. Comparison of Multiple-Criteria Models
   E. Framework: How Useful?
   F. Managing and Avoiding External Control

II. Questions in Organization Theory
   A. What are the major determinants of organizational effectiveness?
   B. What are the relationships between these determinants?
   C. What makes one organization effective, and another ineffective?
   D. What is the applicability of this knowledge to practical problems?

III. Summary

WHAT IS ORGANIZATIONAL EFFECTIVENESS?

Introduction

The fact that some organizations are measurably more effective than others is a basic assumption of economic and organization theory, and indeed, it has been implicit throughout this book. For example, our contentions that turbulent environments require more "organic" structures, that technology, structure, and effectiveness are related, and that some leaders are more effective in some situations than others all assume that effectiveness is an end product that can be defined and measured.

Therefore, it may come as a surprise that the literature concerning the definition and measurement of organizational effectiveness is somewhat inconclusive. Various models and criteria of effectiveness have been proposed, and yet little consensus exists on the definition or measurement of this crucial variable.[1] Many effectiveness criteria and measurement problems have been proposed, and the purpose of this chapter is to discuss some of this information. Our objective here will be to develop a clearer understanding of (1) what organizational effectiveness is, and (2) how the material in the last 14 chapters relates to it. We begin with a discussion of single-criterion and multiple-criteria measures of effectiveness.

Single-Criterion Measures of Effectiveness

Profit maximization. Early models of organizational effectiveness generally focused on a single criterion of organizational success. The most popular of these was (and probably still is) *profit maximization.*

The idea that firms seek to "maximize profits" and that effectiveness should primarily reflect profits is a fundamental assumption accepted by most economists. Technically, they assume that the object of the firm is to obtain as large a difference as possible between total revenue and total costs, provided that the difference is greater than or equal to zero.[2]

Yet even though profit maximization is the most familiar criterion of organizational effectiveness, no one has yet shown that firms do in fact act as if they seek to maximize profits at the exclusion of other, equally important goals, and, in fact, economists themselves disagree as to the supreme position of profit maximization. William Baumol, for example, suggests that firms seek to maximize not their profits but their *sales revenue,* on the assumption that the managers who run our large organizations (as opposed to the stockholder-owners) want their firms as large as possible.[3] And many economists point out that "profit maximization" is as much a convenient device as an unassailable assumption. Stigler, for example, says:

> The extent to which the entrepreneurial behavior can be explained by efforts to maximize profits is a celebrated debating ground for economists. We shall nevertheless use this assumption without extensive defense, and on two grounds. First, and most important, it yields a vast number of testable con-

clusions, and by and large these conclusions agree with observation. Second, no other well-defined goals have yet been developed and given empirical support.[4]

Similarly, Ferguson notes:

> Without doubt, not all producers try to maximize profits at all times. Entrepreneurs may indeed be seekers after multiple goals. Nonetheless, a business cannot long remain viable unless profits are earned; and it is a very unusual businessman who treats profits in a cavalier fashion. . . . Whether profit maximization is a reasonable assumption is a question long debated in economics. Several important criticisms have been brought to bear; however, these criticisms do not overcome the supremely important fact that the assumption of profit maximization is the only one providing a general theory of firms, markets, and resource allocation that is successful in both explaining and predicting business behavior.[5]

Satisficing. Organization theorists have proposed various alternatives for evaluating the effectiveness of organizations, but perhaps the most complete and enduring argument against profit maximization has been proposed by Herbert Simon. According to Simon, managers (and firms) do not maximize but instead "satisfice." That is, "we must expect the firm's goals to be not maximizing profits but attaining a certain level or rate of profit, holding a certain share of the market or a certain level of sales."[6] Firms do not seek to maximize profits, in other words, but instead set a minimum level of acceptable profits and, once this is met, do not aggressively seek to exceed this level.

One example that may support this position was a phenomenon that occurred immediately after World War II. At one point, the price of new cars was actually lower than that of used cars, and the explanation for this, say proponents of "satisficing," is that car manufacturers set a target level of acceptable profits and did not seek to exceed this level. Contemporary examples include the recent attempts by large oil firms to depress reported profits, and by auto insurers in Florida to reduce their "excessive" profits by returning huge sums to their customers. Of course, these examples may simply reflect, say, attempts by the firms to develop better "public relations," rather than satisficing behavior.

Other single-criterion measures. Many other single-criterion measures have been proposed. For example, in one recent review, John Campbell identified 19 different variables that have been used to reflect organizational effectiveness. The most widely used were:

> *Overall performance* as measured by employee or supervisory rating
> *Productivity* as measured typically with actual output data
> *Employee satisfaction* as measured by self report questionnaires
> *Profit, or rate of return* based on accounting data
> *Withdrawal* based on historical turnover and absenteeism data [7]

Other measures of organizational effectiveness are presented in Table 15-1.

TABLE 15-1

A Partial Listing of Single-criterion Measures of Organizational Effectiveness

Overall Effectiveness	The degree to which the organization is accomplishing all its major tasks or achieving all its objectives. A general evaluation that takes in as many single criteria as possible and results in a general judgment about the effectiveness of the organization.
Quality	The quality of the primary service or product provided by the organization. This may take many operational forms primarily determined by the *kind* of product or service provided by the organization.
Productivity	The quantity of or volume of the major product or service that the organization provides. Can be measured at three levels: individual, group, and total organization. This is not a measure of efficiency; no cost output ratio is computed.
Readiness	An overall judgment concerning the probability that the organization could successfully perform some specified task if asked to do so.
Efficiency	A ratio that reflects a comparison of some aspect of unit performance to the costs incurred for that performance. Examples: dollars per single unit of production, amount of down time, degree to which schedules, standards of performance, or other milestones are met. On occasion, just the total amount of costs (money, material, etc.) a unit has incurred over some period can be used.
Profit or Return	The return on the investment used in running the organization from the owners' point of view. The amount of resources left after all costs and obligations are met sometimes expressed as a percentage.
Growth	An increase in such things as manpower, plant facilities, assets, sales, profits, market share, and innovations. A comparison of an organization's present state with its own past state.
Utilization of Environment	The extent to which the organization successfully interacts with its environment, acquiring scarce, valued resources necessary to its effective operation. This is viewed in a long term, optimizing framework and not in a short-term, maximizing framework. For example: the degree to which it acquires a steady supply of manpower and financial resources.
Stability	The maintenance of structure, function, and resources through time and more particularly through periods of stress.
Turnover or Retention	Frequency or amount of voluntary terminations.
Absenteeism	The frequency of occasions of personnel being absent from the job.
Accidents	Frequency of on-the-job accidents resulting in down time or recovery time.

TABLE 15-1

A Partial Listing of Single-criterion Measures of
Organizational Effectiveness (*cont.*)

Morale	A predisposition in organization members to put forth extra effort in achieving organizational goals and objectives. Includes feelings of commitment. Morale is a group phenomenon involving extra effort, goals communality, and feelings of belonging. Groups have some degree of morale while individuals have some degree of motivation and satisfaction. By implication, morale is inferred from group phenomena.
Motivation	The strength of the predisposition of an *individual* to engage in a goal-directed action or activity on the job. This is not a feeling of relative contentment with various job outcomes as is satisfaction, but more akin to a feeling of readiness or willingness to work at accomplishing the job's goals.
Satisfaction	The degree of feeling of contentment felt by a person toward his organizational role or job. The degree to which individuals perceive they are equitably rewarded by various aspects of their job situation and the organization to which they belong.
Internalization of Organizational Goals	The acceptance of organizational goals by individuals and units within the organization. Their belief that the organization's goals are right and proper.
Conflict-Cohesion	A bipolar dimension defined at the cohesion end by an organization in which the members like one another, work well together, communicate fully and openly, and coordinate their work efforts. At the other end lies the organization with verbal and physical clashes, poor coordination, and ineffective communication.
Flexibility-Adaptation	The ability of an organization to change its standard operating procedures in response to environmental changes, to resist becoming rigid in response to environmental stimuli.
Evaluations by External Entities	Evaluations of the organization or organizational unit by those individuals and organizations in its environment with which it interacts. Loyalty to, confidence in, and support given the organization by such groups as suppliers, customers, stockholders, enforcement agencies, and the general public.

Source: J. P. Campbell, "Research into the Nature of Organizational Effectiveness: An Endangered Species?" (unpublished manuscript, University of Minnesota, 1973). Reproduced in Steers, *Organizational Effectiveness* (Santa Monica: Goodyear, 1977), pp. 40-41.

In summary, many "single-criterion" measures of effectiveness have been proposed and used. However, none have proved to be entirely satisfactory as the sole or universal measure.

Multiple-Criteria Measures of Effectiveness

Even though single-criterion measures of organizational effectiveness are still widely used, most of the modern effectiveness models measure effectiveness as a function of *several* criteria, such as productivity, flexibility, and stability.

The idea that managers do in fact pursue multiple goals simultaneously has received some support in research studies. In one study, George England surveyed organizational goals as expressed by American managers. He found that managers rated a variety of goals, including "organizational efficiency," "high productivity," "profit maximization," and "organizational growth," as both highly important and significant for corporate success. And in a recent literature review, Richard Steers surveyed multiple-criteria models and found that each model defined effectiveness in terms of *several* interdependent factors (like productivity and flexibility). However, there was very little consistency between models; his findings are summarized in Table 15-2.[8]

We will briefly discuss three illustrative examples of multiple-criteria effectiveness models—models that try to define and measure organizational effectiveness in terms of several criteria simultaneously—in this section.

The Yuchtman-Seashore model. Yuchtman and Seashore reject the idea that managers seek to attain any single goal. Instead, they see the organization as an open system, and view effectiveness in terms of how successful the organization is at acquiring "scarce and valued resources." As a result, they define organizational effectiveness largely in terms of "bargaining position," and:

> The concept of "bargaining position" implies the exclusion of any specific goal (or function) as the ultimate criterion of organizational effectiveness. Instead it points to the more general capability of the organization as a resource-getting system.[9]

According to these writers, a firm's bargaining position is itself determined by several factors, including how efficiently it uses its resources. This conception of organizational effectiveness thus focuses not on the specific goal toward which the organization is striving, but rather on the organization's behavior, "conceived as a continuous and never-ending process of exchange and competition over scarce and valued resources."[10] To these writers, *the successful acquisition of scarce and valued resources* and the *control of its environment* are thus the two major criteria of organizational effectiveness.

The Bass model. Psychologist Bernard Bass says that traditional effectiveness indexes like productivity or profits are not sufficiently broad for evaluating the success of an organization.[11] Instead, an organization's effectiveness should also reflect "the worth of the organization to its individual members and the worth of both individual members and the orga-

TABLE 15-2

Evaluation Criteria in Multivariate Models of Organizational Effectiveness

Study and Primary Evaluation Criteria	Type of Measure *	Generali- zibility of Criteria †	Derivation of Criteria ‡
Georgopoulous and Tannen- baum (1957) Productivity, Flexibility, Absence of organizational strain	N	A	Ded.; followed by ques- tionnaire study
Bennis (1962) Adaptability, Sense of identity, Capacity to test reality	N	A	Ded.; no study
Blake and Mouton (1964) Simultaneous achievement of high production-centered and high people-centered enterprise	N	B	Ded.; no study
Caplow (1964) Stability, Integration, Volun- tarism, Achievement	N	A	Ded.; no study
Katz and Kahn (1966) Growth, Storage, Survival, Control over environment	N	A	Ind.; based on review of empirical studies
Lawrence and Lorsch (1967) Optimal balance of integration and differenciation	D	B	Ind.; based on study of 6 firms
Yuchtman and Seashore (1967) Successful acquisition of scarce and valued re- sources, Control over environment	N	A	Ind.; based on study of insurance agencies
Friedlander and Pickle (1968) Profitability, Employee satis- faction, Societal value	N	B	Ded.; followed by study of small businesses
Price (1968) Productivity, Conformity, Morale, Adaptiveness, Institutionalization	D	A	Ind.; based on review of 50 published studies
Mahoney and Weitzel (1969) General business model Productivity-support- utilization, Planning, Re- liability, initiative R and D Model Reliability, Cooperation, Development	D	B, R	Ind.; based on study of 13 organizations
Schein (1970) Open communication, Flexi- bility, Creativity, Psycholog- ical commitment	N	A	Ded.; no study

TABLE 15-2

Evaluation Criteria in Multivariate Models of Organizational Effectiveness (*cont.*)

Mott (1972)
  Productivity, Flexibility,
  Adaptability
	N	A	Ded.; followed by questionnaire study of several organizations

Duncan (1973)
  Goal attainment, Integration,
  Adaptation
	N	A	Ded.; followed by study of 22 decision units

Gibson *et al.* (1973)
  Short-run
  Production, Efficiency,
   Satisfaction
  Intermediate
  Adaptiveness, Development
  Long-run
  Survival
	N	A	Ind.; based on review of earlier models

Negandhi and Reimann (1973)
  Behavioral index
  Manpower acquisition,
  Employee satisfaction,
  Manpower retention,
  Interpersonal relations,
  Interdepartmental relations,
  Manpower utilization
  Economic Index
  Growth in sales, Net profit
	N	B	Ded.; followed by study of Indian organizations

Child (1974, 1975) Profitability, Growth	N	B	Ded.; followed by study of 82 British firms
Webb (1974) Cohesion, Efficiency, Adaptability, Support	D	C	Ind.; based on study of religious organizations

* N = Normative (what firms *should* do) model; D = Descriptive (what firms *do*) models.

† A = All organizations; B = Business organizations; C = Religious organizations; R = Research and development laboratories.

‡ Ded. = Deductive, Ind. = Inductive.

Source: Richard Steers, "Problems in Measurement of Organizational Effectiveness," *Administrative Science Quarterly,* Vol. 20, No. 4 (December 1975), 549.

nization to society." Specifically, an organization should be evaluated in terms of:

1. The degree to which it is productive, profitable, self-maintaining, and so forth;
2. The degree to which it is of value to its members; and
3. The degree to which it and its members are of value of society.

Bass believes that these have become recognized criteria of organizational effectiveness, as substantiated by several facts. For example, he notes that federal and state worker-safety and antitrust laws assume that an organization's worth to the individual and to society are both important effectiveness criteria. And even though Bass's work on effectiveness was begun over 25 years ago, his criteria make even more sense today. For example, a multitude of new laws have been enacted establishing the "social responsibility" of business, with the goal of ensuring the worth of the organization to society. Other laws, like the Occupational Safety and Health Act and the Civil Rights Act, are aimed at ensuring the worth of the organization to its individual members. Similarly, interest is increasing among organization theorists and managers in the concept of "quality of work life." Prof. J. Lloyd Suttle defines this as "the degree to which members of a work organization are able to satisfy important personal needs through their experiences in the organization," and many today are coming to view this as an important criterion of organizational effectiveness.[12]

Currently, therefore, there is obviously more interest—even more than when Bass proposed his three criteria in the early 1950s—in measuring an organization's effectiveness not just in terms of productivity, but in terms of the organization's worth to its individual members, and to society as a whole.

The Bennis model. Warren Bennis says the basic flaw in present effectiveness criteria is their inattention to the problem of adapting to change.[13] In his view, "the main challenge confronting today's organization, whether it is a hospital or a business enterprise, is that of responding to changing conditions and adapting to external stress," and measures of organizational effectiveness must therefore include criteria like adaptability and problem-solving ability. He bases his argument on the findings of writers like Emery and Trist, who, as we saw in Chapter 3, found that the environments in which organizations are operating are becoming increasingly uncertain and turbulent.

Bennis feels that the "methodological rules" and problem-solving techniques an organization uses are the critical determinants of its effectiveness. According to him, these rules and procedures closely resemble the rules of inquiry that are an implicit part of scientific investigation, and therefore:

. . . the rules and norms of science may provide a valuable, possibly necessary model for organizational behavior.[14]

Organizations must exhibit two basic aspects of the scientific approach, says Bennis, if they are to exist in a changing environment. First, there must be an emphasis on scientific methodology, and in particular on the spirit of inquiry and desire for experimentation that characterize the scientific approach. In other words, organizations (and their managers) must be willing to approach problems openly and develop solutions with tentativeness and caution, and having done this, they must be willing to expose their tentative conclusions to empirical testing. It is this constant interplay of hypothesis *development* and *testing*, says Bennis, that is the essence of the scientific approach and a major factor in the effectiveness of organizations.

Second, for this spirit of scientific inquiry to flourish, there must be a certain "democracy" in the organization, one that "accents freedom of opinion and dissent, and respect for the individual." [15] Bennis argues, therefore, that the way organizations can come to grips with their problems and survive and prosper in an uncertain environment is by establishing social conditions in which the scientific attitude flourishes. To Bennis, such social conditions would be built on "Theory Y"–type assumptions and would reflect the organizational trust, supportiveness, and democracy found in organizational models like Likert's System IV.

In summary, Bennis's argument is that the most crucial problem facing organizations is to survive and adapt in a changing environment, and that for them to do so, an open, scientific spirit of inquiry must prevail in the organization. Thus, adaptability, an ability to clearly identify the organizational identity, and the capability for "reality testing"—for correctly identifying problems and their solutions—are the major components of organizational effectiveness, in Bennis's opinion.

Comparison of Multiple-Criteria Models

What conclusions can be drawn from a comparison of multiple-criteria models of organizational effectiveness? There are two points of view. Steers believes that the evidence suggests a "lack of consensus as to what constitutes a useful and valid set of effectiveness measures." [16] Thus, although each of the models shown in Table 15-2 lists three or four criteria of success, there is little overlap across various approaches. Table 15-3 shows the frequency of occurrence of effectiveness criteria mentioned in the 17 models of organizational effectiveness shown in Table 15-2. As you can see, adaptability–flexibility was mentioned most often, followed by productivity and satisfaction. However, only adaptability–flexibility was mentioned in more than half the models. From this, Steers concludes:

> . . . the effectiveness construct is so complex as to defy attempts at model development. Perhaps more flexible, comprehensive models are required.[17]

On the other hand, some writers take a somewhat more positive approach to the question of organizational effectiveness. For example, Jeffrey Pfeffer and Gerald Salancik say that the effective organization is *the one that satisfies the demands of those in its environment from whom it requires support for its continued existence,*[18] a conclusion similar to that reached by Yuchtman and Seashore, with their bargaining approach to effectiveness. Pfeffer and Salancik point out that organizations are faced with frequently competing demands from a variety of interest groups, and that their effectiveness—their ability to create acceptable outcomes and actions—can be measured only in terms of the interest group being considered. For example,

TABLE 15-3

Frequency of Occurrence of Evaluation Criteria in 17 Models of Organizational Effectiveness

Evaluation Criteria	No. of Times Mentioned (N = 17)
Adaptability-Flexibility	10
Productivity	6
Satisfaction	5
Profitability	3
Resource acquisition	3
Absence of strain	2
Control over environment	2
Development	2
Efficiency	2
Employee retention	2
Growth	2
Integration	2
Open communications	2
Survival	2
All other criteria	1

Source: Richard Steers, "Problems in Measurement of Organizational Effectiveness," *Administrative Science Quarterly*, Vol. 20, No. 4 (December 1975), 549.

stockholders of a company may consider effectiveness in terms of profits, or rate of growth. To *employees*, decent wages and quality of work life might be crucial. To the *community* surrounding the firm, the firm's support of community projects, such as Little League baseball teams, might be paramount. In summary, these writers propose a multifaceted concept of effectiveness and hold that managers seek to satisfy several aims (and interest groups) simultaneously.

There is some support for the notion that effectiveness is multifaceted and can be described only with respect to particular interest groups. England (in the study discussed above) found that managers do in fact pursue a variety of goals, and these seem to be aimed at different interest groups. The results of another study (see Table 15-4) point up one of the dilemmas managers face if this multifaceted view of effectiveness is correct. The data from this study suggest that satisfying one group (owner, community, government) implies very little about satisfying any other groups, and that the groups' interests may occasionally conflict. For example, there was some indication that satisfying the owners' goals was occasionally incompatible with satisfying those of the government.

Several conclusions concerning organizational effectiveness seem appropriate. In the broadest sense, the firm's ability to survive and to effectively "bargain" with and adapt to crucial interest groups and create acceptable outcomes and actions is probably an ultimate criterion of organizational effectiveness; this is a basic point made by Yuchtman and Seashore, and by Pfeffer and Salancik. And in this regard, Bennis's prescriptions for

TABLE 15-4

Intercorrelations of Satisfactions of Seven Parties-at-Interest

	Satisfaction of					
	Com-munity	Govern-ment	Cus-tomer	Sup-plier	Credi-tor	Em-ployee
Owner satisfaction	.23 *	—.12	.37 *	.14	.00	.25 *
Community satis-faction		.16	.04	.16	.14	.22 *
Government satis-faction			—.09	.11	.20 *	—.07
Customer satisfaction				.17	.23 *	.23 *
Supplier satisfaction					.08	.17
Creditor satisfaction						.08

* Significant relationships.

Source: Reprinted from Hall Pickle and Frank Friedlander, "Seven Societal Criteria of Organizational Success," *Personnel Psychology,* Vol. 20 (1967), Table 1, p. 171.

organizational democracy and a spirit of scientific inquiry provide one organizational strategy for achieving this ultimate objective.

Beyond this, prescriptions like those of Bass and of economic and organization theorists that focus on one or more specific criteria of effectiveness (like adaptability or profits) are probably all useful, but they reflect only *facets* of organization effectiveness, in that each criterion is relevant to only one or a few of the organization's crucial interest groups.

Framework: How Useful?

How useful is our framework for understanding, explaining, and predicting organizational effectiveness? Two points are relevant here. First, many of the research findings we reviewed supported the relationships hypothesized in our model. The organization's context has been found to influence organizational structure and compliance, for example, and the logical "link" seems to be decision making, communicating, and information processing in organizations. Social influences, including leadership, groups, conflict, and organizational change, have been found to have profound effects on organizational structure, compliance, and effectiveness. The framework thus helps explain the factors that contribute to organizational effectiveness, as well as the systemic nature of the relationships involved. For example, "motivation" alone is not sufficient for high effectiveness, but rather motivation combined with group norms, an appropriate structure, effective leadership, and so forth. Similarly, group processes and adequate incentives can compensate for an inappropriate structure, but an appropriate structure is undermined by conflict and inadequate rewards.

The second thing that can be said about our framework is that it obviously does not fully reflect the complex relationships contributing to organizational effectiveness, nor is it the only simple framework that could be proposed. For example, our framework emphasizes a somewhat defensive posture vis-à-vis the environment. We assume that the organization reacts and adapts to environmental demands by reorganizing, establishing new reward systems, and so on. As an alternative, an organization can take a more active stance. For example, Pfeffer and Salancik recently proposed that organizations can control or modify their environments by, say, entering into mergers or trade associations with competing firms, suppliers, or buyers. How does this point of view compare with ours? What implications does it have for the usefulness of our framework? We turn to these questions next.

Managing and Avoiding External Control

In order to understand organizational behavior, according to Pfeffer and Salancik, you have to understand how the organization relates to the various special-interest groups (suppliers, consumers, government agencies, and so on) that make up its environment.[19] They say that organizations must compete and survive in their environments, and that they can either comply with and adapt to the demands of others, or act to manage the dependencies that create constraints on organizational actions. For example, an organization confronted with a turbulent environment might *adapt* by instituting a more organic structure. On the other hand, it might act to *manage* and reduce the turbulence of the environment by entering into trade agreements with competitors and merging with suppliers.

All organizations are "controlled" to some degree by groups in their environments, and the degree to which any group can control or limit the organization's behavior depends largely on the degree to which the organization depends on the group. To the extent that the organization depends heavily on one or more of these groups, its actions will be limited by their demands, and the more these demands conflict, the more the organization's problems (and uncertainties) will increase. To the extent that there is not a high degree of interconnectedness between the organization and these groups and between these groups themselves, and to the extent that resources are not scarce and power is widely dispersed (rather than concentrated in just one or two groups) the organization will be less dependent on powerful outside groups. And to the extent that it is less dependent on outside groups, the organization will be more of a master of its own fate, will be less constrained by outside forces, will face less uncertainty, and will find it easier to survive. By this line of reasoning, "loose coupling"—a reduction in the degree to which the organization depends on various outside groups—should be one aim of organizations, since it reduces the extent to which the organization's activities are constrained by those groups.

Managing the environment. To survive and prosper, the organization can react to environmental demands defensively, offensively, or both. Defensively, it can engage in organizational change and development, thus changing its structure, reward systems, group norms, and so forth, in such a way that the organization is more appropriate for dealing with its environmental demands. In our first 14 chapters, we generally stressed this defensive posture.

But organizations can also react offensively. And explaining specific ways the organization can act offensively to reduce its dependence on "outside factors" by modifying its environment is one of Pfeffer and Salancik's key themes. They say an organization can manage environmental demands by *avoiding influence, altering dependencies, negotiating with the environment,* or *legislatively creating a new environment.*

First, it can *avoid* or manage the conditions of external control without actually changing those conditions. One way to do this is by playing off the demands of one group against those of another. Thus, an organization faced with an affirmative-action suit might seek to avoid government influence by putting the blame for its hiring practices on the union. Another technique for avoiding influence is to control communications and information so that groups like unions, government agencies, and stockholders have insufficient information on which to hold the organization accountable.

A more potent way to manage environmental demands involves reducing or *altering the organization's interdependencies.* And, according to these writers, "the most effective strategies for dealing with dependence which arises from reliance on a single product or market are those which alter the purpose or structure of the organization so that it no longer requires only a limited range of inputs or serves only a few markets." [20] For example, the organization can diversify, perhaps by adding new products, moving into new geographic locations, or offering products in a wider range of prices: By increasing the number and variety of its customers, the firm becomes less dependent on any one of those customers. Mergers are a second technique for reducing a firm's dependence on outside elements. Thus, by following a strategy of "vertical integration," a car manufacturer might merge with or purchase a steel firm in order to reduce the uncertainties surrounding its steel acquisition. Growth is another technique for reducing dependence, since an increase in size should make the firm more powerful and therefore less dependent on outside elements.

Organizations need not totally absorb crucial outside groups in order to gain some control over them. An alternative is for the firm to *renegotiate its environment*—for example, by setting up trade associations, cartels, trade agreements, coordinating councils, and joint ventures. All these are negotiated agreements through which interdependent firms can coordinate their efforts and thereby reduce conflict and uncertainty.

Finally, organizations can legislatively alter or *create environments.* For example, auto-industry lobbyists try to reduce pollution standards, and apparel manufacturers try to have quotas put on imported clothing.

In summary, Pfeffer and Salancik say that organizational effectiveness is multifaceted, and that since each outside group evaluates the organization by its own criteria, effectiveness is always relative: An organization might be simultaneously effective in the opinion of stockholders and very ineffective from the point of view of community groups or government agencies. Yet the organization cannot depend on just a single group for its support, since, in addition to stockholders, it needs the support of its suppliers, retail outlets, clients, and so forth. The effective firm is thus the firm that can survive and prosper in the face of the competing demands from all influential groups, and the firm that can reduce its dependence on outsiders increases its chances for survival. Four techniques for reducing the uncertainty, interdependence, and conflict in environments are *avoiding* the influence, *altering* the dependencies, *negotiating* with the environment, and legislatively *creating* a new environment.

As an alternative, of course, the firm can also deal with its dependencies through a process of organizational change and development. Structurally, for example, it can establish self-contained, differentiated departments, each of which "co-opts" an environmental segment and pays close and continuous attention to it. It is this more "defensive" approach to survival and effectiveness that we stressed in this book, and that our framework helps to explain. The Pfeffer and Salancik thesis complements our approach (and framework) by stressing that the organization can actively try to modify or control its environment.

Summary. We have concluded that our framework is useful for understanding, explaining, and predicting effectiveness. And we also saw that alternative strategies, including changing (rather than just adapting to) the environment, are not only feasible but necessarily complement the more "defensive" approach implicit in our framework. Before concluding this book, however, it would be useful to briefly address the questions first raised in Chapter 1. We will provide the outlines of some illustrative answers here, and leave a more detailed analysis of these questions for class discussion (see discussion question 5 at the end of this chapter).

QUESTIONS IN ORGANIZATION THEORY

What Are the Major Determinants of Organizational Effectiveness?

There are several sides to this question, as there are to the question, "What is effectiveness?" Effectiveness, we have seen, is always relative, since what is effective to one interest group may be ineffective to another. Overall, it is the organization that can survive and prosper while maintaining the support of influential but competing groups that is effective, and many factors contribute to such effectiveness. In terms of our framework, *structure, compliance,* and *social influences,* including leadership, groups, conflict, and organizational change and development, interact in determining organizational effectiveness. We have also seen that effectiveness can be enhanced through a more offensive posture in which the organization attempts to avoid or manage its environment—for example, by reducing interdependencies through mergers.

What Are the Relationships between These Determinants?

We proposed a framework for relating some of these determinants to each other, and the findings we discussed support the framework. However (as we mentioned above), our framework is simplified, and many other models could be proposed.

What Makes One Organization Effective and Another Ineffective?

This was in many respects the overriding question of this book, and there is no completely satisfactory way to answer it in one paragraph. However, in keeping with our framework, one possible answer would seem to be that the problem of achieving effectiveness is a *systemic* one and that no one factor (structure, compliance technique, leadership, or the like) is by itself sufficient to ensure either effectiveness or ineffectiveness. Instead, the effective firm is the one in which management has been able to balance each of these components in such a way that the organization can effectively cope with the demands of competing special interest groups. With respect to our framework, we found, for example, that group processes could compensate for an inadequate organization structure, just as inadequate motivation or a hostile group could undermine the most effective structure. In this last chapter, we saw that environmental management can influence effectiveness and can either complement or detract from the determinants summarized in our framework. Complicating matters is the fact that an organization that is effective in one situation may be ineffective in another, since contextual dimensions like environment and technology have important implications for organizational structure and management.

What Is the Applicability of This Knowledge to Practical Problems?

The systemic nature of the problem serves to underscore the difficulty of applying organization-theory findings to practical problems. Organizations are managed by people whose abilities for assimilating, synthesizing, and processing information and making decisions is limited and who must therefore make decisions based on simplified models of the real world. If organizational effectiveness depended only on developing an appropriate structure, reward system, or leadership style (or on "optimizing" any or all of these components), attaining effectiveness would be a relatively straightforward matter. Organizational contexts are constantly changing, however, and the determinants of effectiveness act not singly but interdependently. An understanding of the determinants of effectiveness and the relationships between these determinants can therefore be useful for predicting the effects of various actions, but the usefulness is obviously limited by the complexity of the situation confronting the manager.

There is also a measurement problem. Although it is useful to distinguish between uncertain and certain environments, considerate and structuring leadership, unit and mass production, or imposed compliance and self-control, the devices for operationalizing these sorts of features are in a very preliminary state. There are unfortunately few proven devices that managers can use to measure how uncertain their environments are, how much they have decentralized, how considerately they are acting, or just how "structured" their subordinates' jobs are, for example. Until realistic, "on-line" means for measuring such features are developed, practical applications for organization-theory findings will be hampered. On the other hand, we have seen in this book that even with these limitations, a knowledge of the research and findings of organization theory and behavior can enable us to better understand, explain, and predict organizational phenomena. It can, for example, enable us to better design our organizations and to choose an appropriate coordination device. It can help us to choose between the various approaches to ensuring compliance. And it can help us to better manage work groups and intergroup conflict and implement organizational changes.

SUMMARY

As is the case with any theory, an organization theory (or set of theories) is aimed at providing the general relationships or frameworks that allow us to understand, explain, and predict phenomena within the science we are focusing on. This book was concerned with organization theory, which we tentatively define as a framework for understanding, explaining, and predicting organizational effectiveness.

The topics in this book—the "context" of organizations, decision making, organization structure, motivation and compliance, leadership, groups, and change—were chosen on the assumption that they all influence each other, and also affect organizational effectiveness. In analyzing these topics, it was therefore useful to start with a hypothesis that tentatively explained how they relate to each other and to organizational effectiveness, and our hypothesized framework was presented in Figure 1-1.

That framework assumes that the organization's "context"—its environment, technology, and size—influences how it is organized and managed. In Chapter 4, we explained how an organization's "strategy"—its basic long-term plan—answers the question, "What business are we in?"

and thereby determines the environment in which the organization must compete, and its technology and size. In turn, the organization's context has a major influence on how the organization is structured and managed. In firms where efficiency is emphasized, effective organizations tend to be "mechanistic." At the other extreme, in organizations like research labs, with unpredictable, nonroutine tasks, creativity and entrepreneurial activities are emphasized, and to encourage such activities, these organizations tend to be "organic." We cited research findings by Burns and Stalker, Lawrence and Lorsch, Woodward, and Blau in support of our contention that environment, technology, and size do in fact influence organization. In Chapter 5, we concluded that decision making, communications, and information processing ability provide a vehicle for explaining this link between the organization and its context.

In this book, we assume that there are two basic aspects of organizations that organization theorists have focused on: their structure, and how compliance is ensured. In Chapters 6 and 7, we addressed the question of organization structure and design—how to distribute specific tasks and responsibilities among the members of the organization. We discussed structural dimensions like departmentation, span of control, and coordination, and we found that context affects the nature and configuration of these dimensions.

But (our framework assumes) from the point of view of an organization theorist or manager, it is not enough to simply assign tasks to individuals; in addition, one has to ensure that those tasks are in fact carried out—that compliance takes place. Thus, theorists have said that predictability is an essential ingredient of organizations: Each manager must be able to assume that the people he or she directs will comply with orders and carry out their tasks, in such a way that they contribute in an integrated manner to the organization's goals. If orders are not obeyed, there is no way to ensure that the logic of the organization's structure will function effectively. Therefore, we discussed motivation and compliance in Chapters 8, 9, and 10. We distinguished between two broad categories of techniques for ensuring that the basic behaviors required for organizational functioning and effectiveness take place, calling these two imposed compliance and self-control. We found that at one extreme the organization can use extrinsic means for getting employees to comply with rules or directives, either by making them "legal" job demands, by making the employees fear sanctions, or by providing rewards. At the other extreme, the organization can rely on intrinsic means for motivating its employees—for example, by creating situations in which the goals of the organization are synchronous with those of the employee; he then adopts these as his own.

But although establishing an effective structure and ensuring compliance are important determinants of organizational effectiveness, other factors also influence effectiveness often through their effects on structure and compliance. In Chapters 11 through 14, we discussed four such influential factors—leadership, work groups, intergroup conflict, and organization change and development—and particularly focused on how each factor influences organization structure and compliance. The findings we cited confirm the fact that each of these factors can and does influence structure, compliance, and organizational effectiveness. Groups influence their members' attitudes and behavior, for example; intergroup conflict (as between line and staff units) can undermine an otherwise effective structure; and organizational change and development techniques can be used to change the structure, technology, or people in an organization.

In this last chapter, we turned our attention to the concept of organizational effectiveness and concluded that the firm's ability to survive and to effectively "bargain" with crucial interest groups and create acceptable outcomes and actions is probably an ultimate criterion of organizational effectiveness. Thus, prescriptions like those of Bass and of economic and organization theorists that focus on one or more specific criteria of effectiveness (like adaptability or profits) are probably all useful but reflect only facets of organization effectiveness, in that each criterion is relevant to only one or a few of the organization's crucial interest groups. We concluded that our framework is useful for understanding, explaining, and predicting the emergence of organizational effectiveness, but that alternative and complementary explanations exist as well.

As an example, we discussed the work of Pfeffer and Salancik, who assume that organizational effectiveness is multifaceted, and that since each outside group evaluates the organization by its own criteria, effectiveness is always relative: An organization might be simultaneously effective in the opinion of stockholders and very ineffective from the point of view of community groups or government agencies, for example. As a result, these writers imply, simply reacting and adapting to exigencies (as emphasized in our model) are not sufficient for organization effectiveness. Instead, they say, the organization should take a more offensive posture in attempting to control or somehow modify the environment. Four techniques for doing so are avoiding the influence, altering the dependencies, negotiating with the environment, and legislatively creating a new environment.

We saw that structure, compliance, and social influences like leadership and groups interact with each other and with the organization's context in determining organizational effectiveness. Specific implications concerning, for example, how structural dimensions have to "fit" environment and technology, and what motivation and compliance techniques are most appropriate in different situations, were discussed. In addition, we concluded that the problem of achieving effectiveness is a systemic one and that no one factor (such as structure, compliance technique, leadership, or the like) is by itself sufficient to ensure effectiveness or ineffectiveness. For example, group processes can compensate for an inadequate organization structure, just as inadequate motivation or a hostile group can undermine the most effective structure. Although the systemic nature of organizational functioning helps to underscore the great complexities involved in developing a general theory of organizations, it is our conclusion that our framework can help the theorist and manager to understand, explain, and predict organizational functioning.

DISCUSSION QUESTIONS

1. How would you define "organizational effectiveness"?
2. Discuss how organization structure, motivation and compliance, leadership, intergroup conflict, group processes, and organizational change and development each contribute to organizational effectiveness.
3. Explain Pfeffer and Salancik's concept of organizational effectiveness.
4. Using the same chapter titles we used in this book, develop an alternative "framework" to the one we used to introduce each chapter. Are there any new topics you would add? What are they?
5. Answer the questions in organization theory we proposed in chapter one, elaborating on (or arguing against) the answers we gave in this last chapter.

FOOTNOTES

1 Richard Steers, "Problems in the Measurement of Organizational Effectiveness," *Administrative Science Quarterly*, Vol. 20 (December 1975), 546–58; Richard Steers, *Organizational Effectiveness* (Santa Monica, Calif.: Goodyear, 1977); Jaisingh Ghorpade, *Assessment of Organizational Effectiveness* (Pacific Palisades, Calif.: Goodyear, 1971).

2 Richard Bilas, *Micro Economic Theory* (New York: McGraw-Hill, 1967), pp. 150–51.

3 Richard Lipsey and Peter Steiner, *Economics* (New York: Harper & Row, 1969), p. 369.

4 George Stigler, *The Theory of Price* (New York: Macmillan, 1966), p. 177.

5 C. E. Ferguson, *Micro Economic Theory* (New York: McGraw-Hill, 1966), p. 191.

6 Herbert Simon, *Administrative Behavior* (New York: Free Press, 1957).

7 John P. Campbell, "Research into the Nature of Organizational Effectiveness: An Endangered Species?" working paper, University of Minnesota, 1973, quoted in Steers, "Problems in the Measurement of Organizational Effectiveness."

8 G. W. England, "Organizational Goals and Expectant Behavior of American Managers," *Academy of Management Journal*, Vol. 10 (1967). Steers, "Problems in the Measurement of Organizational Effectiveness," *Administrative Science Quarterly*, Vol. 20 (December 1975).

9 Ephraim Yuchtman and Stanley Seashore, "A System Resource Approach to Organizational Effectiveness," *Administrative Science Quarterly*, Vol. 32 (December 1967), 377–95.

10 *Ibid.*

11 Bernard Bass, "Ultimate Criteria of Organizational Worth," *Personnel Psychology*, Vol. 5 (1952), 157–73.

12 See, for example, J. Richard Hackman and J. Lloyd Suttle, *Improving Life at Work* (Santa Monica, Calif.: Goodyear, 1977).

13 Warren Bennis, "Towards a 'Truly' Scientific Management: The Concept of Organization Health," in W. Bennis, *Changing Organizations* (New York: McGraw-Hill, 1966). Reprinted in Ghorpade, op. cit. pp. 116–43.

14 *Ibid.*, p. 128.

15 *Ibid.*, p. 129.

16 See Steers, "Problems in the Measurement of Organizational Effectiveness," pp. 547–51.

17 *Ibid.*, p. 549.

18 Jeffrey Pfeffer and Gerald Salancik, *The External Control of Organizations* (New York: Harper & Row, 1978).

19 Pfeffer and Salancik, *The External Control of Organizations,* p. 257.

20 Pfeffer and Salancik, *The External Control of Organizations,* p. 109. Note that Jay Galbraith makes a similar point when he prescribes "environmental management." See Chapter 4.

INDEXES

Name Index

415

Subject Index